MEDIEVAL NARRATIVES BETWEEN HISTORY AND FICTION

Medieval Narratives between History and Fiction

From the Centre to the Periphery of Europe, c. 1100-1400

Edited by Panagiotis A. Agapitos *and* Lars Boje Mortensen

Museum Tusculanum Press
University of Copenhagen
2012

Panagiotis A. Agapitos and Lars Boje Mortensen (eds.).
Medieval Narratives between History and Fiction:
From the Centre to the Periphery of Europe, c. 1100–1400

Cover design, layout and composition: Erling Lynder
Set in Arno and Jenson Classico
Printed in Denmark by Specialtrykkeriet Viborg A/S
ISBN 978 87 635 3809 1

Cover illustration: Paul Klee, *Hauptweg und Nebenwege*, 1929,
Oil on canvas, 83.7 × 67.5 cm, Museum Ludwig – Köln.
Photo: © Rheinisches Bildarchiv Köln.

This book is published with financial support from
Centre for Medieval Studies, University of Bergen
The Committee on Publishing Strategy of the University of Cyprus
The Faculty of the Humanities, University of Southern Denmark
The Norwegian Research Council

Museum Tusculanum Press
Njalsgade 126
DK-2300 Copenhagen S
Denmark
www.mtp.dk

MIX
Paper from responsible sources
FSC™ C010558
FSC www.fsc.org

Contents

Preface

Not unlike many other collective volumes in the humanities, the present one has been through a long process. That it has been possible to sustain it is first and foremost due to the Centre of Medieval Studies at the University of Bergen (Norwegian Centre of Excellence 2003–12) where one of the editors enjoyed a privileged research environment in terms of resources and inspirational colleagues from a number of disciplines. The first somewhat directionless activities go back to some informal seminars in 2005 in which Paul Gerhard Schmidt and Dennis H. Green among others visited Bergen and gave papers on matters of medieval fictionality. When the two editors met at a more formal workshop in March 2006 the direction and the format of the work slowly began to materialize. In March 2007 the workshop met for a second time in Nicosia, where all papers were discussed, views and thoughts exchanged and a rough form of the book agreed upon.

In contrast to the more conventional collections of contributions gathered within a volume, the present book has a rather unique structure because it includes three different types of papers, each type serving a different function within the book. The first type is the essay-like chapter written by Dennis Green that provided in condensed form the initial point of departure for our discussions; thus the chapter is short and without footnotes. The second type is the focused research paper offering a reading of a text or texts and using specific methods of analysis; these chapters form the main body of the book. The third type is the broad comparative essay written by Panagiotis Agapitos that tries to tie together most points in our discussions and bring them to bear upon the analysis of a large number of texts from Byzantium, medieval France, Germany and Persia; it is thus the longest but also the last in the book. The use of these three different types allows a structured but asymmetrical variety of writing to infuse the book and give it an individual form and – we would like to think – medieval colour. We hope that the readers will enjoy this device, not the only one in the book's structure, as the readers will find out in our introduction.

We are naturally indebted both to the University of Bergen and the University of Cyprus for the support they have given us in various ways. We are also immensely grateful to our co-authors who have put their research into the book and contributed so much in the way of developing and changing our and their colleagues' views. They have shown a lot of enthusiasm and patience during the whole process, and we can only say that it has been a delight to work with them.

Unfortunately, time has taken a heavy toll as three of our distinguished older colleagues will not see the finished product. Dennis H. Green died in 2008 but had already very generously submitted a chapter for us to print which draws on his masterly volume from 2002, *The Beginnings of Medieval Romance: Fact and Fiction, 1150–1220*, which became a major source of inspiration for us. Paul Gerhard Schmidt and Tomas Hägg participated very actively with all their wisdom and experience in our workshops and we are very proud to have them as contributors. Sadly we lost Paul Gerhard in 2010 and Tomas in 2011.

For generous financial support of the publication our sincere thanks go to The Norwegian Research Council, the Centre of Medieval Studies at Bergen, the University of Southern Denmark, and the Committee on Publishing Strategy of the University of Cyprus.

Tine Dam Bendtsen compiled the index very efficiently and on short notice. Her effort shouldered an urgent burden and for this we thank her heartily.

Finally, we would like to extend our gratitude to Marianne Alenius and Jordy Findanis at Museum Tusculanum Press for accepting our manuscript and following it through the final editing.

The editors
Copenhagen and Nicosia,
December 2011

Introduction

Panagiotis A. Agapitos and Lars Boje Mortensen

Events of the past can be re-enacted and historical persons evoked through a variety of media and genres: in conversation, scholarly writing, epic delivery, oratory, theatrical performance, images and so on. Irrespective of medium, a certain selection of the past is made to be present – 're-presented' – for a specific audience. In every case there must be a director or external voice who resides over the selection and emplotment of the material. If the representation is successful the audience will engage in the material to such an extent that the mediation falls out of focus and the audience feels immersed in the unfolding of events – almost as if the events were ordering themselves. But the narrative voice will always be in a position to unmask the illusion that one is present, if only by proxy, at important junctures of history.[1]

A telling example may be provided by Michael Psellos, the eleventh-century Byzantine courtier, philosopher, rhetorician, and statesman with no modest opinion about his own historical significance. His portrayal of the emperor Constantine IX Monomachos (1042–55) is a high point in medieval historiography. Psellos owed his high position at court to this emperor, and, while writing the emperor's history after his death, Psellos appeared to be tormented by the fact that he should return the favour by giving a true account of his apparently misguided if not catastrophic reign. Psellos was fascinated by this man, and he explains how he had previously composed eulogies for him, adhering to the genre of rhetoric. He had indeed been at the court of Constantine Monomachos as an official orator. But the genre of history forced him to include criticism, probably aided both by his self-congratulatory wish to display his insider knowledge (or feigned knowledge) of the administration and his fears of lying in the face of eternal judgement.

After accessing the throne by marrying the empress, Zoe, Constantine

1 For the utility and impact of the concept of representation in historical discourse we rely on Ankersmit (2001). In the context of medieval history and fiction, 'representation' is also a key concept in Morse (1991).

quickly saw to it that his mistress, Maria Sclerena, soon to be acknowledged as the 'Augusta', could take up permanent quarters at the palace. Psellos explains:

> When Constantine and the women [Zoe and her sister Theodora] had decided which apartments each was to occupy in the palace, the emperor had the room in the centre, with the sisters on either side of him, but it was Sclerena who had the most private quarters. And Zoe never visited the emperor's room, unless she had first made sure that he was alone and his lady-love far away. Otherwise she occupied herself with her own affairs. I must now explain what these activities were.[2]

What follows next is an exposé of Zoe's all-consuming passion, namely the production and product development of perfumes. Psellos continues: 'With regard to Zoe's other peculiarities – I must speak of her at rather greater length, while the emperor is still taking his ease with the beloved Augusta – there is not much that I can commend, but one trait never fails to excite my admiration: her piety…'. After this Psellos concludes: 'Having reached this point in our account of the empress, let us return once more to the Augusta and Constantine. Perhaps it may be the reader's wish that we rouse them from their slumbers, and separate them.'

Psellos here invites the readers into the narrative by effectively saying that while Constantine and Maria are amusing themselves in the bedroom, they have time on their hands to hear more about Zoe. By thus pretending that the time of narration overlaps with the unfolding of the narrated events, Psellos shows himself to be the self-conscious director of this play.[3] He is the self-professed truthful historian, but here he is certainly telling us quite directly that the stagecraft is his – we are completely at his mercy, being manipulated by narrative as it were – a manipulation that Psellos expressed in theoretical terms when he discussed the narrative technique of Heliodorus's *Aethiopica* (third to fourth century AD), the 'novelistic' bestseller in Byzantium.[4]

All ancient, medieval or modern historiography naturally implies selection, ordering and emplotment of material, but it is rare that a medieval historian who writes the highest genre of historiography lets the illusion fall like

2 *Fourteen Byzantine Rulers: The Chronographia of Michael Psellus*, trans. E. R. A. Sewter, Harmondsworth (Penguin Classics), p. 186.

3 On Psellos as author of and authorial *persona* in the *Chronography*, see Pietsch (2005).

4 See Agapitos (1998) on Psellos's understanding of rhetorical theatricality.

this – undermining the impression that the narrative is guided by the course of events and the relative importance of the chosen subjects.

Psellos is teasing the reader about the relationship between the representation and the audience. However accurate his historical narration might be, he makes it clear that the storyteller is a decisive factor for our understanding of the past – even when we accept his avowal of truthfulness. What makes history visible and tangible, on the one hand, makes it manipulated and reorganized on the other.

A new constellation arises when the relationship between the representation and the represented is called into doubt – when the story is blending in (what is considered to be) imagined figures and events or when it is perhaps completely fictitious with no claim of referring to an actual past. This situation is debated in another eleventh-century masterpiece, *The Tale of Genji*. The thousand-page novel was composed in Japan some fifty years before Psellos's *Chronographia* by Murasaki Shikibu (c. 970–c. 1030), lady-in-waiting to the empress Akiko. In an intimate and erotically charged conversation in chapter 24, the protagonist, Prince Genji, and his fourteen-year-old adopted daughter, Tamakazura, a voracious reader of romances, exchange views on the value of this kind of writing. Genji squarely states that there is not a shred of truth in those old stories and that their female audience is being deceived. He goes on:

> But amid all the fabrication I must admit that I do find real emotions and plausible chains of events. We can be quite aware of the frivolity and the idleness and still be moved. [...] Sometimes a series of absurd and grotesque incidents which we know to be quite improbable holds our interest, and afterwards we must blush that it was so. Yet even then we can see what it was that held us. [...][5]

Tamakazura angrily retorts '[F]or my part, I am convinced of their truthfulness', and then he begins to argue against himself: 'I have been rude and unfair to your romances, haven't I. They have set down and preserved happenings from the age of the gods to our own. The *Chronicles of Japan* and the rest are a mere fragment of the whole truth. It is your romances that fill in the details'. He continues by stressing the convincing image of good and bad in life that

5 *The Tale of Genji*, trans. Edward G. Seidensticker, New York: Columbia University Press, 1987, pp. 436–8. We are indebted to the commentary on this passage by Morris (1979: 309–23).

the romances depict and that 'to dismiss them as lies is itself to depart from the truth [...]. If one takes a generous view, then nothing is empty and useless'.

Murasaki Shikibu brings out very clearly a number of issues central to recent research into the relations between historiography and fiction, including the present volume. One such issue is the place of court entertainment and the role of aristocratic women – here with a special twist as the deliberations are made by a male character but written by a female author in a work of pure fiction. Another issue is the contrastive and supplementary functions of chronicles and romances; the first are composed in a serious or sacred written language (Chinese in Japan, archaizing Greek in Byzantium, Latin in Western Europe), whereas the vernacular tongue in writing signals a lack of serious purpose. Furthermore, the idea that romances flesh out gaps in chronicles has been seen as an important feature in the rise of vernacular romance in Europe. Finally, what is lost in referentiality (to paraphrase Murasaki in modern terms) is gained in emotional attachment and exemplary value.

LITERARY SPACE, TIME AND IDIOM

The triangular tension between the concomitant and sometimes competing values of entertainment, example and historical knowledge would – in other terms – have been recognized by our two authors who wrote a century or more before the spectacular burst of fictional writing connected to the French, Anglo-Norman and German courts.[6] In the present book, we want to pursue these themes by looking at literature in medieval Europe during the period from roughly 1100 to 1400. However, instead of focusing on one medieval language and its literary products, the book opens up the view on literary space, time and idiom by looking at very different regional cultures, sometimes very far removed from each other. As the title of the book indicates, the contributors primarily focus on the 'periphery' of medieval Europe, 'periphery' because most of the literatures discussed are not part of the Western European canon of literary history.

The disposition of the chapters displays a cyclical motion in space: from the world of Graeco-Roman antiquity to medieval France, then to the Scandinavian lands and from there to south-eastern Europe and Byzantium as the link back to the Graeco-Roman world. This disposition also follows a spiral

6 For a further exploration of this triangle, see Mortensen (1994).

motion in time: successive layers of time from antiquity to late antiquity and from the eleventh to the fifteenth century, with temporal spaces explored in the ninth and the nineteenth centuries.

In the first two contributions Tomas Hägg and Dennis Green set the important, and in many different ways formative, background to the relation between history and fiction in Graeco-Roman antiquity and the French twelfth century, the two 'canonical' phases of the still resilient master narrative about narratives. Hägg concentrates on the figures of Cyrus, Alexander and Apollonius to show the different ways in which 'historical' biography is realized, while Green in his essay draws the broad Latin picture to the 'rise of fiction' in medieval France, including such important texts as the Ovidian corpus, the poetry of Baudri de Bourgueil and also the history of Geoffrey of Monmouth written in the Anglo-Norman kingdom.

Picking up Green's suggestions about this Latin background, a first triad of contributions focuses on different medieval Latin narrative texts in the twelfth and thirteenth century. Paul Gerhard Schmidt studies a variety of 'novelistic' biographical narratives between history and fiction, Päivi Mehtonen offers a theoretical reading of rhetorical fabrication in Geoffrey of Monmouth, while Lars Boje Mortensen examines the status of the 'mythical' past in Nordic Latin historiographical works, such as the anonymous *Historia Norwegie* and Saxo's *Gesta Danorum*.

The second triad takes the reader even further north to the world of Old Norse culture in Norway and Iceland, and to the period from the twelfth to the fifteenth century. Jonas Wellendorf, also bringing in the Latin tradition of late antiquity, looks at fictionality in vision literature written in Latin and Old Norse; Else Mundal broadly discusses the consciousness of fiction in Old Norse literature using an extensive selection from all genres of sagas and various genres of poetry; while Slavica Ranković comparatively examines authentication devices in the sagas of Icelanders and Serbian epic poetry, thus moving the literary camera to the south-east of Europe.

In the last chapter, the readers are led by Panagiotis A. Agapitos to Byzantium and to a study of narratives in different genres (from epic to historiography) between history and fiction in Greek, Arabic, Persian, French and German literature, gradually bringing the book's spatio-temporal movement back to its Graeco-Roman background in the eastern Mediterranean and reconnecting it to the Western medieval world.

This conceptual and structural map of the book aims to question a series of issues concerning the national and curricular practice of medieval literary history. Despite the substantial advances in the literary and cultural interpretations of regional medieval literatures and, more specifically, their narrative texts (for example, French and German romances, Byzantine novels, English and French hagiography, Spanish and French epic, Latin, French and Byzantine historiography), the conventional division of medieval literary production into national 'literatures' taught as autonomous and auto-referential linguistic entities in the respective school curricula persists. And this division obstructs the view from one 'literature' to another, even though, unavoidably, *translatio* (such as from Latin to French or Old Norse, from French to German, from Greek to Arabic, from Italian to Greek) is acknowledged but left at the margin of the broader picture within its national literature. This national-curricular perspective by necessity marginalizes in different ways the international linguae francae such as Latin or Greek, the literary products of which cannot be easily or conveniently assigned to one or the other national literatures of a nineteenth-century ideological frame.

The oppositional notion of centre and periphery is of some importance for the present book, in the sense that it describes a geographic and a conceptual axiom which it will attempt to revise. According to the former, medieval northern France is *the* spatial centre of medieval fiction, while, according to the latter, medieval French epic and romance are *the* canonical genres for examining (*qua* evaluating) 'similar' genres in other medieval literatures. Arthurian romance and, in particular, Chrétien's five romances is a case in point. These texts have been used as the measure by which to judge Arthurian subject matter in German or Old Norse literature, simply because some of the latter texts appear as 'translations' of the former, where the word 'translation' needs substantial qualification in order to stand as an approximate equivalent of the medieval *translatio*. A typical example of such a geographic and conceptual distinction between centre and periphery (implying a qualitative drop in the supposed movement from the former to the latter) is Byzantium: the 'antiquarian' novels of the twelfth century were seen as a degenerate *translatio* from the Ancient Greek novels, while the 'chivalric' romances of the thirteenth to fourteenth centuries were viewed as an inept *translatio* from the French romances. Obviously, such readings completely distort the historical, cultural and literary environments of the 'centre' and the 'periphery'. In this sense, the authors of the present volume see medieval Europe as a broad and open system of distinct and yet interrelated regional cultures that come to display, against nineteenth-century constructions of nations and (non-) national literatures, some highly marked common ways of artistically and intellectually expressing similar preoccupations and needs in societies before the 'advent' of modern times.

It is important, we think, to point out in this context that, in one way or another, all European regional literatures, as well as the Arab and Persian Islamic cultures, derive larger or smaller parts of their educational background from Greek and Roman antiquity.[7] Thus – and this can be seen most clearly in the case of romance – the (pagan) Hellenic world appears in various guises through Latin, French, German, Byzantine and Persian romance. At the same time, it is important to remember that the environments in which texts were copied vary substantially from one region to another – monasteries, lay scriptoria, individual scribes working for specific patrons are all represented in many different ways. Similarly, a great variety of patronage is to be found. The Anglo-Norman, French and German lay courts are a point of departure for studying the rise of romance, but such courts offer only one form of patronage; Byzantium, Serbia and the Persian world give us other vantage points for evaluating the relations between patrons, authors and audiences.

Likewise, in the West, the multiple roles played by Latin learning and language need to be emphasized. It is well known that the creators of the first wave of French romances were clerics with a good Latin education. But their transfer and adaptation of pagan epic narratives and *mores* to a lay audience was only one process mediated through Latin books. Within the present context a number of other processes should be mentioned.

The existence of an ancient fictional literature was less conspicuous in the medieval Latin West than in the Greek (and Arabic and Persian) East, but it was not entirely absent. The late antique novel *Apollonius of Tyre* enjoyed a certain dissemination in Latin from the tenth century onwards. It probably had a limited influence on literary techniques in Latin before the twelfth century, and was taken to be a historical narrative (though suspicious for its simple style and high degree of entertainment). It was often copied among chronicles and it was titled *Historia Apollonii*. But during the twelfth century its subject matter attracted more interest and began to play into the fictional literary space. In the later Middle Ages it won a large reading and listening public across Western Europe through numerous vernacular translations and

7 The importance of the ancient rhetorical heritage for narrative invention is well emphasized by Morse (1991), especially pp. 105–24 (for the Anglo-French realm).

adaptations. Roughly the same trajectory was taken by the Latin versions of the *Alexander Romance*, the most important of which was also called a *Historia (de proeliis)*.[8] Thus, Western authors could not, like the Greek Psellos and some of his colleagues, discern a clear pagan genre of prose fiction. But the two histories in question did provide storytelling material and entertainment based on historical figures for monastic, episcopal and lay patrons from at least the twelfth century.

More formative for Latin authors was, as pointed out by Dennis Green and others, the study of pagan poets, especially Virgil and Ovid. They clearly helped to open up a space for fictional experiments in Latin literature as early as from the eleventh century. This fruitful dialogue with pagan poets – made possible by the paradigm shift in the curricula of eleventh-century cathedral schools – did not cease to have an effect on Latin historical and fictional writing once the main narrative matters had been transferred from Latin to French or German.

Likewise in the thirteenth and fourteenth centuries, Latin remained an important vehicle for the development of fictional forms – but now in a lively exchange with written vernaculars. An obvious example of Latin as the busy junction of a number of vernacular versions is Guido de Colonna's *Historia destructionis Troiae* (1287) with its huge impact on the perception and treatment of the matter of Troy. Equally influential in Western literary history was the development of the *exemplum* genre by the mendicants in the thirteenth century. This forerunner of the *novella* – often with historical settings but also marked as fictional ('once upon a time') – got its most important collection in the early fourteenth-century Latin *Gesta Romanorum*.

Only a few of these Latin themes are explored in the present book, but they need to be remembered here as part of the invitation to reconstruct a more open narrative of European literature. They serve to remind us that Latin literature underwent a dynamic change together with vernacular writing and that we still need to worry about the role of Latin after its earlier virtual monopoly had been broken. In the West we find some of the same tensions between linguistic registers, varieties of patronage and types of performance, as Agapitos sets forth in his chapter on Byzantine fiction. But the function of Latin in the West differed to a large degree from that of the high-register classicizing of Greek in Byzantium – not least in northern Europe.

8 For these texts and their medieval fortunes, see Schmeling (1999), Stoneman (1999), Archibald (1999) (all in the fine volume on Latin fiction edited by Heinz Hofmann (1999)).

In comparison to the Romance regions, the Germanic- and Celtic-speaking North were much more alienated from the sacred and authoritative written language by the simple fact that it had no recognizable relation to spoken languages. The performative and compositional interface between written stories and lived literature thus presented new challenges – which might help to explain the fact that Irish, Anglo-Saxon, Old and Middle High German and Old Norse were all comparatively early in producing a host of translations (and adaptations) of Roman and biblical narratives. This transfer, however, did not completely halt a continuous harvesting from the Latin canon (pagan and Christian), not even in the most distant periphery of western Europe, namely Norway and Iceland where a strong and distinct vernacular narrative literature emerged, especially in the thirteenth century. To catch a glimpse of the situation, it is tempting to quote a well-known saga passage – the deathbed scene of the Norwegian King Håkon Håkonsson (reigned 1217–63):

> Afterwards that same night the course of his sickness began to get heavier, and then he took to his bed the second time, and men thought then that his sickness began to be much worse. In the sickness he let Latin books be read to him at first. But then he thought it great trouble to think over what that meant. Then he let be read to him Norse books, night and day; first the sagas of the saints; and when they were read out he let be read to him the tale of the kings from Halfdan the black, and so on of all the kings of Norway one after the other.[9]

During his long reign Håkon had presided over a cultural programme, a small-scale *translatio studii* from France to Norway which included building styles and literature. A number of French romances (as chivalric sagas, *riddarasögur*) and Marie de France's *Lais* were translated and performed at the Norwegian court, and simultaneously a number of great local sagas had been taken down in writing. The literary world of Håkon and his court was therefore both rich and trendy, and it is no accident that he wanted reading at his deathbed. As transpires from the passage, Latin reading was relevant but difficult, and there was plenty of written Norse to choose from. The gloom of the moment called for serious historical events in the form of saints' lives and stories of Norwegian kings, rather than romance entertainment. Taken together with the

9 *The Saga of Hacon*, trans. G. W. Dasent, London, 1894, p. 366.

fact that this was the very period where the Icelandic family saga flourished (although probably not disseminated outside of Iceland), the passage shows that written narratives in Old Norse culture covered the entire spectrum from the strong truth claims of saints' lives and historical kings through semi-historical family stories to fictional adaptations of French romance.[10]

In this context of different literary environments – synchronically situated in space – it is worth pointing to the comparative approach taken up by Slavica Ranković in her chapter. The Serbian oral material from the early nineteenth century (and the particularly well-documented background of its transfer into the written medium) is of great relevance here because it can show how oral or orally derived 'texts' might display revealing similarities across time. The similar authentication devices concerning the storyteller's claim for 'truth', developed within two absolutely unrelated oral cultures, can teach us a lot about socio-cultural mentalities in pre-modern times.

The inclusion of Serbian oral poems and their comparison to Norse sagas points to the similar approach taken up by Panagiotis A. Agapitos in his chapter. Byzantium is another medieval culture, marginalized in previous scholarship, even though it was the major economic and military power of the early medieval world until the early eleventh century. Byzantium was, during the entire high and later Middle Ages, also the centre in the cultural exchanges between Latin, Greek and Arabic cultures. 'History' and 'fiction', as poles of opposition, were viewed by Byzantine intellectuals in quite different terms, as were the notions of 'vernacular' and 'non-vernacular' language, while the cultural 'centralization' of the empire, as opposed to the 'fragmentation' of the Western and the Eastern worlds, offers an excellent paradigm for approaching the subject of the present volume in an extended comparative manner.

Comparisons, obviously, have their limits. But the broad, interconnected space of medieval Europe offers a fairly solid spatial frame for such an approach. Similarly, the period c. 1100–1400 offers a satisfactory chronological frame for our investigations. It is a time that opens and ends with major political and economic changes all over Europe and the Middle East, marking gradual changes in the forms of governance and patronage. Needless to say, such a generalization must be qualified for every individual region within this medieval chrono-geography, but we hope that the present book will give the

10 This spectrum is surveyed in Else Mundal's contribution in the present volume.

opportunity to its readers to see more of the similarities than the differences traditionally explored in previous research.

HISTORY AND FICTION

Having sketched the linguistic, textual and socio-literary space that is covered in this volume, we can return to the overriding general question of the rise and function of fictional modes within the field of historical narratives. It is perhaps useful first to remind ourselves that the notion of fiction, even by the best historical reading of the evidence for medieval concepts and practices, cannot help but have modern connotations.

The present surge of interest in the whole phenomenon of medieval fiction is, at least partly, inspired by trends that emphasize the subjective, creative, identity-shaping and highly selective aspects of discourses on the past (as in postcolonial and cultural memory studies). Serious corrosion is showing in the once proud structure that upheld such a clear dichotomy between the scholarly and the literary practice of history. The modern habit of drawing a demarcation line between the two came into being with the simultaneous upgrading of history to a university and school discipline and the rise of the historical novel in the first half of the nineteenth century, both of course serving patriotic aims in the post-Napoleonic reorganization of European identities.

Furthermore, it was in the second half of the nineteenth century that history systematized its key metaphors ('sources', 'method', 'reality') – still in force but now frozen – and underpinned them with a body of theoretical ideas that were strongly patterned on scientific vocabulary and procedures. Especially the idea of a historical 'truth' to be found out there (as in the natural world), however imperfectly, colours much of our understanding of the boundary between history and historical romance. When we confront medieval texts claiming to be true accounts of the past, our immediate reaction may be that the medieval idea of 'truth' is theological and hence more abstract and immovable than the one implied in our scholarly search for the 'truth' in a particular, concrete historical case. But, in fact, the reverse argument could be made.

As will also appear from the studies in this volume, the medieval experience of historical knowledge was in general much more 'embodied' and concrete than the modern one. The past beyond living memory existed only through certain physical remains, through storytellers (or actors) who were met face-to-face, or through unique manuscript books being handled by specialists in the flesh (see the section below on authentication).[11] Modern historical experience, in contrast, relies on a disembodied truth, or at least an ideal search for historical truth. Through institutions and a multitude of absent professionals, a scholarly discourse perceived as mental and abstract sets the standards. When popular cultural forms (like historical movies) play with history and fiction, it happens in a field where appeals can always be made to the real professional practice of history. This is not to say, of course, that modern historical discourse is perceived to be of one mind, but the salient point here is simply that an ideal abstract discourse is seen as the ultimate guarantor of the past and that the distance between the representation(s) and the represented has grown enormous. In the Middle Ages the distance was so small that the representation and the represented shared the same body and thus often looked almost identical.

In short, there is no Archimedic point in conceptual and literary history from which we can dissect medieval narratives; we will, as it were, always be intruding observers because our interest in medieval truth claims must entail an application of and reflection on our own terms which serve both as vehicles to enter and to exit a medieval storyworld. We must try to shed our notions of 'historical truth' as an ideal abstract account covering all thinkable historical processes and matching 'the reality' on one hand, while, on the other, we have to acknowledge that our interests and even our concepts are, in fact, related to pre-modern ones – even if only distantly so.

A similar impasse faces us when considering the contrasting term, fiction. In non-technical modern discourse 'fiction' and 'literature' are often equated. One result of this is that it can be quite hard to explain to modernists that one is dealing with medieval literature – and under this heading also with chronicles purporting to tell the truth. A conceptual miscommunication of the same type can arise when discussing the matter with medievalists in the history department who acknowledge that medieval historians used literary (or rhetorical) devices but tend to ascribe most of these to the fictional pole of the spectrum. This modern application of 'literary' as almost meaning 'fictional' can of course be cleared up if we switch to a more specialized mode of speaking. But again, even within a specialized scholarly field with well-defined rules

11 Some of these physical aspects are well treated by Otter (1996).

there will never be a *tabula rasa* that contains no traces of modern connotations.

Recent research: Some landmarks

Although historians have been very active in rekindling interest in a number of formal aspects and rhetorical strategies of medieval historiography,[12] most of the groundwork in the last two or three decades on the relationship between history and fiction in medieval narratives has, perhaps not surprisingly, come from the field of literary history. One impulse behind this research is the attempt to understand the prehistory of the eighteenth- and nineteenth-century novel. This is clear, for instance, in an influential article from 1982 by Per Nykrog, 'The Rise of Literary Fiction'. Here we already find several key elements that recur in scholarship from the 1990s and 2000s: a passing but rather dismissive reference to fiction in antiquity;[13] an insistence on defining fiction as written, not oral, and as the product of an author in contrast to the traditional storyteller; the importance of the matters of Rome and of Britanny (and the role of Geoffrey of Monmouth); and, not least, the dominating figure of Chrétien de Troyes who in the 1160s and 1170s created a whole new literary idiom to be imitated for centuries to come.

From the 1990s books and articles on medieval literature with 'fictionality' in the title began to proliferate. In addition to the question of novels before the novel, more theoretical approaches in a wider field of studies now inspired medievalists. The breakthrough of literacy studies made itself felt (e.g. the influence of Goody, Havelock, Clanchy, Stock and others), as did reception studies (e.g. Jauss) and more general literary issues of fiction and imagination (e.g. Iser). A number of rich studies of differing opinions were published, one in English by Morse (1991),[14] but especially in German with a focus on Middle High German literature, for instance by Haug (1995, 2002), Knapp (1997 and 2005), Knapp and Niesner (2002), Heinzle (1990), Grünkorn (1994), and Burrichter (1996). Although no clear consensus of the definition and explanation of fiction in medieval romance seems to have emerged, these contributions

12 A few more comprehensive works may be mentioned: Breisach (1985), Guenée (1980), Kersken (1995), Goetz (1999), Ljubarskij (1998).

13 In accordance with one group of scholars he pronounces Petronius's *Satyricon* as the first known fictional work (p. 594); but see Hägg's contribution in this volume about biographical fiction (and Hägg 1983 and 2004 for studies on the early Hellenistic novel).

14 Focused entirely, in spite of its broad title, on Anglo-French literature (and its Latin background) from c. 1100 to 1600.

brought to the fore both important terminological problems and a mapping of the key generic issues in the voluminous German romances from the decades around 1200 as well as their background in francophone literature. Some of the debated issues of general interest include whether fictionality in the romances should mainly be defined through intratextual or extratextual features (or some combination of them) and whether it is possible, or even desirable, to harmonize vernacular romance poetics with the theoretical vocabulary dealt with in Latin rhetorical treatises (old and new) – in particular the triad of *historia*, *fabula* and *argumentum*?

The status of the triad around 1200 was perceptively dealt with in a separate study by Päivi Mehtonen (1996) which brought forward not only the relevant documentation but also provided an analysis of the tensions between 'old concepts and new poetics'. The existence of a relationship between the two, however, was taken for granted in her context, as her primary material was not vernacular romances but contemporary Latin didactic poems on rhetoric and poetics. The impulse from the reading of the classics for the romance poets proper was also highlighted in an important (but somewhat neglected) study by Francine Mora (1994) who showed the heavy reliance by the *Roman d'Eneas* poet (c. 1160) on exegetical practices in Anglo-Norman and French schools around the middle of the twelfth century – thus contributing again to answering the genetic question of the rise of the romance.

While many of these studies treated Latin writing as a theoretical backdrop for the practice of vernacular fiction (the French and German romances), new ground was broken by Monika Otter (1996) in a study on how not only Geoffrey of Monmouth, but other Anglo-Norman Latin writers of the twelfth century like William of Malmesbury and Walter Map would play with fictionality and referentiality. While not everyone would agree with her ingenious readings, it was important for the first time to move the fictionality debate out of the Latin/vernacular deadlock.[15] The rise of fictionality should be discussed across the linguistic spectrum of the inventive twelfth century and should deal with contemporary historiography as part of an ensemble.

A recent book by Robert Stein (2006), *Reality Fictions* (also on French and Anglo-Norman material but including some texts from the eleventh century), should be recommended for some of the same reasons: the chronology and

15 Although Morse (1991) had already moved in this direction, but without concrete demonstration.

boundaries between historiography, epic and romance are problematized; Latin and Old French examples are used in between each other; and fictional literature is read as a symptom of shifting power systems, among which the intersections between clerical and secular power are blurred in a suggestive manner. Similarly, Laura Ashe has produced very fruitful analyses of literary and historical discourse in her 2007 book *Fiction and History in England, 1066–1200*, showing how a new sense of 'Englishness' was developed in French and Latin, especially from the 1170s in texts with different truth claims – again within Anglo-French confines in terms of both subject matter and modern scholarly traditions.

Drawing on the German discussions of the 1990s and on a large corpus of texts in both French and German, Dennis H. Green published his magisterial book *The Beginnings of Medieval Romance: Fact and Fiction, 1150–1220* in 2002 – a book which has been a major inspiration behind the present collection.

Green puts forward this definition: 'Fiction is a category of literary text which, although it may also include events that were held to have actually taken place, gives an account of events that could not conceivably have taken place and/or of events that, although possible, did not take place, and which, in doing so, invites the intended audience to be willing to make-believe what would otherwise be regarded as untrue.' This definition absorbs the medieval conceptual triad of *historia, fabula* and *argumentum*, but, more importantly, it professes a completely contractual approach to fiction: there are no inherent traits in a text which make it fictional (and exactly the same text can, in principle, be historical for one audience and fictional for another), nor is the inventiveness of the author of relevance. It all resides in a contract between author/storyteller and a specific audience (in practice the contract often has to be decoded from the text and intertexts if clear extratextual evidence is missing).

Armed with this approach, Green was able to make progress in various directions. On one side he placed very creative accounts, like Geoffrey's *History* or hagiographical rewritings (where we can often de-mask the authorial inventiveness), squarely on the side of history: for their immediate patrons and audience such texts were written to be and taken to be true accounts – they are 'fabricated' in Green's term, but not fictional. Another strength of his approach is that he acknowledges the importance of the study of Virgil (cf. Mora 1994) and Ovid in the eleventh- and twelfth-century schools and shows how fictionality already emerged in some Latin writing in the eleventh century.[16] Furthermore he upgraded the importance of the *romans d'antiquité* (between c. 1150 and 1170) as they were the locus of the first vernacular experiments of episodic fiction – passages within a basically historical account based on Virgil, Statius, or writers on Troy and Alexander in which the authors were elaborating love stories or travelogues which were understood to be invented for the occasion. This again was the point of departure for the full-fledged fiction that arose from stories around the (equally historical) King Arthur in the material deriving from Geoffrey's *History* (c. 1136) and his vernacular mediator Wace (1155). The twelve years' peace during the reign of Arthur provided an ideal narrative gap for placing all the fictional adventures of his knights – a practice that in turn led to a more or less consistent 'interfictive world' of Arthurian stories at Anglo-Norman, French and German courts.

Green points to an intra-discursive and an extra-discursive explanation for the burst of fiction in the central period from c. 1150 to 1220. The gaps in historical accounts were important as the point of departure both for incipient and full-fledged fiction. In this sense, a rich historical storyworld was a necessary condition for the development of a fictional one. In line with his definition of fiction as determined by a specific audience and its expectations, Green finally points to the social conditions necessary for the writing of romances. From around the middle of the twelfth century lay courts in England, France and Germany in effect appropriated literacy. Musical and literary entertainment had always been available, but now the literate clergy provided a bridge to bookish learning through vernacular adaptations from Latin books. The courtly interest in love and war was served very well by focusing on pagan stories and the made-up world of Arthurian knights – thus liberating a non-clerical approach to learning and entertainment coming from books.

The present collection attempts to supplement these important scholarly developments during the last two decades. It is, of course, not surprising that scholars have focused on romances in French and German in the crucial period from c. 1150 to 1220, which is a defining moment in those two vernacular literatures and which had a deep impact on many European literatures in a wider perspective. By broadening the chronological and geographical scope in the manner described above, we hope to be able to open some more space for literatures outside the French, English and German curricula – literatures

16 Tyler (2005) provides another fine example of eleventh-century Latin play with fictionality within history inspired by Virgil.

which have been so dominating in the discussion of medieval fictionality that the peripheral literatures have been marginalized more than they deserve.

In addition, the ongoing general discussion of the tension between fictional and historical narratives in the Middle Ages might benefit from the analyses presented here. Let us just highlight a few themes that could be of wider interest.

Narrative gaps

Gaps unaccounted for in important historical narratives prove to be a major inspiration for authorial inventiveness, and sometimes for fiction. This works in a 'negative' way when the audience is missing a key link between elements in an authoritative story – most famously in the frustrating gaps in the lives of Christ, Mary and the disciples, which were filled by a number of *apocrypha*. The opposite, positive way would be the case developed by Green with the twelve years' peace during the reign of Arthur which does not leave any narrative loose ends but simply some time to be filled with endless new adventures.

The vision genre studied by Wellendorf actually began with a negative biblical gap: what did Paul experience when he was taken to the heavens? Later vision literature often made it clear that the visions described took place in very specific 'historical' circumstances (and were recorded in annals). The visionary's experience or the author's inventiveness, however, never became fictional, for the otherworld that had been experienced or made up had to conform to existing standard descriptions in order to inspire confidence.

Another narrative gap, this time a positive one, is employed by the author of the Latin novel *Dolopathos* (c. 1200) presented in Schmidt's contribution. The lack of detailed knowledge about the life of the pagan wise man and poet Virgil could cast him in various heroic roles – such as the one in *Dolopathos*. Furthermore, ignorance about Sicily during the reign of Augustus provided a nice spatial gap: it was conveniently close to Rome for the Roman part of the plot, and it was conveniently distant to allow for a previously unheard-of ruler. Another great hero of the empire, Constantine the Great, naturally attracted much attention, not least in the city he founded. As mentioned in the study of Byzantine fiction by Agapitos (pp. 263–4 below), the narrative pause created by the chronicler Manasses (c. 1150) makes room for a digression, but not for any unprecedented stories as Constantine's well-documented life and status as a saint seems to have excluded such a possibility.

Narrative gaps of enormous extension opened up when historians like

Geoffrey of Monmouth and Saxo Grammaticus (c. 1200) decided that their nations went as far back as the Trojan War. This was both a great opportunity and a great challenge to convincingly synchronize more than a thousand years of history for which the records were very scarce or entirely missing. Geoffrey had to navigate in relation to the existing master narrative by Bede, whereas Saxo had an almost open sea before him. Mehtonen and Mortensen describe some of their rhetorical strategies for achieving this, but in both cases their fabrications were not meant to be seen through – a process that can perhaps be approached in a more sympathetic vein by the concept of mythmaking or mythopoiesis.[17]

A fictional filling of a gap, however, took place in late medieval Iceland with the popular fornaldarsagas – the sagas of ancient times, as described by Mundal. Dealing not only with the pre-Christian North, but with the period before the settlement of Iceland (late ninth century), the stories had plenty of opportunity to indulge in the fantastic and incredible, obviously with the connivance of the audience.

Authentication

Prefaces to medieval historical writing are full of authentications, most notably in the recurring triad of *scripta, audita, visa* as the three accepted media of raw narrative material.[18] That this was of great concern for all kinds of writers about the past – whether slavishly copying older texts, moulding interviews and songs into a literary narrative, inventing new material with or without the complicity of an intended audience – is connected to the 'embodied' nature of medieval discourse. Trust depended on trustworthy men, and if they did not show up they were represented by proxy – either by writs or books or by a messenger who could point back to them. These legal face-to-face mechanisms also dominated historical discourse. There was no scholarly discipline of history and hence no institutionalized abstract vocabulary and disembodied ideals that could function as effective last resort appeals for any truth claim; it had to be men or concrete books (or other objects) speaking for men.

It is therefore not surprising that most of the contributions in this collection touch on issues of authentication devices. Ranković devotes her chapter to an analysis of such devices in two orally-derived epic traditions, those of the Icelandic family sagas and the Serbian epic songs. She uncovers an 'arms race'

17 Mortensen (2006).
18 Cf. Guenée (1980: 77–109); Mortensen (2008).

between devices used by singers/storytellers and truth expectations by the primary audience. In disclosing this rich array of techniques, she introduces the term fictional and factual 'attractor' and explains how both ends of the scale were always ready to come into play. The similarities between the two literatures – with a more complex array of devices than some of the canonical European medieval epics – can be partly accounted for by rich transmission and partly by structures in the societies whose identities the songs and stories were meant to serve.

Another twist in the authentication of oral narratives is studied by Wellendorf. Visions of the otherworld were, on the one hand, completely uncontrollable personal accounts; on the other they reported on an eternal and unchangeable phenomenon. This made authentication especially precarious and it is clear that they – like the contemporary miracles – always left room for scepticism. The conformity of the account with others was, paradoxically, one sort of authentication. Another was a physical mark or object carried over from the other world – much like miracle stories in hagiography and historiography.[19]

Passing from *audita* and *visa* to *scripta* we face a remarkable series of authentications from non-existent books. To put this 'old-book' device in perspective, the more typical situation in the Latin West should first be mentioned: In the Old English translation of the early fifth-century apologetic world history by Orosius (c. 900), the phrase 'says Orosius' is used time and again. Similarly in the Middle High German *Kaiserchronik* (c. 1150), a voluminous verse history on the late antique Empire in particular, the phrase 'says the book' is reiterated. In both instances we are reassured that what comes out of this vernacular book really is grounded in a Latin book (which is in fact not always the case in the *Kaiserchronik*). Any historical narrative about the distant past would routinely be expected to derive from ancient authoritative writings – as was also the case for the *romans d'antiquité* (see Agapitos's contribution pp. 254–63).

When Geoffrey of Monmouth and Saxo Grammaticus composed elaborate 'prehistories' of the Britons and the Danes, they seem to have faced the problem of authentication in an acute way. Both came up with radical solutions which are discussed in Mortensen's chapter. Geoffrey turned the 'Latin-book-behind-my-narrative' on its head by claiming that he was translating an old book in the vernacular (not accessible to anybody else) into a Latin history

19 Cf. Otter (1996).

– thus both authenticating and disowning his own narrative. Saxo ingeniously hinted that the records used by him for the earlier parts of the history – runic inscriptions and songs in the vernacular – amounted to a 'book' *in spe*, thereby presenting himself as a simple mouthpiece, but also as the producer of the book that finally materialized.

References to an ancient book also appear in the early eleventh-century Persian historical epic by Firdowsi, and in blatant fictions, like the thirteenth-century Latin romance *Gesta Herewardi* (see Schmidt below pp. 76–7) and Chrétien's unprecedented Constantinopolitan romance, *Cligés* (for Firdowsi, *Cligés* and more, see Agapitos below, pp. 254–63).

The obsession with the authority of the book and the imaginative power of the idea of a lost book whose remnants are saved by the good services of our author testify not only to a Christian or Muslim habitus with the sacred book as the last resort, but also – from the point of view of literary history – to worlds where books were numerous enough for unheard-of specimens to be probable and where they were still unique and precarious as in any manuscript culture. For the fiction of a lost book to be relevant, we have to be in a world of good libraries and literary refinement, as can be seen in the case of Philostratus's book about Apollonius of Tyana as discussed in Hägg's contribution. His example is that of a second-century (AD) Roman literary salon in which Philostratus claims to have access to an otherwise unknown diary by a certain Syrian Damis who had attended the philosopher-hero Apollonius of Tyana.

Rhetorical elaboration

A final common trait of the texts discussed in this volume is really too great a field to be treated in passing, but it should at least be mentioned. Although there is no simple relationship between the application of rhetorical techniques of elaboration and the degree of fictionalization in a historical narrative, there is certainly a tendency for authors of fiction to visualize more. However, some plainly historical texts – like certain Latin and Greek chronicles and various sagas of kings – do include descriptions of the physical appearance of protagonists as a matter of course. But visualized scenery, descriptions of artifacts and contraptions, and similar rhetorical brilliance became a stock element in a number of twelfth- and thirteenth-century novels or romances (see especially the chapters by Schmidt and Agapitos). These sometimes found a literary point of departure in the *ekphraseis* of ancient epic and, not least, in the Hellenistic novel. Such elaborate visualization both utilized the narrative gaps opened up by history, and catered for a sensual and emotional desire for the 're-presentation' of a glorious past so common to lay (or partly lay) audiences.

But *ekphraseis* and other visualizations are only a subset of wider rhetorical elaboration (*amplificatio*). Speeches, dialogue, and direct or indirect characterization also belong here, and they were widely used in a number of basically historical narratives to enliven them or to introduce partial fiction.[20] They could also be used in a non-fictional (but inventive) mode, like that of Geoffrey of Monmouth and Saxo Grammaticus (see the chapters by Mehtonen and Mortensen). Saxo provides an extreme example of what might be termed moral amplification: the lessons to be drawn from a character or a turn of events are repeatedly rephrased to become exemplary catalogues of vices and virtues.

It is our hope – as already stated – that the present collection will broaden the basis for the debate on fictionality and historicity in medieval narratives on the empirical level of European (and partly, Middle Eastern) literary history and also, through comparison, offering a bearing on some theoretical issues of definition, conceptual history, and the discourse on the past in pre-modern Europe.

We have found the contractual approach advocated by Green very useful for most of our materials, and we have also been able to see – from the peripheries – what a crucial moment the later twelfth century was for the rise of new fictional forms from historical narratives. On the other hand, there was no one rise of fiction. The literatures of classical Greece and Rome, of Byzantium and Persia, all developed forms of fiction well before the French and German romances – as was the case in eleventh-century medieval Latin literature. In the literatures of the North, only beginning around 1100, the impact of the cultural centres was naturally very great on both genres and literary devices, but apart from the oral negotiations that we can glimpse behind the sagas of Icelanders, the North only seems to have produced fiction recognizable as such in the later Middle Ages. Fictional (written) literature, it appears, is dependent both on the availability and relevance of models and a certain proliferation of books, and also on the development of aristocratic audiences who introduce books into their entertainment.[21]

20 Cf. Kalinke (2006: 471).
21 Or audiences consisting of non-aristocratic gentry as in Iceland.

Finally we would like to stress that even if progress can be made in identifying fictional forms, they should, more than ever, be studied together with other types of texts concerned with narratives of the past such as epic and chronicles. As is also apparent from the studies presented here, there is a significant overlap of rhetorical techniques between the genres and approaches to the past and there are mixtures of fiction, mythopoiesis and referential history. The tension between referentiality and imagination is never ultimately released or resolved in discourse about the past. Even with different truth claims, both sides of the scale still share – as they did in the Middle Ages – the same task of shaping identities: by representing a certain past or representing a certain canon of texts, a certain language and linguistic register, identity markers are being made. All narratives under discussion here are moralizing and lead the audience to a contact – through language, names of people and places – with the local past.

References

Agapitos, Panagiotis A. (1998) 'Narrative, Rhetoric, and "Drama" Rediscovered: Scholars and Poets in Byzantium Interpret Heliodorus', in Richard Hunter (ed.), *Studies in Heliodorus* (Cambridge Philological Society. Supplementary Volume, 21), Cambridge: Cambridge Philological Society, pp. 125–56.

Ankersmit, Frank R. (2001) *Historical Representation*, Stanford: Stanford University Press.

Archibald, Elizabeth (1999) '*Apollonius of Tyre* in the Middle Ages and the Renaissance', in Heinz Hofmann (ed.), *Latin Fiction: The Latin Novel in Context*, London: Routledge, pp. 229–37.

Ashe, Laura (2007) *Fiction and History in England, 1066–1200*, Cambridge: Cambridge University Press.

Breisach, Ernst (ed.) (1985) *Classical Rhetoric & Medieval Historiography* (Studies in Medieval Culture, XIX), Kalamazoo: Medieval Institute Publications.

Burrichter, Brigitte (1996) *Wahrheit und Fiktion. Der Status der Fiktionalität in der Artuslitteratur des 12. Jahrhunderts*, Munich: Fink.

Goetz, Hans-Werner (1999) *Geschichtsschreibung und Geschichtsbewusstsein im hohen Mittelalter*, Berlin: Akademie Verlag.

Green, Dennis H. (2002) *The Beginnings of Medieval Romance: Fact and Fiction, 1150–1220* (Cambridge Studies in Medieval Literature, 47), Cambridge: Cambridge University Press.

Grünkorn, Gertrud (1994) *Die Fiktionalität des höfischen Romans um 1200*, Berlin: Erich Schmidt Verlag.

Guenée, Bernard (1980) *Histoire et culture historique dans l'Occident médiéval*, Paris: Montaigne.

Haug, Walter (1995) *Brechungen auf dem Weg zur Individualität. Kleine Schriften zur Literatur des Mittelalters*, Tübingen: Niemeyer.

Haug, Walter (2002) 'Geschichte, Fiktion und Wahrheit. Zu den literarischen Spielformen zwischen Faktizität und Phantasie', in Franz Peter Knapp and Manuela Niesner (eds.), *Historisches und fiktionales Erzählen im Mittelalter*, Berlin: Duncker & Humblot, pp. 115–31.

Hägg, Tomas (1983) *The Novel in Antiquity*, Berkeley: University of California Press.

Hägg, Tomas (2004) *Parthenope: Selected Studies in Ancient Greek Fiction (1969–2004)*. Edited by Lars Boje Mortensen and Tormod Eide, Copenhagen: Museum Tusculanum Press.

Heinzle, Joachim (1990) 'Die Entdeckung der Fiktionalität. Zu Walter Haugs "Literaturtheorie im deutschen Mittelalter"', *Pauls und Braunes Beiträge* 112: 55–80.

Hofmann, Heinz (ed.) (1999) *Latin Fiction: The Latin Novel in Context*, London: Routledge.

Kalinke, Marianne (2006) 'The Genesis of Fiction in the North', in John McKinnell, David Ashurst and Donata Kick (eds.), *The Fantastic in Old Norse/Icelandic Literature: Sagas and the British Isles* (Preprint papers of The 13th International Saga Conference, Durham and York 6–12 August 2006), Durham University, pp. 464–78.

Kersken, Norbert (1995) *Geschichtsschreibung im Europa der 'nationes'. Nationalgeschichtliche Gesamtdarstellungen im Mittelalter*, Cologne: Böhlau.

Knapp, Franz Peter (1997) *Historie und Fiktion in der mittelalterlichen Gattungspoetik. Sieben Studien und ein Nachwort*, Heidelberg: Carl Winter.

Knapp, Franz Peter (2005) *Historie und Fiktion in der mittelalterlichen Gattungspoetik (II). Zehn neue Studien und ein Vorwort* (Schriften der Philosophisch-historischen Klasse der Heidelberger Akademie der Wissenschaften, 35), Heidelberg: Carl Winter.

Knapp, Franz Peter and Manuela Niesner (eds.) (2002), *Historisches und fiktionales Erzählen im Mittelalter*, Berlin: Duncker & Humblot, pp. 63–72.

Ljubarskij, Jakov (1998) '*Quellenforschung* and/or Literary Criticism: Narrative Structures in Byzantine Historical Writings', *Symbolae Osloenses* 73: 5–73.

Mehtonen, Päivi (1996) *Old Concepts and New Poetics:* Historia, Argumentum, *and* Fabula *in the Twelfth- and Early Thirteenth-Century Latin Poetics of Fiction* (Societas Scientiarum Fennica. Commentationes Humanarum Litterarum, 108), Helsinki: Societas Scientiarum Fennica.

Mora, Francine (1994) *L'Enéide médiévale et la naissance du roman*, Paris: PUF, Perspectives Littéraire.

Morris, Ivan (1979), *The World of the Shining Prince: Court Life in Ancient Japan*, 2nd edition, Harmondsworth: Penguin.

Morse, Ruth (1991) *Truth and Convention in the Middle Ages: Rhetoric, Representation, and Reality*, Cambridge: Cambridge University Press.

Mortensen, Lars Boje (1994) 'The Glorious Past: Entertainment, Example or History? Levels of Twelfth-Century Historical Culture', *Culture and History* 13: 57–71.

Mortensen, Lars Boje (2006) 'Sanctified Beginnings and Mythopoietic Moments: The First Wave of Writing on the Past in Norway, Denmark, and Hungary, c. 1000–1230', in Lars Boje Mortensen (ed.), *The Making of Christian Myths in the Periphery of Latin Christendom (c. 1000–1300)*, Copenhagen: Museum Tusculanum Press, pp. 247–73.

Mortensen, Lars Boje (2008) 'From Vernacular Interviews to Latin Prose (c. 600–1200)', in Else Mundal and Jonas Wellendorf (eds.), *Oral Art Forms and their Passage into Writing*, Copenhagen: Museum Tusculanum Press, pp. 53–68.

Nykrog, Per (1982) 'The Rise of Literary Fiction', in Robert L. Benson and Giles Constable (eds.), *Renaissance and Renewal in the Twelfth Century*, Cambridge, MA: Harvard University Press, 593–612. [Repr. Toronto University Press, 1991.]

Otter, Monika (1996) *Inventiones: Fiction and Referentiality in Twelfth-Century English Historical Writing*, Chapel Hill and London: University of North Carolina Press.

Pietsch, Effie (2005) *Die* Chronographia *des Michael Psellos: Kaisergeschichte, Autobiographie und Apologie* (Serta Graeca, 20), Wiesbaden: Ludwig Reichelt Verlag.

Schmeling, Gareth (1999) 'The History of Apollonius, King of Tyre', in Heinz Hofmann (ed.), *Latin Fiction: The Latin Novel in Context*, London: Routledge, pp. 141–52.

Stein, Robert M. (2006) *Reality Fictions: Romance, History, and Governmental Authority, 1025–1180*, Notre Dame: University of Notre Dame Press.

Stoneman, Richard (1999) 'The Latin Alexander', in Heinz Hofmann, *Latin Fiction: The Latin Novel in Context*, London: Routledge, pp. 167–86.

Tyler, Elizabeth M. (2005) 'Fictions of Family: The *Encomium Emmae Reginae* and Virgil's *Aeneid*', *Viator* 36: 149–79.

Historical Fiction in the Graeco-Roman World: Cyrus, Alexander, Apollonius

Tomas Hägg

Literary fiction is, of course, as old as literature itself. Hesiod lets the Muses inspire both what is true (ἀληθέα) and 'many false things similar to genuine ones' (ψευδέα πολλὰ ... ἐτύμοισιν ὁμοῖα) (*Theogony* 27–28).[1] Exactly what is meant by this distinction is unclear, but it seems likely that narrative epic, or some kind of it, is the target of Hesiod's 'false things similar to genuine ones'.[2] Does Hesiod mean that he himself tells the truth, while Homer just presents lies? However that may be, we proceed directly to Homer's *Iliad* and apply to it instead the three basic modes of narration (*tria genera narrationum*) distinguished between in antiquity: *historia*, *fabula* and *argumentum* (with the Greek equivalents ἱστορία, πλασματικόν or δραματικόν, and μῦθος). They are first to be found in the rhetorical treatise *ad Herennium*,[3] in the early first century BC, and then reappear with occasional variations in many Greek and Latin authors, to be codified in the early seventh century AD by Isidore of Seville.[4] No doubt, the *Iliad* would qualify as *historia*, defined (with Dennis Green in *The Beginnings of Medieval Romance*) as 'a true record of events that [have] actually taken place, but at some distance in time from present memory'.[5] That is, at least, the way most contemporary Greeks (though perhaps not Hesiod and his kind) will have looked upon it. That gods appear on earth in disguise would be no obstacle (as it became later),[6] nor the vivid scenes from the gods'

1 Trans. Glenn W. Most (Loeb Classical Library).

2 For discussion, see Bowie (1993: 20–2).

3 *ad Her.* 1.13: *Fabula est, quae neque veras neque veri similes continet res, ut eae sunt, quae tragoedis traditae sunt. Historia est gesta res, sed ab aetatis nostrae memoria remota. Argumentum est ficta res, quae tamen fieri potuit, velut argumenta comoediarum.*

4 *Etym.* 1.44.5. For a detailed account (with full bibliography) of the concept *tria genera narrationum* and its application from Hellenistic times onwards, see Cizek (1997: 275–87). On this concept as applied to the history of the ancient novel, see Barwick (1928).

5 Green (2002: 3).

6 See Dennis Green's contribution in this volume, pp. 54–5.

life on Mount Olympus. In the famous words of Herodotus, Homer and Hesiod created the Greek pantheon and, he continues, 'told us what they look like' (εἴδεα αὐτῶν σημήναντες).[7] Accordingly, Homer's account of their intervention in the Trojan War would by definition be realistic and true.

If we apply the same grid to the *Odyssey*, it might also be defined as *historia*, though with large inserts of *fabula*, recounting 'fictitious events that neither [have] taken place nor could have conceivably done so'.[8] These are to be found in greatest concentration in the so-called Apology (*Od.* 9–12), Odysseus's own tale to the Phaeacians about his marvellous adventures among Lotus-Eaters, Cyclopes, and other fabulous creatures, and about his visit to the ghosts of the Underworld. The fact that this is an ego-narrative, which contains numerous markers of a traveller's tale – in contrast to the impersonal, objective-sounding account of much of the epic – will have made the original listeners, as well as later readers, understand and enjoy it as *fabula*.

To find a clear example in Greek literature of the third mode of narration, *argumentum*, defined by Green as 'dealing with events that [have] not happened, but could have', we go to the late fourth century and Menander's 'New Comedy'. The 'Old Comedy' of Aristophanes, at least the specimens that have come down to us, had in turn been a mixture of *historia* and *fabula*; but Menander and his colleagues put on stage fictitious private persons in realistic-looking Athenian surroundings, with intrigues focusing on everyday topics like love, marriage and money. Aristotle acutely notes this important innovation in the dramatic art. After formulating his famous distinction between history as relating to particulars (τὰ καθ' ἕκαστον), poetry to the universal (τὰ καθόλου) – 'the kinds of things which it suits a certain kind of person to say or do, in terms of probability or necessity' – Aristotle continues (*Poetics* 9, 1451b11–15):

> In comedy, this point has by now become obvious: the poets construct the plot on the basis of probability (διὰ τῶν εἰκότων), and only then supply arbitrary names (τὰ τυχόντα ὀνόματα); they do not, like iambic poets, write about a particular person (τὸν καθ' ἕκαστον). But in tragedy they adhere to the actual names (τῶν γενομένων ὀνομάτων).[9]

7 Herodotus 2.53.2, trans. Robin Waterfield (Oxford World's Classics).
8 Green (2002: 3 f.).
9 Trans. Halliwell (1995).

In fact, a couple of hundred years after Aristotle wrote this, in the late hellenistic period, there emerged a new Greek prose genre which, exactly like New Comedy, put private persons with arbitrary names in the lead and involved them in erotic intrigues and thrilling adventures, with the whole Mediterranean world as a setting.[10] This is what we now, in the absence of an ancient term, call 'the Greek novel' – the closest ancient Greek prose comes to pure *argumentum*.

This 'ideal' Greek novel of love, travel and adventure is the most well-known and most well-defined of the Greek fictional genres in prose. Immediately preceding it in time, we find the fantastic travel tales of the Hellenistic period, recounting voyages to distant islands where people live under paradisical, utopian conditions.[11] In addition, we have the three works of historical fiction that will be my main concern here, the *Cyropaedia* of Xenophon, the *Alexander Romance* of Pseudo-Callisthenes[12] and *Apollonius of Tyana* by Philostratus. These three, though widely different in many respects, all purport to recount the lives of world famous men – a Persian king, a Macedonian world conqueror and a Pythagorean sage.

XENOPHON'S *CYROPAEDIA*

The *Cyropaedia* or 'Education of Cyrus' was written by Xenophon of Athens about 360 BC. It tells the life of King Cyrus the Great, the founder of the Persian empire, who lived in the sixth century (d. 530 BC). So a Greek author writes, for Greek readers, about a Persian ruler, from a distance in time of some 200 years. Both factors, difference in ethnicity and distance in time, would seem to leave fictionality much scope. But Xenophon is a prose author whose earlier production was much devoted to the recording of facts. In the *Anabasis*, he described his own achievement in leading Greek mercenaries back home after a failed military expedition against the Persian king. All the way, he referred to himself as 'Xenophon', in the third person, stressing his documentary purpose. In the *Memorabilia* he purported to give a true portrait of his master, Socrates, in competition with the idealizing pictures being promulgated by Plato and other Socratics. His *Hellenica* was a work of contemporary history, beginning where Thucydides had ended his account of the Peloponnesian war.

10 This viewpoint is developed in Hägg (1974). See further Reardon (1991).
11 See Holzberg (1996: 621–32).
12 The work was falsely attributed to Callisthenes, the Alexander historian (d. 327 BC).

Minor works of Xenophon are devoted to household, riding, hunting, strategy, finances, state constitutions, statesmanship and statesmen, most of them styled as factual accounts.

With this reputation, now at the end of his life, he sends out a large work, in eight 'books' or about 350 printed pages, on the great Persian ruler. He adopts his usual style, and he prefaces his work with a discussion of various political systems and how authority is established. He then singles out Cyrus as the ideal ruler who managed to acquire and keep together an empire of many nations. Finally, he states his intentions with the book in the following way (*Cyr.* 1.1.6):

> So on the grounds that this man was worthy of wonder, we examined (ἐσκεψάμεθα) who he was by birth, what his nature was, and with what education he was brought up, such that he so excelled in ruling men. Whatever we have learned (ἐπυθόμεθα), therefore, and think we know about him, we shall try to relate.[13]

There is no warning here about this work being anything but a fact-orientated description of the king's life, to the best of the author's ability.

The work continues in the usual historiographical style. If only we accept the conventions of ancient historiography, allowing large quantities of directly quoted speech and occasional insights into people's thoughts and feelings, both without indication of sources, this will no doubt have been read as *historia*. The aim of the work, as indicated in the preface, is to investigate what natural endowments this excellent ruler had, how he was educated for his task, and in what manner he then commanded his armies and governed his people. Cyrus is meant to be a model for other rulers, whether in state or household, and if the audience had experienced the description as fictitious, in the sense of contrary to historical truth, much of the point would have been lost.

Yet, on closer inspection, much of the *Cyropaedia* may be revealed as the work of the author's creative imagination. To what degree a contemporary Greek reader of Xenophon's work would have been able to detect this is difficult to know. But those who remembered Herodotus's account of the same Cyrus in the first book of his *Histories* will have noted a number of incompatible facts. So will presumably those who had read the more recent pictures of

13 Trans. Ambler (2001), modified.

Cyrus in Ctesias's *History of Persia* or in a monograph entitled *Cyrus* by the Socratic writer Antisthenes.[14] Of the two latter works only fragments remain, but Herodotus has survived to allow detailed comparison. Some of the differences between his and Xenophon's accounts of Cyrus may be due to Herodotus having got things wrong or using *his* authorial freedom, others to the existence of different, contradictory Persian sources. Among these Xenophon, with his personal knowledge of Persia, may have made his informed choice. But there are also a number of places where, in all likelihood, Xenophon deliberately creates a fictitious world around his hero in order better to convey his message about leadership. It shall suffice just to mention a couple of his more obvious inventions.

Although Herodotus and Xenophon, with one important exception, present the same named members of Cyrus's family, the characterization and roles of the family members differ widely.[15] In Herodotus, Cyrus's grandfather Astyages is a cruel oriental despot who orders his daughter's new-born son Cyrus to be killed. Cyrus's father Cambyses, in turn, is a low-class Persian whom the king only reluctantly allows as the princess's husband in obedience to a threatening dream. Little Cyrus is secretly saved, against his grandfather's orders, and grows up incognito with simple people, like another Moses. The supernatural in the form of dreams and omina around the child's birth plays an important part in Herodotus's story. In Xenophon, in contrast, Cyrus's family background is completely normal and invariably royal. Astyages, King of Media, is here the affectionate grandfather who teaches young Cyrus mores while the boy stays at his court; and his son-in-law Cambyses is King of Persia. In addition, Xenophon has introduced into his narrative a fictitious uncle of Cyrus, a brother of his mother, called Cyaxares, who plays an important part throughout the work as a contrast and foil to Cyrus.

We have, then, a number of historical characters – with τὰ γενόμενα ὀνόματα ('the actual names') – whose personalities have been changed to suit the idealizing purpose of the biography, and one brand-new family member who was invented to serve the needs of the literary characterization of the hero. Moreover, Cyrus's death is as much restructured as were his birth and childhood; while Herodotus lets his Cyrus die violently on the battlefield, Xenophon orchestrates a harmonious family scene where the king on his deathbed looks back on his own life, gives personal and political advice to

14 On Antisthenes' *Cyrus*, see Gera (1993: 8–10).
15 See Due (1989: 54–62, 118–21).

his two sons, speaks of the immortality of the soul, and arranges for his burial – an ideal leader to the bitter end (*Cyr.* 8.7).

It is not unlikely that fourth-century readers of the *Cyropaedia* who had Herodotus fresh in their memories and noted the differences thought Xenophon to be the more reliable recorder of facts. Such was his authorial image. The supernatural elements and folktale motifs are gone, the account is matter-of-fact, with much serious discussion of educational, ideological and strategic topics. This will have lent credibility to the biographical narrative as well. The fact that much of this sixth-century Persian setting is anachronistic as well as anachoristic, displaced in both time and place, need not have disturbed the general Athenian reader much. As is well known, Xenophon's work enjoyed great success well into the modern period, but then as a mirror-of-princes.[16]

THE *ALEXANDER ROMANCE* OF PSEUDO-CALLISTHENES

The *Alexander Romance* is a very different affair than the *Cyropaedia*. It is an anonymous work, with its roots in the centuries immediately following the death of the great world conqueror; but the earliest version that has been transmitted is not older than c. 300 AD (the *terminus ante quem* is the Latin translation of Iulius Valerius, early or mid-fourth century). Its title in the early manuscript tradition, possibly the original one, is Βίος Ἀλεξάνδρου τοῦ Μακεδόνος, *Life of Alexander of Macedon*. My comments will mainly refer to the two oldest extant recensions, labelled A (from an extant eleventh-century manuscript, its *codex unicus*) and b (reconstructed from several manuscripts),[17] and leave out of account the many adaptations and translations that followed through the Middle Ages. As an anonymous work of popular literature, with no obvious 'original' or authoritative version, it had the kind of open textual tradition that allowed copyists, redactors and translators free hands to omit, change and add.[18] Whether that liberal attitude indicates that it was received and read as fiction in the Middle Ages, rather than history, is a question that I prefer to leave open.[19] My own speculation about reader responses will be restricted to the ancient – Hellenistic and imperial – audiences.

The basis for the work is believed to have been a Hellenistic biography

16 Cf. Tatum (1989).

17 On the various Greek recensions, see most recently Jouanno (2002).

18 On the concept 'open text' and its relevance to the *Alexander Romance*, see Konstan (1998).

19 Cf. Cizek (1997: 299–304).

(βίος) of Alexander, romanticized in comparison to the more factual accounts written by the Alexander historians proper, in particular those who had followed Alexander on his campaigns, but also writers of the imperial period, such as Plutarch, Arrian and Curtius Rufus.[20] There is no quite clear-cut distinction, however, in this respect between the 'histories' and the 'romance'. In the histories, too, the historical account is sometimes contaminated with the Alexander legend, which obviously originated already in the lifetime of the hero himself. In Plutarch, whose biography of Alexander is often based on the lost Alexander historians, there are some anecdotes that nicely illustrate Alexander's and his friends' own awareness of the nascent myths around him. While Alexander liked to play out his divine status before orientals, he was ironic about it in the presence of his compatriots. Once, when hit by an arrow, he remarked: 'What you see flowing here, my friends, is blood and not "ichor, which flows in the veins of the blessed gods".'[21] Similarly, long after Alexander's death it happened that Onesicritus, one of the Alexander historians, read aloud from his history to Lysimachus, once Alexander's bodyguard and now king of Thrace. When he came to his description of Alexander's encounter with the queen of the Amazons, Lysimachus smiled gently and said: 'And where was I at that time?'[22] Although told by some of the Alexander historians, Plutarch reports, the Amazon episode was by several others considered to be πλάσμα, 'fiction' (Plut. *Alex.* 46.1). Such source criticism, of course, is totally alien to most parts of the *Alexander Romance*, where the legend is increasingly blown up, rather than allowed to be punctured, as by Alexander's and Lysimachus's remarks in Plutarch.

The Hellenistic *bios* that was (presumably) the point of departure for the late antique *Alexander Romance* was characterized by a straining for effects and sensation typical of the so-called 'pathetic' or 'tragic' historians of the Hellenistic period. To this narrative core was added, at some point,[23] a collection of fictitious letters between Alexander and the Persian king, Darius;

20 I largely follow the analysis of the *Alexander Romance* presented by Merkelbach (1977). For the romance's vacillation between history and fiction, see Stoneman (1994); for its status in relation to the *tria genera narrationum*, see Cizek (1997: 291–306).

21 Plutarch, *Alexander* 28.2, trans. Robin Waterfield (Oxford World's Classics); the Homeric quotation is from *Iliad* 5.340.

22 Ibid., 46.2.

23 When this happened is a matter of contention. Stoneman (1991: 14–17) dates the *Romance*, 'in substantially its present form' (that is, the version present in ms. A), to third-century BC Alexandria. Others attribute the combination of the various constituents to the redactor of c. AD 300, or somewhere between these extremes.

part of the action is narrated within these letters. Long letters of a different character were added as well, addressed to Alexander's mother Olympias and his teacher Aristotle. This is where we find much of the well-known fantastic tales about Alexander's experiences in the east, about his advance towards the edges of the world and of human existence, and about his quest for immortality (esp. 2.32–33, 36–41).[24]

The style in these tales is quasi-scientific and matter-of-fact, as suitable when the alleged addressee is Aristotle and the writer his student,[25] but what is reported is typical *fabula* material and will have been recognized as such: Alexander encounters twelve-metre-tall men with arms shaped like saws, men without heads, monsters and invisible spirits, magic stones and rivers, and birds and trees speaking with human voices. He descends in a glass jar to the bottom of the sea, he flies high up into the sky in a basket carried by large white birds. These are first-person narratives of the same character as Odysseus's Apology and the fabulous accounts of travels to utopian islands. Contemporary readers will not have mistaken the signals: this is *fabula*. Strabo, the geographer who wrote in the Augustan period, ironizes over this kind of teratology in the Alexander historians (2.1.9); others, with a more developed sense of humour, will have taken it as entertaining stories.

But was the original *bios* itself, as far as we can extract it from the various accretions, read as fiction or fact? The very beginning about Nectanebo, the last Pharaoh of Egypt, being the real father of Alexander instead of King Philip, most likely belongs to the early additions to the historical core.[26] This erotic 'novella' is part of an Egyptian nationalistic legend, with magic, astrology and significant dreams at play. This legend intrudes at other places of the Life as well. The defeated Egypt takes its revenge on the victorious Macedonian dynasty by showing that Alexander was in fact of Egyptian royal lineage. Contrary to what it may look like, it is Egypt that has conquered the world.

The Nectanebo novella, it should be added, does nothing to enhance Alexander's status as the son of a god, whether Zeus, Ammon or Sarapis. On the contrary, Olympias's belief that it is the god Ammon who visits her in the night and fathers her child, as she had been foretold in a dream, is exposed as pure fraud. The reader knows all along that Nectanebo himself plays the part of the god whose prophet he pretends to be. He is a magician who makes the

24 Cf. Romm (1992: 108–16); Stoneman (1994: 125–7).
25 Cf. Romm (1992: 112).
26 See Merkelbach (1977: 77–83).

queen see Ammon coming to her in a dream, but in the actual intercourse that makes her pregnant Nectanebo himself impersonates the god, with no supernatural assistance. Astrology, magic and dreams, on the other hand, are narrated as pure facts which the reader is expected to take at face value. As Alexandru Cizek notes, for what might have been a sacred *fabula* the author has substituted a novelistic *argumentum*.[27] Nonetheless, this new beginning (1.1–7), perhaps added as much for its narrative attraction as a spicy 'Milesian tale' as for nationalistic reasons, programmes the reader to expect something quite different from the *historia* that follows.

In the earliest reconstructable recension, to which manuscript A is our prime witness, the story starts with Pharaoh Nectanebo, without any preamble. The redactor behind the next recension, b, has obviously felt the need both to tell the reader that the book is in fact about Alexander, and to strengthen the rhetoric of authentication. For the latter purpose, he states (1.1):[28]

> We begin with his family (γένος) – and the identity of his father. People generally (οἱ πολλοί) are under the misapprehension (ἀπατῶνται) that he was the son of King Philip. This is not true (οὐκ ἀληθὲς οὖν τοῦτο). He was not the child of Philip but rather, as the wisest Egyptians say (λέγουσι), the son of Nectanebo, conceived after he had been driven from his throne.

'People generally', of course, is unanimous Greek tradition; as the authority for the sensational revision of history that the *Romance* is going to propagate, the redactor invokes local Egyptian expertise. No evidence or argument is offered, what is true or not is decided by the nationality of the preferred source and the contrast between experts, 'the wisest', and 'people', οἱ πολλοί.

The alleged underlying *bios*, on the other hand, which we can only hope to retrieve by analysis and dissection of the earliest extant recensions, probably began with Philip being warned by a dream and an omen that his wife is expecting a son who will subdue all the peoples of the east, but then turn back and die young (cf. 1.8, 1.11). The *bios* went on telling about Alexander's birth and childhood (1.13 ff.). This description, as preserved in both A and b, though idealized according to the conventions of Greek *encomia*, does not contain anything supernatural. Alexander's greatest feat is taming his father's man-eating horse, Bucephalus, at the age of fourteen or fifteen. He also wins

27 Cizek (1997: 294).
28 Trans. Dowden in Reardon (1989) and Hansen (1998), modified.

the chariot race at the Olympic Games – by killing his main competitor. By cunning and force, he reconciles his estranged parents. After Philip has been killed, Alexander avenges and succeeds him, and his career as destroyer of revolting Greek cities and world conqueror can begin.

Many of the main facts of the historical Alexander's campaigns are told in the *Romance* as well, though the sequence is often altered (and the recensions vary wildly between them), not to speak of the many imaginative reinterpretations and added picturesque details. In addition, however, we find obviously unhistorical episodes. For example, on his march eastwards Alexander makes a spectacular deviation: he sets out by sea from Asia Minor to Sicily and goes on from there to subdue Rome. On the way he receives the city's capitulation: 'We too shall crown your head, Alexander, king of the Romans and of all the earth' (1.29).[29] Such a western detour of course never happened; but it was part of Hellenistic and Roman historical speculation what course world history would have taken if Alexander had really chosen to confront Rome. If he had not died so young, it was thought, it would have been logical for him to go on to conquer the western Mediterranean as well.[30] The original *bios* may have been less drastic in this case than the later *Alexander Romance*: there is a Hellenistic historical tradition that already at this very point, before Alexander had won his decisive victories over the Persians, the Romans sent a letter of submission to him, accompanied by gifts.[31] It is likely that such notions about how the Romans feared Alexander were cherished in the centuries when the Hellenistic kingdoms gradually succumbed to the Romans, as wishful thinking and a sort of compensation for their present humiliation.

Whatever the exact contents of the supposed original *bios*, it will no doubt have been read as *historia* by its Hellenistic audience. What may seem to us as romantic construction or as unrealistic omniscience on the part of the narrator belonged to the conventions of contemporary historiography. When it comes to the *Alexander Romance* proper, with its blend of erotic novella, tragic history and fabulous letters, I would be less confident. Perhaps we should take recourse to a fourth mode of narration, the recounting of a story that is true in a higher sense, even if it includes obviously supernatural elements and even if many details, when viewed in isolation, may appear incredible. In an Egyptian nationalistic context – where scholars tend to situate the emergence of the

29 Trans. Stoneman (1991).

30 Cf. e.g. Arrian, *Anabasis of Alexander* 7.1.3.

31 See Merkelbach (1977: 17, 33). Cf. Memnon of Heraclea 18.2 (*FGrH* 434); Arr. 7.15.5.

Alexander Romance – this charismatic hero will no doubt have passed as the 'true' Alexander, descended from the last pharaoh, the conqueror not only of Greece and the Orient, but also of Rome, the fearless explorer of the unknown and the master of the elements.

Alternatively, we may with Alexandru Cizek regard the *Alexander Romance* as a composite work in which *historia, argumentum* and *fabula* dominate by turns and where one looks in vain for any unifying principle: 'The chief characteristic of the Pseudo-Callisthenes is in its Protean mutability and incompleteness; because of its structure it could, according to Aristotelian standards (*Poetics* 1451b 33), be viewed as a monstrous ἐπεισοδιώδης μῦθος [a plot with episodes loosely placed next to each other]'.[32] Interestingly, according to Cizek, the composite form opens for different choices in the medieval reception. For instance, 'the Nectanebo novella is taken over without reservation in the Latin novelistic versions, whereas the Alexander compositions in the vernacular often fade it out, sometimes even polemize against this liar's tale (*Lügengeschichte*)'.[33] The explanation, according to Cizek, may be that the Latin-writing clerics did not mind that Alexander was belittled; in fact, such an *argumentum* which caricatured the theogamy might be quite amusing. In chivalric epic, on the other hand, Alexander as the ideal knight needed a dignified descent, and the epic needed a beginning that might be read as *historia*. The amalgam thus falls apart again, partly along the lines of the *genera narrationum*.

PHILOSTRATUS'S *APOLLONIUS OF TYANA*

The *Life of Apollonius of Tyana* is a large work, about the size of the *Cyropaedia*. It was written about AD 220, allegedly by order of Empress Julia Domna (d. AD 217). Its subject is the Pythagorean sage who lived some 150 years earlier. We shall see in some detail how Philostratus expresses himself when he explains what occasioned his work and establishes his scholarly credentials. After a prologue about Pythagoras (1.1), he moves on to Apollonius and the deplorable fact that people generally (οἱ ἄνθρωποι) mistake this genuinely wise man for a magician (1.2.1–2). He continues (1.2.3–3.2):[34]

32 Cizek (1997: 292).
33 Cizek (1997: 295).
34 Trans. Jones (2005), modified.

I have therefore decided to remedy the general ignorance and to give an accurate account (ἐξακριβῶσαι) of the man, observing the chronology of his words and acts, and the special character of the wisdom by which he came close to being thought possessed and inspired. I have gathered my materials from the many cities that were devoted to him, from the shrines that he set right when their rules had fallen into neglect, from other people's reports about him, and from his own letters. These he wrote to kings, sophists, philosophers, Eleans, Delphians, Indians, and Egyptians, on the subject of gods, about customs, morals, and laws, setting upright whatever had been overturned among such people.

But my more detailed information I have gathered as follows. There was a certain Damis, not devoid of wisdom, who once lived in Old Ninos (= Hierapolis in Syria). This man became a disciple of Apollonius and wrote up (ἀναγέγραφεν) not only his journeys, on which he claims (φησί) to have been his companion, but also his sayings, speeches, and predictions. The notebooks containing these memoirs (τὰς δέλτους τῶν ὑπομνημάτων τούτων) were unknown until a member of Damis's family brought them to the attention of the empress Julia. Since I was a member of her salon (τοῦ περὶ αὐτὴν κύκλου) – for she admired and encouraged all rhetorical discourse – she set me to transcribe (μεταγράψαι) these works of Damis and to take care over their style (τῆς ἀπαγγελίας), since the style of the man from Ninos was clear but rather unskillful.

I have also read the book of Maximus of Aegeae, which contains all that Apollonius did in Aegeae, and the will written by Apollonius himself, which gives an idea of how inspired (ὑποθειάζων) he was in his philosophy. Moeragenes does not deserve attention: he wrote four books about Apollonius and yet was greatly ignorant about the man. So much for the way I gathered these scattered materials (ξυνήγαγον ταῦτα διεσπαρμένα) and for my care in assembling them. May my work bring honour to the man who is its subject, and profit to those with an inclination to learning, for they really might learn things quite new to them.

With only few adjustments to contemporary taste, this might as well be read today in the introduction to a scholarly biography. We miss, perhaps, the exact source references in footnotes and bibliography, but all the essential rhetoric to inspire confidence in the writer and authorizing his narrative is present. The impetus to write the book stems from the queen whose confidence the author enjoys. He has used a variety of sources, written as well as oral, among them letters, a will and unpublished memoirs; he has travelled to the places his subject visited; he dismisses one earlier biography of Apollonius as limited in scope, another as useless because ignorant. The contrast to the rudimentary claims to credibility that introduce the *Cyropaedia* and the *Alexander Romance* is significant. We are in a cultural context of quite another intellectual ostentation than either Xenophon's Athens or Pseudo-Callisthenes's Alexandria.

In view of all this scholarly apparatus, it is ironic to note – or perhaps exactly what we should expect – that so much of the story is clearly fictitious. Even the alleged primary source and eyewitness, the Hellenized Syrian Damis who wrote in a poor Greek style, is most probably an invention by Philostratus. In consequence, the queen's role must also be part of the fiction; but Iulia Domna was dead when Philostratus wrote the Life and could not protest. Apparently, Damis and his memoirs were fabricated both to authorize the account and to have a companion to whom Apollonius could expound his wisdom. The dialogue between the master and his naive disciple, quoted directly from the alleged memoirs of Damis (but stylistically improved by order of the queen!), is thus an ingenious literary device to characterize Apollonius. At the same time, it provides unchallengeable authentication of this ultimate description of Apollonius's personality and travels.

Authorial interventions with scholarly discussion of sources to establish what is historical truth are recurring elements throughout the book. For instance, when on their journey to India Apollonius and Damis arrive at Mount Nysa, the mythical birthplace of Dionysus, the report that Alexander the Great had climbed the mountain and celebrated Bacchic rites on its top is rejected as untrue. On the contrary – as the inhabitants of Nysa themselves now tell Apollonius and Damis – Alexander had realized that the sight of vines after so long time would make his men homesick and desirous to drink wine again instead of water. Therefore he had hastened to leave Nysa, after only praying to Dionysus and sacrificing at the foot of the mountain. Philostratus adds (2.9.3):

> I am aware that this account of mine will displease some people (οὐκ ἐς χάριν ταῦτα ἐνίοις γράφων), but those who were on Alexander's campaign falsified this part of it too (οὐδὲ ταῦτα ἐς τὸ ἀληθὲς ἀνέγραψαν). I by contrast am bound to the truth (δεῖ δὲ ἀληθείας ἐμοὶ γοῦν), and if those historians too had honoured (ἐπῄνεσαν) it, they would not have deprived Alex-

> ander of this additional praise. For rather than climbing the mountain and holding revel, as they assert (λέγουσι), it was a nobler act, I think, to ensure the endurance of his army by not climbing it.

Philostratus is obviously anxious to distance himself from the legends and lies that surround Alexander's eastern campaign in order to lend credibility to his own writing project. His hero, it is true, travels in Alexander's footsteps, but we are to understand that his own account, in contrast to that of the Alexander historians, is based on critical examination of the sources.

Indeed, the faked scholarly apparatus that pervades Philostratus's work is sorely needed, for the story includes both the incredible and the supernatural. Apollonius, who was probably a magician of no more than local fame, is exalted to a global celebrity who converses with the kings of Persia and India and with Roman emperors and philosophers. In the style of a Greek sophist, he dispenses advice in religious, philosophical and political matters. He has both prophetic and healing gifts and is endowed with unusual magic faculties, he disappears and reappears at his own discretion, and is taken up to heaven after his last act of disappearance.

Paradoxical facts of oriental flora, fauna and minerals are described in quasi-scientific detail. Such paradoxographical writing was a genre of its own in the Hellenistic and Roman periods, appearing both as separate collections of 'mirabilia' and within larger works of other kinds, from science to entertainment.[35] Philostratus shares his taste for such wonders of nature with, among others, the novelists Achilles Tatius and Heliodorus.[36] Yet, for all his fascination with the material and delight in serving his readers the most sensational details, he is anxious to keep his own credibility intact. Thus, when Apollonius checks with the Indian philosopher Iarchas a whole list of 'great and incredible (ἄπιστα) things', Philostratus lets the Indian give a carefully qualified answer (3.45.2–46.1):

> As for animals, plants, or fountains which you have seen while coming here, what can I tell you? It is now up to you to describe them to others. But I have never heard of an arrow-shooting animal or fountains of liquid gold

35 The term παραδοξογράφος is not attested until Tzetzes, *Chil.* 2.35.151 (twelfth century), but the adjectives παράδοξος, ἄπιστος and θαυμάσιος appear in titles of the separate works. For a survey with copious bibliography, see Schepens and Delcroix (1996).

36 See Rommel (1923).

> in these parts. But as for the stone that attracts and binds other stones to itself, you should not disbelieve (ἀπιστεῖν) that, since you may both see the stone and admire all its properties.

And there follows a detailed description of all the stupendous powers of this *pantarbe* stone. But Iarchas's answer implies that while many false tales circulate about Indian paradoxa, all the phenomena described by Philostratus, with Damis's memoirs as his source, are in fact real and true, because Apollonius and Damis have actually 'seen them' during their travels! Time and again, such indirectly authenticating elements are incorporated into the narrative.

There are other features as well that bring the *Life of Apollonius* closer to the sophistic novels of the period, among them its great size (biographies were mostly much shorter); but there are no subplots, nor is there, more importantly, any love motif that guides and structures the narrative. Apollonius himself is an ascetic, and when love is referred to in the *Life*, it is as a negative and destructive force. Ewen Bowie is probably right in asserting that Philostratus 'develop[ed] a fictitious account which did not consistently parade its fictionality by alluding to the novels but dissimulated it by aping historical writing'.[37]

The *Life of Apollonius* has been described as 'a sort of Alexander-romance with the elegance of the *Cyropaedia*'.[38] It has in common with the *Romance* its geographical pattern, with India as the eastern limit and *Aithiopia* (Nubia) as the southern, and there are frequent significant allusions to Alexander and his feats as Apollonius and Damis are proceeding eastwards.[39] The authors let Alexander and Apollonius share an ethnographical and teratological obsession, making the incredible credible through a scientific jargon. In Alexander's case, as mentioned, this jargon is meant to illude the impact of his teacher Aristotle on him, while Philostratus is a typical exponent of the paradoxographical and ekphrastic habits of the Second Sophistic. Yet, in spite of such thematic similarities, the two works are wide apart in most respects, one popular and truly chaotic in its extant versions, the other sophisticated in the extreme, also in its apparent formlessness.

The *Life of Apollonius* could no doubt be read as *historia*, and more easily so than the *Alexander Romance*, not least because of its recurring discussion

37 Bowie (1994: 195).
38 Anderson (1986: 232).
39 See Bowie (1994: 195).

of sources. It is also instructive to compare it to the *Cyropaedia*. The two have in common, of course, the distinct and authoritative authorial voice that the *Romance* lacks. Philostratus, like Xenophon, had factual accounts on his list of publications, among them the *Lives of the Sophists*, and could be expected to deliver the documentary account of the life of the Pythagorean sage that he advertises in his introduction. Now, to judge from the medieval manuscript tradition, the title of the work did not include the word *bios*, but confined itself to the ambiguous preposition ἐς, 'about', followed by ethnicon and proper name: τὰ ἐς τὸν Τυανέα Ἀπολλώνιον. The title has been variously interpreted as 'On Apollonius of Tyana', 'In Honour of A. of T.', or 'The Stories of A. of T.',[40] and Philostratus's sophistic-minded readers may well have expected something rather more ingenious and exciting than a factual account of the sage's life. Philostratus may have intended his work to be read in different ways: as a documentary biography – thus, as *historia* – by more naive readers who were apt to be impressed by his learned apparatus and would believe in the supernatural ingredients as well, or as a brilliant sophistic display – as *argumentum*, partly even *fabula* – by the literary connoisseurs who took the hints and appreciated the clever deceit.[41]

VARIETIES OF HISTORICAL FICTION IN ANTIQUITY

So far, I have been content to refer to the three works as specimens of 'historical fiction', rather than calling them 'historical novels', as often happens in modern descriptions. I prefer to refrain from that more specific term because they are in any case not very *typical* historical novels, as this prolific subgenre of the novel has been shaped since Sir Walter Scott. The recipe followed by Scott and his successors is, in brief terms, the following. The historical background of the story – the war, the uprising, etc. – is with few exceptions historically correct, in the sense that it adheres to the picture that a contemporary audience would recognize from their history books. The actual plot, however, is usually invented and features private persons of no (or scant) historical record. The particular appeal of this kind of historical novel is generated when the invented indivuals are affected by the historical events and mingle with the well-known historical actors. There are, in fact, some works of ancient fic-

40 For the first interpretation, see Hägg (2004: 387 n. 24) and Jones (2005: 3 n. 1); for the second, Anderson (1986: 121) and Swain (1999: 157 n. 1); for the third, Bowie (1994: 189).

41 See Bowie (1994: 196).

tion that follow this recipe rather closely, and it is useful to compare our three specimens with these in order to come closer to a definition of their kind of fictionality. We thus leave the *genera narrationum* distinction to apply instead definitions that have been worked out in a modern literary context.

At the beginning of this chapter, I mentioned briefly the so-called 'ideal' Greek novels of love, travel and adventure and noted that they are the closest ancient Greek prose comes to pure *argumentum*. They deal with events that have not happened, but *might* have (Aristotle's οἷα ἂν γένοιτο, *Poet.* 9, 1451b5). One of the five extant novels, Achilles Tatius's *Leucippe and Clitophon*, is set in the contemporary world, two others are 'free floating in a timeless Hellenism': Xenophon's *Ephesiaca* and Longus's *Daphnis and Chloe*.[42] But the remaining two, Chariton's *Callirhoe* and Heliodorus's *Aithiopica*,[43] plus one that we only have in a fragmentary form, *Parthenope*,[44] answer rather closely to what is today understood as historical novels. We shall look more systematically at the main criteria for such a classification[45] and at the same time apply the test to the three works under scrutiny here.

Time. The action of the 'historical' novel should be set at least one or two generations back, it should be 'researched rather than remembered'[46] and communicate a sense of the past as past. This applies to all three, if only we understand the concept 'research' in a Graeco-Roman context. The *Cyropaedia* is set 200 years back, *Apollonius* 150, and the *Alexander Romance* 600, if we go for the earliest recension we actually possess (the first *Life of Alexander* may have been created just a generation or two *post eventum*). The *Romance* gives a sense of a legendary past. The two other authors make clear that they did not themselves experience the figures they describe, but rely on historical sources (Philostratus explicitly, Xenophon by implication).

Characters. The typical historical novel deals with fictitious characters in a historical setting. The focus of attention is the personal experiences and concerns of private individuals. Real historical figures appear as well, but not as the main characters. The fictitious characters mingle with those known from the history books. This is where all our three works fail in the test (in sharp contrast to the 'ideal' historical novels, in particular *Parthenope* and *Callirhoe*).

42 Thus Morgan (1993: 200).
43 All five are available in English translation in Reardon (1989), *Callirhoe* also (with the Greek text) in Goold (1995).
44 See Stephens and Winkler (1995: 72–100) and Hägg and Utas (2003).
45 For this classification and a detailed discussion, see Hägg (1987).
46 The phrase from Sanders (1978: 11).

The main characters – Cyrus, Alexander, Apollonius – are themselves historical, however unhistorical the actual treatment of them may be, and so are most of the people around them. The fictitious uncle in the *Cyropaedia* and the note-taking disciple Damis in Apollonius are not marked as unhistorical; and it is not *their* concerns, but those of the historical hero that dominate the narrative.

Setting. Typically, the specific action of the historical novels takes place against a background of well-known historical events, 'mingled with and affecting the personal fortunes of the characters'.[47] Our three works indeed deal with historical events, in particular the *Cyropaedia* and the *Alexander Romance*. But the chief movers of these events are identical with the main characters, so the tension otherwise achieved by the juxtaposition of the real and the imaginary is again missing. The *Life of Apollonius* is perhaps closer in this respect, since its hero is an advisor and commentator on historical events, but mostly not their cause himself. A realistic geography too is part of the setting criterion. All three fulfil this demand as they are set in a clearly identifiable Mediterranean and Oriental world with real cities, rivers, and mountains named along their routes (though the geography of the *Alexander Romance* is sometimes confused).

Truth or historical probability. This last criterion is the most subjective one, and dependent on the readers, as discussed in connection with each work. What the naive reader finds probable or true will not necessarily satisfy the more sophisticated reader; and the author may play on several kinds of audience, as was argued above with regard to Philostratus.

Consequently, our three works of historical fiction do not qualify as typical historical novels, as the genre has been understood since Walter Scott. Furthermore, it is possible to argue that they are not 'novels' at all, since they lack a real plot, such as the love intrigue of the ideal novels. They are closer to an epic like the *Odyssey*, but they lack the *nostos* or homecoming motif that makes that epic into something more than an episodic sequence of travel adventures. Instead, it is the whole life span of the main character, from birth to death, that is the narrative backbone of the three works. For its unity, each work is dependent on the consistency of its central character.[48] Such consistency is achieved by Xenophon and Philostratus, while the *Alexander Romance*, as an open text, admits several different Alexanders, as different source material comes to the

47 The phrase from Fleishman (1971: 3).
48 Cf. Bowie (1994: 190).

fore. If a generic label is required, that of 'life' or 'biography' is the obvious one for all three works, though it needs to be qualified by something like 'romanticized', 'pseudo-documentary', or even 'fictitious'. There remains, as the easiest expedient, simply to speak of them as works of 'historical fiction'.

'Fiction', then, used in a global, non-technical sense. It covers both what Dennis Green calls fabrication, 'not meant to be seen through or called into question',[49] and the types that reveal themselves as fiction to the audience, or at least to part of it. The *Cyropaedia*, I would argue, is mainly fabrication. The readers were to believe that Xenophon had access to privileged information, otherwise his demonstration of the education of the ideal leader would have been less effective: Cyrus's historical success proves the validity of the educational method described. Philostratus probably had a more mixed audience in mind. Some of his readers will have been as sophisticated as he was himself, and with them he had a kind of contract. He knew that they knew that much was invented, and they relished the deceit as well as the story as such; while others would buy the scholarly documentation and believe that they were now being served the whole truth about the Pythagorean sage. The *Alexander Romance*, as always, is the most complicated case. We may perhaps speak of a kind of contract there too, originally: a contract between a conveyor of a nationalistic myth and his like-minded audience that made even the *fabula* constituents 'real'. Yet there are so many layers in the transmitted composition and too much fluctuation between the various narrative modes to make any one definition possible.

References

TEXTS

Philostratus, *Life of Apollonius of Tyana* (Τὰ ἐς τὸν Τυανέα Ἀπολλώνιον), was critically edited by C. L. Kayser in Bibliotheca Teubneriana, Leipzig: Teubner, 1870, but is now most conveniently available in the bilingual edition in the Loeb Classical Library by Jones (2005).

Pseudo-Callisthenes, *The Alexander Romance* (Βίος Ἀλεξάνδρου), is transmitted in several different Greek recensions. The oldest, A, was edited by Wilhelm Kroll, *Historia Alexandri Magni (Pseudo-Callisthenes)*, vol. I: *Recensio vetusta*,

49 Green (2002: 187).

Berlin: Weidmannsche, 1926, with English translation by Haight (1955). For the reconstruction of this recension, there are two further witnesses, the Latin fourth-century translation of Iulius Valerius, ed. Rosellini 2004, 2nd edition, and a fifth-century Armenian version, translated by Wolohojian (1969). The text of Rec. b was edited by Leif Bergson, *Der griechische Alexanderroman Rezension b*, Stockholm, Gothenburg and Uppsala: Almqvist & Wiksell, 1965. The text of ms. L was edited, with German translation, by van Thiel (1974); English translation by Stoneman (1991) and by Ken Dowden in Reardon (1989), reprinted in Hansen (1998).

Xenophon, *Cyropaedia* (Κύρου παιδεία), is available in several critical editions, among them, E. C. Marchant, *Xenophontis Opera omnia*, vol. IV, Oxford: Clarendon Press, 1910, and M. Bizos and É. Delebecque, Xénophon, *Cyropédie*, vol. I–III, Paris: Les Belles Lettres, 1971–78. The most recent English translation is Ambler (2001). There is a bilingual edition in the Loeb Classical Library by Miller (1914).

STUDIES

Ambler, Wayne (trans.) (2001) Xenophon, *The Education of Cyrus*, Ithaca and London: Cornell University Press.

Anderson, Graham (1986) *Philostratus: Biography and Belles Lettres in the Third Century A.D.*, London: Croom Helm.

Barwick, Karl (1928) 'Die Gliederung der narratio in der rhetorischen Theorie und ihre Bedeutung für die Geschichte des antiken Romans', *Hermes* 62: 261–87.

Bowie, Ewen (1993) 'Lies, Fiction and Slander in Early Greek Poetry', in Christopher Gill and T. P. Wiseman (eds.), *Lies and Fiction in the Ancient World*, Austin: University of Texas Press, pp. 1–37.

Bowie, Ewen (1994) 'Philostratus: Writer of Fiction', in John R. Morgan and Richard Stoneman (eds.), *Greek Fiction: The Greek Novel in Context*, London and New York: Routledge, pp. 181–99.

Cizek, Alexandru (1997) 'Die *tria genera narrationum* und die Alexanderstoffe: Ein Beitrag zur Poetik des antik-mittelalterlichen Alexanderromans', in Michelangelo Picone and Bernhard Zimmermann (eds.), *Der antike Roman und seine mittelalterliche Rezeption*, Basel, Boston and Berlin: Birkhäuser Verlag, pp. 273–306.

Due, Bodil (1989) *The Cyropaedia: Xenophon's Aims and Methods*, Aarhus: Aarhus University Press.

Fleishman, Avrom (1971) *The English Historical Novel: Walter Scott to Virginia Woolf*, Baltimore: Johns Hopkins University Press.

Gera, Deborah Levine (1993) *Xenophon's Cyropaedia: Style, Genre, and Literary Technique*, Oxford: Clarendon Press.

Goold, G. P. (ed. and trans.) (1995) Chariton, *Callirhoe* (Loeb Classical Library, 481), Cambridge, MA and London: Harvard University Press.

Green, Dennis H. (2002) *The Beginnings of Medieval Romance: Fact and Fiction, 1150–1220* (Cambridge Studies in Medieval Literature, 47), Cambridge: Cambridge University Press.

Hägg, Tomas (1974) 'Aristoteles och den grekiska romanen', in *Kungl. Vetenskaps-Societeten i Uppsala, Årsbok 1974*, pp. 46–52.

Hägg, Tomas (1987) '*Callirhoe* and *Parthenope*: The Beginnings of the Historical Novel', *Classical Antiquity* 6: 184–204. [Repr. in Tomas Hägg, *Parthenope: Selected Studies in Ancient Greek Fiction (1969–2004)*. Edited by Lars Boje Mortensen and Tormod Eide, Copenhagen: Museum Tusculanum Press, 2004.]

Hägg, Tomas (2004) 'Apollonios of Tyana – Magician, Philosopher, Counter-Christ: The Metamorphoses of a Life', in Tomas Hägg, *Parthenope: Selected Studies in Ancient Greek Fiction (1969–2004)*. Edited by Lars Boje Mortensen and Tormod Eide, Copenhagen: Museum Tusculanum Press, pp. 379–404.

Hägg, Tomas, and Bo Utas (2003) *The Virgin and Her Lover: Fragments of an Ancient Greek Novel and a Persian Epic Poem* (Brill Studies in Middle Eastern Literatures, 30), Leiden: Brill.

Haight, Elizabeth Hazelton (trans.) (1955) *The Life of Alexander of Macedon* by Pseudo-Callisthenes, New York: Longmans.

Halliwell, Stephen (ed. and trans.) (1995) Aristotle, *Poetics*, in Aristotle, vol. XXIII (Loeb Classical Library, 199), Cambridge, MA and London: Harvard University Press.

Hansen, William (ed.) (1998) *Ancient Greek Popular Literature*, Bloomington and Indianapolis: Indiana University Press.

Holzberg, Niklas (1996) 'Utopias and Fantastic Travel: Euhemerus, Iambulus', in Gareth Schmeling (ed.), *The Novel in the Ancient World*, Boston and Leiden: Brill (revised and augmented paperback edition, 2003), pp. 621–32.

Jones, Christopher P. (ed. and trans.) (2005) Philostratus, *Apollonius of Tyana*, vol. I–II (Loeb Classical Library, 16–17), Cambridge, MA and London: Harvard University Press.

Jouanno, Corinne (2002) *Naissance et métamorphoses du Roman d'Alexandre. Domaine grec*, Paris: CNRS Éditions.

Konstan, David (1998) 'The *Alexander Romance*: The Cunning of the Open Text', *Lexis* 16: 123–38.

Merkelbach, Reinhold (1977) *Die Quellen des griechischen Alexanderromans* (Zetemata, 9), 2nd edition, Munich: C.H. Beck.

Miller, Walter (ed. and trans.) (1914) Xenophon, vols. V–VI: *Cyropaedia* (Loeb Classical Library, 51–52), Cambridge, MA and London: Harvard University Press.

Morgan, John R. (1993) 'Make-Believe and Make Believe: The Fictionality of the Greek Novels', in Christopher Gill and T. P. Wiseman (eds.), *Lies and Fiction in the Ancient World*, Austin: University of Texas Press, pp. 175–229.

Reardon, B. P. (ed.) (1989) *Collected Ancient Greek Novels*, Berkeley, Los Angeles and London: University of California Press.

Reardon, B. P. (1991) *The Form of Greek Romance*, Princeton: Princeton University Press.

Romm, James S. (1992) *The Edges of the Earth in Ancient Thought: Geography, Exploration, and Fiction*, Princeton: Princeton University Press.

Rommel, Hans (1923) *Die naturwissenschaftlich-paradoxographischen Exkurse bei Philostratos, Heliodoros und Achilleus Tatios*, Stuttgart: Kohlhammer.

Rosellini, Michela (ed.) (2004) Iulius Valerius, *Res gestae Alexandri Macedonis translatae ex Aesopo Graeco*, 2nd edition, Berlin: K.G. Saur.

Sanders, Andrew (1978) *The Victorian Historical Novel 1840–1880*, London: Macmillan.

Schepens, Guido, and Kris Delcroix (1996) 'Ancient Paradoxography: Origin, Evolution, Production and Reception', in Oronzo Pecere and Antonio Stramaglia (eds.), *La letteratura di consumo nel mondo greco-latino*, Cassino: Università degli Studi di Cassino, pp. 373–460.

Stephens, Susan A., and John J. Winkler (eds.) (1995) *Ancient Greek Novels: The Fragments*, Princeton: Princeton University Press.

Stoneman, Richard (trans.) (1991) *The Greek Alexander Romance* (Penguin Classics), Harmondsworth: Penguin Books.

Stoneman, Richard (1994) 'The *Alexander Romance*: From History to Fiction', in John R. Morgan and Richard Stoneman (eds.), *Greek Fiction: The Greek Novel in Context*, London and New York: Routledge, pp. 117–29.

Swain, Simon (1999) 'Defending Hellenism: Philostratus, *In Honour of Apollonius*', in Mark J. Edwards, Martin Goodman and Simon Price (eds.), *Apologetics in the Roman Empire: Pagans, Jews, and Christians*, Oxford: Oxford University Press, pp. 157–96.

Tatum, James (1989) *Xenophon's Imperial Fiction: On the Education of Cyrus*, Princeton: Princeton University Press.

Thiel, Helmut van (ed. and trans.) (1974) *Leben und Taten Alexanders von Makedo-*

nien. Der griechische Alexanderroman nach der Handschrift L (Texte zur Forschung, 13), Darmstadt: Wissenschaftliche Buchgesellschaft.

Wolohojian, Albert Mugrdich (trans.) (1969) *The Romance of Alexander the Great* by Pseudo-Callisthenes, translated from the Armenian version, New York and London: Columbia University Press.

The Rise of Medieval Fiction in the Twelfth Century

Dennis H. Green

No matter whether we see it in terms of a renaissance or not, the twelfth century produced a number of pathbreaking innovations, not least in the field of literature. Amongst these I include such radical changes as the emergence of secular themes meant explicitly for an audience of laymen, the rising importance of vernacular literature alongside the hitherto dominant role of Latin, the explosion of written literature for these laymen in addition to the oral tradition on which they had previously relied, and also, for my purposes by no means least, the development of fictional literature in addition to historical works, or rather works which claimed to be historically true or were regarded as such. The first beginnings of some, but not all of these changes can be traced back to the last decades of the eleventh century, so that strictly speaking we are talking of what I should call 'the long twelfth century', similar to what modern historians term 'the long nineteenth century', stretching for them from the French Revolution to the outbreak of the First World War.

To talk of a renaissance of the twelfth century, however, has one advantage for me, since it points to the undeniable influence of Latin in this period, not merely in literature itself, but also in rhetoric, poetics, commentaries, as well as in the way in which vernacular cultures go to school with the Latin tradition at large. This is particularly true of the phenomenon of fiction itself, known to classical antiquity in different guises in individual works, but also in theoretical discussion, both in Greek and in Latin. For the Middle Ages, at least before the fuller recovery of Aristotle in the thirteenth century, this amounted to an influence of Latin on the rise of vernacular fiction in the twelfth century. I shall start by considering two Latin authors, well known in this period by

* This paper is based on my book *The Beginnings of Medieval Romance: Fact and Fiction, 1150–1220*, published by Cambridge University Press in 2002 and reproduced in this form by permission. Further details and bibliographical reference can be found there.

their important role in the teaching of schools, by their recurrence in *accessus* literature, and by their vernacular adaptations to medieval and courtly interests in the twelfth century.

My first example is Ovid who at one point in his *Amores* (III 12) admits that he could have chosen to treat of historical themes (he mentions Thebes, Troy, Caesar), which means, in accordance with the three types of narrative, *genera narrationis*, postulated by classical rhetoric, themes that are a true record of events that had actually taken place. Instead, Ovid says that he will sing only of the woman Corinna, but adds significantly that, since he is a poet, he should not be believed as a witness and that no credence should be attached to what he says. What he terms the fertile licence of poets is then contrasted explicitly with the historical reliability (*historica fides*) which he disclaims for himself. Ovid concludes this telling passage by admitting that his praise of the poetic figure Corinna is no more than a lie, but a lie in a special sense. It is not a deliberate deception on his part, since any fault lies with the credulity of his audience which prevents them from seeing the obvious, namely that his words are untrue. In other words, they should have realized, as did the Roman historian Velleius Paterculus, that love-poets declaim nothing in their own person (*nihil ex persona poetae disserunt*). Significantly, it is a historian who sees through the statement of a poet making use of fiction. In pointedly insisting that the untruth of his poetry should have been seen through and that his audience should not have deceived themselves Ovid is making a claim which is central to any definition of fictionality, that it depends on a tacit contract between author and audience in which each wittingly plays his part.

To show that Ovid's attitude in this poem must have been known in the Middle Ages, especially to Latin poets or those who had received a clerical education (in which Ovid played a prominent part), it is by no means enough to rely on such a general statement as that the twelfth century, with the importance it attached to the literary theme of love, was an *aetas Ovidiana*. We have to go much further and be more precise. We can do this in the case of a Latin poet active towards the end of the eleventh century, Baudri de Bourgueil. As a poet dealing with the theme of love he is well acquainted with Ovid and even calls himself 'a new Ovid'. More precisely, he follows the Roman poet's *Heroides* in himself composing two pairs of letter-poems, one claiming to be between Paris and Helen and the other between Florus and none other than Ovid himself. However, Baudri also takes the further step necessary if we are to draw a parallel between him and Ovid with regard to fictionality. Like Ovid in the *Amores,* Baudri makes his position unmistakably clear. He admits that he writes about things as if they were true, attributing to various *personae* in his poems words and sentiments which are not true, but made up: 'Believe me, I do not speak the truth, I make everything up' (*Crede michi! Non uera loquor magis omnia fingo*). At another point he likewise insists that his love-poems are not private confessions, that if he were really in love he would not make a public show of it. Like his Roman master, Baudri disclaims factual, autobiographical truth in favour of fiction, but takes care to make his position clear to his audience. What he says in his poetry may not be true, but he cannot be accused of deliberately hoodwinking the audience.

My second example concerns a Latin author of just as much importance in the twelfth century as Ovid, namely Virgil or, more specifically, his *Aeneid.* With this work and what it could offer medieval authors we must shift our focus on the rise of fiction somewhat. Although Ovid could refer to the difference between historical reliability and poetic licence and make it clear that his writing belonged to the latter camp, this was very much in passing and referred at the most to *one* of his love-poems (and was similarly taken up by Baudri in one of his). With the *Aeneid,* however, we are dealing by contrast with a large-scale epic in which the juxtaposition of historical truth and poetic fiction in the same work presented problems of a different magnitude altogether.

On a number of counts Virgil could propose historical veracity for his account of Rome's origins and find acceptance for it. In that his story proceeded from the Trojan War there was little doubt in antiquity (or in the Middle Ages) about its historical basis. When Dido pronounces her curse on the faithless Aeneas, she vows enmity between her people and his, which transposes her on to the plane of history, initiating the historical opposition of Carthage to Rome. In another way, past is linked with present by the prophecy made by Aeneas's father, Anchises, pointing to future fulfilment in Virgil's own day in the person of Augustus, the poet's own patron. The parallels drawn between the events in Aeneas's day and the Augustan present serve a twofold purpose: they confer authority on the emperor by suggesting his descent from a semi-divine hero, but also on Virgil's account by embedding it in what was regarded as history. By virtue of all this, Servius, an early and arguably the most important commentator on the *Aeneid,* regarded Virgil as presenting history in his epic.

The same view could still be held in the Middle Ages when this work was discussed. For Eberhard the German it was *historialis apex*, the peak of history. Konrad von Hirsau held that Virgil derived his material and overall intention from history, while a commentary attributed to Anselm of Laon even correlates the events in Virgil's work chronologically with ones reported in the Old Testament and regarded beyond all doubt as historically true.

But that is not all, and if it were there would be no place for Virgil in the context of fictionality. Servius does not simply say that Virgil presented history, he also adds that he did so not openly, but as a poet. One reason for this incipient mistrust of Virgil's depiction of events is his imitation of Homer, himself exposed to criticism in antiquity for having the gods intervene in human affairs. Thus Servius, when Virgil reports on Venus talking to herself, comments sceptically: 'This is fictitious. How should the poet know?'

Not merely because of this presence of the pagan gods, medieval reactions to this aspect of Virgil's epic can be even more marked and frequent. Otto von Freising goes beyond Servius in explicitness by saying that Virgil mixes *res gestae* (historical events that actually took place) with *res fabulosae* (what was invented). Bernardus Silvestris draws a similar distinction. Referring to the widespread view in the Middle Ages that Dares Phrygius, regarded as a reliable historian of the Trojan War giving an eyewitness account, was more trustworthy than Homer, he says that Virgil wrote 'not always, as with Dares, in accord with the truth of history'. At a later point Bernardus makes the distinction quite clear: 'It is historical that the Greeks conquered Troy, but fabulous what is recounted of the honesty of Aeneas'. Another reason for doubting Virgil's historical reliability is the fact, well known to medieval commentators, that he wrote to please or flatter his patron, Augustus. These doubts can even extend to a striking feature of the Roman poet's composition technique, his employment of the *ordo artificialis*, for this was regarded, already with Servius, as a poetic rather than historiographic technique, which explains why John of Salisbury describes this mode of presentation as 'under the cloak of fictional invention' (*sub involucro fictitii commenti*). The juxtaposition of history with inventions which these remarks, stretching from antiquity to the twelfth century and beyond, illustrate is summed up, once again, by Bernardus Silvestris, who judges Virgil as having interspersed historical material with his own inventions (*ficmenta*).

That this conjunction of historical with invented material amounted to fiction was already clear in antiquity can be seen in what Macrobius has to say about the *Aeneid*, specifically on the complicity between Virgil and his audience in understanding the Dido episode. For Macrobius, as for others in his day and in the Middle Ages, this episode has no historical substance. In the first place, Macrobius argues that Dido and Aeneas were not even contemporaries. But he is also fully aware of the highly literary manner in which Virgil has composed this episode, borrowing the outline of the love-affair from the *Argonautica* of Apollonius of Rhodes and applying what was narrated there of Jason and Medea to Aeneas and Dido. Macrobius sees that this is the technique of an author of fiction, disposing of material from different sources, literary and historical, for his own purposes with no regard for overall historical truthfulness. He expresses this happily not in the terminology of literary criticism, but in the language of wine-growing: 'He did not make his vintage from the vine of one grower'. Macrobius therefore feels justified in terming Virgil's resulting work a *fabula*, but is particularly illuminating about the way in which this *fabula* was received, not simply by himself alone, but by the whole world (*universitas*). Everyone knows this *fabula* to be false and is aware that it presents only the appearance of truth (*species veritatis*), as if it were true (*pro vero*). They know this because of their knowledge that Dido was chaste and laid hands on herself to protect her honour. Nonetheless, the beauty of Virgil's poetic account (*pulchritudo narrandi*) is so great that they suppress within themselves the testimony of the (historical) truth (*intra conscientiam veri fidem prementes*), preferring to celebrate as true the charm of fiction (*malint pro vero celebrari quod pectoribus humanis dulcedo fingentis infudit*). What this detailed account of 'Rezeptionsästhetik' amounts to is clear. Macrobius describes here how in antiquity Virgil's audience were fully aware of the historical truth, but nonetheless accepted his version of events as if it were true, by a process of make-believe of which, according to him, they are fully conscious. In doing this they perform their part of the fictional contract, so that Macrobius can even describe their position as connivance (*conivere*). This assessment of the relationship between author and audience in literary fiction agrees remarkably with the judgement of a modern classical scholar (D. C. Feeney), who speaks of Virgil's 'awareness of the power of his fictive art to command credence even in the face of the audience's knowledge that the anachronistic affair between Aeneas and Dido is the poet's own created fiction'.

We shall look in vain for such a degree of explicitness in the medieval literary adaptations of the *Aeneid* (nor is Virgil himself quite so open, wisely preferring to leave it to the perceptive members of his audience). Macrobius may well have been known in the Middle Ages (Chrétien de Troyes refers to him), but his influence is more to be seen in the commentary tradition, in the *accessus* to classical authors or works, summing up their contents and authorial intention. One such *accessus*, attributed to Anselm of Laon, may not provide us with a near-definition of fictionality, as did Macrobius, but is nonetheless quite clear about the relationship between history and fiction in the *Aeneid*. The *accessus* begins with Virgil's intention. 'For he intended to praise Augustus through his forebears. And he does this by describing the deeds of Aeneas, namely how, after the fall of Troy, he came sailing to Italy after much wandering, and how he made war there against the opposing Rutilians and Latins. Indeed, since he wrote in praise of Augustus, therefore suppressing much historical truth, he quite becomingly added certain poetic fictions ... And truly, if he had only followed the truth of history, he would not certainly have seemed a poet, but a historiographer'. This is followed by the remark, repeatedly also made of Homer, that the *Aeneid*'s heroic deeds on the plane of human action also contain divine characters, so that the work contains both truth and invention (*vera cum fictis*). In this respect, as also in the observation of Macrobius that Virgil has welded together two separate traditions (the heroic history of Aeneas's conquest of Latium and the literary one of his encounter with Dido, based on a transposition from Apollonius of Rhodes), this *accessus* judges the work to be composite and fictional (*compositum et ficticium*). Enough remains of Macrobius's observations to make it possible for this twelfth-century commentator (as for others) to regard Virgil as both a poet and a historian, creating fiction out of a conjunction of invention and truth.

What we have so far seen of the way in which the idea of literary fiction, as conceived in classical antiquity, could be transmitted to the Middle Ages has been confined to commentary on or discussion of classical works themselves. Even in the case of Baudri de Bourgueil's poetry, he sees himself as a second Ovid and follows that poet's example. If we turn now to medieval examples that were conceived to serve medieval interests, the obvious point of departure is those romances of the twelfth century that deal with a classical theme (the examples range from Thebes, Troy, Aeneas to Alexander), but adapt it in a specifically medieval way. My example will be the first vernacular adaptation of Virgil's *Aeneid*, the Old French *Roman d'Enéas*, by an anonymous author, which betrays a similar conflation of history and fiction.

Like Virgil, the French author is concerned with a historical theme, the founding of Rome, but he even goes beyond the Roman author in plotting a historical dimension. He does this by taking his story backwards in time (to what had been the first cause of the Trojan War, the judgement of Paris), but also forwards (to the imperial descendants following from the marriage of Eneas and Lavine). In addition, when Eneas recounts the fall of Troy to Dido he does this in accordance with the conventional medieval view of what constitutes history, with the justification of an eyewitness ('I shall tell you the truth about it, because I was there and saw it and know'). The French author also largely (if not entirely) removes the divine machinery that had proved an obstacle to credibility even in antiquity, before Christianity added a further one in its rejection of any possible intervention by pagan gods.

On the other hand, the French work goes well beyond Virgil in removing or weakening some of his historical features, which does not of itself constitute fiction, but at least assists its development. The central image in the Latin epic, Augustus as the ruler towards whom Roman history has been moving since its beginning, has been removed altogether in the French romance in that the chronological climax towards which it looks at the conclusion comes well before Augustus. Similarly, the goal reached by the French narrative is not the founding of Rome, but the marriage of Eneas and Lavine. When the French author replaces Dido's curse on Aeneas and all his progeny by an act of forgiveness, this may contribute to the courtly tone of the romance, but empties the scene of its historical function of accounting for the future wars between Carthage and Rome.

Much more telling than these admittedly negative changes is the French author's drastic re-working of the second half of the *Aeneid*. The core of this expansion is the figure of Lavine (whom Virgil had hardly mentioned at all) and with her the theme of love. By this creation, a transforming innovation, the author breaks free from a slavish subservience to his source and consults his own artistic interests, the theme of *amor et militia* which dominates the romance genre of the twelfth century. In this fictional invention of Lavine, the French author can be said to be repeating what Virgil had achieved with his fictional discovery of a role for Dido. In doing this he was assisted by what is characteristic of fiction generated by intertextuality. By that I mean that Virgil's text was open to expansion by an author who was concerned, like his audience, with the interplay between *amor* and *militia* soon to be applied by Chrétien de Troyes to Arthurian, not classical themes. To do this, the author of the *Roman d'Enéas* manufactures his own gaps to be filled with the new theme of love (new, that is to say, in this part of the story) by allowing human emotions to come to the fore precisely during the periods of truce coming between the battles of Eneas and Turnus. In these gaps, filled with Lavine's talks with her mother on the phenomenon of love and with her self-analyzing soliloquies, the author draws for the most part on Ovid (whom he had also exploited earlier in depicting Dido's love). Helpful in this respect were Ovid's *Heroides* and their twelfth-century commentaries. Since most medieval *accessus* to the *Heroides* register the fictive nature of the Ovidian epistles, the French author is in fact inventively building his own fiction on a predecessor's fiction. What this procedure further implies should, I hope, by now be clear. Just as Virgil in his depiction of Dido's story turned not to history (this he could not do), but to another literary work, the *Argonautica* of Apollonius, so does the French author later turn to another expressly fictional source, the *Heroides*, for depicting Dido and especially Lavine. Fiction may have found a niche in what was regarded as history, but in addition fiction had the ability to grow out of other fiction.

However important the step taken by this French author towards developing the possibilities of medieval fiction, limits to his inventiveness have to be stressed, not so much in the fact that he was learning from Virgil and from Ovid, but above all in the fact that he was still working on Virgil's material and making use of a pre-existent narrative. Our next step is to look at two narratives in medieval Latin which by their very language were also open to learning from classical Latin, but did this with new material, narratives that arose in the Middle Ages with no precedent in antiquity.

My first example is the beast epic *Ecbasis captivi*. Insofar as it follows, by its very genre, the tradition of Aesop's fables which were regularly quoted as fictitious, this work must be classed as a fiction. Of this genre Quintilian said that the simple-minded take pleasure in what has been made up (*quae ficta sunt*) and Isidore pinpoints the seat of its fictionality in the presentation of animals with the gift of speech. Although the *Ecbasis* therefore belongs to a genre recognized in antiquity as fictional, its novelty lies in the invention of an unprecedented narrative plot with a more ambitious structure than the beast *fabula* conventionally shows. More than that, the author makes his audience aware of his work's status as fiction from the outset. He begins by stating what this work is *not*: he distances himself from what used to be the practice, namely treating deeds that had actually been performed (*res gestae*) and recorded in writing on the basis of what an eyewitness or credible hearsay had reported. What the author keeps aloof from, however, is nothing less than *historia*: not simply because he dismisses *res gestae*, but because his words sum up the traditional view of history. (For Isidore of Seville no one in antiquity wrote history if he had not actually witnessed the events himself, and Konrad von Hirsau describes the historian succinctly as one who writes up what he has seen, *rei visae scriptor.*)

Instead of history, the author says he is presenting a strange fable (*rara fabella*), where the noun denotes a fictional story and the adjective implies that it is not entirely factually reliable. We reach greater certainty when he refers to his work as a lying book (*mendosa charta*), but useful because of its ethical content. For the author to describe his epic as lying hardly amounts to a rejection of its fictional status, since then it could not otherwise be recommended as useful. Nor would the author have concluded by seeing himself in a line with Horace's satires, giving delight as well as instruction. Instead, the word 'lying' was possibly employed because of the lack of a theoretical place and critical vocabulary for medieval fictionality.

As a second example I take the epic *Ruodlieb*, composed towards the end of the eleventh century. Like Chrétien a century later, the author drew upon a variety of different genres, combining material from them to produce a new experimental whole. This material includes such an undoubtedly fictional genre as the folktale or *Märchen*, but likewise the fabliau as well as reminiscences of romances of antiquity. The author also inserts signals to the unreal nature of his narrative: the anonymity of characters, the indefiniteness of time and place, the presence of animals that can speak. Benedikt Vollmann sees all this as typical of the folktale, received as fictional by the audience, which implies a contract or agreement between author and audience, characteristic of fictional writing, as was made clear by Macrobius.

That is not all, however, for the author of *Ruodlieb* complicates matters for us by also adopting material from heroic tradition, regarded by laymen in a still mainly oral society as a trustworthy source of historical knowledge. This was not the case with all clerics, though, and certainly not with the author of *Ruodlieb*, for whom this heroic tradition provided no more than a few random details. If he also makes occasional use of legendary material, this was likewise not because it was regarded as historically true, but because it was free to be adapted across genres to the novel needs of secular literature.

The fictional status of *Ruodlieb* thus rests on a variety of features. It draws much of its narrative from recognizably fictional genres, but even what it adopts from non-fictional sources which were regarded as historical is freely turned to new ends. Behind this novel combination of disparate features lies the invention of a new story, not derived from history or from a source with a reputable truth-status. Although it has been argued from time to time that *Ruodlieb* is a forerunner of the romance of the twelfth century, I think it is more revealing that, like its vernacular counterparts a century later, it made use of fictionality to experiment with new narrative possibilities.

We saw in the case of the medieval adaptation of Virgil's *Aeneid* that one growth point of fiction lay in gaps which existed or could be imagined in the Latin work. I propose to come back to this point, this time with regard to Arthurian material, but once more in the development of a vernacular work from a Latin one. The examples I have in mind are the *Roman de Brut* of Wace and his source, the *Historia Regum Britannie* of Geoffrey of Monmouth.

Wace presents his work as a translation of what the twelfth century for the most part regarded as a historical text, so that he feels justified in claiming the truth of what he recounts. True both to his source and to historiographical practice of his day, Wace gives a chronological sequence of historical events and of successive rulers of England, even to the point, like Geoffrey again, of synchronizing the events of his history with ones in biblical and classical history. So concerned is he to claim the truth for his work that he can at times criticize his sources over details, especially over the final disappearance of Arthur and the tales that have gathered around the king. Like William of Malmesbury, the leading English historian of the time, Wace therefore draws a firm distinction between the historicity of Arthur himself and the *fabulae* that have attached themselves to him. In all probability it was as a historian that Wace was commissioned to write by Henry II of England, so that past glory, above all in the figure of Arthur, could be seen reflected in the Anglo-Norman present.

This last point is particularly relevant to where Wace goes noticeably beyond what was to be found in Geoffrey's Latin text, namely the descriptions of courtly splendour. These descriptions are largely located in a twelve-year period of peace coming between Arthur's victorious campaigns in various parts of Europe, but for Wace they serve a highly topical purpose. The cultural hegemony of Henry II's court was to a large extent made possible, as it was for Arthur, by a period of peace at the beginning of his reign, when Wace was writing. In other words, these courtly embellishments are not simply fanciful additions to history; instead, they serve as links between past and present. This is a clear shift of emphasis by comparison with Geoffrey but, as with medieval adaptations of the *Aeneid,* it still remains within the unchanged framework of historical events. These descriptions of Wace are simply descriptions; they do not amount to a fictional reshaping of the narrative.

From our point of view, that looks very much like a wasted chance on Wace's part, a window of opportunity which he failed to exploit. What he does with this gap of twelve years' peace in Arthur's campaigning is to use it as a focus for Arthur's courtesy, for the Round Table (Wace is the first to introduce this emblem of Arthur's court) and, in Gauvain's praise of peace as opposed to Cador's impatience for renewed warfare, for the themes of love and knightly adventure. In refusing to narrate these adventures because of what he saw was their transparently fabulous nature, Wace provided, however inadvertently, an opening in which the romance fiction that developed soon after him could find a home. What with Geoffrey of Monmouth and still with Wace was a gap in historical time was free to be appropriated for imaginative time by Chrétien and others who situated their romance fictions precisely in this period left open by historiography. That Chrétien's romances were felt to belong in this period of peace was recognized by a thirteenth-century scribe (Bibl. Nat. fr. 1450) who inserted Chrétien's works in a collective manuscript that runs chronologically from the *Roman de Troie* through the *Roman d'Enéas* to Wace's *Roman de Brut,* placing Chrétien precisely in the period of Arthurian peace in the last work. Freed from any obligation to historical veracity, Chrétien could now develop the themes of *amor* and *militia* that concerned his audience, but had not been tackled by Wace.

Looking at Geoffrey, Wace and Chrétien (one writing in Latin, the others in the vernacular) in this way plots a progressive move away from *historia* and towards *fabula.* Geoffrey presents us with a period of peace in the middle of a series of historical campaigns, but this period is not treated by him in any detail, apart from the odd mention of Arthur's court. In the likewise historical work of Wace, these years are also an interval in Arthur's wars of large-scale conquest, but are filled with significantly more detail (the Round Table, court life in much fuller detail, the conjunction of love with chivalry, the fables that deal with this period, even if they are rejected as untrue). The position with Chrétien, although emerging from this, is quite different. With him we find ourselves exclusively within the period of peace, without any treatment of the framing campaigns and any mention of Arthur as a *dux bellorum.* What is given in Chrétien's works corresponds to the gap in Geoffrey's account, but fleshed out with the adventures that Geoffrey had not mentioned and Wace had omitted to treat. With Chrétien we have moved from the realm of history to that of fictional adventures.

To conclude at this point, just when we reach Chrétien de Troyes, the all-important progenitor of the Arthurian romance, may seem like stopping just where I should have started my observations on the rise of fiction in the twelfth century. There are, however, several reasons why I have focused rather on the prehistory of Chrétien's fictionality. An elementary one is the simple fact that, despite the immense amount of scholarly attention this author has rightly attracted, we still possess no monograph devoted to the role of fiction in his artistry. That surely is a task awaiting Romanists and does not rightly fall to a Germanist. Another reason was my wish to stress that Chrétien had predecessors in the elaboration of what fictionality could offer to authors of narrative works, not merely in antiquity but also in medieval Latin (after all, he refers to Macrobius and translated Ovid). This emphasis is meant polemically as criticism of an American scholar of medieval French literature who has recently argued, quite unconvincingly, that Chrétien was really an oral poet, a jongleur with no literate education who acquired scraps of Latin-based knowledge only by conversation with clerics at court.

Returning Chrétien to the Latin tradition from which he emerges enables us to plot his position in literary history with greater precision. I have attempted this in one respect by placing him in a line going back to Geoffrey of Monmouth and Wace, but there is another context in which Latin tradition plays a greater part than in Geoffrey's Latin history. We have been concerned with two types of romance: romances with a classical theme (even though I have looked at only the *Roman d'Enéas*) and Arthurian romances (even if only implicitly by reference to Chrétien). As far as fictionality is concerned, there is a clear difference between these two types of romance. The antique model finds room at the most for what could be called episodic fiction within a given overall plot which could not be changed in its outlines, whereas the Arthurian model was bound to no traditional plot and could therefore dispose freely of its material. These two models differ in the extent to which they realize the possibilities of fiction. The antique romance remains externally referential (its events were regarded as historically true), while the narrative of the Arthurian romance is self-referential. The former was seen as history, but with fictional insertions, while the latter is fiction with the possible addition of historical touches.

Where, before Chrétien's works, we do find more than episodic or incipient fiction, informing the whole structure and permitting invention without ties to historicity, is in such medieval Latin epics as *Ecbasis Captivi* and *Ruodlieb* (to these *Ysengrimus* could possibly be added). However few these 'forerunners' may be, they suggest that here, too, Latin literature, although soon to be overtaken by the vernacular, was still in the lead. It is this which makes me doubtful whether Walter Haug, with reference to Chrétien, is correct in speaking of his 'discovery of fiction', rather than of his 'discovery of vernacular fiction'. In acting as a bridge between Latin and the vernacular, the French poet was performing one of the culturally most important tasks of the cleric at the court of the lay aristocracy.

Fictionality in the Medieval Latin Novel

Paul Gerhard Schmidt

For Michele Feo
in recognition of
a long friendship

For a long time the existence of medieval novels and romances in Latin has been neglected by scholarship. Usually, Geoffrey of Monmouth's *Historia regum Britannie* and the *Ruodlieb* have been seen as the only representatives of this literary genre.[1] Hagiographic and historical 'romances' such as the *Gesta Herewardi* and the *Vita Haroldi* generally remain unmentioned, likewise the translations of Arthurian romances into Latin.[2] There are some forty works that would need to be considered as fictional narratives in Latin, but in this chapter I shall concentrate on four twelfth- and thirteenth-century texts belonging to different genres. Studies on fictionality in medieval literature written almost exclusively by specialists in Middle High German are usually concerned solely with works in the vernacular and pass over Latin literature.[3] In Dennis H. Green's book *The Beginnings of Medieval Romance*, for example, (Pseudo-)Turpin's chronicle of Charlemagne and Roland is not dealt with, nor is the text I want to contrast with it, the novel *Dolopathos*. This is indicative of the current practice of scholars studying vernacular narratives towards medieval Latin as marginalized from 'national' literatures. However, at least three of the four texts I will be discussing in the present essay would in my opinion stand the bid for classification as fictional narratives according to the criteria described by Green in his contribution to the present volume.

1 See, indicatively, Ziolkowski (1997: 308).
2 Schmidt (1995, 2003); Day (2005).
3 Instead of referring to Walter Haug's much outdated hypothesis about the discovery of fictionality in the twelfth century, stated by the author himself to be scantily supported, I use the collection published by Knapp and Niesner (2002), in which Haug, amongst other things, tries to invalidate the arguments of his critics; similarly I refer to Green (2002) and Knapp (1997 and 2005).

CHARLEMAGNE AND ROLAND

Let us begin with Turpin. Since 1865 the author of the *Historia Karoli Magni et Rotholandi* has no longer been known as Turpin, but as Pseudo-Turpin. In renaming the author, Gaston Paris wanted to make clear that the work could not possibly have been written by the contemporary of Charlemagne, Archbishop Tilpin of Rheims. The very fact that the *Historia* had been conceived in the lifetime of Charlemagne had ensured its wide circulation in the medieval period, for according to ancient and medieval thinking the best historian was the man who had been an eyewitness of the events recorded by him. The work had great influence on the custom of pilgrimage to Santiago by virtue of Charlemagne being called upon in a vision of the apostle James to rid his tomb of its appropriation by heathens.

And so Charlemagne journeys to Galicia and Spain, conquers many cities and has the captive foes baptized by Archbishop Turpin. After Charlemagne has left Spain, the pagan King Aigoland of Africa sets sail for Spain and forces Charlemagne, newly equipped with a great army, to return to Spain, where a full-scale religious conflict between Christians and followers of Islam ensues. After the Christian victory over the army of the African king, a second religious conflict breaks out between Charlemagne's nephew Roland and the giant Ferracutus, in which Roland triumphs, first through words and then by sheer cunning. Charlemagne leaves behind him a liberated Spain. Roland, however, loses his life at Roncesvalles through betrayal by Ganelon.

Anyone appearing to be a contemporary and intimate friend of Charlemagne could be assumed to be reporting the truth as an authentic witness. For this reason the *Historia Karoli* was often copied as a reliable source, with the result that today very nearly 200 manuscripts have been preserved. Let me, by way of comparison, quote the figures for manuscripts of other historical texts of the medieval period. Of Einhard's *Vita Karoli Magni*, which is the work of an undoubted contemporary of Charlemagne, a mere 123 manuscripts and fragments have survived, of the *Breviarium* of late antiquity by Rufus we have 83, and of the *Speculum historiale* of Vincent de Beauvais there are 100 manuscripts. From the ninth, tenth or eleventh centuries there is no manuscript of Pseudo-Turpin's work. The oldest codex is the Codex Calixtinus from Santiago de Compostela, which is believed to date from the period around 1140 or soon afterwards. The *terminus ante quem* for the Calixtinus is the year 1172. From the second half of the twelfth century onwards the *His-*

toria Karoli has been worked with intensively. Extracts from it appear in historical works and encyclopaedias. Around the year 1200 a verse form emerged with the title *Karolellus.*[4] In the *Karolellus* and in many manuscripts which preserve the prose version in a variety of editions the work has a strange ending, which appears separately in the Codex Calixtinus as an appendix, but which was very soon afterwards fully integrated into the work. This ending tells of Turpin's death in Vienne. We have here then the rare, possibly unique, case of an author of a work reporting on his own death. In the medieval period no one seems to have been disturbed by this construct. We are told in this concluding chapter that *nostris temporibus* Turpin's corpse was found entirely undecayed, lying in his bishop's robes in a sarcophagus in a ruined church and that he was translated to another church in Vienne. A person whose body was unaffected by decay gained a reputation for holiness. Through the miraculous conservation of a dead body, apparently sleeping, God was commonly seen then, and even today, as confirming this man's special status as a martyr and the status, too, of any other saint. In Vienne, on seeing the undefiled body, people came to this unsurprising conclusion and honoured Turpin from then on as a saint. The same concluding chapter emphasizes that Charlemagne, too, deserved to be canonized for having fought against the heathens. Considering this comment, it seems probable that the *Historia Karoli Magni et Rotholandi,* written anonymously in Spain, or, as some would have it, by an anonymous monk in Cluny, could be regarded as a publication which advocated and prepared the case for the canonization of Charlemagne.

The canonization of Charlemagne took place at the instigation of Frederick Barbarossa on 29 December 1165. This conferment of sainthood could not properly be proved by reference to Einhard's *Life of Charlemagne,* for Einhard's biography, in a similar fashion to Suetonius's *Lives of the Emperors,* deals primarily with the worldly deeds of a worldly ruler. So, the Pseudo-Turpin emerging just before the canonization was especially welcome to all those who had supported the sanctification of Charlemagne. Also in the period that followed, the *Historia Karoli Magni et Rotholandi* aroused undivided attention. Straight after the canonization, an anonymous author, probably in Aachen, quite possibly a senior cleric in that town, wrote a panegyrical life of Charlemagne, whose chief focus is already revealed by its title: *De sanctitate meritorum et*

4 *Karolellus* atque Pseudo-Turpini *Historia Karoli Magni et Rotholandi,* ed. Schmidt (1996).

gloria miraculorum beati Karoli Magni ad honorem et laudem nominis dei.[5] This *Vita* naturally uses the Pseudo-Turpin and takes over the morally edifying passages *in extenso*. The Pseudo-Turpin works particularly well as a biography of a holy ruler. For in the *Historia*, nocturnal visions bid Charlemagne march in crusade against the heathens. It is in fact a work to be read in the context of the *Reconquista* of Spain. Stories of miracles are reported, such as the one about the lances of Christian soldiers turning green, that is to say that the dry wood of lance-shafts sprouts like a tree in spring and allows green foliage to spring forth. This 'adynaton' is well known in the hagiographic tradition. A grievous sinner, who confesses his serious shortcomings, and wishing to be reinstated in the Christian community, is instructed that his sins will only be forgiven when the dry staff they hand him becomes green again. The repentant sinner does not become discouraged by his father-confessor (in some versions with this motif, the priest is no less a figure than the pope himself). Thereafter he leads a life of the strictest abstinence and unceasing acts of penance. In the course of this, usually only at the very moment of death, the seemingly impossible occurs. In the context of the *Historia Karoli*, the motif is somewhat distorted. For the Christian soldiers do not figure as sinners; for them, only the second part of the motif is valid: they are to be hailed as the chosen ones, the highly favoured. The many visions occurring in the Pseudo-Turpin are borrowed from hagiographic literature. St Dionysius accordingly appears to the ruler in a nocturnal vision; the death of Charlemagne is announced to Turpin when he is bent over in prayer before the altar, in a state of ecstasy.

Despite its wide dissemination, the *Historia Karoli Magni et Rotholandi* has received little attention by scholars. One reason for this is because, until just a few decades ago, forgeries tended to be neglected. The label 'Pseudo-Turpin' could therefore have proved a hindrance to its recognition. A second reason is that no satisfactory text basis was available for closer investigation. For several editions suffered miserably on account of the incompetence and philological inaccuracy of the editors. The *editio princeps* of Sebastiano Ciampi, dating back to about 1822, reveals the autocratic manner of an editor of the nineteenth century who produces a text conforming to his taste but with no reference to its transmission.[6] An edition by Walter Muir Whitehill from 1944, long in the preparation, was a spectacular disaster. This edition was so unreli-

5 Ed. Rauschen (1890); the *Vita Karoli Magni* is now available, on the basis of Rauschen's text, with a translation by Helmut and Inge Deutz (2002).

6 Schmidt (2005).

able that the editor himself stepped in to prevent full circulation of the book and did it so successfully that today only four copies of his edition can be found. Unfortunately the edition based on the Codex Calixtinus published by André de Mandach in 1965 from Adalbert Hämel's posthumous writings in no way lives up to what one might have expected.[7] And so a reconstruction, undertaken with verifiable sources of the *Historia Karoli Magni et Rotholandi*, is still in its infancy. Above all, the intertextual references to spiritual writings remain unauthenticated. I would like to illustrate this by means of two examples. When Charlemagne wanted to avenge the Saracens for the death of Roland in Roncesvalles, a miracle well known for its biblical sources takes place. In order for Charlemagne to catch up with the fleeing enemy during the hours of daylight, the sun stands still in the heavens. While the sun is at a standstill, a day is lengthened to three days, allowing Charlemagne to reach the enemy and slay three thousand of them. As is well known, this is a reference to Joshua 10.12–14, where it is recorded that revenge on the Amorites was only made possible by the fact of the sun's lingering in the heavens: *non fuit ante et postea tam longa dies*. In medieval saints' lives, the *sol immobilis* motif must have been present. Without a long search I have found two examples of it: St Bessarion and St Oringa of Lucca, who admittedly belongs in a period after Pseudo-Turpin. Presumably further parallels could be found in Crusade literature. The search for sources has really not yet begun. I am confident that for many miracles in the *Historia* one could identify models in the Bible and in hagiography, but not in Roman literature.

Concerning the second example that I have chosen, I must confess my desperation. I have not yet been able to trace the model for the following motif. It turns on a deed of Charlemagne's, who wants to outwit, if not totally deceive, God (*De bello Furre*). Before the ruler moves into battle against Furre, the Prince of Navarre, he beseeches God to identify for him those of his troops who will perish against Furre. God fulfils the pious king's request. On the morning before the battle, Charlemagne sees inscribed on the backs of the men destined for death a red cross as a sign. So as not to expose them to death in battle, Charlemagne takes the *morituri* aside and locks them in a church. His calculation is simple: anyone who does not take part in the battle cannot die in it. But God's purposes and ways are unfathomable. As the victorious Charlemagne returns from the battlefield without loss, he discovers that all

7 *Der Pseudo-Turpin von Compostela*, ed. A. Hämel (1965); Spiegel (1993).

150 warriors, whom he believed to be safe in the church, are dead. The author offers no details about how the warriors may have lost their lives. We do not learn either that Charlemagne had been punished in some way for attempting to deceive God. Obviously the death of 150 warriors is punishment enough for him. The source for Charlemagne's stratagem has yet to be traced.

If one day all models and narrative motifs in the Pseudo-Turpin have been established, the anonymous author could not be hailed as a master of fiction but rather as an average compiler, of limited imagination and narrative technique. In my opinion, this Latin text, which bears the ambiguous title *Historia*, does not belong in a history of fictionality. If, as Dennis H. Green has pointed out, *militia* and *amor* are vital components of the medieval romance, then in the case of Pseudo-Turpin we can speak only of *militia* in connection with *fides Christiana*. The battle scenes only occasionally show any originality. Original is the battle against the masks, that is against Saracens masked as devils, who with their terrifying disguise are initially successful against Charlemagne's army, until Charlemagne finds a suitable counter-offensive (*De bello larvarum*). It might conceivably still be possible, in the rich literature of war stratagems, perhaps in Vegetius and other relevant authors, to unearth a source for this style of fighting. Moreover, it should be observed that *amor* is not encountered in this text. The *Orlando innamorato* of Boiardo belongs to a later era.

To make it perfectly plain that I do the *Historia Karoli Magni et Rotholandi* no wrong if I deny it the attributes of a fictional romance, I would like to undertake an experiment. How would the *Historia Karoli* look if one were to strip it of the hagiographic element? We have already been relieved of that task by a Nuremberg physician, Hieronymus Monetarius, whose German name is Münzer. After having studied medicine in Pavia and gaining his degree as a doctor in 1479, he settled in Nuremberg, where he practised as a doctor and soon became rich. As a doctor he was well aware of the danger of illnesses. To avoid the risk of infection when the plague broke out in Nuremberg in 1484, he left his patients and travelled to Italy, on this occasion to Rome, from where he eventually returned once the epidemic in Nuremberg had died down.

In 1494 Münzer/Monetarius withdrew from a new epidemic then raging in Nuremberg and fled to Spain. With a few wealthy friends he toured the land and kept a diary as he went. This diary, which was not published until 1920, in the *Revue hispanique*, reveals his broad interests. It was not a document intended for publication, but a means of retaining his stock of travel experiences. In December 1494 Münzer spent about ten days in Santiago de

Compostela. He put a little drawing of the facade of St James's Cathedral in his diary and had the opportunity of examining the Codex Calixtinus. The *Historia* of Pseudo-Turpin interested him so much that he inserted large sections of it into his diary. He was actually quite selective, not copying out all chapters in their entirety, but for many of these he contented himself with short subject headings. Although Münzer was a devout Catholic, and not a reformer before his time, he omitted many miracles, many moral aphorisms and above all the long disputations between Christians and heathens, in which Roland, like a preacher, enunciates Christian dogma and attempts to persuade the Muslim enemy to accept baptism. With these summarized elements, the *Historia Karoli Magni* in the Münzer version gains in terms of inner coherence and narrative tempo. The tone of a sermon and the monumental character are gone. The text is concerned purely with the *Historia*. In this version, written in the last years of the fifteenth century, the *Historia Karoli Magni* is a text focusing on the military angle, whereas the original can be categorized under the twin headings of *militia* and *fides*. Of course, the term 'legendary romance' might come to mind, but I hesitate a little in labelling the *Historia Karoli Magni* in this way. Since Reinhold Merkelbach we know that romances can additionally carry a religious content, which in the medieval period occurs in no way discreetly, and in the romances about saints quite openly. The *Historia Karoli Magni et Rotholandi* in my view is no edifying romance about two saints, but a work which just as enthusiastically traces the aim of the Christian reconquering of Spain (*Reconquista*) and the propagating of pilgrimages to St James's tomb.

As much as thirty years before Monetarius/Münzer, the Florentine author Donato Acciaiuoli had thought about the Pseudo-Turpin in similar fashion. His *Historia Karoli Magni* of 1461 was guided by Einhard's *Life of Charlemagne* and avoided all the medieval refinements and the hagiographic element. Obviously the legendary side of Pseudo-Turpin meant little to the early modern period. It is striking that this *Historia* was not printed in the period of incunabula, or in the sixteenth, seventeenth or eighteenth centuries. Ciampi's first edition dates from 1822. One might compare that with the 'after-life' of the Greek love romances, with their strong echoes to be detected here and there in Latin translations of the early modern period. Tomas Hägg in *The Novel in Antiquity* has described most vividly the fascination aroused by the Greek romances of love and adventure. The Pseudo-Turpin exercised no such appeal. Anyone interested in Charlemagne read Donato Acciaiuoli or Einhard, both in the end influenced by an ancient author Suetonius. Einhard's *Life of Charlemagne* served as an ideal method of disseminating political ideas, which perhaps explains why it has been frequently reprinted in modern times. In the Napoleonic era, for example, it is seen as a monument to the greatness of German imperial rule in the Middle Ages and was commandeered as a means of spiritual resistance against France. *Sanctus amor patriae dat animum* ('Holy love for the fatherland gives the spirit'): Einhard could well be included under this motto. Pseudo-Turpin by contrast would not have gained a place within the *Monumenta Germaniae Historica,* but rather in the *Acta Sanctorum.*

I would like to add a further word about the Old French version of the cycle of tales about Charlemagne, Roland and Roncesvalles. Where Latin and vernacular versions on the same theme exist, the question of priority is often difficult to establish. In the case of the *Historia Karoli Magni* and the *Chanson de Roland,* the question of the relationship is indisputable. The Old French text claims priority because its composition has been proved to date back to around 1110, whereas Pseudo-Turpin was written at least three decades later in about 1140 or a bit later. The Latin literature, which in many cases precedes it, in this instance postdates the vernacular text by a wide margin of time.

DOLOPATHOS

Concerning the second text, to which I now turn, we again have a Latin and an Old French version, which are much more closely related than are the Pseudo-Turpin and the *Chanson de Roland.* Both works bear the same title, *Dolopathos,* and the one can be described quite simply as a translation of the other.[8] The nineteenth century initially saw priority as resting with the Old French *Dolopathos.* In the meantime, however, it has been proved beyond doubt that the Latin text takes precedence. Before the year 1200 the Cistercian monk John of Haute Seille in the diocese of Metz composed his Latin *Dolopathos,* a version of the story of the Seven Wise Men. About ten years later Herbert translated the text into Old French. His vernacular version was meant as a tribute to the son of the French king, Philippe Auguste, reflecting his princely glory. The romance readily lends itself to this task. The eponymous King Dolopathos – whose name ominously means deceit or pain (*patitur dolum or dolorem*) – is of Trojan stock, with the very best pedigree. At the time of

8 Johannes de Alta Silva, *Dolopathos sive De rege et septem sapientibus,* ed. A. Hilka (1913).

Emperor Augustus, he is king of Sicily, standing out as an ideal ruler who combines in one person all the virtues of a good father towards his subjects. He is successful in battle, wise and mild, exercising the virtue of generosity and the gift of eloquence. He contrives through military victories, through lavish gifts and a persuasive rhetoric to convert his enemies into friends. He treats his subjects as kindly as a father does his children; they respect and love him. As a true knight he protects widows and orphans, helps the oppressed and pursues those who inflict injustice on the weak. Offenders do not escape his wrath. The guilty cannot buy back their freedom. Intercession made by friends cuts no ice with Dolopathos. Boasting noble, or even royal, lineage gives no immunity in the face of rightful punishment. And so it is that an inner peace descends on Sicily under the patronage of this fair-minded king. For the ruler hounds all criminals without mercy and corners them in even the most remote refuges and caves. Those failing to improve are chased from the realm or executed. The farmer can now till his land in peace. The streets are safe, the cities have no need of ramparts, ditches or walls for their defence. Harvests always yield plentifully. Wine, oil and honey flow in abundance. Even Nature shows her very best side. Instead of a sequence of winter and summer there prevails under Dolopathos a steady, temperate spring climate. The peace of Paradise and a return of the Golden Age are the hallmarks of his reign.

In this realm of peace, a veritable Paradise on earth, the manners of men change. Everything points to the fulfillment of carnal desires, for now instead of the war-god Mars, Venus and Cupid are in the ascendant. Youth seeks after the joys of love, the old people recapture the amorous adventures of the past over a glass of wine. Dolopathos recognizes the dangers of easy living and introduces sport and competitive athletics to counter the effects of hedonism: hurling boulders, horse racing, *hastiludia*, that is, tournaments and jousting. For the moral stabilizing of his subjects he educates them in fear of the gods. Almost apologetically the Latin author ventures the thought that at this time Jesus Christ had not yet been born. This means that Dolopathos was only acquainted with polytheism and should not be criticized for this. All would have been perfect had not jealousy moved certain slanderers to plot against Dolopathos and capture the ear of Emperor Augustus. But these dark intrigues are soon unmasked. Dolopathos, having been summoned to the imperial court, after the punishment of the plotters rises in the estimation of the emperor, who marries him to the sister of his wife. For many years the marriage remains childless until at last a son is born. Astrologers, when asked for advice, provide the newborn child with the following horoscope: he will become a great philosopher, will be exposed to a host of setbacks, but will in fact eventually become his father's successor and worship the highest god. Here, too, the author cannot resist a private comment. He explains that the astrologers could not have made these predictions because of their divinatory knowledge. It would have been God himself who spoke through them.

Seven years pass since the birth of the boy, to whom the father had given the name Lucinius. The son was like a light (*lux*) for him, his birth a day of joy. At the age of seven Lucinius is put in the care of the best philosopher of the time; we have here an indirect reference to the education of Alexander the Great by Aristotle. In these days of Emperor Augustus, there is no better educator and no greater philosopher than the poet Virgil. Lucinius is brought to him in Rome, and under his tutelage he makes rapid progress in the liberal arts and in all other branches of knowledge. Thanks to his astrological wisdom Lucinius escapes the scheming of his jealous contemporaries, whom he easily outwits. They want to kill him with poisoned wine but he sees through their trickery and compels them to drink from the deadly chalice themselves.

When he is fourteen, news comes from his father in Palermo that his mother has died and he must return to his homeland. On his taking leave of Virgil, his teacher reminds him that one owes more obedience to one's spiritual father, that is, the teacher, than to a blood-father. Virgil, his guardian, extracts from the departing pupil this promise, to remain silent until he meets his teacher once again. With his father's envoys the dumb Lucinius travels home where he is greeted warmly by Dolopathos (who in the meantime has married again), by his young stepmother and by all the people. In the celebrations held on occasion of his arrival, the youth's silence remains unnoticed. On the following morning the king is devastated when he must conclude that his son has lost the power of speech while in Rome. The young queen promises a remedy. Her maidservants lead Lucinius to his stepmother's apartments, where they try by all means to persuade him to loosen his tongue. One ploy is to set their powers of seduction in motion. The lascivious maidens give him wine to drink, undress before him and try by tactile approach to move him to love-making and to speech. In the midst of this fire (*in igne positus*), Lucinius nevertheless refuses to succumb to desire's flames. In the description of this scene one is unavoidably reminded of chaste Hippolytus or of the steadfast saints who will not let themselves be seduced. Eventually the queen resorts to an extreme measure. Since the chaste stepson had reacted to the enticing servants no more than an inanimate stone, she decides to tempt the *lapis insensibilis* herself. She adorns herself, and as lovely as Helen she approaches Lucinius. With love-potions, magic formulae, words and tears she tries to stir him. And the inevitable happens. What started as play becomes dangerously serious as she burns with searing love for her stepson, who yields not an inch. On being rejected her love is turned into hatred. Like Potiphar's wife in her treatment of Joseph, she throws accusations at her stepson and presses for the punishment of the man she calls her violator. Then the king in utter distress sees himself compelled to sentence his own son to death, for his silence must mean admission of guilt.

The condemned man is to lose his life outside the city of Palermo on a refuse heap. The court and the citizens all want to witness the execution. Lucinius is standing ready on the heap when a venerable old man approaches, recognizable as one of the Seven Wise Men. He demands to hear the reasons for the intended execution of the king's son. And then he recites a tale to the assembled gathering, a tale warning about the impulsiveness and cunning of women. His story proceeds and the whole day passes, so that the execution has to be delayed till the next morning. But the next day brings a further delay because the second Wise Man appears, who in his turn has a tale to tell. In this way seven days are consumed with the tales of the Seven Wise Men. On the eighth day Virgil arrives. He comes sweeping through the air on the back of a bird. Like a *deus ex machina* he resolves all the problems. He releases Lucinius from his vow of silence and exposes the guilt of the mendacious queen, who together with her handmaidens promptly meets her end on the rubbish heap, where she would have had her stepson burned alive.

A fairytale would end at this point. In some circumstances it might go on to report that the young Lucinius celebrated his marriage to a lovely, virtuous young woman. Our romance takes another direction. There is no question of marriage. Lucinius becomes his father's successor, just as the astrologers had prophesied at his birth. In the very same year both his father and his spiritual father, Virgil, die. The blissful conditions on the island of Sicily remain unchanged until the last years of Emperor Tiberius, that is, AD 37. While King Dolopathos had been a pagan, living in the time before Christ's birth, during the reign of his son Lucinius a historical change comes about. News of a world-revolutionizing event is brought to Sicily by a Christian preacher. In long conversations he talks to Lucinius of Christ's suffering and death, about predestination, the Trinity and other Christian dogma. Nor does he omit to mention that heathens like the Sibyl of Tibur or like the Athenians had already announced the coming of an unknown god. Lucinius is already partially converted to Christianity but still craves a miraculous sign. His Christian teacher accedes to this request and in full view of the crowd brings a dead youth back to life. Descending from his bier, he proclaims Christ as the one true God. There are parallels in the Apocryphal Gospels of the apostles of such dramatic and spectacular rising from the dead. Lucinius and his people immediately become baptized. Lucinius hands the government of Sicily to a trusted friend and goes on pilgrimage with his Christian teacher to Jerusalem, where, full of piety, he leads a life pleasing to God and comes to a peaceful end. It could be noted in parentheses that although this romance about the Seven Wise Men originates in the time of the Crusades, it contains no allusion to the presence of the author and no appeal, direct or indirect, for participation in a Crusade.

I have now sketched the framing narrative of the work, which, to my knowledge, has not been taken into account in the investigation of this romance. The interest of literary scholarship was directed exclusively at the interpolated stories concerning the Seven Wise Men and Virgil's speech on the eighth day, a part of the work I have thus far intentionally omitted. Woven into the core material of the romance there are familiar narrative features, for example the *Creditor*, which have had an influential history and broad application. The *Creditor* is the story of the pound of flesh, most famously used in Shakespeare's *The Merchant of Venice*. Virgil's speech known as *Puteus* deals with the adulteress who returning from a nocturnal tryst is barred entry by her husband to the locked house. She threatens suicide and deceives him by tossing a rock into the well. When her husband, thinking that she is drowning, rushes from the house to save her, she slips into the house, locks the door from within, and now in her turn threatens to discredit her husband as an adulterer to the neighbours. There is also narrative material recalling the *Odyssey* and Herodotus, such as Polyphemus and the treasure-house of Rhampsinitus. One cannot be at all sure how such tales reached the Cistercian monk in Lorraine. The narrative technique in all the eight core speeches is masterly. Some of these novellas are concerned with true love and chivalrous life, but all create access to another level of reality in which a human being's resources are fully put to the test.

But I will return to the rather neglected framing narrative, which has not yet been viewed under a fictional aspect. It is concerned of course with a Golden Age, an eternal spring, with the inner security of a land untroubled by interference from outside and with the sensual pleasures of its inhabitants under the heathen King Dolopathos. I bring attention to the omniscient philosopher Virgil, of whom it is affirmed in the framing narrative that he summarized all human wisdom in a single handbook. The author has here depicted a Utopia of joy for all and has idealized Sicily as a kingdom of innocence and plenty. Against this shining epoch before the coming of Christ is set a strangely pale picture of the time beginning with the baptism of Lucinius. His pilgrimage to Jerusalem and his death in a distant country appear like a swan-song, as if Christianity had ushered in a colourless, unexciting existence and flight from the real business of living. The modern reader gets the impression that the romance has turned into a tract or sermon designed to show the superiority of Christianity over heathen polytheism. The single break in the cloud or, if you like, the only real action is the awakening of the dead boy. Everything else lies under a veil of mist. Have we a cleric speaking here, who in nostalgic spirit draws a picture of ancient heathen times now transfigured, and sees Christianity as a descent from the Golden to the Iron Age? I leave the question of decline or decadence open and turn my attention to the final words of the romance, which take up an attitude to the problem of the fictional character of the text.

Johannes de Alta Silva addresses the reader directly with a request that he should not be criticized for having written about the incredible or the impossible (*incredibilia vel impossibilia me scripsisse*). He defends himself with the well-used argument that it is his wish to entertain and be of use to him, the reader (*et delectationem et utilitatem legentium*). And finally with a reminiscence of Isidore he explains the fictional nature of his romance, a genre to which he concedes the full right to transcend reality (*quae etsi facta non sunt, fieri tamen possunt*).[9]

TWO ENGLISH HISTORICAL NOVELS

The writing of historical novels is in no way the privilege of the nineteenth century. The twelfth and thirteenth centuries had already produced the predecessors of Sir Walter Scott and Charles Kingsley. In this context two works which originated in England deserve consideration, works that, while claiming to be

9 Isidore, *Etymologiae* 1.44.5 (definition of *argumentum*).

pieces of fiction, reflect English history. The one romance has as its title *Vita Haroldi* and so far has been published only once, in an inadequate form and in only a small number of copies by Walter de Gray Birch in 1885, with the subtitle *The Romance of the Life of Harold, King of England*. The anonymous author of the *Vita* made use of numerous rumours circulating in England and Scandinavia soon after the battle of Hastings that Harold Godwinson had survived the battle.[10] He allows the vanquished king to pass through a remarkable period of development. Out of a hero bent on revenge and reprisal there eventually emerges a hermit living a blameless life, submitting piously to his fate, who lives on unrecognized until the end of the eleventh century in England and triumphs to such a degree over self-interest that he even prays for the victorious Norman duke. In spite of his defeat at the battle of Hastings, Harold achieved a great victory. He overcame his own ambition. He finds his last resting place in Waltham, where incidentally even today a memorial tablet commemorates the site of his grave in the churchyard. The author of the *Vita* was very probably a canon of Waltham, who surely strove for the canonization of the king.

The return of a dead ruler is no rarity in the medieval period. In this way the legendary Frederick II gained great popularity. In the nineteenth century similar rumours were current about Napoleon, who fleeing from St Helena is supposed to have achieved great military triumphs as Jussuph Pasha in the Turkish army.[11] The adventure story, then, serves frequently as a starting point for constructs which conceive of another historical outcome. The considerable success of the novel *Fatherland* (1992) by Robert Harris exemplifies this mixing of history and fiction at its best. This phenomenon was the subject of a very readable study by Alexander Demandt.[12] Finally, the *Gesta Herewardi* weaves a fascinating romance around a historically verifiable background figure of English history in the years after 1066; it uses scenic devices from Norse sagas and sketches in the life story of a rebel, Hereward, one that takes bloody revenge on the Normans who had occupied his father's estate and beheaded his brother. Employing tricks of all kinds which make him a forerunner of Robin Hood, he can wage guerrilla war (with Ely as his base) against William the Conqueror, until by the agency of his second wife he manages to conclude a peace, not verifiable historically, with the Conqueror. The author of this col-

10 Schmidt (1986).
11 Von Schaden (1910).
12 Demandt (1986).

ourful adventure-laden romance, perhaps a monk of Ely living in the second half of the twelfth century, glorified a knight who thanks to his ingenious wit, proves superior to his foreign enemy. His peace agreement with William can be interpreted as an endeavour to create terms of compensation between victors and vanquished and to engender a common identity. This romance about this hero, still popular today in the east of England, presents fiction as history in the interests of a higher truth.

In his prologue the author uses the popular motif in fiction of the unearthed manuscript, to which he owes his story. But the pages of this manuscript, he suggests, had become mildewed and illegible with damp. Whole pages had become detached and gone missing. The truth of this report can no longer be tested. But a reader with a good literary background knows what one should make of it, especially when, as in this case, it is supported by the note that the author claims to have translated the illegible text from the vernacular into Latin.[13]

References

TEXTS

Gesta Herewardi, ed. C. T. Martin, in Th. D. Hardy and C.T. Martin, Geoffrey Gaimar, Lestoire des Engles, Rolls Series 91, London 1888.

Johannes de Alta Silva, *Dolopathos sive De rege et septem sapientibus*, herausgegeben von Alfons Hilka. Sammlung mittellateinischer Texte 5, Heidelberg: Winter, 1913.

Karolellus atque Pseudo-Turpini *Historia Karoli Magni et Rotholandi*, ed. Paul Gerhard Schmidt. Bibliotheca Teubneriana, Stuttgart and Leipzig: Teubner 1996.

Der Pseudo-Turpin von Compostela, ed. A. Hämel. Aus dem Nachlaß herausgegeben von André de Mandach, Sitzungsberichte der Bayerischen Akademie der Wissenschaften, Phil.-hist. Klasse 1965, Heft 1, Munich: C.H. Beck 1965.

De sanctitate meritorum et gloria miraculorum beati Karoli Magni ad honorem et laudem nominis dei, ed. Gerhard Rauschen, in *Publikationen der Gesellschaft für rheinische Geschichtskunde* 7, Leipzig, 1890, pp. 17–93; the *Vita Karoli Magni* of the twelfth century printed in Aachen, which uses the textual base in Gerhard

13 *Gesta Herewardi* (ed. C. T. Martin, 339): *nichil invenimus preter pauca et dispersa folia partim stillicidio putrefactis et abolitis et partim abscisione divisis.* Schmidt (1985); Kingsley (1884); Rex (2005).

Rauschen, newly published, translated and prefaced by Helmut and Inge Deutz, Siegburg 2002.

STUDIES

Day, Mildred Leake (ed. and trans.) (2005) *Latin Arthurian Literature*, Cambridge: D.S. Brewer.

Demandt, Alexander (1986) *Ungeschehene Geschichte. Ein Traktat über die Frage: Was wäre geschehen, wenn…?*, Göttingen: Vandenhoeck & Ruprecht.

Green, Dennis H. (2002) *The Beginnings of Medieval Romance: Fact and Fiction, 1150–1220* (Cambridge Studies in Medieval Literature, 47), Cambridge: Cambridge University Press.

Hägg, Tomas (1983) *The Novel in Antiquity*, Berkeley: University of California Press.

Kingsley, Charles (1884) *Hereward the Wake*, London. [Repr. Hildesheim: Olms, 1969.]

Knapp, Fritz Peter (1997) *Historie und Fiktion in der mittelalterlichen Gattungspoetik. Sieben Studien und ein Nachwort*, Heidelberg: Winter.

Knapp, Fritz Peter, and Manuela Niesner (2002) *Historisches and fiktionales Erzählen*, Berlin: Duncker & Humblot.

Knapp, Fritz Peter (2005) *Historie und Fiktion in der mittelalterlichen Gattungspoetik (II). Zehn neue Studien und ein Vorwort*, Heidelberg: Winter.

Merkelbach, Reinhold (1962) *Roman und Mysterium in der Antike*, Munich and Berlin: C.H. Beck.

Rex, Peter (2005) *Hereward the Last Englishman*, Stroud: Tempus.

Schaden, Adolf von (1910) 'Jussuph Pascha oder die Geschichte der Flucht Napoleons aus Sankt Helena. Höchst merkwürdige Schicksale des Exkaisers am konstantinopolitanischen Hofe', in Friedrich M. Kircheisen (ed.), *Hat Napoleon gelebt? Und andere kuriose Geschichten* (RARA, Eine Bibliothek des Absonderlichen, 1. Band), Stuttgart, pp. 59–122.

Schmidt, Paul Gerhard (1985) 'Biblisches und hagiographisches Kolorit in den Gesta Herewardi', in Katherine Walsh and Diana Wood (eds.), *The Bible in the Medieval World: Essays in Memory of Beryl Smalley*, Oxford: Clarendon, pp. 85–95.

Schmidt, Paul Gerhard (1986) 'Veritas Naufragatur. Das Leben und die Taten König Harolds von England nach 1066', in *Fälschungen im Mittelalter. Internationaler Kongreß der Monumenta Germaniae Historica* (vol. 1), Munich: MGH, pp. 189–204.

Schmidt, Paul Gerhard (1995) 'Das Interesse an mittellateinischer Literatur', *Wolfgang Stammler Gastprofessur,* Heft 3, Freiburg: Universitätsverlag.

Schmidt, Paul Gerhard (2003) 'Mittellateinische Romane', in Christa Bertelsmeier-Kierst and Christopher Young (eds.), *Eine Epoche im Umbruch. Volkssprachliche Literalität 1200–1300,* Tübingen: Niemeyer, pp. 195–203.

Schmidt, Paul Gerhard (2005) 'Editoren als Zensoren', *Mittellateinisches Jahrbuch* 40: 431–3.

Spiegel, Gabrielle L. (1993) *Romancing the Past: The Rise of Vernacular Prose Historiography in Thirteenth-Century France,* Berkeley: University of California Press.

Ziolkowski, Jan (1997) 'Die mittellateinische Literatur', in Fritz Graf (ed.), *Einleitung in die lateinische Philologie,* Stuttgart and Leipzig: Teubner, pp. 297–322.

Speak, Fiction: The Rhetorical Fabrication of Narrative in Geoffrey of Monmouth

P. M. Mehtonen

With works of imaginative literature there is nothing more ruinous for historical understanding than genre theory or a mindless search for antecedents, origins, and distant parallels. (Bowersock 1997: 14)

When the first-person speaker of the *Historia regum Britannie* (c. 1135–38; hereafter HRB) by Geoffrey of Monmouth repeatedly returns to the question of his low and brief style as well as his consecutive and orderly narrative, he is only being a partly reliable narrator. His style indeed is fairly unornamented and straightforward – in one word, easy (*simplex constructio*)[1] – as long as we follow the narrator's chronicling of the generations of British rulers. Something quite different, however, is going on in the speeches and letters in the text, in other words, in the fictional speech acts of the characters embedded in the first-level narration. In these embeddings not only does the stylistic register shift from simple to complex, but also the mode of representation is altered. The plot no longer follows linear chronology, with an occasional digression back and forth, as in the narrator's discourse. The embedded sections begin to construct modal and alternative courses of events in the speaker's and listeners' minds – things that might, would or must take place (or not). Naturally, some of these possibilities actualize and some do not as the narrative returns to the world of the main plot.

Direct discourse in general and speeches in particular seem to mark overt fictional activity in Geoffrey of Monmouth's HRB, a work which has managed

* This article is part of my larger study, funded by the Academy of Finland.

1 Cf. the division between *simplex constructio* (the simple prose, proper for the general audience) and *appositio* (more complex for the learned audience), in Gervais of Melkley, *Ars poëtica* (1965: 216–7).

to escape univocal genre labels until the present day. By analyzing the speech acts in this 'legendary history', 'epic history', or 'chronicle',[2] it is possible to trace activities in the text which represent an archaic phase in the development of twelfth-century fiction. The word 'archaism' here simply means that the *Historia* keeps strictly and rather mechanistically separate the business of the narrator's and the characters' speech acts. Yet Geoffrey's text contains the crucial elements or 'windows of opportunity' (Green 2002: 187) that later, in the romance and saga narratives, became intentionally blurred or – to be more precise – *the blurring* of which became a poetic device.

The HRB was composed during the first decades of the century that has been referred to as *Epochenwende*, that is, as a transformative period in the Western divorce of fiction from reality. The medieval romance as a genre or mode of fiction arose out of the traditions of ancient Latin and Greek narratives transposed into Latin and vernacular Romance languages, Celtic legends, and contact with historical writing (Green 2002: 134; Marnette 2005: 205). Surprisingly little text-analytical work exists of Geoffrey's frequently and routinely mentioned work.[3] Although it is not the aim of the present essay to participate in genre discussions, it will be necessary to compare the narrative structures of the HRB both to the traditions of fiction and history. The shared challenge of composition for anyone working with narrative structure was aptly formulated by a later saga narrator, returning to the main plot from yet another episode: 'Now the story returns to the point where we left it, for

2 In respective order, Tatlock (1950); Faletra (2000); Weiss (2004: 27). It is customary to notice the influence of classical epic – Virgil, Statius – in the HRB (e.g. Flint 1979: 459–60; Curley 1994: 18); however, it was pointed out already by Pähler (1958: 61–73) that important influences such as Virgil, the Old Testament or the Alexander material were not structural models for Geoffrey of Monmouth's work. The most workable genre definition for the present purposes comes from John O. Ward's article on rhetorical historiography; Geoffrey's *Historia* was 'the first thorough application of the genre of *historia* to patently invented *materia*' (Ward 1985: 103). Cf. also Monika Otter (1996: 79): 'The *Historia*, as many commentators have noted, imitates the formal structures used by such great contemporaries as William of Malmesbury and Henry of Huntingdon; yet it is "emptied" of the referentiality and the truth claims that normally adhere to the form. Nonetheless, it is not devoid of serious intentions [...].'

3 For adequate references, see for instance Pähler (1958: 22–6); Flint (1979: 448–9); (for the spatial poetics and *descriptio* of geography and topography in the HRB) Otter (1996: 69–83); Faletra (2000); Wright (2001: xvi). More generally, I also consider still adequate what Evelyn Birge Vitz (1989: 8) called 'the besetting sin of virtually all modern narrative analysis', namely its tendency to bracket off as irrelevant elements which do not fit the (modern) idea of a narrative. To update this claim we only need to have a look at the entry 'medieval narrative' in a recent handbook of narrative to realize how meagre is the dialogue between medieval studies and mainstream comparativism. See *Routledge Encyclopedia of Narrative Theory*, ed. David Herman, Manfred Jahn and Marie-Laure Ryan, London: Routledge, 2005. For medieval concepts of narration and narrative, see Mehtonen (1996 and 2006); Davenport (2004).

it's not possible to tell two stories at the very same time, even though that may have been the way they happened' (*Göngu-Hrolf's Saga* 1980: 78). Further excitement for the composer is created by *materia* which consists of both historical and fantastic stories, or material both narrative ('x did y') and non-narrative (proverbs, arguments, prophecies).

Geoffrey of Monmouth's solution to the challenge was a sort of frame narrative which opens two dominating spaces with distinctive features: the main, first-level narration of the chronology of the British kings, and the embedded direct speech acts, containing also fabulous *materia*, future tenses, hypothetical events – in a word, embedded worlds within worlds (within worlds). Instances of direct speeches, letters or dialogue introduce present-tense discourse into a past-tense narrative. Unlike in a pure chronicle or simple historical narrative which mainly consist of a sequence of events which 'happen' in the narrated world, the *HRB* also presents events that do not actualize in the plot but are merely imagined, wished for, prophesied or hypothesized about by the characters. As will be suggested in the following pages, this structure in the *HRB* is elaborate, yet rough when compared to the later twelfth-century romances where the narrator's act of narrating is profoundly fused into the narrated world. Consider, for instance, the famous episode in Wolfram von Eschenbach's *Parzival* (in Book IX), where the first-person narrator known as Wolfram enters into a dialogue with Frau Abenteuer, Lady Adventure, inviting her to tell more about the hero. The limits between narrator Wolfram's and Frau Abenteuer's speech acts are far from clear as both the labour and the joy of narrating are divided. In comparison to the early twelfth-century historical fictions (such as the *HRB*), such traffic between the businesses of narrating can be taken to indicate a more advanced administration of the medium of fictionality.

SPEECHES IN HISTORY AND FICTION

Geoffrey of Monmouth's *HRB* was by no means a pioneer work in the use of speeches in a narrative that takes *historia* as one of its models. On the contrary, the work had eminent predecessors both in the tradition of fiction and history writing. By selecting speeches, letters and dialogues as his devices of constructing narrative, Geoffrey is relying on 'a tried device of ancient, medieval, and Renaissance historiography' (Ward 1985: 146, without reference to Geoffrey, though). According to Ward, the speeches served different oratorical functions in the twelfth-century writers he calls 'rhetorical historians' and 'rhetorical chroniclers':

> Speeches, for the rhetorical historian, were a vital creative tool, whether ideological set-pieces such as Frederick Barbarossa's outburst against the Roman citizens or his opening address at the Diet of Roncaglia, Bishop Ulger's declamation in John of Salisbury's *Historia pontificalis* (with its opening use of *repetitio* 'mirum est...'), Queen Ethelburga's decisive speech to her husband in William of Malmesbury, elaborate pre-battle addresses such as the speech of Walter Espec in Aildred of Rielvaux's *Relatio de Standardo*, or architectural fictions such as Urban's speech at Clermont. (Ward 1985: 146)

The quoted passage depicts well the deliberative and epideictic situations of oratory, not only as they were exhibited in historiography but also as taught and exercised in the schools.

Also the *literary* functions of speeches in history are well known at least since Erich Auerbach's studies in *Mimesis*. Not only did direct speech in history – here Tacitus is being discussed – serve in the presentation of ideas, as an access to the thoughts of the supposed speaker, or as rhetorical 'bravura pieces', speeches were also used in the dramatization of events in historiography which required 'grandiloquent speeches, which as a rule are fictitious' (Auerbach 1974: 38).[4] Although thus emphasizing the stylistic and fictional import of speeches, Auerbach also mentions in the same passage 'a certain realism' as one of the narrative effects of speeches. The same effect has been observed in a recent linguistic (pragmatic) study of medieval narrative that analyzes direct discourse in the vernacular French romance from the twelfth century onwards. It has been suggested that certain stylistic elements now considered as characteristic of narrative *writing* (e.g. historical present, or tense usage typical for interior monologue, etc.) may have been adapted ultimately 'from the naturally occurring narratives of everyday speech' (Fleischman 1990: 10). Moreover, direct discourse might give the medieval story '"psychological realism" if not "historical truth"' (Marnette 2005: 204). Although these remarks regarding the reality effect of direct discourse, or medieval narratives as 'natu-

4 See also Harder (1997: 236–7), who has suggested that the speeches in the Byzantine novels resemble the twelfth-century progymnasmata exercises, in the case of overtly fictional letters those of *fabula*.

ral narratives', may also apply to some direct discourses in Geoffrey's *HRB*, this essay is interested exactly in the opposing features of the speeches embedded in the broader narrative frame: the speeches as embryos of techniques that serve overtly fictional and fantastic composition.

The narration which uses agents who speak in their own voice creates a practical as well as theoretical dilemma which is much older than Geoffrey of Monmouth or the rhetorical historians of the twelfth century. Namely, there exists an ancient controversy about the issue of whether the persons' speeches should be accepted in history writing or not. The negative answer is extremely relevant for the study of fiction: if history explores the sequences of cause and effect (as for instance the historian Polybius claimed it should), then the integration of speeches in history betrays the historian's duty. Direct speeches are quite obviously *invented*, showing the historian displaying his oratorical skill instead of the transcription of actual words spoken.[5] Also Lucian ridicules in *The Way to Write History* the would-be historians who want to emulate Thucydides's funeral oration but only manage to make, with their copious flood of rhetoric, oratory a felony – and make the listener weep not from sorrow but from laughter.

What therefore seems a restrictive norm for the historian in fact opens a free space of invention – also of parody – for a fiction writer. Directly reported discourses inside even a chronological narrative allow imaginary courses of events and a range of stylistic choices. This freedom was already celebrated in the ancient Greek and medieval Byzantine novel (romance). As discussed elsewhere in this volume, for instance the ancient *Alexander Romance* contained letters between the protagonist and his teacher Aristotle that were written in a matter-of-fact style, yet fabulous in content.[6] Although such structural design which consists of shifts of style and different *materia* is sometimes not appreciated,[7] it may be here taken as a patent device in the rhetorical fabrication of the plots also in the Middle Ages, not to mention the later development

5 As for Polybius's views, I am here following MacPhail (2001: 7–8).

6 See Tomas Hägg, pp. 31–2 above; see also Reardon (1991: 46) for Philostratus's group of imaginary letters. For discussions of the medieval Latin and vernacular translations and versions of epistolary Alexander material such as *Alexander's Letter to Aristotle about India*, *The Correspondence of Alexander and Dindimus* and *Secreta Secretorum*, see Stoneman (1999a: 168; 1999b: 238, 240, 247).

7 Regarding the *Alexander Romance* a recent commentator judges the movement between the plain, 'historically attested' narrative of Alexander's deeds, on the one hand, and the rhetorical speeches and letters reporting fantastic accounts of exotic people, on the other, as 'abrupt shifts' of content and style and 'not altogether successful' (Archibald 2004: 18).

of the (epistolary) novel.[8] The ancient and medieval Greek novels contained letters where the range of topics varied from foreign and domestic politics to private affairs and love letters; the speeches could serve forensic as well as epideictic purposes in the plot (Reardon 1991: 149–52; Harder 1997: 231, 234–7). Although culturally remote from the topic of this study, it is also relevant to observe here a structural principle regarding the functions of letters in this tradition. As suggested by Harder (1997: 239–40), the function of letters within a Byzantine novel could be that of a *Sekundärgeschichte* which creates a contrast with the main narrative. The letters do not only (or at all) serve the recapitulation of events already narrated in the frame narrative, but may, on the contrary, contain imaginary meetings between characters, or even messages which were never sent and therefore never answered.

Such events, which are non-events in the sense that they do not actualize in the first-level narration of the text, are also important in Geoffrey of Monmouth's *HRB*.[9] It is therefore crucial not to detach the speeches from the immediate narrative context where they were presented, but, on the contrary, to begin from there.

THE FRAMEWORK OF THE SPEECHES: THE STRUCTURE OF A STORYIZED CHRONICLE

The manifest aim of Geoffrey of Monmouth's narrator – at the first-level narration – is to avoid prolixity and obscurity in presentation. He repeats three times the aims of the presentation, claiming to omit material that for instance Gildas the historian has treated 'with sufficient prolixity' (*satis prolixe*); whereas the narrator himself proceeds in a low and brief style (*uil-*

8 The word 'fabrication' should, in this paper, be understood only in the positive sense of 'the rewriting of the mythic and legendary past as part of the creation of a new and miraculous present' (Bowersock 1997: 13. Cf. the more negative definition of 'non-fiction' by Green 2002: 187: 'invention which is a fabrication, not meant to be seen through or called into question and therefore not fiction in the technical sense'). Regarding the epistolary form of direct discourse it may be worthwhile to recall Samuel Richardson's often-quoted passage in the letter-shape preface to the epistolary novel *Clarissa*, where the narrator wishes that the letters were not thought genuine. I owe this reminder to Bowersock (1997: 51), discussing related themes in antiquity.

9 It is important to emphasize that this focus on the 'world-switch' is not based on the referential assumptions regarding the matter-of-factuality of Geoffrey's narrative. Cf. the broader view of 'other worlds' by Otter (1996: 95–6): 'In a sense [...] William [of Newburgh, in attacking the fabulous Arthurian content in the *HRB*] is exactly right: Geoffrey does "dream" another universe in which there is plenty of room for all his "fictions" and "fabulae," as William contemptuously calls them; he is creating, as Bäuml would put it, a "coherent pseudo-reality," or fiction. [...] William of Newburgh objects to Geoffrey because his own view of history is strictly linear'.

iori dictamine; uili stilo breviter; inferiori stilo; HRB: 15, 47, 129–30) – or, as in the variant version of the *HRB*, with 'lucid writing' (*lucide scripti*, Geoffrey of Monmouth 1988: 65). It has been suggested in earlier research that these remarks are partly rhetorical pretence and Geoffrey's parody of the writerly conventions of his predecessors and sources. According to Valerie Flint, 'for all its apparent simplicity', the *HRB* is a work of considerable complexity and erudition (1979: 459). With agreement we must nevertheless ask further: exactly *how* is this 'simplicity' made both apparent and – in some places – absent? The suggested answers will also relate to the distribution of fictionality in the structure of the *HRB*.

For the alleged purposes of the consecutive and brief style in the frame narrative of the *HRB*, the models of chronology and genealogy are well suited. At least at first sight these principles seem to govern the first-level narration of the *HRB* where the remote past is the object. The temporal structure resembles a 'biblical story' (cf. Boitani 1982: 4) in that time moves in one direction only, from the year 1100 BC and from the mythic Brutus to King Cadwallader in the seventh century AD. Yet at the same time the sequential plan forms a fundamentally secular narrative. Genealogy as a structure of the plot or – as observed by Gabrielle Spiegel in the context of the twelfth- and thirteenth-century French chronicle – 'as both a social phenomenon and a literary device', functions to secularize narration of temporal processes by emphasizing the human process of filiation as a metaphor for historical change (Spiegel 1999: 4; 1983: 47, 50).

Both the biblical and secular associations of genealogy are relevant here. The first-level narration of the *HRB* reports past events and the power struggles of the leaders or their heirs by mainly keeping the grammatical tempus of preterit and connecting the events and episodes with deictic adverbs such as *iterum, dum, exin*, and so forth. Yet upon closer scrutiny the consecutive order begins to multiply and break. Firstly, this 'preterit reality' in fact does not consist only of one but three preterit realities, namely those of the kings of Britain, biblical history and the Greek-Roman mythopoetic past which each create their own sparse chronologies along the frame narrative (§22, p. 15; §26–27, p. 17; §28–29, p. 18; §38, pp. 22–23; §64, p. 42; §68, p. 44). These passages do not only make visible the existence of the narrator who holds the strings of the plot in his hands; the passages also remotely resemble the technique of interlaced narrative, as observed by generations of romance scholars particularly in the twelfth-century vulgate version of the Arthurian romances. Interlacing allows transitions in the plot in which 'the writer announces that he is going to stop talking about one thing and turn to something else' as he carries forward several storylines simultaneously and moves from one sequence to another, and then back to the matter left in suspense (Ryding 1971: 70). A primitive form of such transitions is also needed by Geoffrey's narrator since the co-chronologies, as mentioned above, are connected to the main plot only via simultaneity expressed with the emphatic *tunc* ('at that time'; exceptions being e.g. the birth of Jesus *in diebus illis*, §64, p. 42, and the deeds of Peter the Apostle *eodem tempore*, §69, p. 44). Other elements of the plots – characters, events – do not travel between the ontologies of these different preterit realities. As aptly put by Pähler, the synchronic temporal parallels do not form part of Geoffrey's historical narrative itself ('haben mit Geoffreys Geschichtsdarstellung an sich nichts zu tun', Pähler 1958: 71, 82–3). The closest hit in terms of the main plot comes with the mention of Aeneas Silvius, 'son of Aeneas and uncle of Brutus' (§22, p. 74), who reigned in Italy at the time Brutus had built the city of Troia Nova (London) and given the citizens a code of laws. Due to the separate existences of these narratives at the level of plots, this structure does not allow for a linear movement in the HRB as a whole.

Secondly, in addition to the (horizontal) zigzag movement between the aforementioned multiplied chronologies, the HRB also presents a constant (vertical) movement which breaks the linearity of the first-level narration. This consists of the traffic between the story-now – that is, the narrated events – and the speaker-now: the time and event of narrating. Apart from the frequent 'as said above' (*ut predictum est*), also longer narratorial interventions take place:

> If I believed its [the Eagle, *aquila*] sayings to be true, I would not hesitate to hand them down to history with my other material (p. 80).[10]
>
> If I were to describe everything, I should make this history far too prolix. (Trans. P. M. M.)[11]

Although the narrator of the HRB does not participate as a character or contemporary witness in the described events – a criterion of 'vicarious narration'

10 All English translations of the HRB by Lewis Thorpe (1987/1966), unless otherwise acknowledged.

11 *Cuius sermones si ueros arbitrarer, sicut cetera memorie dare non diffugerem* (§29, p. 18). *Quem si omnino describere pergerem, nimiam prolixitatem historie generarem* (§157, p. 112).

(cf. Fleischman 1990: 109–10) – his presence is nevertheless strongly felt in the act of narrating. This is one of the archaic features of narration that gradually disappears in the later tradition of fiction and romance. Sophie Marnette, in analyzing the speech and thought presentation in thirteenth-century French prose romance as a 'historiographical genre', makes interesting observations although not directly in the context of Geoffrey at all. Prose romances as an example of the historiographical genre (the others examined by Marnette are *chansons de geste* and chronicle) are 'historiographical' in the sense that 'they present their stories as based on a unique source both historically and even religiously true'. The first prose romances in French were the Grail romances:

> [T]hese romances use a linguistic medium that had long been associated with the notion of religious and historical truth in Latin and they tell a story that is clearly parallel to the Bible: revealing the veritable events that happened after Jesus' death and the ensuing creation of the fellowship of the Grail. They are all told in a specific way, with the disappearance of references to the *je*-narrator to the benefit of an impersonal narrative voice performatively referring to itself as *le conte* or *l'histoire*. (Marnette 2005: 202)

Yet this does not mean that the visible first-person narrator disappeared from the romance for good. The later prose romances both departed from the Grail thematic and presented themselves at times as translated or transposed by the *je*-narrator (ibid.: 203). This visible agent clearly has functions similar to Geoffrey of Monmouth's narrator (cf. Marnette 2005: 204–5): he is not so much the guarantor of the story's truth but a link on the chain of transmission. This first-person narrator is also very fond of reporting direct discourse and explaining to the reader how he masters the composition of his tale.

Story-wise the main body of Geoffrey's *HRB* could therefore be conceived in terms of the form of a storyized chronicle (cf. Vitz 1989: 109): although the skeleton of the narrative resembles a chronicle as a mainly linear, sequential, chronologically structured and open-ended narrative, the narrative is partially structured by episodes and according to patterns of problem solving and developmental process.[12] Pure chronicle as a form is rare, and perhaps

12 Since the word 'chronicle' is used here simply as referring to a form of narrative, its medieval meanings are not explored here. However, for a relevant twelfth-century opposition between two groups

closest to it in historical fiction come the simple lists of kings in Geoffrey's *HRB* or the genealogies of families in the Old Norse sagas.[13]

It is important to recognize and reassess these microscopic back and forth movements, as identified above, within the macroscopic genealogical design of the text. That is, it is often claimed that genealogy 'necessarily fashions history as linear narrative' (Spiegel 1983: 51), or that the whole narrative of the *HRB* is 'in the correct chronological sequence' (Green 2002: 169) or, even more emphatically, the *HRB* is characterized by 'a relentless sense of linearity'. With the latter claim, Michael A. Faletra argues against an old 'fundamental misunderstanding' according to which the *HRB* as 'the stuff of romance' is digressive and ahistorical. Instead, the text should be seen 'as Geoffrey conceives it: as an epic history marked, like other Anglo-Norman histories, by linearity and continuity' (Faletra 2000: 62–4). However, I have suggested above that it is difficult to affirm from the textual basis how such linearity and continuity is maintained in the *HRB*.[14] Moreover, the question of the digressivity versus linearity as such does automatically relate to the question of historicity versus ahistoricity.[15] There exist digressive genuine histories as well as linear genuine fabulations in the history of Occidental writing.

The textual zigzag movements meddle in the 'relentless' sense of linearity already in the first-level narration of the *HRB*, but they are even more apparent in the speech acts embedded in the main plot.

of historians, the chronicler (who offers *veritatem humili sermone* but speaks *balbuetindo*; Odo of Deuil) and the more eloquent rhetorical historian, see Ward (1985: 148).

13 See for instance *HRB* §52, p. 34: *Huic successit Runo Pereduri filius: cui Gerennus Eliduri filius; post illum Katellus filius suus; post Katellum Coillus; post Coillum Porrex; post Porrecem Cherin. Huic nati fuerunt tres filii, Fulgenius uidelicet atque Edadus necnon et Andragius, qui omnes alter post alterum regnauerunt.*

14 It has been more convincingly argued by Otter (1996: 97) and others that Geoffrey 'both exploits and violates the principle of "transparent", linear history': at the surface he seems to fill the 'gaps' in the earlier histories of England, yet he 'overstuffs' these gaps and historical spaces with his narratives.

15 Nor does genealogy or chronology as structural principles automatically require the linearity of the narrative. In analyzing the types of medieval genealogy as historical and poetological devices, Croenen points out that an 'ancestor-oriented type' gives a specific person a set of prestigious ancestors, whereas a 'descent-oriented type' starts from a specific ancestor and then goes forward to the younger generations. In both types the direction of the narrative is usually (but not necessarily) chronological, although the 'conceptual starting point' is different. In the medieval historiographical tradition, genealogies of the ancestor-oriented types had more appeal since they were easier to compose and conveyed a clearer message when used for political or other propaganda purposes (Croenen 1999: 85–91).

HYPOTHETICAL PLOTS AND UNACTUALIZED POSSIBILITIES

> 'If I had refused to take part in that campaign, then you would have beaten Cassivelaunus.' (Androgeus's letter to Caesar, p. 114)

A complete change of style and form in Geoffrey's *Historia regum Britannie* occurs when the (pseudo)chronological sequencing is replaced by rhetorical order. The text contains a vast proportion of letters and speeches, most of which are direct discourse as reported by the narrator. These are not only the speeches of the kings but also of the mothers of the great men (§ 41: the mother of Brennius and Belinus; §107: Merlin's mother), of anonymous individual characters as well as collective groups (e.g. the Trojans, Roman exiles), or even personified inanimate creatures (the Forest in Merlin's prophecies). Occasionally the speech acts are reported by the narrator in indirect discourse (e.g. §6–8 *et passim*), sections of which tend to be very short in comparison to the direct discourses. The function of the indirect speech acts in the *HRB* is clearly to provide elements which directly advance the plot.[16] Apart from direct and indirect discourses reported by the narrator, there also exist more infrequent combinations – such as speech reported by a character within another speech. Such multiple embedding occurs also in Merlin's prophecies, to be discussed below.

This variety of the thematized fictional speech acts in the *HRB* exhibits a high level of rhetorical specialization – not unlike the earlier *chansons de geste* where the amount of direct discourse is much greater than in the later tradition of romance (cf. Marnette 2005: 192). Not only do the characters in the *HRB* simply 'say', 'answer' and 'argue'; they also proclaim, exclaim, decree, give advice, command (in the second person), lament, swear or beg. They even expressively and dramatically 'bellowed out words again and again' (Corineus's speech, §24, p. 16: *iterum iterumque proclamans librabat*), 'sob aloud'

16 This paper focuses on the vulgate version of the *HRB* (Berne, Burgerbibliothek, MS. 568), but it is interesting to observe differences between nearly contemporary versions. As pointed out by Neil Wright, the editor of both the vulgate and the First Variant Version (an anonymous redaction made between 1138 and the early 1150s), in the variant version some speeches have been abbreviated, omitted, paraphrased indirectly or otherwise altered in form and content. The tone of the speeches in the variant version is 'rather more moral than that of Geoffrey's original'. Another interesting observation is that although the amount of speeches in the variant is smaller than in the vulgate, all the passages in which the variant offers a fuller version of similar material in the vulgate consist of speeches (Wright 1988: viii, xi, xxx, xxxiv).

(Leir's speech, §31, p. 21: *in hec uerba cum fletu et singultu prorupit*), lie, and speak in a prophetic trance (Merlin's speech, §111: *in fletum prorumpens spiritum hausit prophetie et ait*). Among these linguistic performances, the fictive and actual audiences thus no longer follow the preterit reality as such, but are also forced to ponder upon different modal past as well as future courses of events and actions.

As defined by Brian Richardson in the context of modern fiction, the rhetorical sequence of the narrative may be based on the text's argument or demands of thesis/antithesis rather than any temporal structure or fictional probability (Richardson 2005: 169). The most obvious way in which the direct speeches in the HRB deviate from the frame narrative is that they multiply the imaginary courses of events also in the future tense. In other words, they produce conditional sequences ('If you want a lasting peace', 'If any dispute should arise', 'If you change your present plan, then … if not, then…', pp. 62–4) and hypothetical or alternative worlds. Let us have a look at the following examples, the first of which is Brutus's letter to King Pandrasus after the fall of Troy:

> Be moved to pity for them [i.e. those who survived the fall of Troy], and deign to bestow upon them their lost liberty. [1] Give them permission to inhabit the forest-glades which they have occupied in their attempt to escape from slavery. [2] If you cannot grant this, then let them, with your approval, go off to join the peoples of other lands. (pp. 56–7; the bracketed numbers added)[17]

The immediate result of Brutus's request in the storyworld is that neither the first nor the second suggestion is actualized. Instead, Pandrasus is offended by the message, collects an army and attacks the Trojans. Brutus's speech, nevertheless, offers *possible* or *desired* courses of events for the reader's and the fictional audience's imagination to continue or complete. This simultaneity of ideas, conflicting desires and optional *gesta* would be much more difficult to express in direct narration, as already the medieval romancers and saga writers pointed out.

My second example of rhetorical sequencing is Pandrasus's speech, after

17 *Misericordia igitur super eam motus* [1] *amissam libertatem largiri digneris et saltus nemorum quos ut seruitutem diffugeret occupauit eam habitare permittas.* [2] *Sin autem concede ut ad aliarum terrarum nationes cum diligentia tua abscedant* (HRB §8, p. 4; the bracketed numbers added).

the Trojans have captured him. Again, hypothetical and possible courses of events are introduced by one of the characters to the audience:

> Since the gods are hostile to me and have delivered me and my brother Anacletus into your hands, I must obey your command; for, [1] if you meet with a refusal, we shall both lose our lives [...] Since so noble a young man has been able to resist me so courageously, I give him my daughter Ignoge. I also give him gold and silver, ships and corn, and whatsoever you will consider necessary for his journey.
>
> [2] If you change your present plan and prefer to stay with the Greeks, then I grant you a third of my kingdom for you to live in. If not, then I will carry out my promises effectively [...]. (pp. 63–4; the bracketed numbers added)[18]

After the speech, the narration again returns to a more straightforward course: Brutus married Pandrasus's daughter and the Trojans sailed away. But before this is known to the reader, the two alternative courses of future events – as numbered in the quotation – produce suspense: alternatives and places for engaged hearing, reading and deliberation. The real and fictional audiences may wonder whether Pandrasus dies or not (or wish it so, or fear it). And should Brutus and the Trojans choose the fairytale-like destiny of staying in Greece and receiving a third of the kingdom...? While this readerly speculation and speakerly deliberation goes on, the expectation to learn more about the *really* actualizing events increases.

The force of the rhetorical fabrication of the plot, as evident in the examples, emerges from the states of the characters' minds, plans and wishes that do not produce linearity in the structure. By contrast, we follow variations of narrative cul-de-sac and non-events which sometimes only take place in the speech acts (as textual events) but never actualize as events in the narrated preterit reality. These speech acts in the HRB therefore resemble the textual phenomenon labelled as *irrealis narration* in the linguistic study of narrative.

18 *Quoniam aduersi dii me meumque fratrem An<tigon>um in manus uestras tradiderunt,* [1] *parendum est peticioni uestre ne uitam – que nobis arbitrio uestro et adimi et concedi potest si repulsam passi fueritis – amittamus.* [...] *Quia ergo tantus iuuenis tanta probitate mihi resistere potuit, do ei filiam meam Innogen. Do etiam aurum et argentum, naues, frumentum et quicquid itineri necessarium esse dixeritis.* [2] *Et si a proposito uestro diuertentes cum Grecis commanere uolueritis, terciam mei regni partem uobis ad inhabitandum concedo. Sin autem promissa mea effectu prosequar* [...] (HRB §15, p. 8; the bracketed numbers added).

It is separate from narration which uses the preterit and 'suggests verisimilitude' since it is 'the prototypical tense of *realis, historical narration*'. Contrarily, irrealis narration consists of verbalizations of experience that is unrealized 'either because it is predicated as taking place in the future or because it is in some sense hypothetical'. Dreams and visions also belong to the realm of irrealis narration (Fleischman 1990: 104–5, 112).[19]

With such frequent hypothetical and conditional worlds in the HRB we are removed far from the form of a chronicle, or even a storyized chronicle. Instead, the rhetorical sequencing produces latitude for elements that are usually attached to fiction and fantasy: imaginary possible worlds, hypothetical plots and incoherent (even contradictory) claims. In Geoffrey of Monmouth's *Historia* the introduction of such possibilities is the privilege of the embedded rhetorical speech acts.

THE LYING AND OBSCURE SPEAKER

Lying as a speech act in Geoffrey's *Historia* is the characters', not the narrator's, business. In medieval rhetoric and arts of poetry (e.g. John of Garland), lying, *mendacium*, belonged to the vices of narration – those opposing clarity and brevity – along with incontinuity, prolixity and obscurity in writing (cf. Mehtonen 2003: 103–22). Not only do these pitfalls threaten the poet's own writing; according to the medieval *poetriae*, the writer in the process of *inventio* must also be able to recognize and deal with them in the literature already existing, that is, in the *materia* on the basis of which the work will be constructed.

Yet the vices recognized by the Latin textbooks naturally also became virtues in poetic practice. The *claritas-obscuritas* duel should be kept in mind in also considering the structure of the HRB, based on a prompt division of labour. While the narrator allegedly follows the clarity rule (as manifested by himself), the speaking and letter-writing characters are more free to produce verbal prolixity, lofty style, lies, and other questionable speech acts. Nowhere is this as obvious as in the section on Merlin's prophecies, presented as his direct speech. However, the business of lying also characterizes shorter

19 Observe that in Fleischman's scheme (1990: 104), plans – where events are recounted in the future tense – are not strictly speaking narratives. 'All narratives, even those that refer to the future, speak of the unreal as if it were past, as if the events had actually occurred.' In Geoffrey's HRB the modal courses of events also occur in speeches reported by the narrator indirectly (e.g. §59, p. 39), but hardly ever otherwise in the first-level narration.

speeches in the *HRB*, for instance in the episode where two 'ingenious liars' (*fabricatores mendacii*) come to Brennius, in order to break the treaty between him and his brother Belinus. The act of lying in the guise of malicious persuasion takes place in the anonymous characters' speech (§35, pp. 24–5). Apart from mendacious activity, the direct discourses also house a legion of fabulous, visionary or supernatural events – and for the present purposes only those phenomena qualify as supernatural or amazing that are affirmed as such by the narrator of the characters of the *HRB*. In addition, predictions, anticipating future events in the storyworld – whether they actualize or not – are mainly reported as direct or indirect characters' discourse (e.g. §16: Brutus's dream of the ritualistic and poetic exchange between the dreamer and the goddess Diana). The more imaginary direct discourses also include the 'amazing' story of Merlin's mother regarding the fatherless conception of the child (§107: the mother's speech as well as its affirmation by a 'certain Maugantius', both reported as direct discourse).

This activity culminates in the obscure prophecies of Merlin which form the longest directly reported speech in the *HRB*.[20] Before the section, Merlin's amazing skill and his supernatural presence (*numen*, §108, p. 73) have been observed through the other characters' perception.[21] In the prophecies that follow, Ambrosius Merlin is able to transgress all layers of narration. He exists – as a topic and magnet of public fame – in the speaker-now (according to the first-person narrator, Merlin was being 'talked about very much' by people 'of my own generation'; §109, p. 73; trans. 170). Merlin also exists in the preterit reality of the story-now, entering into conversation with King Vortigern. Finally, the obscure and futuristic prophecies that fill the rest of the chapter are presented as Merlin's direct speech. This also is one of the rare places in the *HRB* where the process of communication is highlighted or obfuscated by producing various levels of embedded narratives: Merlin's speech, as reported by the narrator, contains the speech of the Daneian Forest, as reported by Merlin, which contains the Forest quoting itself.

The Daneian Forest shall be wakened from its sleep and, bursting into

20 Also the *Alexander Romance* (1.3, 1.15, 1.33, 1.35, 3.34) contains prophecies and oracular utterances in direct discourse.

21 The same amount of repeated amazement is reported only in the context of King Arthur's deeds later in the work. See for instance Lucius Hiberius's letter to Arthur and the eloquent trope of *gradatio* therein: 'I am amazed at the insolent way... I am even more amazed at the damage which you have done to Rome. When I think about it, I am outraged that you should have so far forgotten yourself...' (230–1).

> human speech, it shall shout: 'Kambria, come here! Bring Cornwall at your side! Say to Winchester: "The earth will swallow you up. [...] The day approaches when your citizens will perish for their crimes of perjury".' (178)[22]

This passage thus forms a tiny Chinese-box narrative, where the layers of fabulous material presented in the future tense are hyperbolized *ad absurdum*. Since the words and commands refer to the future after another future, the Forest both presents the speech act and does not. The speech acts have not actualized yet; they only exist as textual events within the direct discourses.

In the structure and speech acts of the HRB, the narrator's freedom is much more limited than in later and quite different histories of the kings. In Snorri Sturluson's *Heimskringla* (The Chronicle of the Kings of Norway) the narrator reports quite unreservedly in his own discourse about for instance Odin's metamorphic skills or his ability to roll up his ship like a cloth (Ch. 7).

THE RELUCTANT SPEAKER: 'I FEEL MORE LIKE BURSTING INTO TEARS THAN EMBARKING UPON A LOFTY SPEECH'

The final aspect of rhetorical fabrication in the HRB, to be discussed here, deals with the interaction between the narrator's and the characters' reports, and the negation of possible events therein. With the aid of also non-narrative elements such as proverbs the narrator may deny or rudely abandon courses of events affirmed or desired in the direct discourse of the characters.

An ironic antithesis develops between the speech of Guithelinus, the archbishop of London, to the British men and the narrator's argument after the speech. The Romans are about to leave the island, after having 'protected' the Britons and fought their enemies 'for them'. The archbishop has been given the task to speak to the Britons and encourage them to take their destiny into their own hands. The speech of this (rhetorically) reluctant speaker – who 'feels more like bursting into tears than embarking upon a lofty speech [*in excelsum sermonem*]' (HRB §90, p. 59) – reaches its climax in an emancipatory exhortation, directly addressed to the audience consisting of all the military men of Britain assembled in London:

22 *Excitabitur Daneum nemus et in humanam uocem erumpens clamabit: "Accede, Kambria, et iunge lateri tuo Cornubiam et dic Wintonie: 'Absorbebit te tellus. [...] Festinat namque dies qua ciues ob scelera periurii peribunt'"* (HRB §116, p. 79).

> Given that you were only ordinary folk in the days when you possessed soldiers, do you think that for this reason you have lost all claim to manhood? Surely men can be born out of their social caste – a soldier from a farmer, for example, or a farmer from a soldier? Surely a military man can be the son of a shop-keeper, or, for that matter, a shop-keeper the son of a military man? Given the possibility of one caste being born from another, I find it hard to believe that people are such that they can actually lose their manhood. If you are men, then behave like men! Pray to Christ to give you courage and then protect your own liberty! (p. 146)[23]

At this point, the actual reader feels encouraged by this social fairness, together with the fictional audience who applauded loudly and 'were inspired by courage'. However, the short moment of democratic idealism and consensus between the audiences inside and outside the storyworld is disrupted, as the laconic narrator informs the reader:

> However, it is easier for a kite to become a sparrow-hawk than for a peasant to become suddenly an erudite man. He who offers deep knowledge to this man is acting as though he were throwing a pearl among swine. (p. 146, translation slightly altered by P. M. M.)[24]

As this (non-narrative) argument again returns to the narrative mode, the reader learns that destruction is on its way as the Saxons, Scots, Picts and even, according to Geoffrey, Norwegians and Danes, are about to attack from the north.

The use of non-narrative elements such as the proverbs – which in a sense are always true, even tautological – always reveal the presence of the narrator and serve different functions. In the example the narrator effectively *disnarrates* what had just been positively affirmed by the character and believed by the fictive audience: he disnarrates by denying the possibilities that are elsewhere referred to in a hypothetical mode but remain unactualized in the text

23 *Si tempore militum uestrorum fueratis uulgus, putabitis iccirco humanitatem a uobis diffugisse? Nonne homines transuerso ordine nascuntur ita ut ex rustico generetur miles et ex milite rusticus? Miles etiam de mangone uenit et mango de milite. Hac ergo consuetudine quamuis unus ab altero procedat, non existimo esse quod est hominis amittere. Cum igitur sitis homines, habetote uos ut homines et inuocare Christum ut audatiam adhibeat et libertatem uestram defendite* (HRB §90, p. 59).

24 *Set facilius est accipitrem ex miluo fieri quam ex rustico subitum eruditum. Et qui profundam doctrinam ei diffundit idem facit acsi margaritam inter porcos spargeret* (HRB §59, p. 59).

('this could have happened but didn't'; cf. Prince 1988; Richardson 2001). In the quoted examples this effect is produced by the interaction between the characters' and the narrator's words – in other words, as a sort of dialogue not only between the characters' speech acts but also between those at different narrative levels in the structure of the narrative. However, this is basically just an illusion of a genuine dialogue since the narratorial power in the distribution of interpretative comments, partial judgements, or emphasis goes unchallenged.

SPEAKING CHARACTERS IN HISTORY: TEXTUAL SPACES FOR OVERT FICTIONALITY

The shifts between the narrator's storyized chronicling and direct discourse in Geoffrey of Monmouth's *Historia regum Britannie* therefore mark other simultaneous shifts in the grammar and rhetoric of narration: one from the main narrator's voice to the characters', another from the 'reporting' narrator's prose style to the oratorical styles of the epideictic and demonstrative speech acts, yet another from genealogical to rhetorical sequencing of the narrative.

It is an often-acknowledged fact that in the direct discourse the emphasis is usually on the form of reported discourse, whereas speech acts reported indirectly contribute to the content of the plot and events (cf. Marnette 2005: 192). This paper has proposed that in addition to – and inseparable from – the formal stylistic variation at the level of *elocutio*, the shifts between direct and indirect presentation also work as an important structural device in the production of the modal effects of fictionality. For the modern reader it may not be easy to rid oneself of the temptation to take 'realistic' speeches as a norm and read the others as deviations. Yet texts such as Geoffrey's *Historia* persuade the reader to take exactly the opposite route.

References

TEXTS

Geoffrey of Monmouth, *The History of the Kings of Britain. [Historia regum Britanniae]*, trans. L. Thorpe, Harmondsworth: Penguin Books, 1987/1966.

Geoffrey of Monmouth, *Historia regum Britannie* (Berne, Burgerbiliothek, MS 568), ed. Neil Wright, Cambridge: D.S. Brewer, 2001/1985.

Geoffrey of Monmouth, *The Historia regum Britannie of Geoffrey of Monmouth. The First Variant Version*, a critical edition by Neil Wright, Cambridge: D.S. Brewer, 1988.

Gervais von Melkley, *Ars poetica*, ed. Hans-Jürgen Gräbener (Forschungen zur romanischen Philologie, Heft 17), Münster Westfahlen, 1965.

Göngu-Hrolf's Saga, trans. H. Pálsson and P. Edwards, Edinburgh: Canongate, 1980.

John of Garland, *The Parisiana Poetria of John of Garland*, ed. and trans. T. Lawler, New Haven and London: Yale University Press, 1974.

STUDIES

Archibald, Elizabeth (2004) 'Ancient Romance', in Corinne Saunders (ed.), *A Companion to Romance from Classical to Contemporary*, Oxford: Blackwell, pp. 10–25.

Auerbach, Erich (1974/1953) *Mimesis: The Representation of Reality in Western Literature*. Translated by Willard R. Trask, Princeton: Princeton University Press.

Boitani, Piero (1982) *English Medieval Narrative in the Thirteenth and Fourteenth Centuries*. Translated by Joan Krakover Hall, Cambridge: Cambridge University Press.

Bowersock, G. W. (1997/1994) *Fiction as History: Nero to Julian*, Berkeley, Los Angeles and London: University of California Press.

Croenen, Godfried (1999) 'Princely and Noble Genealogies, Twelfth to Fourteenth Century: Form and Function', in Erik Kooper (ed.), *The Medieval Chronicle* (Costerus New Series, 120), Amsterdam and Atlanta: Rodopi, pp. 84–95.

Curley, Michael J. (1994) *Geoffrey of Monmouth*, New York: Twayne Publishers.

Davenport, Tony (2004) *Medieval Narrative: An Introduction*, Oxford: Oxford University Press.

Faletra, Michael A. (2000) 'Narrating the Matter of Britain: Geoffrey of Monmouth and the Norman Colonization of Wales', *The Chaucer Review* 35, no. 1: 60–85.

Flint, V. I. J. (1979) 'The *Historia regum Britanniae* of Geoffrey of Monmouth: Parody and Its Purpose. A Suggestion', *Speculum* 54, no. 3: 447–68.

Fleischman, Suzanne (1990) *Tense and Narrativity: From Medieval Performance to Modern Fiction*, Austin, TX: University of Texas Press.

Green, Dennis H. (2002) *The Beginnings of Medieval Romance: Fact and Fiction, 1150–1220*, Cambridge: Cambridge University Press.

Harder, Ruth E. (1997) 'Die Funktion der Briefe im byzantinischen Roman des 12. Jahrhunderts', in Michelangelo Picone and Bernhard Zimmermann (eds.), *Der antike Roman und seine mittelalterliche Rezeption*, Basel, Boston and Berlin: Birkhäuser Verlag, pp. 231–44.

Hofmann, Heinz (ed.) (1999) *Latin Fiction: The Latin Novel in Context*, London and New York: Routledge.

Kooper, Erik (ed.) (1999) *The Medieval Chronicle* (Costerus New Series, 120), Amsterdam and Atlanta: Rodopi.

MacPhail, Eric (2001) 'The Plot of History from Antiquity to the Renaissance', *Journal of the History of Ideas* 62, no. 1: 1–16.

Marnette, Sophie (2005) *Speech and Thought Presentation in French: Concepts and Strategies*, Amsterdam and Philadelphia: John Benjamins Publishing Company.

Mehtonen, Päivi (1996) *Old Concepts and New Poetics*: Historia, Argumentum *and* Fabula *in the Twelfth- and Early Thirteenth-Century Latin Poetics of Fiction* (Commentationes Humanarum Litterarum, 108), Helsinki: The Finnish Society of Sciences and Letters.

Mehtonen, Päivi (2003) *Obscure Language, Unclear Literature: Theory and Practice from Quintilian to the Enlightenment*, Helsinki: Academy of Sciences and Letters.

Mehtonen, Päivi (2006) 'Poetics, Narration, and Imitation: Rhetoric as *Ars Aplicabilis*', in Virginia Cox and John O. Ward (eds.), *The Rhetoric of Cicero in Its Medieval and Renaissance Commentary Tradition*, Leiden and Boston: Brill, pp. 289–312.

Otter, Monika (1996) *Inventiones: Fiction and Referentiality in Twelfth-Century English Historical Writing*, Chapel Hill and London: The University of North Carolina Press.

Pähler, Heinrich (1958) *Strukturuntersuchungen zur Historia regum Britanniae des Geoffrey of Monmouth*, Inaugural Dissertation, Bonn: Rheinische Friedrich Wilhelms-Universität.

Picone, Michelangelo, and Bernhard Zimmermann (eds.) (1997) *Der antike Roman und seine mittelalterliche Rezeption*, Basel, Boston and Berlin: Birkhäuser Verlag.

Prince, Gerald (1988) 'The Disnarrated', *Style* 22, no. 1: 1–8.

Reardon, P. B. (1991) *The Form of Greek Romance*, Princeton, NJ: Princeton University Press.

Richardson, Brian (2001) 'Denarration in Fiction: Erasing the Story in Beckett and Others', *Narrative* 9, no. 2: 168–75.

Richardson, Brian (2005) 'Beyond the Poetics of Plot: Alternative Forms of Narrative Progression and the Multiple Trajectories of *Ulysses*', in James Phelan and Peter J. Rabinowitz (eds.), *A Companion to Narrative Theory*, Malden and Oxford: Blackwell Publishing, pp. 168–80.

Ryding, W. W. (1971) *Structure in Medieval Narrative*, The Hague: Mouton.

Saunders, Corinne (ed.) (2004) *A Companion to Romance from Classical to Contemporary*, Oxford: Blackwell.

Spiegel, Gabrielle M. (1983) 'Genealogy: Form and Function in Medieval Historical Narrative', *History and Theory* 22, no. 1: 43–53.

Spiegel, Gabrielle M. (1999) 'Theory into Practice: Reading Medieval Chronicles', in Erik Kooper (ed.), *The Medieval Chronicle* (Costerus New Series, 120), Amsterdam and Atlanta: Rodopi, pp. 1–12.

Stoneman, Richard (1999a) 'The Latin Alexander', in Heinz Hofmann (ed.), *Latin Fiction: The Latin Novel in Context*, London and New York: Routledge, pp. 167–86.

Stoneman, Richard (1999b), 'The Medieval Alexander', in Heinz Hofmann (ed.), *Latin Fiction: The Latin Novel in Context*, London and New York: Routledge, pp. 238–52.

Tatlock, J. S. P. (1950) *The Legendary History of Britain: Geoffrey of Monmouth's 'Historia Regum Britanniae' and Its Early Vernacular Versions*, Berkeley: University of California Press.

Vitz, Evelyn Birge (1989) *Medieval Narrative and Modern Narratology*, New York and London: New York University Press.

Ward, John O. (1985) 'Some Principles of Rhetorical Historiography in the Twelfth Century', in Ernst Breisach (ed.), *Classical Rhetoric & Medieval Historiography* (Studies in Medieval Culture, XIX), Kalamazoo: Medieval Institute Publications, pp. 103–65.

Weiss, Judith (2004) 'Insular Beginnings: Anglo-Norman Romance', in Corinne Saunders (ed.), *A Companion to Romance from Classical to Contemporary*, Oxford: Blackwell, pp. 26–44.

Wittig, Susan (1978) *Stylistic and Narrative Structures in the Middle English Romances*, Austin: University of Texas Press.

Wright, Neil (1988) 'Introduction', see Editions, Geoffrey of Monmouth, *The Historia regum Britannie of Geoffrey of Monmouth. The First Variant Version.*

Wright, Neil (2001/1985) 'Introduction', see Texts, Geoffrey of Monmouth, *Historia regum Britannie* (Berne, Burgerbiliothek, MS 568), pp. ix–lxv.

The Status of the 'Mythical' Past in Nordic Latin Historiography (c. 1170–1220)

Lars Boje Mortensen

The enlightenment philosopher, comedy writer, historian, moralist and more, Ludvig Holberg (1684–1754), published his three-volume history of the Danish Kingdom in the years 1732 to 1735 – a period in which the study of history had been professionalized to a certain degree by harvesting the immense learning of seventeenth-century antiquarianism, but still before the arrival of History, the modern scholarly discipline, which would emerge only a century later.[1] For Holberg medieval texts were still 'monuments' and 'writings', not 'sources' – and in this his conceptual framework seemed almost medieval; likewise, the discipline of archaeology was not yet available, so he found himself dealing almost exclusively with texts when confronting his narrative task. He shared these conditions with his medieval and Renaissance predecessors, and to some extent he also shared their nationalist triumphalism. But the Enlightenment rationalism, skepticism, moralism and unsurpassed cross-cultural learning put him in an uncomfortable position when dealing with the origins of Danish history.

There are three 'sects' of historians, he claims, who have dealt with the beginnings of Danish history. This concept – at once connoting for the Enlightenment intellectual the worst of pointless theological disputes – alerts us to his problem. One sect was founded by Saxo Grammaticus and its belief is that Dan was the first Danish king. Many hypotheses have been promoted as to the period in which Dan lived (a thousand years before Christ or perhaps just 300 years?). To speculate in such a way on a king whose existence is uncertain is, Holberg says, as vain as to write dissertations on the properties of the bird Phoenix. The second sect connects the Danish and Swedish

1 Ludvig Holberg, *Danmarks Riges Historie*, Copenhagen 1732–35.

royal genealogies directly to the biblical account and has Gomer founding the Nordic realms at the time of Nimrod. The sect bases its beliefs on a document so poorly forged, says Holberg, that its author 'did not know properly the art of putting a wax-nose on the world'. The third sect is the Icelandic one which claims that the first Danish king was Skjold – giving his name to the dynasty of the Skjoldunger (perhaps better known today as the Scyldings from *Beowulf*) who can then be traced through Icelandic texts.

Holberg plays with the idea of creating a fourth sect, but refrains from doing so as he does not want to stir up more disputes. The Icelandic hypothesis boasts a venerable age (it was for instance promoted by the Danish historian Sven Aggesen writing just before Saxo) and Holberg then decides: 'I adhere to the Icelandic hypothesis in the old history [...] and thus also avoiding Saxo's strange and unhuman fables [...]. But I let go of the Icelandic hypothesis again and follow the order of Saxo when history approaches his time [...]. Hence I am completely Icelandic from King Skjold to Sigurd Ring and become Danish again from this king [...].'[2]

Holberg clearly lived in a time when the traditional paradigm had lost its coherence and persuasiveness and a new paradigm for the oldest parts of history, which turned out to be archaeology, had not yet been devised. He found it impossible not to mock the stories, but equally impossible to substitute them. He had to make his way through by holding his breath and using his wit.

In the present contribution I want to investigate the rise of the old paradigm – the historiographical *ancien regime*, so to speak – by looking at the representation of the distant past in Nordic Latin historiography from the crucial period between c. 1170 and 1220 that brought forth two important works in both Norway and Denmark: the anonymous *Historia Norwegie* (HN) and the chronicle by Theodoricus Monachus, and Sven Aggesen and Saxo Grammaticus respectively. How did the tales of national or dynastic origin find their canonical written forms and what status were they given in comparison with narratives of more recent history? Were they taken to be valid in exactly the same way as literary representations of recent events? Were they presented with a common understanding of their special status, or were they even brought forth tongue in cheek as simply the best available beginning of the story? The recent trends in discussing the rise of fiction in exactly this period – by Otter (1996, 2005), Knapp (1997, 2005), Haug (2002), Green (2002), Stein

2 The edition from 1856, p. 35.

(2006) and others – is a welcome opportunity to rethink and rephrase questions about the status of 'mythical' history in Nordic works. Conversely, I also hope that the texts in question can be helpful in shaping the more general debate of these issues in medieval literary history.

Before proceeding we should remind ourselves how the professional historians who followed Holberg in the nineteenth and twentieth centuries have, in the main, categorized and divided medieval narratives of national origin. As will be clear below, our medieval historians under investigation did not distinguish explicitly between a legendary or mythical past, on the one hand, and a more 'historical' one on the other. For them the real divisions in history were defined by Christian salvation, the arrival of a new people (*HN*, Geoffrey of Monmouth), and the Christianization of one's own nation (Sven, Saxo, *HN*, Theodoricus, etc.). Until recently, however, historical scholarship has routinely divided the chronicles into parts by their historical value *for us*.

For Geoffrey – to take one of the most famous of twelfth-century mythmakers – the denigrating 'pseudo-history' has stuck as the proper characterization, implying at one and the same time that his narrative is lying to us, and that he passes it off as real history.[3] The early parts of *HN*, Sven and Saxo have had a milder fate in Scandinavian scholarship. The fantastic stories are labelled 'sagn' (the best English rendering is perhaps 'folk-tales'), and the entire early parts of their *opera* are known as 'sagnhistorie'. The word derives from 'to say', and has its equivalent in Old Norse (*saga*) and German (*Sage*). Although we place no trust in their historicity, the term is not quite as negative as 'pseudo-history' because there is no implication of intent to deceive. On the contrary, Saxo in particular is seen as performing the valuable task of transmitting a part of ancient Nordic culture – the myths of the pagan Scandinavians – as a counterpart to classical mythology. To be sure, Saxo's mythological tales are most often seen as a distorted, but still valuable, version of the mythology of the *Edda*.[4] Apart from his tales of Odin, etc., his many 'sagn' of early kings and warriors were perceived from the Romantic period on as a treasure of Danish and Nordic folklore;[5] the same holds true for Sven's stories,

3 For instance, Wright (1985: vii); Crick (1989: vii); Christiansen (1981: 27) calls him 'the biggest liar of all'. 'Legend/legendary history' and 'fiction' also has some currency, e.g. Curley (1994: 14 ff.), and Stein (2006: 123–4); cf. the discussion by Green (2002: 169 ff.).

4 See Davidson's valuable commentary with further references (in the translation of Saxo by Fisher and Davidson 1979).

5 Cf. Jørgensen (1931) and Friis (1945); the latter has a richer vocabulary ranging from 'oldhistorie'

whereas the brief chapter on the Ynglinge kings and their Norwegian successors in *Historia Norwegie* was instead dismissed as a pale substitute for similar material in vernacular works (the anonymous work is never labelled a 'saga'). In the twentieth century, however, *HN*'s account has been taken seriously by scholarship because it counts among the earliest testimonies of this tradition.[6]

In recent German scholarship a less valorizing conceptual framework is predominant, as in the admirable overview of the genre of national history by Kersken (1995). Here the past is seen as divided into 'Vorgeschichte' ('prehistory'), 'Vergangenheitsgeschichte' ('ancient history') and 'Zeitgeschichte' ('contemporary history'). As Kersken carefully points out, these are all relative to the respective local historiographical records (and the delimitations are perhaps not quite as straightforward as he makes them).[7] It is clear that this is not a 'native' Romantic conceptualization like the Nordic one.

In the wake of *Mentalitätsgeschichte* and the literary studies emanating from the neo-rhetorical trend (Ernst Robert Curtius, the application of medieval notions of the interpretation of the Bible, etc.) other frameworks developed from the 1970s onwards in Danish and German scholarship. Saxo was again a central figure, Sven appears sporadically, but *Historia Norwegie* (and Theodoricus Monachus) was still completely subsumed under discussions within Old Norse literature. One begins to see the first casual remarks about Saxo's and Sven's use of fiction,[8] but an allegorical reading of the early narratives was more fashionable (Johanneson 1978; Kværndrup 1984, 1999): the 'myths' were not to be taken on the surface level in the 'historical' sense, but were allegories of the medieval 'world view' in various complicated schemes. Thus their purpose was to point to another kind of truth – and consequently not a fictional one, we might add. The significance of the architecture of Saxo's enormous work was established by Skovgaard-Petersen, who also suggested that the first part of Saxo's history was a kind of Old Testament which pointed

through 'historiske romaner' ('historical novels' on Viking chieftains). During a spell in the 1950s and 1960s, the University of Copenhagen even had a chair of 'Sagnhistorie' within the History Department.

6 Cf. Krag (1991).

7 Kersken (1995: 788–91).

8 Christiansen (1981); Skovgaard-Petersen (1981: 127–8): 'So Saxo seems to have relied on a widespread literature, picking out here and there what he wanted for his purpose. If this picture is right, the first eight books of the *Gesta Danorum* are not history in the modern sense of the word, but a sort of fiction, or to put it better, Saxo's legendary history represents a different historical reality from what we know nowadays.' See also Kværndrup (1984: 314) on the fictionality of Sven's 'novels'. Clunies Ross (1992: 59) calls Saxo's myth on Balder 'historicized fiction'.

typologically to the later 'historical' books (as a New Testament fulfillment).[9] Very briefly it can be said that these attempts to come to grips with Saxo's 'mythical history' located it within a learned construction and went beyond the nationalist and Romantic 'transmission of Nordic mythology/folklore' paradigm, thus making Saxo more European than national.

THE TEXTUAL LANDSCAPE

My emphasis will be on three national histories written in Latin: the anonymous *History of the Norwegians,* written in Norway around 1170; the *Brief History of Danish Kings,* composed by Sven Aggesen in Denmark around 1185; and Saxo Grammaticus's voluminous *Danish History,* shaped during the decades around 1200, probably from c. 1180 to 1215. They can all claim status as pioneering works, and they share a feature that I shall discuss at some length because of its relevance for our present topic: the narrative of the distant past is linked to a narrative of the more recent past and even to contemporary events by an authorial effort to unify the entire work in a coherent manner. This means that we can study how the transitions between the various periods are presented and perhaps get some glimpses of the way the author and his contemporary audience viewed the status of the account of the distant past. These three texts are situated in a larger textual landscape of other Latin and Old Norse historiographical and hagiographical works, none of which, however, strive to combine 'Vorgeschichte' with 'Vergangensheitsgeschichte' and 'Zeitgeschichte', although some of them were compiled together or built upon to form comprehensive histories later in the thirteenth century. The brief Latin Chronicle of Lejre (*Chronicon Lethrense*), perhaps as early as 1170, tells various stories from Danish 'prehistory'; it begins explicitly at the time of David with stories mostly of an etymological character (Roskilde was founded by Ro, etc.), but also includes kings and episodes to be developed at length by Saxo. The small collection rounds off before the advent of Christianity and thus does not try to combine ancient with more recent history. Another case in point is the poorly and very partially transmitted *Skjoldungesaga,* covering the kings from Skjold to Gorm, which is believed to have existed around 1200 in Old Norse. It is probably the first vernacular text to deal with kings other than the Norwegian kings (of the Ynglinge stock). By 1250 it may have provided the

9 Skovgaard-Petersen (1969 and 1987); the architectural reading has been refined by Friis-Jensen (1992).

first instalment of Danish history as a prelude to the so-called *Knytlingesaga* beginning with the historical Harald Bluetooth and with a strong emphasis on St Canute (d. 1086).[10] In Iceland and Norway both Latin and vernacular historiography rose to prominence in the decades around 1200. Theodoricus Monachus wrote a brief Latin chronicle of the ancient Norwegian kings in Trondheim around 1180 (see below), and in the 1190s and 1200s a number of biographies on the two heroes of conversion from around the turn of the Millenium, Olav Tryggvason and Olav Haraldsson, were composed in Iceland and Norway, in Latin and in the vernacular. A saga about Olav Haraldsson (the saint) came to form part of the compilation that stands as the culmination of the kings' saga genre: *Heimskringla* from around 1230, which united prehistory, ancient history and contemporary history (up to 1177).[11]

CONTENTS AND AUTHENTICATION

Historia Norwegie

Let us first look briefly at our three main texts and how they accommodate and authenticate their accounts of national beginnings. The anonymous chronicle *Historia Norwegie* is, to the best of our knowledge, the first attempt to put Norwegian history into writing.[12] Its standard title is a modern reconstruction, and to my mind *Historia Norwagensium* (History of the Norwegians) is a more probable suggestion as it better reflects contemporary usage. Only the first book has survived and it covers the story from the foundational dynasty of the Ynglings up to the point where the later saint Olav Haraldsson returned from England in 1015 to claim the Norwegian throne. This first book comprises a little less than thirty pages in a modern edition, and, as the author in the prologue promises to tell the story up to his own age, it is reasonable to surmise that the complete text included two, three or even four books and ran to at least a hundred pages. Two other signs of the ambitions of the author are

10 On *Skjoldungesaga*, see Lund (1984).

11 For some recent surveys with further references: Bagge (1991) (*Heimskringla*); Mundal (2004) (on Kings' sagas in general); Mortensen and Mundal (2003) (literature on St Olav); Mortensen (2005 and 2007b) (on Norwegian and Danish Latin literature). A recent important finding on *Heimskringla* is the doubts raised by Louis-Jensen (2006) about Snorri's responsibility for the entire work.

12 A possible forerunner of uncertain scope is a lost Latin work by the Icelander Sæmund from the 1120s. For the lost twelfth-century Latin literature of Iceland, see Jensson (2004). For details and references regarding HN, see the introduction and commentary in the edition by Ekrem and Mortensen (with translation by Fisher) (2003).

his elaborated and somewhat personal Latin style and the long geographical introduction which makes little sense as prelude to a small work.

Unfortunately we cannot know what the entire canvas looked like. What we do know is that the narrative – as is quite common in medieval historiography – gradually becomes broader and ends with rather detailed and visual accounts of the warrior feats of Olav Tryggvason (995–1000) and Olav Haraldsson (1015–30). The beginnings of the royal lineage is constituted by the 'mythical' kings of Swedish origin who later branched into Norway – the Ynglinge kings, named after their founder King Yngve (Ingui/Yngvi):[13]

> The ancient family of Norwegian kings traced its beginnings from Sweden, from which Trøndelag, the chief law province of Norway, was also settled. King Yngve, who, according to a great many was the first ruler of the Swedish realm, became the father of Njord, whose son was Frøy. For centuries on end all their descendants worshipped these last two as gods.

> Vetus prosapia regum Norwegie a Swethia sumpsit exordium, unde eciam inhabitata est Trondemia, que patria principalis est in Norwegia. Rex itaque Ingui, quem primum Swethie monarchiam rexisse plurimi astruunt, genuit Neorth. Qui uero genuit Froy. Hos ambos tota illorum posteritas per longa secula ut deos uenerati sunt.

The genealogy continues for about two pages through many generations of Swedish kings with brief notices on who begat whom and how they met their end until Halvdan Hvitbein, who was the first to be appointed king in Norway. Five generations down this line we meet Harald Hårfager who allegedly united Norway and is the first historical king according to modern reckoning (dubious dating, sometimes said to have ruled c. 865–c. 933).

The genealogy of the Ynglings appears in other near-contemporary vernacular texts from the brief chapter on the pioneering vernacular Icelandic author Ari Frode (c. 1130), through the Skaldic poem *Ynglingatal*, believed by most to have been composed in the ninth century (but only taken down in writing around 1230), to the famous opening chapter of Snorri's voluminous sagas of the Norwegian kings, *Heimskringla* (c. 1230). The actual development of the genealogy is controversial and need not concern us here; we can simply

13 *HN* 9.1–4.

note that there is a consensus that we are dealing with a written textual relationship between the various versions.[14] In short, this means that the author of *Historia Norwegie* in all probability had a brief written genealogy in front of him (in Latin or Old Norse) when composing the chronicle.

However, he does not tell us as much. The key statement of authentication occurs, not unexpectedly, in the prologue where we are told: 'I shudder at the smarts inflicted by those who might brand me a liar, since I have incorporated on my own account nothing new or unheard of from earlier ages, but have followed the statements of my elders in every respect.'[15] He is relying on *seniorum asserciones*, a phrase that does not strictly exclude written material but the natural interpretation of which would be 'interviews with old wise men'. He implies the technical terms of *historia* and *fabula*, inasmuch as he rejects any criticism of telling falsehoods (he is not *falsidicus*). At one point in the Ynglinge genealogy he refers to a pagan element as plainly false and fantastic (*fabulosum*).[16] But otherwise he presents his account of older history – including that of the missionary kings Olav Tryggvason and Olav Haraldsson – as trustworthy because it relies on the 'statements of the elders'. For the contemporary part of his history, now lost, he explains in his prologue that he draws on his own observations.

Sven Aggesen

Almost around the same time, the first Danish national history came to light, written at the archsee of Lund by Sven Aggesen and entitled *A Short History of the Kings of Denmark* (*Brevis historia regum Dacie*). In contrast to *Historia Norwegie*, it is neither anonymous nor fragmented in transmission. It is a modest but charming little book (c. thirty-five pages.), not without stylistic or literary pretensions, giving us a brief overview from the very beginnings of the dynasty up to the king ruling at the time of writing, Canute VI (1182–1202).

Sven gives the Danish pendant to Norwegian/Swedish Ynglinge genealogy, namely the royal lineage beginning with Skjold – the Skjoldunger of Icelandic poetry, as Sven points out himself (the Scyldings known from *Beowulf*).

14 Cf. Ellehøj (1965), Krag (1991).

15 Prologus 8: *Neque enim laudis auidus ut chronographus existo, neque uituperii stimulos ut falsidicus exorreo, cum nichil a me de uetustatis serie nouum uel inauditum assumpserim, sed in omnibus seniorum asserciones secutus.*

16 9, 5–6: 'Frøy engendered Fjolne, who was drowned in a tun of mead. His son, Sveigde, is supposed to have pursued a dwarf into a stone and never to have returned, but this is plainly to be taken as a fairy-tale' (*Froyr vero genuit Fiolni, qui in dolio medonis dimersus est, cujus filius Swegthir nanum in petram persequitur nec redisse dicitur, quod pro certo fabulosum creditur*).

After a very brief rundown of the first generations, Sven elaborates on two incidents in particular. The first is that of the weak and speechless prince Uffe who suddenly, in a crisis facing the Germans, takes to both speaking and courage and saves the Danes in a duel; the second is placed 'historically' at the time of the German emperor Otto I, and tells of the ruse laid by the Danish queen Thyra who successfully defended Denmark and constructed the bulwark in Southern Jutland called Danevirke. The rest of the narrative – the historical part, in a modern sense, from c. 950 to 1185 is very brief. Sven partly excuses this by referring to his colleague Saxo who was working on a much more ambitious work to cover these events.

There are two key passages that illustrate Sven's attitude towards his material. One is from the preface:

> However, Martianus [Cappella] tells us that 'the statement of the unknown must not appear to be mixed with falsehood,' and lest I should seem to be narrating fable as history, I shall give an abbreviated account of what I have been able to ascertain by questioning aged men and ancient authorities.

> Sed, ut ait Martianus, 'ne incomperta falsitatem admiscere uideatur assertio', et ne fabulose uidear historiam enarrare, quantum ab annosis et ueteribus certa ualui inquisitione percunctari, compendiose perstringam.[17]

Here Sven employs *les mots justes* by saying the he will not tell history (*historiam*) in a fabulous manner (*fabulose*), and his safeguard is the same as that given in *Historia Norwegie*: his authorities are old (and trustworthy) men. He goes on to say that we naturally know most about men renowned for their deeds; the less famous we are forced to pass by quickly. Later in the narrative he elaborates on such difficulties in writing about antiquity (ch. 4):[18]

> However, in case I should be accused of making up stories and telling untruths, by stringing together the reigns of kings whom I have learned to be quite widely separated by intervals of time, and since I may have passed over many illustrious men, owing not to my idleness but to the unfruitful-

17 Prooem (p. 94 in Gertz's edition), translation by Eric Christiansen, p. 48. In Gertz's Danish translation (p. 35) *ab annosis et ueteribus* is taken together to mean 'aged and old authorities', which may be the right solution given the absence of writings to draw on for the early period.

18 Cf. Lukman (1942–44: 603).

> ness of my research, so I leave the inquiry to my diligent successor, that by his careful investigation he may supply what I have left out through memory's eclipse.

> Verum ne fabulose uel mandaciter regum redarguar tempora continuare, quos tamen haut modico distare didici temporum interstitio, cum non pigritia uerum potius referentis inopia multos illustres transcurrerim, diligenti relinquo indagandum successori, ut, quod ex eclipsi pretermisi memorie, sollicita suppleat inuestigatione.[19]

Interestingly, Sven is anxious that he may seem fabulous by not being able to tell us something that really happened in the past.

Saxo

Sven's contemporary successor Saxo Grammaticus – who might be the one hinted at in the passage above – does not appear to have had any troubles with narrative deficiencies. The gap that worried Sven is filled in in Saxo's account with a cornucopia of stories about twenty-seven kings.[20] This is not the place to describe Saxo's 600-page opus in any detail, but a few key facts may be repeated for the sake of the present argument.[21]

The *Gesta Danorum* deals with Danish history from its origins (the eponymous hero Dan) up to 1185. It is divided into sixteen books and the main narrative thread is the series of kings. It is a national history from the vantage point of the kingdom and the *patria*, although many stories are clustered around other towering figures such as Hamlet (Books 3–4), Eric the Eloquent (5), the warrior-cum-poet Starcatherus (6–8) and, not least, from contemporary history, the commissioner of the work, Archbishop Absalon (d. 1201, Books 14–16). Important themes throughout are the gradual acceptance of Christianity, the antagonistic relationship with the German Empire, and an emphasis on warrior virtues such as loyalty, persistence and courage. The structure of the work has been shown to reflect principles relating to both Roman history and the progress of salvation: the reign of the great Frode Fredegod in Book 5 matches that of Augustus and is explicitly said to be contemporary with the

19 Gertz's edition, p. 106; Christiansen's translation, p. 55.
20 Cf. Christiansen's note, p. 114.
21 For major surveys with bibliographies, see Skovgaard-Petersen (1987), Friis-Jensen (1987), Kersken (1995), and the introduction to the new edition (2005) by Friis-Jensen.

coming of the Lord. Books 5 to 8 cover the period of Danish history when the Roman Empire becomes Christian (from Augustus to Charlemagne) and the true religion spreads to the vicinity of the Danish realm. From Book 9 to 12 the Danes are christened and the last quarter of the work (Books 13–16) deals with the period of the Danish archsee in Lund (from 1104).[22]

Had Saxo only been dealing with contemporary history his work would have had very respectable dimensions, but the most remarkable fact about his work is the narrative space he allots to 'prehistory', or 'mythical history', or whichever label we prefer. The first eight books – taking up approximately 250 pages – take us through innumerable generations of pre-Christian Danes, including euhemerized stories of Odin, Thor, Frigg, Frø, Balder and others we know from mythological texts in Old Norse, as well as countless other episodes, often with fantastic features.

According to Norbert Kersken's comprehensive comparison of medieval national histories, both Sven and Saxo placed great emphasis on the distant past (*Vorgeschichte*) in relative terms – around 45 per cent of their narratives are dedicated to early 'history'; but in absolute terms Saxo's opus remains almost unique in high medieval historiography in its devotion of so much space to a distant and pre-Christian past. I shall return to one of his probable sources of inspiration for this, Geoffrey of Monmouth, but first we must take a look at Saxo's formulas of authentication.

Concerning the older parts of the Danish past, Saxo claims in the prologue that two kinds of monuments were available, namely old Danish songs (which were sometimes carved into stone) and the 'treasure-house of the Icelanders' – a people who had collected admirable knowledge of their own as well as of other nations' history. Saxo obviously used the poets of old in the first eight books because this is where we find Saxo's Latin poems which are renderings of the old songs. The key passage of the prologue explains:

> Adhering to the footprints of these men [i.e. the Danes of an older age], as if to books from antiquity, and following their sense with the true steps of a translator, I have assiduously rendered one poem by another; my chronicle, relying on these aids, should be recognised not as something freshly

22 For the significance of sixteen books, see Skovgaard-Petersen (1969 and 1987), Mortensen (1987), Friis-Jensen (1992). Book 14 is approximately six times larger than the other books, which makes the last quarter of the series almost half of the entire work.

compiled but as the utterance of antiquity; this book is thereby guaranteed to give a faithful understanding of the past, not a frivolous glitter of style.

> Quorum uestigiis ceu quibusdam antiquitatis uoluminibus inherens tenoremque ueris translationis passibus emulatus metra metris reddenda curaui, quibus scribendorum series subnixa non tam recenter conflata quam antiquitus edita cognoscatur, quia presens opus non nugacem sermonis luculentiam, sed fidelem uetustatis notitiam pollicetur.[23]

As can be seen from the Latin, Saxo, unlike Sven, avoids the standard vocabulary *historia* in contrast to *fabula*, but he makes the same point, only with his usual *copia* and variation: he provides trustworthy knowledge (*fidelis notitia*) of the distant past (*antiquitas/uetustas*) because he is relying on authentic utterances of the past (*antiquitus edita*). There is no excuse for the numerous fantastic metamorphoses, efficient pagan magic, etc. – he is telling a true story about the past. Similarly there is no sharp division between the various periods of 'antiquity' – the Icelanders, for instance, may have provided material for the first eight prosimetric books as well as for the later books.

To sum up so far, all three pioneering histories clearly insist that they are reporting *historia* – facts about the past (distant and nearer). They all seem to be aware that objections may be voiced, that, indeed, they may be reproducing *fabulae*, but the firm response is a reference to the authority of their informants (old songs, old men). There is no hint whatsoever that the first parts of their narratives are dealing with 'legends', 'myths', 'sagas', 'sagn', 'prehistory' or whichever term we might prefer.

On the other hand, all three authors seem to be aware that sanctioning orally transmitted stories or songs by putting them into parchment books is a delicate matter. Before we proceed, we must make a brief detour around the status of the handwritten book and its monumentalization of stories previously floating in oral space.

ORALLY TRANSMITTED STORIES, LISTS OF KINGS AND LATIN BOOKS

The performer of a traditional oral epic text guaranteed the truth of his story through his social role and the established rules of this sort of literary commu-

23 Praefatio 1.3, translation by Fisher, p. 5, but here in the revised version published in Friis-Jensen (2004: 133).

nication. Other minor oral genres – the joke, the anecdote, the story illustrating a proverb, etc., which were performed by non-professionals as well – must often have been communicated with a clear common understanding of fiction. Performer and genre conventions could place the narrative in its correct place on the spectrum – although it is often difficult for modern researchers to reconstruct. Moreover the performer would be able to play on ambiguities in the story matter as well as in the interface with specific audiences (see Ranković's chapter in this volume).

But with the arrival of the book as a container of stories and the subsequent indeterminacy of sender, voice and audience (implied and real) the equation could become even more entangled. Furthermore, in an established culture of books, with a hierarchy of texts and canonical selections, the role of intertextuality provides for ever more refined play with the scale of history and fiction. In western Christendom the role of the Latin parchment book as the source of revelation and as liturgical guide – especially before the significant expansion of (vernacular) literature in the thirteenth century – lent at least a 'connotative' authority to narratives written in the holy language in venerable books kept in monasteries and bishop's palaces. This is not to say that fiction (and forgeries) could not develop in Latin books – they did (cf. the chapters by Green and Mehtonen) – but it does mean that concerns of putting down blatant untruths in a holy medium exerted a pull in the opposite direction. The 'performer' of a Latin parchment book (i.e. the author and later copyists/compilers/readers/storytellers) was by default believed to monumentalize useful and beneficiary knowledge. Play with fiction, interest in pagan poets, etc. (as discussed in Green's chapter) were important phenomena in the eleventh and twelfth centuries,[24] but it should not be forgotten that even sophisticated authors operated in a world where the Latin parchment book usually radiated truth and salvation by its very presence.

The relationship between stories that were just told and those which were codified is well put by Adam of Bremen (c. 1075):[25]

> The Danish king whose memory should last long and who holds in his memory the entire history of the barbarians as if it were written down, told

24 See also the interesting discussion of eleventh-century fiction in Tyler (2005).

25 *Gesta episcoporum* ... II, 43 (41): *Narravit nobis diu memorandus rex Danorum et qui omnes barbarorum gestas res in memoria tenuit, ac [si] scriptae essent,* [...]. [...] *multa in hunc modum per diversas Sclavorum provintias tunc facta memorantur, quae scriptorum penuria nunc habentur pro fabulis.* Cf. Johanek (2002: 14).

> us [...]. [M]any events like this are remembered as having taken place in various provinces of the Slavs, but they are now regarded as fables because of the lack of written accounts.

Unlike Adam, the Nordic historians of the twelfth century could not afford the luxury of automatically consigning orally transmitted stories to the damnation of being *fabulae* (nor did Adam himself in practice). But when stories took the step from oral circulation (often in vernacular) to calligraphed eternity on the parchment page, they were in a sort of limbo between oral fluidity and damnation, on the one hand, and scriptural solidity and salvation on the other. This precarious crossing is probably reflected in the fact that most authors who played such an admirable creative role in composing fresh accounts of the distant past are sometimes very reluctant to tell us that their material does not come out of a book.[26]

Most famously Geoffrey of Monmouth makes it clear in his *History of the Kings of Britain* (1136–38) that he had borrowed a certain book in the British language which he translated into Latin. The elaborated series of fabrications and inventions about the pre-Anglo-Saxon past – effectively creating a civilization to mirror the present Norman civilization – are presented as a translation from a book. Geoffrey even ends (in one version) by daring his prominent historian colleagues William of Malmesbury and Henry of Huntingdon: they should write about Anglo-Saxon kings but stay clear of the British past because they do not possess the old Welsh book given to Geoffrey by his patron, Walter, archdeacon of Oxford!

To mention just one other instance of creative historical writing from the twelfth century: the Bavarian *Kaiserchronik* (c. 1150) constantly refers to 'daz buoch' from which this voluminous poetic account of Roman emperors from Caesar up to 1147 was allegedly 'translated' from Latin into German. There is no doubt that the multilayered work drew on many written and oral stories, but the illusion that this came out of one book seems to have been important as authentication.[27]

Saxo likewise strains himself to paint a picture of ancient Danish literacy (poems, rocks, treasure-house of the Icelanders) without, however, committing himself to any concrete reference. As shown by Friis-Jensen in a recent

26 The fear of lying in a book in an ecclesiastical setting is further discussed along these lines in Mortensen (2007a).

27 Cf. Johanek (2002: 14–15) and Vollmann (2002: 71).

article, Saxo presents his early books as a compilation from the authority of old men 'following their sense with the true steps of a translator', and wants to project the image of a book of the North corresponding to the 'book of Rome', and, in the last resort, to the Book of God. His lack of direct reference to classical authors (in spite of his heavy stylistic reliance on Valerius Maximus and others) is caused by his desire to not destroy the illusion of the classical solidity in his own work – almost as if his book should pose as having been authored by the same eternal voice as the book of Rome.[28] Saxo's book remedies the lack of Danish fame, but paradoxically, this feat is almost concealed by appealing to another 'book' that preceded his.

In these three instances we are dealing with very long 'inventive' narrations of a distant past. In the case of smaller works, the pressure to pretend that there was a book behind the book seems to have been much easier to manage.

Theodoricus Monachus wrote the brief *Account of the Ancient History of the Norwegian Kings* (*Historia de antiquitate regum Norwagiensium*) around 1180. He deliberately gave up writing about Norwegian origins on account of the lack of books. We have no knowledge about the era preceding Harold Fairhair (i.e. before the late ninth century). He says:

> Because it is clear that no established succession of the royal line existed in this land before the time of Haraldr Fair-hair, I have begun with him; [...] It is therefore clear from these accounts [...] that before the days of Haraldr there were in this land men mighty in war, but that, as I have said, a dearth of writers has effaced any remembrance of them.[29]

> Sed quia constat nullam ratam regalis stemmatis successionem in hac terra extitisse ante Haraldi pulchre-comati tempora, ab ipso exordium fecimus. [...] Liquet itaque [...] ex his fuisse etiam ante tempora Haraldi in hac terra in bellicis rebus potentes viros, sed ut diximus illorum memoriam scriptorum inopia delevit.

Theodoricus furthermore straightforwardly states – much like *Historia Norwegie* and Sven Aggesen – that he is relying on orally transmitted history

28 Friis-Jensen (2004), esp. pp. 134–5.

29 Theodoricus Monachus, ed. Storm (1880), pp. 3–4, translation by McDougall and McDougall (1998: 1–2).

('audita conscripsimus'). He also refers to a written list of kings as his point of departure for the Harold Fairhair dynasty that he is following through his booklet. A lot of speculation has surrounded the pioneering historians' use of written 'sources' – especially because they can be caught using written material without giving credit (and vice versa as we have just seen). To offer a balance, however, I think that they shared the working condition of having lists of kings (and sometimes of other rulers, abbots, bishops, etc.), but all the early narrative had to be filled in from interviews of knowledgeable storytellers, from listening to professional poets, and through authorial invention and amplification.

In the case of Geoffrey there is agreement that his infamous book 'in the British language' never existed as such, but could have been a dossier in British consisting of some documents and lists, i.e. nothing resembling his fantastic Latin narrative, but a means for orienting himself in names and places.[30] Saxo's situation probably did not differ very much. There is good reason to suppose that he possessed a list of the Skjoldunge kings (as did Sven), but like Geoffrey he also had to make a lot of rearranging, amplification and invention in order to put out a grand rhetorical narrative. As stated above, it is fairly certain that the author of *Historia Norwegie* had access to a list of the Ynglinge kings – but as far as we can see he did not elaborate much on it.

Modern scholarship has been obsessed with identifying the written 'sources' underlying the narratives – a concept that gives wrong connotations because such small scraps as these medieval historians had (like lists of kings) – acted as one limited means of structuring their stories, not as *the* window to the past as modern historical scholarship imagines once it has established which sources are good. The wish to be able to bypass our narrative monuments through source analysis has been too strong. *Historia Norwegie* and Sven Aggesen did not bother to boast about their written 'sources' although these did help them, whereas Saxo and Geoffrey in various ways claim to rely on a book before their own in which 'antiquity' was already represented in its full rhetorical splendour. The scale of their respective enterprises seems to have called for another kind of authentication than those we find in the more modest narratives of origins (*HN* and Sven).

30 Cf. Curley (1994: 10–13); Otter (2005: 119–20).

FICTION OR HISTORY? THE EVIDENCE OF NARRATIVE TECHNIQUES

When we ask the question again about the status of the distant past in these narratives, we cannot do so without relating the discussion to the idea of the rise of fiction in twelfth-century courtly literature which has become prominent within the last ten years. Even if we do not support any strong version of this thesis, the discussions about the significance of a new aristocratic audience influencing the status of written narratives are important enough to be drawn into an analysis of contemporary historical writing – in Latin and in the vernacular. If we think of the Nordic authors in question here, there is a general consensus that they and their commissioners were top-level people who had spent time in northern France (Theodoricus Monachus, Sven Aggesen, Saxo) or perhaps Saxony (the author of *Historia Norwegie*) between c. 1150 and 1190, exactly the time and place when the vernacular revolution took place (in both French and German). It would be odd if they had not taken any notice of this entertaining literature and the way it was exchanged and developed at major and minor courts. Even if their own output was primarily composed in a milieu of secular clergy, the warrior stories (and, indeed, ideals) it contained must have had a courtly resonance in Denmark and Norway. Furthermore, the narrative structure or technique might very well have been influenced from contemporary Latin or vernacular literature.

With these conceptual and historical distinctions in mind the first step in our investigation should be a descriptive one: what is hinted about the status of the distant past through the authorial voices and the narrative techniques in our three histories?

Historia Norwegie

After the prologue and geographical introduction, *Historia Norwegie* begins its narrative in chapter 9 (out of seventeen extant chapters) with the heading *De ortu regum* (the headings are probably original). It is initially stated that the Norwegian royal line originated in Sweden and that the first ruler 'according to a great many' was King Inge (ancestor of the Ynglings). The narrative pattern of chapters 9–11 is easily perceived as distinct by the reader, medieval or modern. Witness for instance 9.9–11:

> He was the father of Visbur, whose sons burnt him alive with all his hirdsmen, so that they might attain their inheritance more swiftly. His son

> Domalde was hanged by the Swedes as a sacrificial offering to Ceres to ensure the fruitfulness of the crops.

> Hic genuit Wisbur, quem filii sui cum omni curia sua, ut cicius hereditarentur, uiuum incenderunt. Cuius filium Domald Sweones suspendentes pro fertilitate frugum Cereri hostiam obtulerunt. Iste genuit Domar, qui in Swecia obiit.

Name, ancestry, and the manner (or place) of death are the stable and almost exclusive elements in this genealogy. The wording – with the often repeated *genuit* – plays very directly on the biblical genealogies (Gen. 5 and Matt. 1.1–17). This takes us through the Swedish Ynglinge kings (ch. 9) and the list continues in the same manner after they branch off to Norway (ch. 10) up to Halvdan the Black. Chapter 11 tells of Harald Fairhair who is traditionally alleged to have unified Norway. It also maintains the same style as the genealogy and gives a list of his sixteen sons, but, in contrast to the Ynglinge genealogy, the author lets us in on the fact that 'there are many marvellous recollections of him, which would take too long now to relate individually'. The genealogical format is also abandoned inasmuch as we are not told about the way Harald passed away, only that he had sixteen sons and ruled for seventy-three years! In the subsequent chapters on the deeds of his various sons, the genealogical element is still there, but the narrative opens up significantly. The language register and the authorial voice do not change dramatically, but longer periods are called for to explain more complicated occurrences than who begat whom, and the narrator is occasionally displayed on a meta-level as a providential and moral voice.[31]

It is fair to say that the genealogical chapters 9–10 (with 11 as a transition) stand out, and that no attempt has been made to hide the different status of the Ynglinge past. On the one hand, the reader is left with the impression that we know very little about these rulers – there is not much more to tell, as was the case for Harald Fairhair. We are, as it were, on rather thin ground. On the other hand, the special style and biblical allusions create a monumentalization of the distant past. The genealogy springs to our eyes almost as a quotation from some venerable ancient authority and is thus beyond our author's

31 For instance 13.10.

control.[32] By thus 'quoting' antiquity he makes sure that the little we know is unquestionable and worthy of Latin and biblical monumentalization.

Sven Aggesen

Sven's working conditions appear to have been similar to that of the author of HN, but his narrative technique in *Historia brevis* is somewhat different. His first chapter (after the prologue) deals briefly with the first generations of the Skjoldunger, but it does so in a language more varied than *HN*'s genealogy of the Ynglings and without its biblical allusion. Already in chapter two and three, Sven fleshes out at great length the story of King Vermund and his son Uffe (see above). In chapter four we return to more brief notes about Uffe's successors, but again the narrative opens up in chapter five (on Queen Thyra). Thus Sven obviously tries to subsume the earliest history under his ordinary diction and to make it memorable by telling two stories at greater length. Another feature singles Sven out from both *HN* and Saxo: the authorial voice enjoys a much stronger presence. In the above-quoted passage from chapter four, he candidly admits the problems he has with his material and tells us that others will be able to handle it better. This voice returns several times, and in later chapters it is even used as authentication ('saw myself....' and similar).[33] If the reader focuses on the whole text, he will construe the authorial *persona* from all these instances and will know that Sven is a knowledgeable man whose judgement, on the early part of Danish history as well, deserves respect. Implicitly, then, Sven glosses over the difficult status of the distant past by not producing a simple list and by enlivening the narrative with good storytelling, dialogue and speeches. On the explicit level he admits that others can do better than he in digging up genealogies and stories from the distant past, but what he does write at least is supported by the integrity of the explicit authorial *persona*.

Saxo

Turning to Saxo we face a more difficult task. Are there distinct features in the literary techniques that are inescapable signposts for medieval and modern readers which suggest that Saxo was less certain about the distant than the recent past – and that he strived for a different kind of representation of it? A

32 Again with the exception of the comment on the fabulous pagan element in 9.6 quoted above.

33 Cf. ch. 10, reference to Saxo; ch. 14, on Sven's grandfather; ch. 19, where Sven confirms Queen Sophia's beauty.

systematic study would take up a whole monograph, and I can only make and exemplify a few general observations here.

It is clear that there is both a formal and a content-determined caesura between Books 8 and 9: the first eight books (except 3 and 4) are written as a prosimetrum and contain highly elaborate Latin poems – or 'renderings' in Saxo's words – of ancient poems in the vernacular. Furthermore, the Danish kings learn of Christianity towards the end of Book 8 and gradually embrace it from Book 9 and on (9.4.36). The poems and their functions have been analyzed thoroughly in a number of studies by Friis-Jensen (chiefly 1987, but also 2004 and elsewhere) and it is clear that Saxo has capitalized on the additional effect of poetic monumentalization of the distant past by emulating Virgil, Horace and other figures of the Roman Parnassus. In this context we can draw a parallel to HN's use of a biblical register in the easily identifiable unit on the Ynglinge genealogy: the constraints of the material in a 'marked form' (genealogical list, vernacular poetic diction) are used as a means to express the *ipsissima verba* of antiquity in another marked form, namely in Latin with its proper register of antiquity which connotes a biblical or Roman past.[34]

Apart from these rather clear distinctive features between Books 1–8 on the one hand and 9–16 on the other, any reader of Saxo will first and foremost be struck by the remarkable unity in narrative technique, the prose style and by the specific flavour of the moralizing voice which pervades the entire work. This moralizing voice is so often explicit ('through this we can see that cowardry never pays off,' or similar) that the reader cannot help but gradually incorporate its morality even when it is only implicit. This feature is one of many which shape the unity of *Gesta Danorum*. Not even such a tempting distinction as supernatural/natural between the two main parts will work because the existence of supernatural forces is acknowledged throughout, be it in the numerous workings of pagan wizards or those of Christian martyrs. The underworld journey of Hadding (1.8.14) and the fight between Asvid and Asmund in their grave (5.11.3 ff.) are as real as the dream of Bishop Sven of Roskilde in which he saw the collapse of the church while it was happening in reality (11.12.1–2), the posthumous miracles of St Canute the King (11.15.1–3) and the escape of the demon disguised as a black animal after the destruction of the pagan Svantevit's effigy in Rügen (14.39.32). The display of traditional,

34 A similar point can be made about the catalogue of warriors which is presented as a 'quotation' from the poet and warrior Starkad (8.2.1–8.3.12, the battle of Bråvalla).

simple virtues in the earlier books is equally matched by the exposition of the stern rectitude of the heroes of the later books, especially that of Archbishop Absalon.

However, there are still some points of narrative technique where one might try to slip in a knife between two stones of Saxo's well-polished edifice. Among these, I think, are: (1) Explicit authorial deliberations and reservations, (2) 'Narrative grounding', and (3) Amplification.

A somewhat long quotation which is significant in many respects may introduce the first feature:

> I intend to touch briefly on their activities [the giants Vagnhofth and Hafli], but, in case I should seem like a brash inventor of tales which strain men's credulity, it is worth telling you that at one time there were three amazing species of wizard, each practising their own miraculous illusions.
>
> The first of these were creatures of monstrous size, whom the ancients called giants, far surpassing human beings in bodily stature.
>
> Second were those who obtained the leading expertise in haruspicy and were masters of the Delphic art. Although in frame they yielded precedence to the former, they excelled them in acuteness of intellect. Between these and the giants there were interminable battles for supremacy, until the diviners won victory over the monster race and appropriated not only the right to rule but even the reputation of being gods. Both these types, being dexterous in deceiving the eye, were clever at counterfeiting different shapes for themselves and others, and concealing their true appearance under false guises.
>
> The third class, bred from an intermingling of the other two, reflected neither the size nor the magic arts of their parents. Nevertheless, minds deluded by their legerdemain believed in their divinity.
>
> It is not surprising that barbarians yielded to their weird hocus-pocus and were led into the rites of a debased religion, since even the intelligent Romans were seduced into worshipping similar mortals with divine honours. I mention these matters so that when I write at length of portents and marvels the incredulous reader may not contest them. After this digression I shall take up my narrative.
>
> Quorum summatim opera perstricturus, ne publice existimationi contraria aut ueri fidem excedentia fidenter astruere uidear, nosse opere

pretium est, triplex quondam mathematicorum genus inauditi generis miracula discretis exercuisse prestigiis.

Horum primi fuere monstruosi generis uiri, quos gigantes antiquitas nominauit, humane magnitudinis habitum eximia corporum granditate uincentes.

Secundi post hos primam physiculandi solertiam obtinentes artem possedere Phitonicam. Qui quantum superioribus habitu cessere corporeo, tantum uiuaci mentis ingenio prestiterunt. hos inter gigantesque de rerum summa bellis certabatur assiduis, quoad magi uictores giganteum armis genus subigerent sibique non solum regnandi ius, uerumetiam diuinitatis opinionem consciscerent. Horum utrique per summam ludificandorum oculorum peritiam proprios alienosque uultus uariis rerum imaginibus adumbrare callebant illicibusque formis ueros obscurare conspectus.

Tertii uero generis homines ex alterna superiorum copula pullulantes auctorum suorum nature nec corporum magnitudine nec artium exercitio respondebant. His tamen apud delusas prestigiis mentes diuinitatis accessit opinio.

Nec mirandum, si prodigialibus eorum portentis adducta barbaries in adulterine religionis cultum concesserit, cum Latinorum quoque prudentiam perlexerit talium quorundam diuinis honoribus celebrata mortalitas. Hec idcirco tetigerim, ne, cum prestigia portentaue perscripsero, lectoris incredula refragetur opinio. His pretermissis propositum repetam.[35]

A digression of a similar scope is found in Book 5 (5.5.2–5.5.5) when the figure of Starkad is introduced. Both his physical and mental stature were larger than that of ordinary people, but he was not, as popular opinion has it (*fabulosa autem et uulgaris opinio*), descended from giants (the first group above, the 'jætter'/'jötnar'). This false opinion leads to a digression on the pagan wizards, among them Thor and Odin, belonging to the second group in the above quotation (the 'aser', 'æsir'). Saxo is at pains to explain that Odin and Thor cannot be equivalent to Jove and Mercury even if the names of the weekdays might at first suggest this (because Thor's day is Jove's day and Thor is not the father, but the son of Odin).

These two digressions are not only key passages for understanding Saxo's

35 1.5.2–1.5.6; translation by Peter Fisher, pp. 21–2.

euhemerizing interpretation of pagan beliefs and the status of this aspect of the past, but they also give us glimpses of authorial deliberations and reservations. It should be emphasized at once that Saxo's literary *persona* is of a completely different kind than Sven's, who places himself and his family in the midst of the narrated history as eyewitnesses. The authorial *persona* in Saxo is a moralizing entity at a considerable remove from both action and reader. One might say that the *persona* is completely subsumed under the moralizing perspective that encompasses most of the stories told. In this sense it is impersonal and very indirect. But a slightly more direct version of it surfaces now and then in the early books in order to bridge the gap between traditional memory and Saxo's time (as in the above case of belief in the pagan gods), or to mediate or decide between various versions of a story. It frames some stories by saying, with a hint of reservation, 'tradition has it that…' (*tradunt veteres, ferunt quidam, fert/prodit/perhibet antiquitas, si fame credi fas est*);[36] in some instances it leaves the choice to the reader, in others it expresses the author's own scepticism. In Book 3 (4.8) we are told how Odin finally succeeded in his amorous advances towards a Russian princess through a ruse, but there is another version of that story which is then told (*aliam quoque ea de re opinionem subtexere non pigebit*). In another passage we hear of a ferocious dog belonging to a certain Bjørn (6.2.5); it is said to have savaged several times no less than twelve people in one attack, but 'the reader must be the judge of that as it is tradition rather than established fact' (*sed quoniam tradita magis quam cognita referuntur, fidem arbiter penset*). A final example shows how the author dismisses a given story: in Book 6 (7.10) Starkad is reported to have hollowed out a boulder (still to be seen) and left his bodily imprint by simply leaning on it; the authorial voice is sceptical and advances the theory that it must have been the work of a conscious human effort (*Ego autem hanc imaginem humana arte elaboratam reor, cum ueri fidem excedere uideatur, insecabilem petre duritiam ita cere molliciem imitari potuisse, ut solo innitentis contactu humane sessionis speciem representaret habitumque perpetue concauitatis indueret.*)

The upshot of this tendency to mediate the incredible in the earlier books engenders in the reader's mind a slightly less certain authorial voice than in the later books. Although expressions such as those quoted are not frequent, the careful reader does get the impression that some of the stories chosen by Saxo can only claim good probability, not entire certainty. It is important to

36 For example 6.5.6, 6.6.1, 6.7.5, 7.1.1.

note that this is not because of their fantastic elements but because of a precarious transmission. It is not a different kind of truth that applies, but the vision of the distant past can occasionally be clouded by a lack of good witnesses. This implicit admission does not strike the reader of the later books – here miraculous and incredibly heroic events are also sometimes underlined by the authorial voice, but we are reassured that they are warranted by the most reliable witnesses.[37]

My second point, 'narrative grounding', also addresses a difference of degree between the early and the later books. What I am thinking of here is the grafting of disparate narrative units onto a larger framework: to which degree are smaller units grounded in a narrative logic on a larger scale? Following this enquiry systematically would demand a large and formal investigation, and my only contention here is that the earlier books leave the reader floating, as it were, in a more undetermined narrative space. Most episodes are rather brief and they do not seem to be linked strongly either by the logic of emplotment, explicit chronology, or other manifest frameworks. Very often discrete narrative units are felt to be interchangeable.

A peculiar feature of the *Gesta Danorum* is that it avoids datings: they would infringe stylistically on the polished Roman monument. There is, as noted above, an internal chronological architecture in the work, but only one date is given, in the midst of the peace of Frode, the time when the Creator (*auctor temporum*, 5.15.3) made his earthly appearance. Therefore Saxo's antiquity is presented *prima facie* as independent from external chronology and events from biblical or other ancient history. The narrative thread throughout is the reigns of kings – this is the chief handle offered to the reader on his or her way through the maze. Each episode is subsumed under a reign, but in the early books the relation between the reign and the important stories is often vague. Medieval readers must have been struck by the effect created by Saxo's continual addition of episodes with 'about the same time' (*interea, inter haec, post hoc, quo peracto, eodem tempore*, etc.). This associative style is gradually counterbalanced by figures with a greater narrative mass such as Hamlet (Books 3–4), Eric the Eloquent (5) and Starkad (6, and partly 8) – but even here the interchangeability of episodes is often striking. Compared to the later books, especially 11–16 (representing half of the whole work due to the oversized Book 14) in which Saxo is approaching or drawing directly on

37 For instance the heroic deeds of Aslak warranted by Absalon (11.5.1): *qua res ueri fidem excederet, si non Absalon auctor suis eam relatibus tradidisset.*

living memory and an enormous wealth of stories, the narrative flow is of a different order. In the later books, medieval as well as modern readers are more comfortable, I think, because of larger narrative units that support the reading of the smaller ones which makes the narrative logic more easily recognizable, and simply because we have a historical knowledge which supplies a skeleton narrative independent of Saxo's. When St Canute is introduced (11.8.1) Saxo states, 'I have now come to Canute' (*Veniam nunc ad Kanutum*) – which is what most knowledgeable readers expect; this is contrasted with introductions in the earlier books: even if we did expect to hear about Odin, Balder, Hamlet, etc., we are surprised that they should enter the story exactly at this point. Therefore, I think it is reasonable to suggest that our expectations in the later books are grounded both in external relevant knowledge anticipated by Saxo, and by the logic of emplotment: What happened to the traitor after the battle? How did they return from overseas? Who was elected bishop when the old one passed away? Structural predictability is greater and the reader tunes in to a more solid rhythm. This is not to say that in the later books Saxo does not spring surprises or that he does not sometimes prefer shortcuts that leave our obvious plot questions unanswered, but this does mean that he honours our expectations much more regularly and on a larger narrative level than in the earlier books.

The general stylistic unity of the *Gesta Danorum* in terms of vocabulary and syntax is reinforced on the level of narrative technique by the presence throughout the work of features such as dialogue, indirect and direct speech (including lengthy set pieces in both registers), digressions/diatribes and *ekphraseis*, a distant moralizing and gnomic authorial voice, the balance of narrative and argumentative sections, and the absence of quotations, summaries and anticipations.

My third point deals with such an omnipresent technical feature which is connected to the matters of authorial voice and narrative grounding – and again we are talking about a difference in degree suggested here on the basis of an impressionistic reading rather than a systematic formal investigation. One of the defining characteristics of Saxo's style is his strong penchant for amplification. Let us see one in its full glory (5.1.2):

> Koli's wife was Gøtvara, who flaunted her outstanding eloquence so much that she would quell anyone, however fluent and articulate. She was proficient in disputation and had plentiful resources in every type of argument.

> A warrior with words, she was armed with an equal battery of questions and stubborn replies. Though she never fought in battle, no one could vanquish this woman, whose tongue provided her with arrows. Some she confuted by her unremitting audacity of speech, others she entwined within the meshes of her ironies and strangled in nooses of sophistries. A sprightly-witted woman, highly skilled in making or breaking agreements, she would manipulate the sting inside her mouth to be effective either way; for this reason she was adept at striking alliances or dissolving them as she plied the ambivalent trade of her tongue for one or the other.

> Uxor Colonis erat Gøtwara, que eximie procacitate facundie quantumlibet disertos ac loquaces eneruare solebat. Altercando quippe efficax erat et in omni disceptationum genere copiosa. Pugnabat siquidem uerbis, non modo questionibus freta, uerum etiam peruicacibus armata responsis. Imbellem nemo foeminam debellare poterat, a lingua spicula mutuantem. Quosdam uerbositatis petulantia refellebat, alios ueluti quibusdam cauillationum nexibus implicatos fallaciarum laqueis strangulabat. Adeo uegetum mulieri ingenium fuit. Ceterum condere pacta aut rescindere prepotens erat, utriusque horum efficaciam oris aculeo gestans. Quippe disiicere foedera ac sociare callebat. Ita ad utrumlibet anceps lingue commercium fuit.

What Saxo is saying here, in effect, is that Gøtvar had a sharp tongue (and this element is important for what follows). As a recent Danish translator has hinted, such passages are amongst the most difficult to handle because modern languages are much more sparing with the rhetoric of *copia*; it is almost impossible to avoid a comical effect.[38] This *amplificatio* of a simple meaning, however, serves several important purposes in the rhetoric favoured by certain Roman authors (like Valerius Maximus) and their twelfth-century imitators. On the surface level the expatiation itself naturally adds weight to the subject and the narrative. For a medieval imitator of a certain difficult 'manierist' style like Saxo, it furthermore proves that the full range of Roman vocabulary must be activated to properly represent the local past. For a modern reader without inculcated respect for *copia*, a passage as the one above tends to highlight emptiness rather than fullness. But for someone with the same rhetori-

38 Peter Zeeberg, in the introduction to the translation (2005: 34–5).

cal schooling as Saxo it would rather foreground the rich gnomic and moral potential of ancient tales. So many variants of *bonmots* and such a display of vocabulary plenitude was in fact part of ancient Danish history – it is not to be seen as a coincidental 'mental' description of a past phenomenon, rather the proverbial Latin wording embodies the essentials of a paradigmatic past.

Amplification is certainly a feature that pervades Saxo's work from beginning to end, but I would like to suggest that there is a preponderance of the full form in the earlier books.[39] This could be interpreted as a reaction to a lack of material on the part of Saxo, but what is interesting in this context is the effect that it creates. In a traditional modern reading we would add this feature to other dubious talents of Saxo's – those of invention and fabrication, even perhaps as his worst 'fictional' habit. From the standpoint of *Quellenforschung*, however, he is not telling a number of untruths about the past here, he is only inflating a single fact or invention. But the intended effect is rather the reverse, namely to represent the past as already included in a rich learned conceptualization: it is a property of the past to be represented through such language and it enhances the exemplary and gnomic value of the distant past. If I am right in pointing to more consistent amplification in the earlier books, this can be construed as a deliberate effect in representing ancient history in a different colouring than the more recent one.

Having looked briefly at the seams between various narrative parts that do, after all, show in the three chosen works, some common elements can be pinpointed. As has been evident, I have not included much discussion of 'source' problems for our authors. These can naturally not be disregarded completely, but they remain a speculative field, and no matter what the authors' 'source' situation might have been, it seems legitimate to analyze the effect rather than the genesis of their elaborate narratives. Their efforts were, in the main, designed to merge a wealth of 'traditional' material into one master-story and to conceal the disparate nature of its original elements. What I am proposing here is that they did not quite succeed, or they did not dare to succeed completely (see below). But I do not think that the reader's task is as easy as Auerbach eloquently states:

39 In the earlier books there are good examples in the poems, especially the two longest ones, Bjarkamålet (2.7.4–2.7.28 on martial courage) and the Lay of Ingellus (6.9.3–6.9.16 on decadent lifestyle); in the prose some examples from Book 6 are: 6.5.19 (on insidious fighting), 6.6.1 (on the effeminacy of Ingellus), 6.8.6 (on the modesty of Starkad), 6.8.7 (on fancy German cooking), 6.19.17 (on Ingellus's change of heart). In the later books I have only noted longer amplifications in 11.1.1, 11.2.2, 11.10.1, 12.3.5 (the devotion of Bodil).

> Now the difference between legend and history is in most cases easily perceived by a reasonably experienced reader. It is a difficult matter, requiring careful historical and philological training, to distinguish the true from the synthetic or the biased in a historical presentation; but it is easy to separate the historical from the legendary in general. Their structure is different. Even where the legendary does not immediately betray itself by elements of the miraculous, by the repetition of well-known standard motives, typical patterns and themes, through neglect of clear details of time and place, and the like, it is generally quickly recognizable by its composition. It runs far too smoothly. All cross-currents, all friction, all that is casual, secondary to the main events and themes, everything unresolved, truncated, and uncertain, which confuses the clear progress of the action and the simple orientation of the actors, has disappeared. [...] Legend arranges its material in a simple and straightforward way.[40]

As hinted, some of this holds true for Saxo, although much less clearly than in the ideal world of Auerbach (and perhaps he would simply claim that Saxo is writing history *tout court*). Sven Aggesen and Saxo both admit to some uncertainty in dealing with tales from the most distant past through a common positioning of the authorial *persona* (even though their characteristics and transparency are quite different). *Historia Norwegie* and Saxo share the feature of setting the distant past somewhat apart by 'quoting' it: the Ynglinge genealogy and Saxo's poems are presented as authentic voices from the past, made even more authentic through a Latin adaptation which displays them as voices from a biblical or Roman past. Finally one can find shades in Saxo's otherwise very unifying style and narrative technique which make for a slightly different (but discernible) reader response to the prose narrative of the early

40 Translation by Willard R. Trask, *Mimesis: The Representation of Reality in Western Literature*, Princeton 2003/1953, p. 19. 'Nun ist der Unterschied zwischen Sage und Geschichte für einen etwas erfahrenen Leser in den meisten Fällen leicht zu entdecken. So schwer es ist, und so sorgfältiger historisch-philologischer Ausbildung es bedarf, um innerhalb eines geschichtlichen Berichts das Wahre vom gefälschten oder einseitig beleuchteten zu unterscheiden, so leicht ist es im allgemeinen, Sage und Geschichte überhaupt auseinanderzuhalten. Ihre Struktur ist verschieden. Selbst da, wo sich die Sage nicht sogleich durch Elemente des Wunderbaren [supernatural], durch Wiederholung bekannter Motive, durch Vernachlässigung örtlicher und zeitlicher Bedingungen oder ähnliches [different narrative grounding] sofort verrät, ist sie doch meist an ihrem Aufbau schnell zu erkennen. Alles Querlaufende, aller Reibungswiderstand, alles Sonstige, Sekundäre, welches in die Hauptereignisse und Hauptmotive hineinspielt, alles Unentschiedene, Gebrochene und Schwankende, welches den klaren Gang der Handlung und die einfache Richtung der handelnden Personen verwirrt, ist ausgewachsen. [...] Die Sage ordnet den Stoff in eindeutiger und entschiedener Weise' (Auerbach 1946: 21–2).

books (weak narrative grounding and more amplification). Many parts of the first eight books, with a preponderance in the first three, give themselves away as the first tentative glimpses of Danish history.[41]

THE INFLUENCE OF GEOFFREY OF MONMOUTH

Before concluding I would like to get back to the larger European picture, mainly in the guise of Geoffrey of Monmouth. Ever since Jørgensen (1931), it has been repeated that Geoffrey probably exerted some sort of influence on Sven and especially Saxo, and this was corroborated in an article by Lukman in 1944 where he showed that a Danish official genealogy from the 1190s referred directly to King Arthur as represented by Geoffrey. Since then no investigation has been carried out, although the general knowledge of the overwhelming twelfth-century European reception of Geoffrey has been amply documented recently (Crick 1989 and 1991). Geoffrey's history not only provided the point of departure for vernacular Arthurian romances but also became the single most popular Latin piece of historical writing in the entire Anglo-Norman realm with reception in Saxony as well. To this should be added that it was paraphrased in Old Norse around 1200 (*Breta sögur*),[42] and its prophecies were referred to in *Historia Norwegie*. It is almost nonsensical to assume that Saxo (and Sven) did not know it well – they had both studied in northern France in the 1170s or 1180s. If Saxo knew it, a number of things would follow for our evaluation of the 'mythical' part of his history, because Geoffrey is the only Latin historical writer of the twelfth century whose 'prehistory' can match that of Saxo.[43]

Although Geoffrey's *History* (written c. 1136–38) – with all its material on the exiled Trojans in England, the long genealogy of otherwise unknown rulers, some of whom conquered Rome, the prophecies of Merlin and the tales of Arthur – did encounter famous criticism for being a *fabula* by William of Newburgh around 1200, there is a large consensus that his history – no matter how fabricated – was taken, to all effects and purposes, as a true account of the distant past of insular history throughout the Middle Ages, and that its urgent topicality of defining insular identity during the twelfth century made

41 I am grateful to Peter Zeeberg for discussions about this.

42 For a recent survey, see Würth (1998).

43 I am only touching on a few points here that concern the topic of fictionality. In Mortensen (2007c), I have discussed other similarities between Geoffrey's and Saxo's Histories.

it much more than simply an entertaining book.[44] As Dennis Green puts it: 'In view of this we may take Geoffrey's work, as most of his contemporaries did, as (fabricated or imperfect history), but not, as is occasionally the case in scholarship, as fiction in the technical sense with which we are concerned.'[45]

I do not see any difficulty in aligning the author of *HN*, Sven Aggesen and Saxo with the mainstream medieval understanding of Geoffrey – and consequently also to view him as a great source of inspiration for them (especially Saxo) to tell ancient national history at length – as history and not as fiction. Geoffrey, however, does not display any of the three features in Saxo I have looked at above (uncertainty of voice, weak grounding of narrative units, or a certain telling stylistic penchant in the early books). The difference here can tell us something about the choices faced by Geoffrey and Saxo.

The reason for Geoffrey's extreme certainty of voice is partly explained by the above-mentioned claim of a book in the vernacular from which he allegedly translated his entire text (mentioned in chapters 2, 177, 207–208), except the prophecies of Merlin which are purported to have been translated from somewhere else (cf. 109–110).[46] This illusion is often easy to see through, but perhaps also easy to oversee, which is what contemporaries including Saxo might have done. For modern readers the obvious heavy dependence of Geoffrey on Virgil[47] as well as the allusions to and quotations from Lucan and Juvenal immediately make his claim of a vernacular book suspect. The dependence on a series of works of Latin literature seems to be very direct and, to say the least, very strange as a defining feature of a hypothetical vernacular text from the eleventh century or earlier. But what we tend to identify on a formal level medieval scholars may have simply recognized as a natural reflection of the importance of Virgilian and Trojan influence on the 'content' level – that is, once you believe in the importance and plausibility of a Trojan origin it is no great surprise to find this corroborated in a previously overlooked old book in the vernacular. For medieval readers, as far as they noticed, Geoffrey's entire narrative was in quotation marks – it was simply antiquity itself

44 Cf. Crick (1991: 224–6) and (1992), Curley (1994), Green (2002: 169–74) with further references.

45 Green (2002: 170); he refers to those who agree with his view and to those who describe it as fiction in a broader sense than Green's definition. Cf. also Stein (2006: 123–5) who falls into the latter category.

46 The authorial interventions have been discussed by Blacker (1994: 17–24), but I think she underplays the degree to which the authorial voice was formally bound by its pretending to be a translator only. I am not aware of any systematic investigation of the instances where he almost crosses the line and undermines the illusion.

47 Cf. Stein (2006: 123).

telling its authoritative tale. A probable explanation for Geoffrey's claim has been offered by Curley who thinks that he did in fact have a miscellany in the British language available and that he used it for genealogies, names, etc., but certainly not for the narrative itself.[48] In any case, the ruse provided Geoffrey with an excellent starting-point for his assertive authorial voice as well as his stylistic unity which no doubt impressed twelfth-century readers, probably including Saxo. Without recourse to such a claim, Saxo had to acknowledge the deficiency of his 'book' behind the book – it only gave him runic inscriptions and orally transmitted poems. He had no alternative to signal his uncertainty and his only very partial quotation of antiquity itself. Still Geoffrey could have given immense inspiration for Saxo's scheme to out-Roman the Romans and to report a wealth of details from the long gone past.

By way of conclusion I would like to expand on two suggestions I have made previously.[49] The first one is related to the narrative analysis and suggests that the readers tuned in differently to the first very distant stories. This does not mean that another category of truth was applied,[50] nor that a contract of fiction prevailed here, only that Saxo was not quite alone in accepting a slightly different type of aesthetics for those early parts. The other one involves the commissioners and primary audience more directly. Instead of announcing the early books as instances of fiction in the same degree as Chrétien de Troyes's romances, I think that one should take into account that Saxo (like other contemporary historians in similar positions) were socially empowered to make choices for local mythopoiesis: if anything should be said authoritatively about the distant past, they were the professionals to do it. Faced with a bewildering variety of local stories, the best representative of the Latinate elite secular clergy was the one to do it – much like Virgil was empowered by Augustus to forge the most fitting version of Aeneas's coming to Italy. A certain amount of fabrication on behalf of the author was agreed upon in the peer group – this was the best representation of the distant past formulated by the best man. A full moralizing, exemplary and poetic vision of the distant past (and in Geoffrey's case a prophetic vision of the future) should be in the hands of professionals who were trained in scriptural exegesis and classical rhetoric.

Even if the narratives discussed here can in no way be categorized as fic-

48 Curley (1994: 10–13).
49 Mortensen (1994, 1997, 2006 and 2007a).
50 *Pace* Steblin-Kamenskij (1973).

tion in Dennis Green's sense (nor as *argumentum* for that matter), they do partake in the contemporary movement of European literature: without the inspiration from European developments like Geoffrey and his general influence on written historical and fictional discourse, it is unlikely that the narratives in HN, Sven Aggesen and especially Saxo would have turned out the way they did. All the authors in question were anxious to transfer old stories in a fitting form to the parchment, but it was a precarious business to pass such stories off as being completely on the level with contemporary tales. Both Geoffrey's book and perhaps our authors' knowledge of the writing down of real fiction gave them the necessary courage to venture along a path of fabrication and mythopoiesis warranted by the best possible informers and by their own position as appointed sanctified mythmakers. There was no contract of make-believe between Saxo and his intended audience, but there was a contract between Saxo and his patrons that *he* was enabled to represent the Danish past to the best of his heuristic and rhetorical powers.

References

TEXTS

Chronicon Lethrense is edited by Gertz 1917–18, vol. 1, pp. 43–53.

Geoffrey of Monmouth, *Historia regum Britannie*. This is the traditional title, but the new standard edition has chosen *De gestis Britonum: The History of the Kings of Britain*. Edition by Michael D. Reeve, translation by Neil Wright, Woodbridge: The Boydell Press, 2007.

Historia Norwegie is edited by Inger Ekrem and Lars Boje Mortensen with a translation by Peter Fisher, Copenhagen: Museum Tusculanum Press, 2003.

Saxo Grammaticus, *Gesta Danorum – Danmarkshistorien* is edited by Karsten Friis-Jensen with a Danish translation by Peter Zeeberg, 2 vols., Copenhagen: Gad, 2005. I have quoted from the English translation: *The History of the Danes*, vol. 1: English text. Translation by Peter Fisher, edited with a commentary by Hilda Davidson, Cambridge: D.S. Brewer, 1979. Friis-Jensen's edition of the Latin text will soon reappear in Oxford Medieval Texts with a revised complete parallel translation into English by Peter Fisher.

Saga of the Scyldings/Skjoldunger. The remains and later paraphrases of this mostly lost text are translated into Danish in *Skjoldungernes saga. Kong Skjold og hans slægt – Rolf Krake – Harald Hildetand – Ragnar Lodbrog*. Translated by

Karsten Friis-Jensen and Claus Lund. Edited by Claus Lund, Copenhagen: Gad, 1984.

Snorri Sturluson, *Heimskringla* is edited by Finnur Jónsson, vols. 1–4, Copenhagen: Gad, 1893–1901. There is an English translation by Lee M. Hollander, *Heimskringla: History of the Kings of Norway*, Austin: University of Texas Press, 1967.

Sven Aggesen, *Historia brevis regum Dacie* is edited by M. Cl. Gertz 1917–18: 94–141 in two separate versions. I am quoting from the X-version which also lies behind the Danish and English translations: M. Cl. Gertz in *Sven Aggesøns historiske Skrifter*, Copenhagen 1916–17, and Eric Christiansen, *The Works of Sven Aggesen, Twelfth-Century Danish Historian*, London: Viking Society for Northern Research, University College London, 1992.

Theodoricus Monachus, *Historia de antiquitate regum Norwagiensium* is edited by Gustav Storm, pp. 1–68 in *Monumenta Historica Norvegiae*, Kristiania, 1880. [Repr. by Norsk historisk Kjeldeskrift-Institutt, Oslo 1973.] There is an English translation by David McDougall and Ian McDougall: Theodoricus Monachus, *Historia de antiquitate regum Norwagiensium: An Account of the Ancient History of the Norwegian Kings*. Translated and annotated by David and Ian McDougall, with an introduction by Peter Foote, London: Viking Society for Northern Research, University College London, 1998.

STUDIES

Auerbach, Erich (1946) *Mimesis. Dargestellte Wirklichkeit in der abendländischen Literatur*, Berne: A. Francke.

Bagge, Sverre (1991) *Society and Politics in Snorri Sturluson's 'Heimskringla'*, Berkeley: University of California Press.

Blacker, Jean (1994) *The Faces of Time: Portrayal of the Past in Old French and Latin Historical Narrative of the Anglo-Norman Regnum*, Austin: University of Texas Press.

Christiansen, Eric (1981) 'The Place of Fiction in Saxo's Later Books', in Karsten Friis-Jensen (ed.), *Saxo Grammaticus: A Medieval Author between Norse and Latin Culture*, Copenhagen: Museum Tusculanum Press, pp. 27–37.

Clunies Ross, Margaret (1992) 'Mythic Narrative in Saxo Grammaticus and Snorri Sturluson', in Carlo Santini (ed.), *Saxo Grammaticus. Tra storiografia e letteratura*, Rome: Il Calamo, pp. 47–59.

Crick, Julia (1989) *The Historia regum Britannie of Geoffrey of Monmouth III: A Summary Catalogue of the Manuscripts*, Cambridge: D.S. Brewer.

Crick, Julia (1991) *The Historia regum Britannie of Geoffrey of Monmouth IV: Dissemination and Reception in the Later Middle Ages*, Cambridge: D.S. Brewer.

Crick, Julia (1992) 'Geoffrey of Monmouth, Prophecy and History', *Journal of Medieval History* 18: 357–71.

Curley, Michael J. (1994) *Geoffrey of Monmouth*, New York: Maxwell Macmillan International.

Ellehøj, Sven (1965) *Studier over den ældste norrøne historieskrivning*, Copenhagen: Munksgaard.

Friis, Oluf (1945) *Den danske Litteraturs Historie, I, Fra Oldtiden til Renæssancen (c. 1615)*, Copenhagen: H. Hirschsprungs Forlag.

Friis-Jensen, Karsten (1987) *Saxo Grammaticus as Latin Poet: Studies in the Verse Passages of the Gesta Danorum*, Rome: Bretschneider.

Friis-Jensen, Karsten (1992) 'Saxo Grammaticus's Study of the Roman Historiographers and his Vision of History', in Carlo Santini (ed.), *Saxo Grammaticus. Tra storiografia e letteratura*, Rome: Il Calamo, pp. 61–81.

Friis-Jensen, Karsten (2004) 'Adhering to the footprints of these men as if to books from antiquity ...', in Marianne Børch (ed.), *Text and Voice: The Rhetoric of Authority in the Middle Ages*, Odense: University Press of Southern Denmark, pp. 121–37.

Gertz, Martin Clarentius (ed.) (1917–18) *Scriptores minores historiæ Danicæ medii ævi*, vol. I, Copenhagen: Gad. [Repr. Selskabet for udgivelse af kilder til dansk historie, Copenhagen, 1970.]

Green, Dennis H. (2002) *The Beginnings of Medieval Romance: Fact and Fiction, 1150–1220*, Cambridge: Cambridge University Press.

Haug, Walter (2002) 'Geschichte, Fiktion und Wahrheit. Zu den literarischen Spielformen zwischen Faktizität und Phantasie', in Franz Peter Knapp and Manuela Niesner (eds.), *Historisches und fiktionales Erzählen im Mittelalter*, Berlin: Duncker & Humblot, pp. 115–31.

Jensson, Gottskalk Thor (2004) 'The Lost Latin Literature of Medieval Iceland: The Fragments of the Vita Sancti Thorlaci and Other Evidence', *Symbolae Osloenses* 79: 150–70.

Johanek, Peter (2002) 'Die Wahrheit der mittelalterlichen Historiographen', in Franz Peter Knapp and Manuela Niesner (eds.), *Historisches und fiktionales Erzählen im Mittelalter*, Berlin: Duncker & Humblot, pp. 9–25.

Johannesson, Kurt (1978) *Saxo Grammaticus. Komposition och världsbild i Gesta Danorum*, Stockholm: Almqvist & Wiksell.

Jørgensen, Ellen (1931) *Historieforskning og historieskrivning i Danmark indtil aar 1800*, Copenhagen: Den danske historiske Forening.

Kersken, Norbert (1995) *Geschichtsschreibung im Europa der 'nationes'. Nationalgeschichtliche Gesamtdarstellungen im Mittelalter*, Cologne: Böhlau.

Knapp, Fritz Peter (1997) *Historie und Fiktion in der mittelalterlichen Gattungspoetik. Sieben Studien und ein Nachwort*, Heidelberg: Carl Winter.

Knapp, Franz Peter (2005) *Historie und Fiktion in der mittelalterlichen Gattungspoetik (II). Zehn neue Studien und ein Vorwort* (Schriften der Philosophisch-historischen Klasse der Heidelberger Akademie der Wissenschaften, 35), Heidelberg: Carl Winter.

Krag, Claus (1991) *Ynglingatal og Ynglingesaga. En studie i historiske kilder* (Studia humaniora 2), Oslo: Universitetsforlaget.

Kværndrup, Sigurd (1984) 'Den første nordiske renæssance', in *Dansk litteraturhistorie 1: Fra runer til ridderdigtning o. 800–1480*, Copenhagen: Gyldendal, pp. 305–78.

Kværndrup, Sigurd (1999) *Tolv principper hos Saxo. En tolkning af Danernes Bedrifter*. Copenhagen: Multivers.

Louis-Jensen, Jonna (2006) 'Heimskringla – et værk af Snorri Sturluson?', in Jonna Louis-Jensen, *Con Amore. En artikelsamling udgivet på 70-årsdagen den 21. oktober 2006*. Edited by Michael Chesnutt and Florian Grammel, Copenhagen: C. A. Reitzels Forlag, pp. 217–32. [The article was first published in *Nordica Bergensia* 14 (1997): 230–45.]

Lukman, Niels (1942–44): 'Saxos Kendskab til Galfred af Monmouth', *Historisk Tidsskrift* 10. R., 6: 593–607.

Lund, Claus (1984) 'Indledning', in *Skjoldungernes saga Skjoldungernes saga. Kong Skjold og hans slægt – Rolf Krake – Harald Hildetand – Ragnar Lodbrog*. Translated by Karsten Friis-Jensen and Claus Lund. Edited by Claus Lund, Copenhagen: Gad, pp. 9–42.

Mortensen, Lars Boje (1987) 'Saxo Grammaticus' View of the Origin of the Danes and His Historiographical Models', *Cahiers de l'institut du moyen-âge grec et latin* 55: 169–83.

Mortensen, Lars Boje (1994) 'The Glorious Past: Entertainment, Example or History? Levels of Twelfth-Century Historical Culture', *Culture and History* 13: 57–71.

Mortensen, Lars Boje (1997) 'Det romerske epos som historisk og litterær kilde i højmiddelalderen', in Minna Skafte Jensen (ed.), *Homer gennem tiden. Historie eller fiktion*, Copenhagen: Museum Tusculanum Press, pp. 46–57.

Mortensen, Lars Boje (2005) 'Den norske middelalderlitteratur på latin', in Steinar Imsen (ed.), *Den kirkehistoriske utfordring*, Trondheim: Tapir, pp. 139–46.

Mortensen, Lars Boje (2006) 'Sanctified Beginnings and Mythopoietic Moments: The First Wave of Writing on the Past in Norway, Denmark, and Hungary, c. 1000–1230', in Lars Boje Mortensen (ed.), *The Making of Christian Myths in the Periphery of Latin Christendom (c. 1000–1300)*, Copenhagen: Museum Tusculanum Press, pp. 247–73.

Mortensen, Lars Boje (2007a) 'From Vernacular Interviews to Latin Prose (ca. 600–1200)', in Else Mundal and Jonas Wellendorf (eds.), *Oral Art Forms and their Transmission into Writing*, Copenhagen: Museum Tusculanum Press, pp. 53–68.

Mortensen, Lars Boje (2007b) 'Højmiddelalderen 1100–1300', in Klaus P. Mortensen and May Schack (eds.), *Dansk litteraturs historie, bind 1: 1100–1800*, Copenhagen: Gyldendal, pp. 52–90.

Mortensen, Lars Boje (2007c) 'Saxo og Geoffrey af Monmouth', *Renæssanceforum – Tidsskrift for renæssanceforskning* 3: 22 pp. [www.igl.ku.dk/~pade/renaessanceforum/]

Mortensen, Lars Boje, and Else Mundal (2003) 'Erkebispesetet i Nidaros – arnestad og verkstad for olavslitteraturen', in Steinar Imsen (ed.), *Ecclesia Nidrosiensis 1153–1537. Søkelys på Nidaroskirkens og Nidarosprovinsens historie*, Trondheim: Tapir, pp. 353–84.

Mundal, Else (2004) 'Sagalitteraturen', in Odd Einar Hagen (ed.), *Handbok i norrøn filologi*, Bergen: Fagbokforlaget, pp. 267–303.

Otter, Monika (1996) *Inventiones: Fiction and Referentiality in Twelfth-Century English Historical Writing*, Chapel Hill and London: University of North Carolina Press.

Otter, Monika (2005) 'Functions of Fiction in Historical Writing', in Nancy Partner (ed.), *Writing Medieval History*, London: Hodder Arnold, pp. 109–30.

Skovgaard-Petersen, Inge (1969) 'Saxo, Historian of the Patria', *Mediaeval Scandinavia* 2: 54–77.

Skovgaard-Petersen, Inge (1981) 'The Way to Byzantium: A Study in the First Three Books of Saxo's History of Denmark', in Karsten Friis-Jensen (ed.), *Saxo Grammaticus: A Medieval Author between Norse and Latin Culture*, Copenhagen: Museum Tusculanum Press, pp. 121–33.

Skovgaard-Petersen, Inge (1987) *Da tidernes Herre var nær. Studier i Saxos historiesyn*, Copenhagen: Den danske historiske Forening.

Steblin-Kamenskij, Michail Ivanovic (1973) *The Saga Mind*, Odense: Odense University Press.

Stein, Robert (2006) *Reality Fictions: Romance, History, and Governmental Authority, 1025–1180*, Notre Dame: University of Notre Dame Press.

Tyler, Elizabeth (2005) 'Fictions of Family: The *Encomium Emmae Reginae* and Vergil's *Aeneid*', *Viator* 36: 149–79.

Vollmann, Benedikt Konrad (2002) 'Erlaubte Fiktionalität: Die Heiligenlegende', in Fritz Peter Knapp and Manuela Niesner (eds.), *Historisches und fiktionales Erzählen im Mittelalter*, Berlin: Duncker & Humblot, pp. 63–72.

Wright, Neil (1985) 'Preface', in *The Historia Regum Britannie of Geoffrey of Monmouth I: Bern Burgerbibliothek, MS 568*, Cambridge: D.S. Brewer.

Würth, Stefanie (1998) *Der 'Antikenroman' in der isländischen Literatur des Mittelalters: Eine Untersuchung zur Übersetzung und Rezeption lateinischer Literatur im Norden*, Basel: Helbing & Lichtenhahn.

True Records of Events that Could Have Taken Place: Fictionality in Vision Literature

Jonas Wellendorf

The Christian tradition of vision literature begins with the short passage in Paul's second letter to the Corinthians (12:2–4) where he states that he was caught up to the third Heaven, and there in Paradise 'heard the secret words which man is not permitted to utter' (*audivit arcana verba quae non licet homini loqui*). Although this prohibition does not extend to the things Paul saw, the second letter to the Corinthians gives no description of the sights in the third Heaven or in Paradise, nor does Paul leave us with other accounts of this experience.

Subsequent writers have attempted to fill this narrative void in the Scriptures with an account of Paul's experiences, and in a similar way later writers told other stories that were hinted at but absent from the canonical writings. Thus we now have a series of apocrypha that were widely read and by and large accepted by the church, although they were not considered canonical. Among such writings one can find accounts of the birth and childhood of Mary, what happened during the three days between the descent of Christ to the dead and the resurrection, and what Paul experienced in the third Heaven and Paradise, and many other tales. The development sketched for the apocrypha is in this way somewhat similar or analogous to the one described by Dennis Green in his contribution to the present volume and elsewhere: existing or imagined gaps in transmitted authoritative Latin works could be filled with largely fictitious accounts by subsequent writers.

In the case of Paul's otherworldly experiences, the narrative gap or potential was (ful)filled by *Apocalypsis Pauli* (*The Apocalypse of Paul*). In some manuscripts the account of Paul's revelation proper is preceded by a short prologue that tells the story of how this report of his revelation was miraculously discovered in a marble chest in the foundations of Paul's house in Tarsus together with the sandals he used to wear while spreading the word of God.[1] This miraculous discovery is supposed to have taken place in 388.

The account itself begins with the complaints by Creation, represented in turns by the Sun, the Moon and the Stars, the Ocean and the Waters, and finally the Earth, over the evil ways of mankind. An account follows outlining how each night the angels bring the Lord reports about the deeds of man. Paul is then led to Heaven by an angel, and looking down at the earth he sees what befalls a righteous and a wicked soul respectively the moment they depart from their bodies at death. After having visited Enoch and Elijah in the Paradise that is situated in the third Heaven, Paul is led to the Land of Promise where the marvellous City of Christ is situated, built of gold and encircled by twelve walls. He meets the prophets, the children slain by Herod, the just, etc. At an altar placed in the centre of the city, David sings in honour of the Lord. From the City of Christ Paul is led across the ocean that encompasses the earth to the dark and terrifying place where the souls of the ungodly and the sinners are imprisoned. A long and detailed description of the various categories of sinners and their torments is presented, including a description of deep pits and rivers of fire, worms, torturing angels and other unpleasantries. Paul cries for all the sinners and on their behalf beseeches God for mercy. He is joined in his prayers by the archangel Michael and the rest of the heavenly hosts, and finally the Son of God descends from Heaven and grants the sinners Sunday respite, which means that they are allowed one weekly day of rest from their torments, analogous to the day of rest observed and enjoyed by the living. After this the angel takes Paul to the Paradise where Adam and Eve sinned. He meets the Virgin Mary, the Patriarchs, Moses and many other characters from the Old Testament.

Exactly when and where *The Apocalypse of Paul* was composed remains an unsettled issue. Augustine was familiar with a text bearing the same name, but he was definitely not favourably inclined towards it; rather the opposite. In his treatise on the Gospel of John, he writes:

> Untrustworthy men have, with the most foolish presumption, fabricated an *Apocalypse of Paul* which is full of I don't know which fables, and which the sensible church does not acknowledge. They say that this was what he was referring to when he said that he was carried off into the third Heaven

1 See Piovanelli (2000).

> and there heard the ineffable words which man is not permitted to utter. Their audacity would to some extent have been tolerable if he had said that he heard what was not *yet* permissible to utter, but since he said what is not permissible to utter, who are then those who so shamelessly and unfortunately dare to utter them?

> uani quidam Apocalypsim Pauli, quam sana non recipit ecclesia, nescio quibus fabulis plenam, stultissima praesumptione finxerunt, dicentes hanc esse unde dixerat raptum se fuisse in tertium caelum, et illic audisse ineffabilia verba quae non licet homini loqui. Vtcumque illorum tolerabilis esset audacia, si se audisse dixisset quae adhuc non licet homini loqui; cum uero dixerit: quae non licet homini loqui, isti qui sunt qui haec audeant impudenter et infeliciter loqui? (*In Iohannis evangelium tractatus*, ch. 98.8)

Similarly, the Gelasian decree *De libris recipiendis et non recipiendis*, traditionally dated to 496, enumerates a *Revelatio, quae appellatur Pauli apocryfa*, 'an apocrypha revelation ascribed to Paul', among the books that are not accepted by the Roman Church and are to be avoided because they are written by heretics or schismatics (53). Both quotations most likely refer to the same *Apocalypsis Pauli* as the one we know today. Dismissals by such authoritative and widespread texts suffice to show that there was general dissatisfaction with the text and its contents from the official side of the church. In spite of this unease, *The Apocalypse of Paul* enjoyed enormous popularity later on in the Middle Ages. Particularly popular was the shorter version called *Visio Pauli*. This work contained only the description of the visit to the place of the damned and (in most versions) the account of the destinies of the righteous and the wicked soul at the moment of death. It circulated throughout the Latin West in numerous Latin as well as vernacular versions and redactions.[2] This means that the text had now liberated itself, at least partly, from the biblical framework where a visit to the third Heaven was presupposed. Around 1200 knowledge of *Visio Pauli* had even spread to the northern periphery of Europe, and in the Old Norwegian book of homilies the rubric *Visio sancti Pauli apostoli* (148) can be found, indicating some kind of knowledge of this text. That the heading is not in fact followed by the promised text, but by an Old Norse ren-

2 See Jiroušková (2006) for a study and an edition of the Latin text and medieval German and Czech translations. Jiroušková underlines that the *Visio Pauli* is not to be seen only as an abbreviation of the apocalypse, as it also contains new material not found in the apocalypse.

dering of another vision, the *Visio Philiberti*, shows that the scribe's knowledge of the text was superficial at best; perhaps he was only familiar with it from second-hand accounts. Actual preserved versions of a translation into Old Norse, known under the title *Páls leizla*, are not preserved in manuscripts earlier than the fifteenth century.[3]

In the passage from Augustine quoted above, the apocalypse of Paul is characterized as a text full of *fabulae*, that is, according to the widespread definition, descriptions of 'events that are neither true nor verisimilar'.[4] Yet how could Augustine be so certain that *The Apocalypse of Paul* was a *fabula*? After all, the text describes something that happened to Paul fourteen years before the writing of the second letter to the Corinthians.[5] If this 'something' ever took place, it must have been an experience as much as it was an event, and even Paul himself is uncertain as to whether he was *in corpore* or *extra corpus* during it. Only the Lord knows, he says.[6] This uncertainty as to the whereabouts of Paul's body during the rapture allows us to assume that there were no witnesses, as any spectators certainly would have noticed if Paul had been carried away *in corpore*, and would have been able to inform him afterwards.[7]

In other words, the problem with *The Apocalypse of Paul*, and with much of the later vision literature, is how the reader can possibly evaluate the truthfulness, or lack thereof, of an account of a personal experience about a contact with the divine or the transcendent to which there might not have been any witnesses, and how it is possible to categorize any text as 'truth' or 'lie'. In the case of the brief account in the letter to the Corinthians, this did not, of course,

3 Tveitane, the editor of the Old Norse version, argues that the text had already been translated before 1200. In a monograph on the Old Norse reception of vision literature, a revision of my doctoral thesis on the same subject (Wellendorf 2009), I argue for a later date.

4 The characterization of *fabula* as a type of narration follows the *Rhetorica ad Herennium*, as quoted by Mehtonen (1996: 149).

5 See II Cor 12:2: *scio hominem in Christo ante annos quattuordecim* [...] *raptum eiusmodi usque ad tertium caelum*... The customary medieval (and modern) interpretation of this passage is that Paul is speaking about himself in the third person in accordance with *vitra manna háttr*, 'the manner of wise men' as it is formulated in the Old Norse *Páls saga postula II* (267).

6 *sive in corpore nescio, sive extra corpus nescio, Deus scit.*

7 Augustine's main objection to the text was that Paul was forbidden to reveal what he saw and that this is revealed in the text despite this prohibition. This criticism is in fact anticipated and countered in the apocalypse itself, where, while in the third Heaven, the guiding angel in ch. 21.1–2 says to Paul: 'Look, no matter what I show you in this place and no matter what you hear, you must not tell it to anyone.' And he led me and he showed me, and there I heard the words that man is not permitted to utter. And again the angel said: 'Follow me once more and I will show you the things that you can speak freely of, and that you ought to tell...', *'Vide quaecunque nunc ostendero tibi in hoc loco, et quaecunque audieris, ne indices ea hominibus in terris'. Et duxit me et ostendit mihi, et audiui illuc uerba quae non licet homini loqui. [2.] Et iterum dixit: 'Adhuc enim sequere me, et monstrabo tibi quae enarrare palam et referre debeas...'* (*Apocalypsis Pauli*, 212).

pose a serious problem to medieval readers since this text is considered to be among the canonical writings and consequently true by definition. Augustine also devotes the entirety of the twelfth and final book of his *De Genesi ad litteram* (*On the literal meaning of Genesis*) to elucidating aspects of the biblical passage, in particular the Paradise to which Paul was rapt. In the same connection he outlines his theory of the different kinds of vision: the corporal, spiritual and intellectual.

Nevertheless, Augustine saw the *Apocalypsis Pauli* as a *fabula* and thereby not only as a fabrication but a lie as well; to him at least, this meant that it had no value as a means of propagating correct behaviour.[8] Others must have had a more favourable view of the text, since it could not have attained such a wide circulation otherwise.[9]

As time went by the *Apocalypsis Pauli*, and in particular the *Visio Pauli*, became the foundation of an entire genre of otherworldly journeys.[10] Unlike the *Apocalypsis Pauli*/*Visio Pauli*, these texts are not designed to fill gaps in existing narratives but are independent texts in their own right, and usually they communicate an edifying message about otherworldly reward or retribution that follows as a consequence of deeds done in this earthly life.

Still, views differ as to whether the visions of this genre are to be regarded as true or fabricated. Thus, at one end of the scale Ciccarese (1987: 9–12) argues that visions belong to the realm of literature. At the other end we find Dinzelbacher (1981: 64) who argues against such a classification of vision literature when he states that 'any text that presents itself as describing a genuine experience can claim to be regarded as a testimony of experienced reality, as long as no serious suspicions arise'. More recently he has suggested that parallels between existing visions 'are explained not so much by the fact that the authors of these texts rewrote older models – something that does happen – but mainly because the same emotional experiences lead to the same descriptions' (Dinzelbacher 1999: 44). Accordingly, he divides the large corpus of visions he considers in *Vision und Visionsliteratur im Mittelalter* into two major groups called 'experienced visions' and 'literary visions' respectively (Dinzel-

8 See Knapp (2005: 101).

9 Jiroušková (2006: 423) quotes interesting marginalia from manuscripts of the *Visio Pauli*, which shows that the scribes, or their commissioners, were not always comfortable with individual points in the text.

10 In the following the terms 'vision' and 'vision literature' are restricted to the type of visions that describe an otherworldly journey. This group of visions corresponds to what Dinzelbacher (1981) labels 'Type I' in his typology of visions or texts of the same kind as those treated by Carozzi (1994).

bacher 1981: 13–28).[11] He presents very useful lists of all the visions known to him, but one consequence of his emphasis on the (historical) experiences behind the visions is that the visions are listed chronologically according to the year in which they were supposedly experienced. If the emphasis had been on the more literary aspects of the texts, one could have arranged them according to when they were written down or perhaps by the earliest manuscript testimonies.

TRUTH CLAIMS AND AUTHENTICATING DEVICES

The body of vision literature consists of rather heterogeneous material and the texts ought not be treated *en masse* as a completely unified corpus. Rather, each text needs to be considered both on its own as well as in relation to the genre it is a part of. It is nevertheless possible to make some generalizations, which I shall do in the following. In general, no secure criteria exist for evaluating whether or not a specific vision is a faithful reproduction in writing of an actual experience or not. It is indeed questionable whether such a faithful reproduction in speech or even in writing is possible at all. An experience such as a vision will, because of its transcendent nature, lie beyond what can be expressed in words – at least for an individual without special training – and since the visionary journeys of the kind described in these texts are experienced most often by people who only have one such experience (according to the texts at least), the visionaries will usually not have been able to acquire the proficiency needed to express the ineffable in words.[12] Therefore it is necessary to leave the question of the historicity of individual visions behind and instead turn to the question of how the visions were regarded by their authors and audience. Whether the visions are 'true' or not, they must be seen as true articulations of the notions of the beyond that circulated at the time of their composition, and to a certain degree they must have been structured by the historical realities under which they were composed, transmitted and read.

Taking the point of departure in one of the customary medieval divisions of the various types of literature, namely the distinction between the three kinds of narrative *historia, argumentum* and *fabula,* we find that vision litera-

11 Some of the 'experienced visions' are even labelled 'fake' or 'possibly fake'.

12 The situation is somewhat different in the case of the mystic visionaries who experienced numerous visions. Thus Birgitta of Vadstena is supposed to have been the recipient of more than 700 visions. In sharing these visions with others, she must have acquired the proficiency necessary to express these experiences in words along the way.

ture does not readily fit into any of the categories. *Historia* was regarded as the narration of events that actually had taken place, *argumentum* as the narration of events that could have taken place but did not, and finally, as already mentioned, *fabula* recounted events that were neither true nor verisimilar.[13]

To classify all the visions as *fabulae* is inconceivable since such occurrences certainly would have been regarded as possible in a world ruled by an omnipotent God who already had taken Paul on a trip to the third Heaven and back again. That it had happened once meant that it could happen again. Furthermore, visions are mentioned in historical records such as annals and other very factual writings. In the Icelandic annals known as *Konungsannáll*, for example, one can find the entry *Leizla Duggals á Írlandi*, 'the vision/rapture of Tundale in Ireland', under the year 1149 (114).[14] A full account of the event referred to in these annals can be found in *Visio Tnugdali*, a vision which is set in Ireland in the year of 1149 and in all likelihood written in the same year.[15] Another set of Icelandic annals, the *Flateyjarannáll*, are the only Old Norse-Icelandic annals with the entry *Leizla Karls keisara*, 'The vision/rapture of Emperor Karl'. This is entered under the year of 889 (III: 514) and in all likelihood refers to the vision known as *Visio Karoli Crassi*.[16]

Works that are historical by designation, such as *Speculum historiale* by Vincent of Beauvais, also occasionally include visions.[17] Due to their inclusion in annals and other historical writings, it would seem as though *historia* was a suitable category for the visions because it was possible to experience a vision, literary narrations of such experiences could fall into the realm of *historia* as with any other narration of events that really had taken place in the past.

On the other hand, it is possible that some written visions were not based on real experiences but were invented by their authors or by the authors of the sources they used (invented in the sense that they lack a foundation in an

13 The characterization of the various types of narration in the main follows the *Rhetorica ad Herennium* as quoted by Mehtonen (1996: 149) and the treatments of this and similar passages by Green (2002: 3 ff.).

14 These annals are preserved in a manuscript that has been dated to c. 1300–28. Other Icelandic annals record this event as well, as do some continental annals. A few references can be found in Röckelein (1998: 144).

15 'This vision was seen in the year 1149 after the incarnation of the Lord', *Visa est namque ipsa visio millesimo centesimo quadragesimo nono ab incarnatione domini anno...*, *Visio Tnugdali*, 4–5. On the problems of dating the vision, see Picard and de Pontfarcy (1989: 17–29).

16 By this time the emperor Charles the Fat was already dead, so the vision has been slightly misdated in the Old Norse reference. The vision is usually dated to 885.

17 The majority of the visions that were translated into Old Norse can in fact be found in *Speculum historiale*. Most visions in Old Norse were not translated from *Speculum historiale*, but their appearance in this work shows that the visions preserved in Old Norse were among the most well-known visions.

event or experience that actually took place at some time in the past). These texts would then belong to the realm of *argumentum*. Unfortunately, as has already been mentioned, there is no way of knowing whether actual visionary experiences lie behind the individual visions or not, even though some texts might seem more fabricated than others to a modern reader. Visions were time and again regarded with suspicion. The author of one early thirteenth-century vision, *Visio Thurkilli*, writes that almost every vision has its sceptics.[18] From time to time even recorders and transmitters of visions suspected that a particular vision was untrue.[19] At least two possibilities seem to have been present: the vision could have been untrue because it was a false vision or illusion, in the sense that it did not come from God but from demons, or it could have been made up. The distinction between true and false visions (and dreams) – that is, visions (and dreams) originating from God on the one hand and from demons on the other – is a fundamental one, but at the same time it must have been extremely difficult to determine the origin of a particular experience, although according to the *Dialogues* of Gregory the Great, this was somewhat easier for saints.[20]

One writer who expressed doubts about the truthfulness of the vision he recorded was the priest Sigar, who, in 1126 (or shortly thereafter), wrote down the account of the vision of a fourteen-year-old Northumbrian boy by the name of Orm. In his prologue Sigar expresses some hesitation regarding the truthfulness of the vision, but he leaves it up to his readers, and in particular his commissioner and superior Simeon of Durham, to evaluate the vision for themselves (*Visio Ormi*, 76). Which conclusion Simeon reached in this matter is unknown. But Simeon, who was a chronicler himself and wrote a history of the Church of Durham (*Historia Dunelmensis Ecclesiae*), included a number of visions of the same kind as the vision of Orm in his *Historia*. Thus if he had continued his *Historia* until the time of Orm's experience chances are that he might have included an account of his vision as well.[21]

Even some of the people who had visions seem to have been in doubt about the divine origin of them. One example of this is found in *Visio Walteri*, which

18 ... *fere de omni revelatione a quibusdam dubitatur* (*Visio Thurkilli*, 4).

19 Schmidt (1978: 52) presents a particularly good example of this.

20 *Sancti autem uiri inter inlusiones atque reuelationes ipsas uisionum uoces aut imagines quodam intimo sapore discernunt, ut sciant uel quid a bono spiritu percipiant, uel quid ab inlusione patiantur* (*Dialogi* IV: 50).

21 A treatment of the vision of Orm and of the visions recorded by Simeon can be found in Carozzi (1994: 426–36).

is preserved in some manuscripts containing *De miraculis libri duo* by Peter the Venerable. In the middle of the night a creature appears to Walter and promises to make him wiser than any other living person if only Walter will follow him. This generous offer naturally makes Walter suspicious and the being swears that he is sent by God. Even this oath is not enough for Walter; he wants to be entirely certain, and cautiously asks for twenty-four hours to think the matter over. The following day he summons the monk (who later acts as the informant for the author of the *visio*) and two clerks. They sprinkle him with holy water and read selections from the Scripture over his head. Thus protected he awaits his nightly visitor (*Visio Walteri*, 723), who turns out not to be an evil spirit after all, but the penitent soul of a prince who died before he had time to confess the grave sins he had committed (726).

To counter the doubt that might arise regarding the veracity and truthfulness of the individual visions, some redactors or authors repeatedly state that what they write really is the truth. One example is found in a letter from Richard of St Vannes, reproduced by Hugh of Flavigny in his *Chronicon*, in connection with a record of a vision experienced in 1011 by one of the local monks, claiming: *Sane nemo autumet, hic aliquid falsatis esse permixtum, aut a veritate aliquatenus credat alienum, quoniam sicut audivimus, vidimus* (381), 'Really, no-one would say that this is confused with lies, or that it contains information that is not in accordance with the truth, since I heard it in this way, and saw it'. Furthermore, Richard stresses – five times on a single page (Hugh of Flavigny, *Chronicon*, 381) – that several brothers witnessed the incident, and emphasizes that he did not change as much as a single word in the account (382). This vision is quite unusual in so far as Richard, who wrote down the vision, claims that he sat by the side of the ecstatic monk while he was experiencing the vision, and that the unconscious monk, by the workings of the Holy Spirit, simultaneously narrated not only what he saw but also his conversations in the beyond.

Another method for stressing the veracity of the vision is found in the vision of the peasant Gottschalk, *Visio Godeschalci*. The vision is supposed to have taken place late in 1189. The most recent editor of the text dates the written composition to the later half of the following year, 1190 (*Visio Godeschalci*, 29). Here the anonymous canon who recorded the vision informs us of how he sat continuously by Gottschalk's sickbed and *ex ore ipsius seriatim visionem fideliter signavi* (150), 'from his very mouth faithfully recorded the vision in its right order'. He also assures his readers that Gottschalk is a simple peasant and therefore too stupid to tell a lie.[22]

A different strategy of authentication is used in the Carolingian *Visio Wettini* in which the reader is informed about the dangers inherent in not believing in visions. One of the tormented souls Wetti hears about in the beyond belongs to a certain bishop who refused to believe in the truthfulness of a vision once told to him. The bishop rejected this vision with the following words: *Deliramenta* [...] *somniorum non sunt adtendenda* (271), 'one should not pay attention to the nonsense of dreams'. As a consequence of his carelessness and disbelief, the bishop must pay the penalties of his damnation in the afterlife.[23] The message to the audience here is obvious: Believe in visions or you will suffer.

This need for authenticating devices and their use in the texts gives a very strong indication that it was not only possible but perhaps even common to doubt the veracity of a vision. And since there would be no point in calling what everyone knew to be a fictitious narration a lie, as is the case with *argumentum* (a narration of events that could have taken place but did not), the visions would seem to belong to the category of *historia* rather than *argumentum*.[24]

Within this threefold division, the visions seem to fit best as *historia*, but such a classification does call for some qualifications. When reading through a number of visions, one soon notices the great similarities between individual narratives, even though unique traits are found in most visions as well. These similarities stem partly from the fact that the authors were familiar with other visions, and used them as models for their own writings. If, in addition, a particular vision resembled another already well-known vision, its general trustworthiness would be greatly enhanced.[25] At first a particular vision might not fit directly into the standardized and expected framework of the genre, but during its subsequent transmission it

22 ... *nam persone simplicitas in corde versute loqui nescientis* (150). Simplicity on behalf of the visionaries seems to be a good argument for the trustworthiness of a vision. Much earlier Augustine used this claim as well in *De genesi ad litteram* 12.2.4 where he tells about a peasant who had a vision. This peasant was 'such a simple believer that I listened to him, as if I had myself seen what he said that he had seen', *verum tam simpliciter fidelis, ut eum sic audirem, ac si illud quod se vidisse narrabat, ipse vidissem* (*PL* 34, col. 455).

23 ... *suae damnationis poenas luit* (*Visio Wetini*, 270).

24 Even so, the possibility always existed that an audience would mistake fiction for *historia*.

25 See e.g. Ehlen (1998).

might be revised and reworked in order to gain greater similarity with the already known tradition of vision literature.[26]

This harmonization with the already known body of vision literature began with the authors of the original visions and must be regarded as one of the characteristic features of the process of literalization when the texts were committed to writing. Sometimes accounts of visions circulated widely orally or in written form before an author took care to write them down. Some even complained that the versions circulating were not in accordance with what really happened, and would therefore offer a corrected version. This is the case with *Visio Ulrici* and *Visio Alberici.*

Later writers continued this same process of streamlining the visions. But it was not only the authors of visions who knew earlier visions and used them as models. The person claiming to have had a vision might be familiar with the genre and its requirements as well. Whatever experience he or she might have had, the interpretation and verbalization of the experience would, to a high degree, have been predetermined by this very knowledge of how a vision should be structured. At the very least this knowledge of the usual structure of visions would have provided a necessary framework for the interpretation and the first narration of a visionary experience.

This is where the *historia* classification fails. The authors of *historia* were allowed a certain amount of embellishment so that their texts could fulfil the double purpose of being educational as well as entertaining.[27] Even the works of poets are classified under *historia* by Isidore of Seville, the difference between poets and the prose writers being primarily that the poets made use of oblique expressions (Grünkorn 1994: 44). This difference between poet and historian is, in other words, seen first and foremost on the formal level of expression, even though the content they present might well be the same. A similar strict dichotomy between form and content is found in the preface to *Visio Tnugdali* when Marcus, the author or recorder of the vision, states: 'The pen is ours, but the work is of Christ', *Noster enim stilus, set Christi est opus* (*Visio Tnugdali*, 4). Such a strict division between form and content is clearly

26 This can be readily seen if, for example, one compares the Vision of Gunthelm in its most original known version with the version of Vincent of Beauvais' *Speculum historiale* (1965: 29, chs. 6–10), where Vincent has left out a long passage with an allegorical interpretation concerning the sight of an angel leading the sun across the sky. Such allegories are usually not found in vision literature.

27 One version of the prologue to the Old Norse translation of *Visio Tnugdali* claims that the text is written 'for the entertainment, bettering and consolation of men', *til skemtanar ok umbóta mönnum ok hugganar* (*Duggals leizla*, 2).

incompatible with more recent attitudes towards texts, where any clearly demarcated division between content and form is seen as problematic – since most present-day readers would surely agree that the form in which a text is presented imbues meaning in the work as well as the content. Nevertheless, if one would want to venture an attempt at sifting the contributions of Christ from those of the author/recorder in a specimen of vision literature such as *Visio Tnugdali*, one would necessarily begin by stripping the text of its linguistic form, since this is clearly one of the elements that Marcus, the pen and the author or recorder of *Visio Tnugdali*, contributed himself as he claims to have translated the vision from a vulgar tongue (in this case Irish) into Latin: ... *de barbarico in latinum*... (4). Next one would have to strip the text of all rhetorical embellishments – devices Marcus used to great effect throughout his text. What would be left is an imagined plain narrative consisting of an introductory preface, the geographical location of the vision and a framing narrative about a sinful man who loses his consciousness during a meal and wakes up three days later, whereupon he initiates a new and better life. The account of the visionary experience itself is framed by this narrative. The visionary core of this text and many other visions is typically highly episodic and usually consists of a longer or shorter row of scenes or stations in the otherworld that might be separated by shorter intermezzos describing how the visionary and his guide move from one location to the next. In *Visio Tnugdali*, and the many other visions imitating the structure of the corresponding section of *Visio Pauli*, the scenery with its torments or pleasures at the individual stations is described first. This *ekphrasis* is typically followed by an exposition of the meaning of the sights and the reasons why souls had ended up in this location. The exposition usually takes the form of a monologue by the guide or a dialogue between the visionary and his guide. Due to the highly standardized nature of this part of the visions, it must be regarded as a formal element dictated by the requirements of the genre as well. The various sights themselves, apart from how they are described, are highly standardized as well, and texts often mention the wonderful scents, shining light and *loci amœni* as key elements in the regions of the saved and an immersion in unpleasant substances or exposure to tormenting creatures in the regions of the damned. Plenty of room is left for the ingenuities and inventiveness of the authors in these sections, particularly in the descriptions of the hellscape. Nevertheless, I would argue that this is a part of the formal aspects of the visions as well.

In cutting the visions to the bone in this admittedly rather simplistic and reductionist fashion, all that is left is a framing narrative and maybe the intangible, transcendent, original religious experience of an otherwise unknown individual, covered by multiple layers of formal elaboration. This framing narrative will, of course, have been structured by the author/recorder as well, so one must separate story from the plot (the story being the actual sequence of events and the plot the structuring of those events). After this stripping of elements, the actual historical kernel – the work of Christ – is rendered negligible and most difficult to pin down. But still, despite this lack of palpable historical fact, the authors/recorders of the visions consistently maintain that their narratives are true, such as when Marcus, the author of *Visio Tnugdali*, describes the result of his literary efforts as 'true/certain/trustworthy material', *certa materia* (4). A conflict seems to exist between the stereotyped contents of the various texts and the assurances of the authors or redactors about the truthfulness of the accounts.

MORAL TRUTHFULNESS OF THE CONTENT

Disagreement of a similar nature between authorial claims and the actual content is also found in hagiographical writings, and because visions often are treated among the legendary genres, along with saints' lives, miracles and other kinds of texts, it is worthwhile to examine how the tension between truth claims and non-historicity is tackled by the authors and students of hagiography.

Stories of particular saints or their miracles were often more or less explicitly copied or transferred from one saint to another.[28] In these cases it must have been as obvious to medieval readers as it is to modern ones that the authors simply copied the stories and miracles they thought were suitable from one *vita* to another. Alternatively, if the story of one saint resembled that of another, a hagiographer would rarely hesitate to point this out. In Old Norse hagiography this is particularly apparent in the youngest version of the life of Guðmundr the bishop, *Guðmundar saga D*.[29] The author of this saga continuously refers to other saints who have worked miracles that are similar to those worked by Guðmundr, and in one instance he copies a long passage

28 Some good examples of this can be found in Delehaye (1955: 95–100).

29 Bishop Guðmundr of Hólar (d. 1237), despite several attempts from the Icelanders and much activity in the sphere of miracle working, never received a canonization. The D-version of his saga is dated to shortly after 1343.

from the life of St Nicolas to the life of Guðmundr almost verbatim, changing only the name of the hero of the text (see Wellendorf 2009: 268–300). To counter possible criticism of his biographical and hagiological methods, the hagiographer could have referred to I Cor 12:12–20 and I Rm 12:4–5 where Paul writes about the unity between the individual limbs and the body as a whole, as did the anonymous author from Whitby in *Earliest Life of Gregory the Great*:

> So let no one be disturbed even if these miracles were performed by any other of the saints, since the holy Apostle, through the mystery of the limbs of a single body, which he compares to the living experience of the saints, concludes that we are all 'members one of another'. [...] Hence we know too that all saints have everything in common through the love of Christ of whose body they are members.
>
> Sed neque et illud moveat quemquam si quid horum de alio quolibet sanctorum fuisset effectum, cum sanctus apostulus per mysterium unius corporis membrorum, sanctorum scilicet vitam conparando concordat ut simus ad invicem alter alterius membra. [...] Inde etiam scimus sanctorum esse omnia per caritatem corporis Christi, cuius sunt membra communia. (130–1, text and trans.)

For all intents and purposes, this unity between the saints makes it of secondary importance whether a particular miracle was performed by this or that saint, since, as Ward puts it: 'What was said about one saint could equally well be said about the other' (1982: 210).

The earliest life of Gregory is a relatively old text (c. 710) and a quite idiosyncratic one in many ways.[30] Even so, utterances along the same lines can be found in much later Old Norse writings as well. This shows that the views presented by the anonymous monk of Whitby were far from unique, even though they might not be as clearly formulated elsewhere. Thus in the Icelandic manuscript *Flateyjarbók* (c. 1387–95), the compiler has inserted a discursive passage attributed to Styrmir Kárason (d. 1245) at the end of the additions to

30 Lapidge and Love (2001: 212) write about this *vita*: 'Miracles are attributed to Gregory which he could never have performed: but the author reports these on the pretext that, even if what is recorded in the *vita* about Gregory did not in fact pertain to him, there is nevertheless no doubt that it was true of him (ch. 30: *si quid horum quae scripsimus de hoc viro non fuit ... de illo eius etiam esse in magno dubitamus minime*)'.

the saga about St Óláfr. In this paragraph he comments on the veracity of the events narrated:

> Take now from the complete story of King Óláfr that which seems to you likely to be true, because in old sagas many things become mixed up. And that is not unlikely when oral tradition is all people have to rely on. But people should firmly believe in the truthfulness of the best things that are said about King Óláfr. I also expect that St Óláfr will not mind if some things are false, because it was done more for the sake of entertaining people than out of malice towards the king or to some evil end.[31]

> Hafið nú þat af samsettri sögu Óláfs konungs allri saman sem yðr lízt sannligt vera, þvíat í fornum sögum verðr mörgu saman blandat. Er þat ok eigi ólíkligt þar er menn hafa sögusögn eina til, en því trúi menn fastliga at þat mun allt sannast er frá Óláfi konungi er bezt sagt. Væntir ek þess ok at hinn heilagi Óláfr mun eigi fyrirkunna menn þó at nökkut sé falsligt í, þvíat menn hafa þat meir gert fyrir sakir skemmtanar mönnum enn til áleitni við konunginn eðr nökkurra illenda. (*Saga Óláfs konungs hins helga*, 695)

Here the most truthful account of St Óláfr is equated with the one that depicts him in the best, or in the most favourable, way. The passage is thus a means to defend a certain degree of inventiveness and freedom in relation to actual events on behalf of the saga author or compiler. As Rowe (2005: 266–7) notes, this passage is even more striking when seen in the immediate context of the manuscript, since it comes directly after the lengthy praise of St Óláfr's virtues and other accomplishments in the governmental and missionary fields. A similar but even more outright discursive section can be found in *Guðmundar saga B*.[32] The author steps back from his narrative, gives a summary of the miraculous healings and prophecies of Guðmundr and appends the following comment:

> But even though some people might consider this a lie, an innumerable multitude of men still believe that this saga is true, and as long as Chris-

31 Translation from Rowe (2005: 266). 'Oral tradition' is used to translate Old Norse *sögusögn*. Another possible translation would be 'hearsay' or 'second-hand information', in the sense that the informants were not eyewitnesses to the action.

32 The B version of the saga of Bishop Guðmundr of Hólar was written shortly after 1320 and has been characterized as an 'unsuccessful attempt to write a saint's life' (Stefán Karlsson 1993: 246). It has not yet been published in its entirety.

tianity lasts the number of people who believes this account will remain the majority. Now it is not possible to follow each opinion, since each has his own, and therefore more about Guðmundr will be written, so that it might instruct and delight those who believe this saga with good intentions, because all men know that every good thing that is said about God and his saints is true, and therefore it is good to believe the good things and bad to believe the bad things, even though they might be true. But the worst is to believe bad lies, and yet it happens that many good men believe lies, and it is not fitting if men distrust what is good and true, but trust what is evil and untrue.

En þótt sumum mönnum þykki þat nú sem lygi sé, þá er þat þó ótalligr fjöldi manna, er trúa enn þessa sögu sanna, ok svá mun jafnan meðan kristin strendr, at þeir munu fleiri, er trúa þessi frásögn. Nú má því eigi at hvers manns orði fara, at sitt þykkir hverjum satt, ok skal af því nú enn ríta fleira frá Guðmundi biskupi, at þeim veri at gagn ok gaman, er trúa með góðum hug þessi sögu, því at þat vita allir menn, at þat er allt satt, er gott er sagt frá Guði ok hans helgum mönnum, ok er því gott góðu at trúa, en illt er at trúa illu, þótt satt sé, ok allra verst því, er illt er logit, ok verðr þat þó mörgum góðum mönnum, at trúa því er logit er, ok verðr þá eigi rétt um skipt, er menn tortryggja þat, er gott [er] ok satt, en trúa því er illt er ok logit. (I: 592)

The message the anonymous author of *Guðmundar saga B* here intends to convey is difficult to translate, but the essence seems to be that as long as good things are written about the saints they are considered to be true as well. In practice this means that the historicity of an event described – whether it actually took place and did so in the manner described in the saga – is irrelevant. What is more important is that it is good (*gott*). From this the author continues to say that it is evil (*illt*) to believe evil things said about the saints (*illu*) even though they might be true (*satt*) as well. Even worse is to believe that which is *both* evil and untrue (*þat er illt er ok logit*). This means that all good things are true, no matter how loose their connection to the historical reality might be; whereas all bad things as a matter of definition are wrong or false, even though they might be (historically) true.

The truthfulness of a narration is thus not tied to the description of the historical facts on the surface level of the text, but is rather to be sought at a deeper moral or religious level. Thus the presence of an eternal truth compensates for the lack of historicity.[33] This way of looking at a narrative as 'good' and 'true' is clearly at odds with modern ways of thinking. But even though many of the lives of saints from the early church – presumably those favoured by the Old Norse translators[34] – might be more or less made up without any firm basis in a historical reality, it should be kept in mind that narratives such as saints' lives can be considered truthful without being factual at the same time. Similarly Ward writes about yet another group of texts: 'The miracles of the Virgin [...] were only "true" in the sense of being consistent with their context and embodying certain truths that could best be apprehended through them – contextual truths that are a long way from simple associations of events and records' (1982: 211).

This means that the designation 'fiction', when applied to saints' lives such as the monograph *Sacred Fictions* by Coon (1997),[35] cannot be thought of in terms of the plausible fiction of the historical novel, but rather as a truthful fiction[36] where the intended audience of the texts encounters an ahistorical but eternal truth. The hagiographic genre makes room for fictionality at the historical level without losing its truthfulness. Vollmann (2002) speaks in this regard about an 'allowed fictionality', and this fictionality is allowed as long as the narrative is morally good or edifying; and saints' lives usually are both.

This defence of the hagiographers' relaxed attitude to what we would label historical truth is readily transferable to vision literature. What it does not explain is why the redactors or authors at the same time were so eager to situate their texts in a definite historical context. But hagiographers were no less eager to do the same, which means that this objection applies to vision literature as well as to saints' lives.

Visions are rarely capable of developing typology in the same way as saints' lives, but like saints' lives they could use other visions to corroborate the truthfulness of the content of a particular vision. Thus in the late twelfth-

33 One might agree with Geary (1990: 10): 'When he [the hagiographer] did incorporate particular details and accurate descriptions, one might almost say that the author failed in his craft, because such details turn the reader's mind from the eternal ideal to the fleeting moment of this world.'

34 The earliest Old Norse preserved hagiography (c. 1150–1250) consists primarily of lives of the apostles (and other biblical characters) and fourth-century martyrs (see Wellendorf 2010). The majority of the texts are – if not completely then partially – largely fictitious.

35 Justifying the use of this designation, she writes at the end of her introduction: 'In short, all saints' lives are rhetorical, didactic, and constructed. They are sacred fictions, not factual accounts of human achievement' (Coon 1997: xxi).

36 Cf. Francis (1998: 421).

century *Visio Godeschalci B*, the author or recorder writes that although the vision he describes is hard to believe, 'we should not doubt the veracity of this vision, because we read that similar things have happened to others' (198).[37] What is most important here as an authenticating device is that the visions tell the audience what they already know, and thus confirm their belief instead of confronting it with new and hitherto unheard of details about the otherworld. In this way the writers of visions were 'more concerned about the truth of the teaching found in the vision than in whether the vision was being recounted "wie es eigentlich gewesen ist"', as McGinn notes about other kinds of visions, namely those experienced by the late medieval mystics (2005: 236).

In some cases, material that is not in accordance with the common faith still surfaces in the written texts and the author/redactor of the vision must deal with it. An illustrative example of this is found in *Visio Walteri*. During his vision Walter is told how the damned souls will fall into the great pit on Judgement Day and then turned into demons. To this the (anonymous) authorial 'I' adds the following comment:

> Here when I had objected to Walter that this departed from the truth – 'Will the men', I say, 'who die not remain men?' – he persistently affirmed that this was what he [the otherworldly guide] had said. This might possibly be accepted if understood in the figurative sense; that men are said to be turned into demons, in the same way as the devil in a figurative sense is called man, as in 'Rise Lord so that man does not prevail' (Ps 9:20) and 'The hostile man sowed weeds [among the wheat]' (Mt 13:25). But let us return to the story, after this Walter said...

> Hic cum obiecissem Gualtero, quod hoc dissonet a vero, 'Neque' inquam 'homines, qui peribunt, homines non erunt', constanter affirmavit, quod sic ille dixerit. Quod bene fortassis per figuram potest accipi, ut sic homines fieri dicantur demones, sicut diabolus per figuram dicitur homo ut 'exurge Domine non prevaleat homo' (*Ps* 9,20) et ‚inimicus homo superseminavit zizinia' (*Mt* 13,25). Sed ut ad narrationem redeamus, post hec Gualterus dixit... (725)

37 *Nec tamen diffidendum est vera esse, que dicit, eciam si racio difficile reperitur, cum similia quibusdam accidisse legamus.*

In this way the author saves the potentially dubious contents of the vision by arguing that one should not interpret the passage literally, but rather figuratively. That authors of visions have to resort to the figurative sense of the events described in visions is quite unusual within this genre; usually the stories are to be taken at face value. But this might be taken as an indication of the willingness of this particular author to disseminate the vision in the raw form in which he heard it himself, rather than interfering with it.[38]

That the author is eager to fit the story into the accepted and well-known visionary and biblical framework for a vision is apparent from a remark in the beginning of the same vision. When Walter tells how the otherworldly guide leads him away, the author asks whether his body remained in his bed during the vision. Clearly the aspect is of interest to the author because of the passage in Paul's second letter quoted above (in note 6) where Paul states that he does not know whether he was carried away with his body or not. But just as Paul was uncertain about this, so was Walter (723). Thus the text offers no new knowledge about this point, but what it says fits readily within the well-known biblical framework.[39]

Returning to the threefold division of narrative presented above, it seems clear that visions do not readily fit into any of the three types, but must belong somewhere between *historia*, the true record of events that had taken place, and *argumentum*, the narration of a fictitious event that could have taken place. Were we to conceive of a category between the two, fitting for visions as well as hagiographic writings in general, it could be defined as 'a true record of events that could have taken place'. In other words, what we find in the visions is somewhat analogous to the truth clothed in lies that, according to Thomasîn von Zerklaere, was to be found in romances,[40] although the setting is naturally different in the case of visions. In contradistinction to romances, visions

38 Other authors/redactors seem to have had exacted less restraint. Interesting in this connection is Otloh of St Emmeram who concludes the preface to his *Liber visionum tum suarum tum aliorum* ('Book of his own visions as well as those of others') with a remark that although he has written everything as it was seen, he has abbreviated and left out the parts that were not edifying (*... ad aedificationem nullam pertinere*), with the edification of believers as the stated purpose of Otloh's book. On one possible meaning of *aedificatio* in this context, see Joyce (2007: 89–94).

39 This concern for the whereabouts of the body during visions is also found in a few other texts, such as *Visio Ulrici* (written around 1246, but seen in 1240) where the passage from Paul's letter is directly quoted (210). Most often, however, it is, clear that the body is left behind.

40 Quoted by Haug (1997: 237–8). The quotation concerns romances and is from his book on courtly etiquette, *Der Welsche Gast* (1215), but equally valid for vision literature. Thomasîn acknowledges that even though the romances are fabricated, they still contain truths. But he also suggests that readers, as soon as they have gained the most basic understanding, move on to heavier reading material (ll. 1107–1126).

might be historically true, but morally speaking they are, as long as they have the right origin, certainly true. In written form, visions were presented as accurate accounts of historical events and a number of literary and structural devices were used to attain this goal. At the same time, however, the visions were structured to a very high degree by the constraints and conventions of the genre to which they belonged and many things needed to be considered. If a particular detail in the initial account of a vision was not in accordance with what was expected, the detail was likely to be suppressed by the author/redactor/scribe, or somehow explained away. The most important aspect for the recorders and authors of visions seems to be the truthfulness of the lesson one could learn from the visions, i.e. that they were edifying. To attain this goal the historical truth might have to yield. In this way the visions seem to rest on the boundary between *historia* and *argumentum*, at times one prevailing over the other.

References

Many visions are only available in their original Latin versions (those used here are listed below), but collections of visions translated into modern languages have appeared in English (Gardiner 1989), German (Dinzelbacher 1989), French (Micha 1992) and Italian (1987). A separate translation of *Visio Tnugdali* into English has been published by Jean-Michel Picard and Yolanne de Pontfarcy (1989). A comprehensive list of editions of visions in Latin can be found in Dinzelbacher (1981: 13–28). Since 1981 a number of new editions have appeared and references to some of these can be found in the bibliography to *The Revelation of the Monk of Eynsham* (2002); more recent are the editions of *The Vision of the Monk of Wenlock* (2005) and *Visio Pauli* (2006).

TEXTS

Apocalypsis Pauli, ed. Claude Carozzi in *Eschatologie et au-delà: Recherches sur l'*Apocalypse de Paul, Aix-en-Provence: Publications de l'Université de Provence, 1994: 186–262.

Augustinus, *De Genesi ad litteram*, ed. J. P. Migne, *Patrologia Latina* 34. Paris, 1844–65. The *Patrologia Latina Database* is issued by ProQuest Information and Learning Company (http://pld.chadwyck.co.uk/).

Augustinus, *In Iohannis evangelium tractatus CXXIV*, ed. D. R. Willems, *Corpus Christianorum, Series Latina* 36, Turnhout: Brepols, 1954.

De libris recipiendis et non recipiendis, ed. Ernst v. Dobschütz in *Das Decretum Gelasianum de libris recipiendis et non recipiendis*, Leipzig: J. C. Hinrichs'sche Buchhandlung, 1912.

Duggals leizla, ed. Peter Cahill in *Duggals leiðsla, Rit* 25, Reykjavík: Stofnun Árna Magnússonar, 1983.

Earliest Life of Gregory the Great by an Anonymous Monk of Whitby, ed. Bertram Colgrave, Cambridge: Cambridge University Press, 1985. [First published in 1968.]

Flateyjarannáll in *Flateyjarbók: en Samling af norske Konge-Sagaer med indskudte mindre Fortællinger om Begivenheder i og udenfor Norge: samt Annaler.*

Flateyjarbók: en Samling af norske Konge-Sagaer med indskudte mindre Fortællinger om Begivenheder i og udenfor Norge: samt Annaler, ed. Carl Rikard Unger and Guðbrandur Vigfússon, Christiania: Malling, 1860–69.

Gregory the Great, *Dialogi*, ed. Adalbert de Vogüé, Paris: Les éditions du cerf, 1978–80.

Guðmundar saga B in *Biskupa sögur*, ed. Jón Sigurðsson and Guðbrandur Vigfusson, Kaupmannahöfn: Hið íslenzka bókmenntafélag, 1858–78.

Hugh of Flavigny, *Chronicon*, ed. Georg Heinrich Pertz, *MGH, SS* VIII, Stuttgart: Anton Hiersemann, 1963.

Islandske Annaler indtil 1578, ed. Gustav Storm, Oslo: Norsk historisk kjeldeskriftsinstitutt, 1977. [First published in 1888].

Konungsannáll in *Islandske Annaler indtil 1578.*

Otloh of St Emmeram, *Liber visionum tum suarum tum aliorum*, ed. J. P. Migne, *Patrologia Latina* 146, Paris, 1844–65. The *Patrologia Latina Database* is issued by ProQuest Information and Learning Company (http://pld.chadwyck.co.uk/).

Páls leizla, ed. Matthias Tveitane in *En norrøn versjon av Visio Pauli*, volume 3 of *Årbok for Universitetet i Bergen. Humanistisk serie 1965*, Bergen: Norwegian University Press, 1965.

Páls saga postula II in *Postola sögur: Legendariske fortællinger om Apostlernes liv, deres kamp for kristendommens udbredelse samt deres martyrdød*, ed. Carl Rikard Unger, Christiania: B. M. Bentzen, 1874.

Saga Óláfs konungs hins helga: Efter pergamenthåndskrift i Kungliga biblioteket i Stockholm Nr. 2 4to, eds. Oscar Albert Johnsen and Jón Helgason, Oslo: Jacob Dybwad, 1941.

The Revelation of the Monk of Eynsham, ed. Robert Easting, Oxford: Oxford University Press, 2005.

The Vision of the Monk of Wenlock, ed. Patrick Sims-Williams in 'A Recension of Boniface's Letter to Eadburg about the Monk of Wenlock's Vision', in *Latin Learning and English Lore: Studies in Anglo-Saxon Literature for Michael Lapidge I*, ed. Katherine O'Brien O'Keeffe and Andy Orchard, Toronto: University of Toronto Press, 2005.

Vincent of Beauvais, *Speculum Historiale*, Graz: Akademische Druck u. verlagsanstalt, 1965. [First published in 1624.]

Visio Alberici, ed. Paul Gerhard Schmidt in 'Visio Alberici: Die Jenseitswanderung des neunjährigen Alberich in der vom Visionär um 1127 in Monte Cassino revidierten Fassung', *Sitzungsberichte Wissenschaftlichen Gesellschaft an der Johann Goethe-Universität Frankfurt/Main* 35, 1997, pp. 149–212.

Visio Godeschalci, ed. Erwin Assmann, *Godeschalcus und Visio Godeschalci: mit deutscher Übersetzung, Quellen und Forschungen zur Geschichte Schleswig-Holsteins* 74, Neumünster: Wachholtz, 1979.

Visio Gunthelmi, ed. Giles Constable in 'The vision of Gunthelm and Visions Attributed to Peter the Venerable', *Revue Bénédictine* 66 (1956): 92–114.

Visio Ormi, ed. Hugh Farmer in 'The Vision of Orm', *Analecta Bollandiana* 75 (1957): 72–82.

Visio Pauli in *Die Visio Pauli: Wege und Wandlungen einer orientalischen Apokryphe im lateinischen Mittelalter unter Einschluß der alttschechischen und deutschsprachigen Textzeugen*, ed. Lenka Jiroušková, Leiden: Brill 2006.

Visio Thurkilli, ed. Paul Gerhard Schmidt, Leipzig: Teubner, 1978.

Visio Tnugdali, ed. Albrecht Wagner, Erlangen: Andreas Diechert, 1882.

Visio Ulrici, ed. Johannes Grabmayer in 'Visio quam Ulricus sacerdos vidit. Die Vision des Propstes Ulrich von Völkermarkt im Jahre 1240', *Mediaevistik* 9 (1996): 209–15.

Visio Walteri, ed. Paul Gerhard Schmidt in Wilhelm Heizmann et al. (eds.) *Runica – Germanica – Mediaevalia*, Ergänzungsbände zum Reallexikon der germanischen Altertumskunde 37, Berlin: De Gruyter, 2003, pp. 722–6.

Visio Wettini ed. Ernst Dümmler in *Poetae Latini aevi Carolini (II)*, MGH *Poetae Latini medii aevi* II, Berlin, 1884.

Vulgata, ed. R. Gryson et al., Stuttgart: Deutsche Bibelgesellschaft, 1994.

STUDIES

Carozzi, Claude (1994) *Le voyage de l'âme dans l'au-delà d'après la littérature latine (V^e–XIIIe siècle)*, École française de Rome.

Ciccarese, Maria Pia (1987) *Visioni dell'aldilà in occidente: Fonti, modelli, testi* (Biblioteca patristica), Firenze: Nardini Editore.

Coon, Lynda L. (1997) *Sacred Fictions: Holy Women and Hagiography in Late Antiquity*, Philadelphia: University of Pennsylvania Press.

Delahaye, H. (1955) *Les légendes hagiographiques*, 4th edition (Subsidia hagiographica 18), Bruxelles: Société des Bollandistes.

Dinzelbacher, Peter (1981) *Vision und Visionsliteratur im Mittelalter*, Stuttgart: Anton Hiersemann.

Dinzelbacher, Peter (1989) *Mittelalterliche Visionslitteratur: Eine Anthologie*, Darmstadt: Wissenschaftliche Buchgesellschaft.

Dinzelbacher, Peter (1999) *Die letzten Dinge: Himmel, Hölle, Fegefeuer im Mittelalter*, Freiburg: Herder.

Ehlen, Thomas (1998) 'Vision und Schrift – Interessen, Prozeß und Typik der Verschriftlichung hochmittelalterlicher Jenseitsreisen in lateinischer Sprache am Beispiel der "Visio Edmundi monachi de Eynsham"', in Thomas Ehlen, Johannes Mangei and Elisabeth Stein (eds.), *Visio Edmundi monachi de Eynsham: Interdisziplinäre Studien zur mittelalterlichen Visionsliteratur*, Tübingen: Gunter Narr Verlag, pp. 251–300.

Francis, James A. (1998) 'Truthful Fiction: New Questions to Old Answers. On Philostratus' *Life of Apollonius*', *American Journal of Philology* 119: 419–41.

Gardiner, Eileen (1989) *Medieval Visions of Heaven and Hell: A Sourcebook*, New York: Garland Publishing.

Geary, Patrick J. (1990) *Furta sacra: Thefts of Relics in the Central Middle Ages*, revised edition, Princeton: Princeton University Press.

Green, Dennis H. (2002) *The Beginnings of Medieval Romance: Fact and Fiction, 1150–1220*, Cambridge: Cambridge University Press.

Grünkorn, Gertrud (1994) *Die Fiktionalität des höfischen Romans um 1200*, Berlin: Erich Schmidt Verlag.

Haug, Walter (1997) *Vernacular Literary Theory in the Middle Ages: The German Tradition, 800–1300, in Its European Context*. Translated by Joanna M. Catling, Cambridge: Cambridge University Press.

Hughes, Shaun (2005) 'Late Secular Poetry', in Rory McTurk (ed.), *A Companion to Old Norse–Icelandic Literature and Culture*, Malden, MA: Blackwell Publishing, pp. 205–22.

Jiroušková, Lenka (2006) *Die Visio Pauli: Wege und Wandlungen einer orientalischen Apokryphe im lateinischen Mittelalter unter Einschluß der alttschechischen und deutschsprachigen Textzeugen*, Leiden: Brill.

Joyce, Ellen (2007) 'Speaking of Spiritual Matters: Visions and the Rhetoric of Reform in the *Liber Visionum* of Otloh of St Emmeram', in Alison I. Beach (ed.), *Manuscripts and Monastic Culture: Reform and Renewal in Twelfth-Century Germany*, Turnhout: Brepols, pp. 69–98.

Knapp, Franz Peter (2005) *Historie und Fiktion in der mittelalterlichen Gattungspoetik (II)*, Heidelberg: Universitätsverlag Winter.

Lapidge, Michael and Rosalind C. Love (2001) 'The Latin Hagiography of England and Wales (600–1550)', in G. Philippart (ed.), *Hagiographies*, vol. III, Turnhout: Brepols, pp. 203–325.

McGinn, Bernard (2005) 'Visions and Visualizations in the Here and Hereafter', *Harvard Theological Review* 98, no. 3: 227–46.

Mehtonen, Päivi (1996) *Old Concepts and New Poetics:* Historia, Argumentum, *and* Fabula *in the Twelfth- and Early Thirteenth-Century Latin Poetics of Fiction*, Helsinki: Societas Scientiarum Fennica.

Micha, Alexandre (1992) *Voyages dans l'au-delà: D'après des textes médiévaux IVᵉ–XIIIᵉ siècles*, Paris: Klincksieck.

Picard, Jean-Michel and Yolanne de Pontfarcy (1989), *The Vision of Tnugdal*, Dublin: Four Courts Press.

Piovanelli, Pierluigi (2000) 'The Miraculous Discovery of the Hidden Manuscript, or the Para-Textual Function of the Prologue to the *Apocalypse of Paul*', in G. J. Brooke and J.-D. Kaestli (eds.), *Narrativity in Biblical and Related Texts*, Leuven: Leuven University Press, pp. 265–82.

Rowe, Elizabeth Ashman (2002) '*Sörla þáttr*: The Literary Adaptation of Myth and Legend', *Saga-Book* 26: 38–66.

Rowe, Elizabeth Ashman (2005) *The Development of Flateyjarbók: Iceland and the Norwegian Dynastic Crisis of 1389*, Odense: The University Press of Southern Denmark.

Röckelein, Hedwig (1998) 'Geschichtsbewußtsein in hochmittelalterlichen jenseitsvisionen', in Hans-Werner Goetz (ed.), *Hochmittelalterliches Geschichtsbewußtsein im Spiegel nichthistoriographischer Quellen*, Berlin: Akademie Verlag, pp. 143–60.

Schmidt, P. G. (1978) 'The Vision of Thurkill', *Journal of the Warburg and Courtauld Institutes* 41: 50–64.

Stefán Karlsson (1993) 'Guðmundar sögur biskups', in Phillip Pulsiano (ed.), *Medieval Scandinavia: An Encyclopedia*, New York and London: Garland Publishing, pp. 245–6.

Vollmann, Benedikt Konrad (2002) 'Erlaubte Fiktionalität: Die Heiligenlegende', in Franz Peter Knapp and Manuela Niesner (eds.), *Historisches und fiktionales Erzählen im Mittelalter*, Berlin: Duncker & Humblot, pp. 63–72.

Ward, Benedikta (1982) *Miracles and the Medieval Mind: Theory, Record and Event, 1000–1215*, London: Scholar Press.

Wellendorf, Jonas (2009) *Kristelig visionslitteratur i norrøn tradition* (Bibliotheca Nordica 2), Oslo: Novus forlag.

Wellendorf, Jonas (2010) 'The Attraction of the Earliest Old Norse Vernacular Hagiography', in Haki Antonsson and Ildar H. Garipzanov (eds.), *Saints and Their Lives on the Periphery: Veneration of Saints in Scandinavia and Eastern Europe (c. 1000–1200)*, Turnhout: Brepols, pp. 241–58.

The Growth of Consciousness of Fiction in Old Norse Culture

Else Mundal

The development of fiction in Old Norse culture (medieval Norway and Iceland) can be investigated from two rather different points of view. We can look for what we, scholars in modern times, regard as fiction in Old Norse texts, or we can look for signs which indicate the presence of a consciousness of fiction in Old Norse texts and their social setting. My focus in this article will be on the latter, how fiction and a consciousness of fiction developed, in which kinds of texts, and how fiction is signalled by the authors. Related to these topics is the question of the possible restrictions on fiction in Old Norse culture. What scholars have regarded as fiction is another question than the consciousness of fiction in the Old Norse society, but the two topics are related, and cannot be entirely separated. Some scholars – both scholars in the past and scholars of today – seem to assume that people in the Middle Ages had more or less the same understanding of what fiction was as we have today, a discussion to which I will return below. Another view that has had some adherents is that people in the Middle Ages – or in the early Middle Ages – were not able to distinguish between historical truth and fiction, and consequently there was no consciousness of fiction either.

In discussing the existence – or the development – of fiction in Old Norse culture, the notion of 'fiction' has been closely connected to the changing view of the historical reliability or even 'truth' of the different saga genres. The *fornaldarsǫgur* ('sagas of ancient times') were discounted as historical sources even before the scholarly debate began in the early eighteenth century.[1] This late medieval saga genre (the first written sagas of this type may have originated around the middle of the thirteenth century) deals with events which for the most part took place in mainland Scandinavia before the settlement in

1 See *Árni Magnússon, Brevveksling med Torfæus* (Copenhagen, 1916), quoted and commented on in Mundal (1977: 13–16).

Iceland (in the late ninth century). The stories are told in a non-realistic mode, and fantastic and supernatural elements are frequently used. Sagas of kings (a productive genre from the late twelfth century up to the 1260s) have never been completely rejected as historical accounts. However, sagas – or chronicles – about kings may differ greatly from each other. Some of these sagas or chronicles tell about kings who lived long ago, others about contemporary kings or kings in the recent past. The few existing Latin chronicles in particular may have a brief form,[2] but the sagas in Old Norse normally have a broader narrative style with developed scenes, dialogues, descriptions of characters and other elements that cannot be historically true in a narrow sense – at least not in the cases where these texts describe events in the distant past.

Another genre that has never been rejected as history is the so-called contemporary sagas. These sagas were written as individual sagas in the thirteenth century, but are in most cases preserved only in the compilation *Sturlunga saga* from the end of the century. They describe events in Iceland in the authors' recent past. The authors themselves may have witnessed the events they are telling about, or they may have the stories from first-hand eyewitnesses. These are facts that contribute to the reliability of these sagas. On the other hand, it is obvious that both sagas of kings and contemporary sagas were in many cases written by great artists who had ambitions far beyond enumerating historical facts. The question of the relationship between fiction and history in the Middle Ages is therefore a highly relevant one in connection with these genres.

Like the Icelandic contemporary sagas the most famous Old Norse narrative texts, namely the sagas of Icelanders,[3] describe Icelandic heroes, in most cases chieftains or sons of chieftains; but these sagas from the thirteenth century – or in some cases later – are concerned with long-past events that took place in the time of settlement in Iceland:[4] feuds between two or more Icelandic families, and other events which took place in the period from the last part of the ninth century to the first part of the eleventh century. There is thus a long stretch of time between the events that are described and the time of the authors – roughly 200–400 years. The literary form of these sagas, however, conveys a much more trustworthy impression than the *fornaldarsǫgur*. The

2 Cf. Mortensen's contribution in the present volume.

3 The term 'family sagas' was previously the most common genre term; this genre is now also called 'sagas about early Icelanders'.

4 The settlement started in the late ninth century and continued on into the tenth century.

sagas of Icelanders are written in a realistic mode, the so-called saga realism, with a modest use of fantastic elements compared to the *fornaldarsǫgur*. Typical of the saga style, and most developed in the sagas of Icelanders, is a seemingly objective author who reports what once could be seen or heard and only in exceptional cases reveals what people thought. The seemingly objective descriptions may have contributed to the impression of trustworthiness. The view regarding the historical accuracy of the sagas of Icelanders has changed over time, and not only once. The sagas of Icelanders have been characterized as fiction by some scholars in some periods of time, and as history – or some kind of history – by other scholars belonging to other schools and periods.

The more doubt one casts on the historicity of a text or a genre, the easier it is to classify the literature in question as fiction. This means that there have been only a few objections to characterizing the *fornaldarsǫgur* as fiction of some sort. As regards the sagas of Icelanders, the classification of this literature as fiction has been, and is, both complicated and disputed.

The scholarly debate on the presence and the development of fiction in Old Norse culture has concentrated on these two genres, the *fornaldarsǫgur* and the sagas of Icelanders, plus a third genre, the *riddarasǫgur* (sagas of chivalry) – which originated in the translations of French poems into Old Norse prose in Norway in the thirteenth century, but later became a productive genre in Iceland (see below).

THE PERCEPTION OF 'HISTORICAL TRUTH' IN OLD NORSE CULTURE

In addition to the questions of whether a text should be regarded as history or fiction, and whether by 'fiction' we mean a text that people in the Middle Ages looked upon as fiction or a text scholars in modern times regard as fiction, there is the important question of how widely or narrowly we define the concept of 'history'. A narrow definition of history will leave us with a lot of medieval texts that must be regarded as some sort of fiction – at least from a modern point of view. A broader definition of history will make it possible to include a text in history that contains many details which cannot be true in a narrower sense. How history or historical truth was understood in Old Norse culture is therefore closely connected to the question of whether there was a consciousness of fiction in this culture, and, if so, how a fictional text, or oral story, was recognized by the audience and signalled by the author or the storyteller.

In the scholarly discussion of whether some of the saga genres should be regarded as fiction or history, scholars have normally taken their point of departure in the understanding of these two concepts in their own time. In an article published in 1967 the Russian scholar Mikail Steblin-Kamenskij put the question:

> Must he [the scholar] not, contrary to usual practice, begin with what these works were intended to be by their contemporaries, rather than with what they seem to be to us? Is not a literary work, generally speaking, something which is meant to be this or that for its contemporaries, rather than something which is this or that in itself? (Steblin-Kamenskij: 1967: 77)

Steblin-Kamenskij followed up this discussion in his later book *The Saga Mind* (1973).[5] He argued that people living in a mainly oral culture in the early Middle Ages divided oral stories, as well as written stories, into other categories than we do in modern times. According to Steblin-Kamenskij, people in the Middle Ages were not able to distinguish between historical truth in a narrow sense, 'the exact report of what has occured', and an image of the past 'in all its fullness' reproduced by a creative author. The last kind of truth – which from a modern point of view was a kind of fiction – he called 'artistic truth'. However, since people in the Middle Ages did not distinguish between these two kinds of truth, they recognized only one kind, which he labelled 'syncretic truth' (Steblin-Kamenskij: 1973: 22).

Steblin-Kamenskij's term 'syncretic truth' could have been useful as a label for a kind of truth in saga literature which comprised both historical truth – in a narrow as well as in a broad sense – and fictional stories about the past in which people were supposed to believe, had it not been for his view that this was the only kind of truth that existed in Old Norse society. Steblin-Kamenskij's reason for introducing the term 'syncretic truth', that people in the Middle Ages were not able to distinguish between different kinds of truth, has been criticized by many scholars, first by Peter Hallberg (Hallberg 1974). Since the concepts of 'fiction' and 'historical truth' must be seen in relation to each other, there is good reason to look for a consciousness of historical truth – or even different kinds of historical truth – before investigating the concept and the consciousness of 'fiction' in Old Norse culture.

5 Original title *Mir Sagi* (1971).

If we take a look at a few Old Norse texts in which the authors themselves comment on the truth of their own text, I think that it becomes obvious that the authors – and their audience – were able to distinguish between history in the narrow sense, as the exact report of what has occurred, and stories that could be more or less true. A good example of this can be found in the oldest preserved work in Old Norse, Ari fróði's *Íslendingabók* ('Book of the Icelanders'), written in the 1120s. In the prologue of the work Ari says that whatever is wrong in the book should be replaced by what proves to be more correct.[6] Statements like these are often found in prologues of medieval texts; they are stereotypes, but not without meaning.[7] Whether the authors really meant that others were free to correct their text or not, such phrases demonstrate that writers in the Middle Ages were conscious of the fact that some information in a text could be unreliable. In chapter 1 of *Íslendingabók* Ari mentions his sources: they are old people with a good memory who possessed knowledge about many things and told the truth.[8] The fact that he mentions his sources and the importance attached to good memory, learning and truthfulness shows the same awareness as in the prologue of the distinction between historical truth in a narrow sense and stories that were not reliable, or not reliable to the same degree.

Around 1180 the Norwegian monk Theodoricus wrote his chronicle *Historia de antiquitate regum Norwagiensium*. In chapter 1 he mentions the year 858 as the year when King Haraldr Finehair came to power, and he says he has come to this result by asking the Icelanders who know more about such things than others.[9] In the prologue of his work he mentions that the Icelanders remember the past in their poetry.[10] Here he probably expresses the same trust in the skaldic poetry's capability for preserving historically true accounts over time as Snorri Sturluson did later (see below).

However, Theodoricus admits that since there were no written sources from that time, the exact year of King Haraldr's reign is impossible to know for certain. As we can see, Theodoricus has faith in the tradition, but he is very

6 'En hvatki es missagt es í frœðum þessum, þá es skylt at hafa þat heldr, es sannara reynisk' (*Íslendingabók* I1: 3. Here and later there are references to chapters in the text, to pages in the footnotes).

7 See Sverrir Tómasson (1988: 155–63). This book offers an overview and discussion of prologues in Old Norse literature.

8 *Íslendingabók* I1: 4.

9 Storm (ed.) (1880: 6).

10 *qui hæc in suis antiquis carminibus percelebrata recolunt* (Storm (ed.) 1880: 3).

well aware of the fact that historical accuracy is not easily combined with oral culture.

Snorri wrote his sagas of kings in the 1220s and around 1230. In the prologue to both *Heimskringla* and *The Separate Saga of St. Óláfr*,[11] it is obvious that the author is aware of the fact that stories can be more or less true. Snorri's belief in the truth of skaldic poetry about contemporary events is well known, and he quoted skaldic stanzas throughout his sagas as proof of the truth of his stories. He regarded these compact oral texts that obey a number of formal rules as nearly equivalent to written sources in terms of their ability to pass on historical truth in a narrow sense. In his prologues Snorri gives his reasons for trusting his sources,[12] showing that he is conscious of historical truth in a narrow sense.

At the same time Snorri admits in his prologues that he has included stories about times of old

> with which people have entertained themselves; and although we do not know for sure whether these accounts are true, yet we know that old and learned men considered them to be so.[13]

If we look at how Snorri worked – which we are able to do because we know many of his written sources – we can see that Snorri often made changes. He could, for instance, change or add dialogues, put in descriptions of characters, provide causal links, and so on.[14] Of course Snorri was aware that the elements which he himself had added to the text were not historically true in a narrow sense, and a Norwegian or Icelandic thirteenth-century audience would probably have understood that many elements in a saga text did not correspond precisely to actual events or verbal exchanges that had taken place. Still Snorri, and other saga authors, presented their sagas as true stories, or history, and they could do this because they obviously operated with a concept of 'historical truth' both in a narrow and in a broad – in fact in a very broad – sense.

11 Published with the title *Den store saga om Olav den hellige* by Oscar Albert Johnsen and Jón Helgason (Oslo, 1941).

12 Finnur Jónsson (ed.) (1911: 2–3).

13 'er menn hafa haft til skemtanar sér, en þó at vér vitim eigi sannyndi á því, þá vitum vér dœmi til þess, at gamlir frœðimenn hafa slíkt fyrir satt haft' (Finnur Jónsson (ed.) 1911: 1). Translations from Old Norse and Scandinavian languages are my own if not stated otherwise.

14 See Lie (1937). Snorri and other authors within Old Norse culture were not the only ones who allowed themselves rewritings of this kind. This was also widely accepted among authors of medieval Latin chronicles; see O'Connor (2005: 116).

The ability to distinguish between history in a narrow and a broader sense, or between reliable stories and stories that could not be trusted, could of course be seen in connection with the arrival of writing and the written culture to which the authors mentioned above belonged. As we have seen, Theodoricus explicitly mentioned the lack of written sources as the reason for not being able to guarantee the exactness of his chronology. On the other hand, it does not seem reasonable that the *ability* to distinguish between strictly historical accounts and less reliable stories came as a result of written culture. The question of truth and lies was something people had to face in everyday life – in medieval oral culture as well. However, there was no *possibility* for the storyteller in the oral culture to distinguish between historical truth and lies except in cases when he could narrate events that he himself had experienced, or when he could build his story upon reports from other trustworthy eyewitnesses; but most stories told in Old Norse saga literature – and in the oral tradition on which the authors built – were not stories about the present or the recent past, they were stories about the remote past.

Skaldic poetry may have been regarded as more reliable than other forms of oral tradition long before the time of Theodoricus and Snorri, but as the examples above clearly show, people in the Old Norse written culture were aware of the fact that the written document helped to preserve exact reports of what had occurred in quite another way than oral tradition, and there is no reason to believe that the insight that oral tradition changed came as something new with the written culture. It is to underestimate the people in Old Norse society to believe that they regarded the truth in stories about the remote past to be of the same kind as the truth in stories about yesterday. The broad meaning of 'historical truth' found in Old Norse culture has nothing to do with *ability,* but rather with *possibility*. People in the Old Norse oral culture possessed the concept of 'history' that functioned in an oral culture. The arrival of writing made it possible to pass on history in a more narrow sense, but the old concept of history continued to be the one commonly used in stories about the past – and in fact Old Norse society continued to be mainly an oral culture for a long time after the arrival of writing.

It seems at first glance that people in Old Norse culture did not distinguish between more or less true stories, with the word *saga* referring to all of them. I will come back to the question of whether, within the broad category of saga, and in spite of the common term, characteristics can be found that signal different truth claims in different groups of saga literature.

It is a fact that even within the sagas of kings the notion of 'historical truth' seems to have a very broad meaning, and these sagas seem to embody much which we, from a modern point of view, would classify as fiction. However, the attitudes to historical truth in modern times and in the Middle Ages are perhaps not so different from each other as it would seem at first glance, and it is important to stress that both in the Middle Ages and in more recent times the concept of 'historical truth' may differ from one context to another. In modern times even a rather narrow definition of historical truth would normally include more than an enumeration of facts. The term 'history' also includes the scholars' theories about what happened and why. Writing history involves conjuring up a convincing image of the past and explaining historical processes. Historians of today present their sources, their theories, their discussion of problems and their solution, or their view of what happened and why. Snorri – and other authors of sagas – presented their theories and their view of what had happened in the form of a story, and we are no longer able to distinguish between historical facts, the author's sources and the author's theory of how things had most likely happened and why.[15]

If we compare Old Norse texts, and the division of these texts according to their attitudes towards factuality, to classical texts and their division into *historia, argumentum* and *fabula,* a difference appears. The Old Norse word 'saga' covers the whole spectrum. The question of truth and fiction is obviously not the most important criterion for dividing texts into groups of texts or into genres. In the Old Norse corpus there is no sharp division between what is defined as *historia* in the classical tradition (the exact report of what has occurred) and *argumentum* (a story that is not necessarily true, but which might be true). What is presented as truth, but probably as slightly different kinds of truth in different groups of sagas, covers both *historia* and *argumentum* – and probably even cuts into *fabula* as well (a story that is not true and that could not be true). The saga authors, and especially the authors of sagas of Icelanders – and before them probably the sagatellers too – seem to have taken delight in the border area between the real and the fantastic. We find exaggerations of different kinds, often in descriptions of the deeds of the heroes, which are almost unbelievable. We find stories about the hero's struggle with the dead in the grave mound, a few instances of stories about trolls, and so on. A characteristic of the so-called realistic saga genres is that

15 See Mundal (1994); Bjarni Guðnason (1979).

this literature, which is also presented as some sort of history, challenges the borderline of realism. This is not necessarily a sign that the authors and their audience were not aware of this borderline or that it was not important. On the contrary, this playing with the boundaries between the real and the fantastic, the balance on the edge so to speak, even in texts that claim to tell of true events, may very well indicate an awareness of this line. However, the division into categories of texts in Old Norse culture does not conform with the categories in modern culture nor with the categories in classical culture. This fact is a complicating factor when discussing 'history' and 'fiction' in an Old Norse context.

SAGAS OF ICELANDERS – FACT OR FICTION?

As already stated, the sagas of Icelanders, such as the famous *Egils saga* (dated by most scholars to the 1230s) and *Njáls saga* (from the last decades of the thirteenth century), have been classified as fiction during different periods and by scholars belonging to different schools.

As early as in the last decades of the eighteenth century and the turn of the nineteenth century a group of German scholars deprived saga literature of its value as a historical source. One of these German scholars, August L. Schlözer, argued that the saga literature imitated continental (*Provençale*) literature (Schlözer 1771), and in his important book *Die Edda,* Friedrich Rühs (1812) characterized the sagas of Icelanders as *romane* (novels). The reason for reconsidering the view of saga literature – which, with the exception of the *fornaldarsǫgur,* had been regarded as some sort of history up to that time – was partly due to the disbelief in the oral tradition's ability to preserve historical truth. According to these scholars, in the time before the arrival of writing there was no real history. Another reason for their consideration of saga literature – or at least the sagas of Icelanders – as fiction was the artistic form and literary quality of these texts. In his book from 1812 Rühs asked: 'Is it ever possible for a historical subject to be treated in a poetical and true manner?' (Rühs 1812: 282). Rühs's answer was 'no', or at least he was very doubtful whether one could combine a poetic and a faithful treatment of the same matter. The narrow meaning of 'historical truth' among these scholars in the last phase of the Enlightenment not only made room for fiction, but made it necessary to label texts that built on oral tradition telling about the remote past as something other than 'history'.[16]

During Romanticism, the contrast between 'history' and 'fiction' subsided. Only one year after Rühs published his book, he received an answer from the Danish theologian and saga scholar, later bishop, Peter Erasmus Müller in a work called *Ueber den Ursprung und Verfall der Isländischen Historiographie*.[17] According to Müller, history was the third and final phase in a development from *contemporary story* through *tradition* to *history*. It was thus the author of genius who lifted the tradition up to the higher level of history. Müller would not deny that an exact report of what had occurred was historical truth, but believed that the real and true history emerged when the author of genius reconstructed his image of the past on the basis of the fragmented truth from the oral tradition. Müller's view is representative of the view of saga literature in his period. A similar view of the development of the oral tradition is found in Niels Matthias Petersen's literary history *Bidrag til den oldnordiske Literaturs Historie* (1866).[18] He called the three phases in the development *beginning of a saga*, *saga* and *history*. The last phase in the development was characterized thus:

> The storyteller becomes aware of the idea of the period, he appropriates this idea and reproduces it; he connects the fragments, the incomplete, he gives life to the characters. An idea appears in the story. The story becomes critical history with historical art. The saga becoms history.[19]

Petersen in fact characterized the best of the sagas of Icelanders as 'perfect historical novels'.[20]

In Carsten Hauch's *Indledning til Forelæsning over Njalssaga og flere med den beslægtede sagaer*,[21] which can be called the first analysis of a saga of Icelanders as a work of art, we find the same combination of literary art and history. In

16 The Enlightenment was in fact passè when Rühs published his book in 1812. His view of 'historical truth' and the saga literature is more representative of the previous decades.

17 This work was later published in Danish in a slightly reworked version in *Nordisk Tidsskrift for Oldkyndighed* I (1832) with the title *Om den islandske Historieskrivnings Oprindelse, Flor og Undergang*.

18 The book was published four years after the author's death.

19 Petersen (1866: 182).

20 Petersen (1886: 220).

21 The lecture course about *Njáls saga* and other sagas of Icelanders was given at the University of Copenhagen during the winter of 1848/49. The lectures were later printed in *Afhandlinger og æsthetiske Betragtninger* (1855).

Njáls saga in particular, Hauch saw the work of an artist, especially in what he called 'an artistic plan' (*En kunstforstandig Plan*). Hauch characterized *Njáls saga* as epic fiction.[22] However, he shared the Romantic understanding of 'history' with other scholars of his time. The sagas could therefore be both history and literary art at the same time.

The discussion of whether the sagas of Icelanders were history *or* fiction became a matter of discussion again late in the nineteenth century. In this period the concept of 'history' was used in a more narrow sense than during the Romantic era. Now Icelandic scholars, the so-called Icelandic school, took the lead in the saga debate. The scholars belonging to this school attached less importance than scholars in the previous period to the oral tradition on which the authors had built, and placed more importance on the role of the authors and the written composition. They emphasized that the sagas of Icelanders were created by authors who, to a lesser or greater extent, had drawn on an oral tradition, but that there had been no oral equivalents to the written sagas. The saga view of the scholars belonging to the Icelandic school has been labelled as 'book prose', the older view as 'free prose'.[23] However, in spite of the fact that the adherents of the book prose school were very critical of the value of sagas of Icelanders as historical sources, and held the view that the author's contribution was significant, most of them were reluctant to speak of them as fiction. Nevertheless, some scholars did. In 1928 the Danish literary historian Paul V. Rubow published a short article, 'Den islandske familieroman',[24] in which, as the title indicates, he regarded the sagas of Icelanders as historical novels, and he argued that the whole genre was modelled on the translated *riddarasǫgur*. This theory was never accepted, but led to a discussion that focused on the possible fictional nature of these sagas. In his book *Hrafnkatla* (1940), Sigurður Nordal argued that *Hrafnkels saga* was composed without basis in oral tradition, the author's only sources were some names and a few facts that he had found in *Landnámabók*.[25] Bjarni Einarsson's view of *Egils saga*, which he defended in his doctoral thesis in 1971,[26] was that the saga was comprised of a large number

22 He labelled the saga *episk Digtning* or *episk Poesie*.

23 The terms 'book prose' and 'free prose' were introduced by Andreas Heusler (1914). See also Mundal (1977: 141–64).

24 The article was first published in *Tilskueren*, May 1928, and republished in *Små kritiske breve*, 1936.

25 Óskar Halldórsson (1976) later maintained that the author built on tradition.

26 A revised version of Bjarni Einarsson's doctoral thesis from the University of Oslo, 1971, was published in 1975.

of older written sources from which the author borrowed motifs and plots. The rather extreme form of the book prose theory, for instance found in the two books of Sigurður Nordal and Bjarni Einarsson, is sometimes referred to as the *fiction theory*.

Another scholar who has argued that the sagas of Icelanders must be regarded as fiction is Fritz Paul (1971; 1982). In his article from 1982, Paul is very conscious about the fact that a medieval text can only be seen as fiction when the author intended it to be fiction and the audience received it as fiction (Paul 1982: 53). In his argumentation he emphasizes the form and narrative art of the sagas of Icelanders, especially this genre's references to its sources, which with few exceptions were references to the oral tradition of the type 'people say' or 'some people say [...], other people say'. He held these references to be fictitious. The sagas of Icelanders shared this kind of references with the *fornaldarsǫgur*, the fictionality of which – according to Paul – was recognized in the Middle Ages (Paul 1982: 66). In the sagas of kings, which were regarded as history, the references to sources were normally of another type, namely to persons and books. Paul admits that in the saga texts themselves it is not easy to find indisputable evidence of the authors' consciousness of their fictional character. However, the logical conclusion that the authors must have reflected on their own way of writing forms part of his argumentation. Whether or not the audience of the sagas perceived the signals of fictionality is – according to Paul – more uncertain.

Recently Torfi Tulinius has placed emphasis on the fictional character of the sagas of Icelanders, especially *Egils saga* (Torfi Tulinius 2002/1995; 2004). As he sees it, the literary form, or structure, of these sagas reveals their fictional character. The authors of both the sagas of Icelanders and of the *fornaldarsǫgur* were writing fiction. The goal of the authors of both genres was to create meaning for people in their own time:

> Like the legendary sagas, the Icelandic family sagas are also fictions, but the degree of complexity with which they mediate reality is greater. The *fornaldarsögur* project the aspirations and preoccupations of the thirteenth century onto heroes of the distant past, in quite an overt fashion. The Íslendingasögur also project a certain ideal into the past, but into the near past. They also project the tensions and preoccupations of thirteenth-century society, but in a more covert fashion. (Torfi Tulinius 2002: 294)

There is no doubt that the sagas of Icelanders are written in a highly developed artistic form, but to see an artistic form as an indication of fiction is in my opinion problematic.

Even so, it must be admitted that scholars who have regarded sagas of Icelanders – or at least some of these sagas – as fictional have from one point of view done so with good reasons. It is obvious that the sagas of Icelanders are works by authors who have added much of their own material. However, when these texts are characterized as fiction, in most cases it is on the basis of an analysis of the literary form that is found to be more similar to fiction than to history in modern times. When Paul, for example, takes the references to tradition in the sagas of Icelanders as evidence of the fictional character of the genre, it must be seen as an interpretation. It is very hard to find in these texts anything that clearly indicates that the authors – or their audience – in the Middle Ages regarded them as anything other than history – though history in a very broad sense of the word. In the last decades of saga research this is a fact that has been emphasized by many scholars.[27]

It may be that many sagas of Icelanders contain very little that is historically true in the narrow meaning of the word and that they come close to historical novels when judged from a modern point of view. However, it is problematic to talk of these sagas as fiction as long as no clear consciousness of fiction is reflected in the texts. Within this genre we never find prologues in which the author declares his intention to write history, but neither does he undermine the impression that he wants to do so. Some of the characteristics of the genre that have been used to argue that the authors as well as their audience understood these sagas as dealing with historical events are, for instance, that the names of the main characters in the sagas of Icelanders are in most cases found in *Landnámabók,* the intention of which was to give a survey of the settlers in Iceland. The fact that long extracts from sagas of Icelanders were copied into different, younger redactions of *Landnámabók* is a strong indication that medieval readers took these sagas to be true. Many of the saga characters occur in more than one saga, and it would be strange if a great number of authors had come to an agreement about a common fictitious cast of characters. References to the type of oral tradition that employs 'people say' have been mentioned. Even though such references may

27 See especially Meulengracht Sørensen (1993: 58 f.) for a discussion of this problem. For another approach to fictionalizing features in the sagas of Icelanders, see the analysis by Ranković in the present volume.

in many cases be false and inserted by the author to strengthen his credibility, most scholars will – contrary to Paul – agree that such references are meant to signal trustworthiness, not fiction. There may, however, be many elements in the sagas of Icelanders that not even the more naive members of the audience would believe to be authentic in every detail, for instance long dialogues, descriptions of clothes and other information about how people were dressed on a certain occasion, and so on. However, fictional elements of this kind (which also occur in sagas of kings) are hardly important when it comes to the question of whether or not a saga would be regarded as historical or fictional – by the author as well as by his audience. The crucial question may be how fictional elements were used. If such embellishment were regarded as appropriate for reconstructing a full picture of what had happened in the past, this use of fiction would serve the historian's purpose and be included in history. Therefore it seems that stories about the past, like the sagas of Icelanders, could include a lot of fiction as long as the stories were believable – or nearly believable – and were used to give life to historical persons and events from the past. (For more on the sagas of Icelanders, see Ranković in the present collection).

NORDIC GENRES BETWEEN HISTORY AND FICTION

Steblin-Kamenskij did not thematize fiction in connection with the saga literature. Since people in the Middle Ages, as he saw it, were not able to distinguish beween historical truth (in history) and artistic truth (in fiction) he characterized the artistic truth in saga literature as 'latent fiction'. He admitted, however, that in the genre of the *fornaldarsǫgur* we have something that comes close to real fiction. These sagas did not lay claim to truthfulness, therefore the fiction in these texts was consciously recognized as fiction, and the syncretic truth, which according to Steblin-Kamenskij was the basis for this group of sagas as well, 'gives way to an embryonic form of artistic truth' (Steblin-Kamenskij 1973: 41).

Whether it is fiction in an embryonic form or not that is found in the *fornaldarsǫgur*, this genre is undoubtedly the right place to start looking for a consciousness of fiction in Old Norse society, and there may be other interesting texts as well. Eddic poems, especially the heroic poems, should be seen in connection with the *fornaldarsǫgur*. In my opinion there is no reason to look for the embryonic form of fiction only in the written culture. I will argue that a consciousness of fiction in all likelihood existed in the Old Norse oral culture as well.

An often quoted and very illustrative example of how the *fornaldarsǫgur* – or the oral traditions behind the *fornaldarsǫgur* – were valued in Old Norse society can be found in the contemporary saga *Þorgils saga ok Hafliða*. The passage mentions the entertainment at a wedding at the farm Reykjahólar in Iceland. The wedding took place in the year 1119, and the saga was written in the thirteenth century, according to most scholars around 1240. The author who wrote *Þorgils saga ok Hafliða* would, of course, not have had first-hand knowledge about what happened at a wedding more than a hundred years ago. The passage is first and foremost evidence of attitudes towards this sort of literature in the author's own time. As a short introduction to the passage we find some reflections from the author about truth and lies.[28] The narrative continues as follows:

> Hrólfr from Skálmarnes told the saga about the Viking Hrǫngviðr and Óláfr, king of the *liðsmenn*, Þráinn's breaking of the grave mound and Hrómundr Gripsson, together with many stanzas. King Sverrir was entertained by this story, and he said that such untrue stories were amusing. But still people can trace their family back to Hrómundr Gripsson. The priest Ingimundr presented the story about Ormr Barreyjarskáld and many stanzas and a good *flokkr* [skaldic poem of a special type], which Ingimundr had composed, at the end of the saga, and yet many wise men consider this saga to be true.[29]

From the short passage we can draw the conclusion that at least the first-mentioned saga is a saga of the *fornaldarsaga* type. However, the story that is characterized as a *lygisaga*, 'an untrue story', is not a written text, but an orally told story. This oral story Hrólfr put together or composed himself ('sjálfur saman setta'). The wording 'sjálfur saman setta' has given rise to debate, and

28 Sverrir Tómasson (1988: 214–15 and 316–17) has suggested that the discussion about truth and lies indicates that the author regarded the saga, which was composed by Hrólfr af Skálmarnesi, as belonging to the category of *argumentum*.

29 'Hrólfur af Skálmarnesi sagði sögu frá Hröngviði víkingi og frá Ólafi liðsmannakonungi og haugbróti Þráins og Hrómundi Gripssyni og margar vísur með. En þessari sögu var skemmt Sverri konungi og kallaði hann slíkar lygisögur skemmtilegar. Ok þó kunna menn að telja ættir sínar til Hrómundar Gripssonar. Þessa sögu hafði Hrólfur sjálfur sanan setta. Ingimundur prestur sagði sögu Orms Barreyjarskálds og vísur margar og flokk góðan við enda sögunnar er Ingimundur hafði ortan og hafa þó margir fróðir menn þessa sögu fyrir satt' (*Sturlunga saga* I: 22).

the meaning is not absolutely clear. It does not necessarily mean that he created the whole story himself. He had probably chosen stories from an older oral tradition – both in prose and stanzas – changed it and added something of his own so that Hrólfr became the creator of this particular story. The same creative authorship which is normally attributed to authors of written fiction is here attributed to the storyteller.

The attitude to historical truth in the saga told by Hrólfr af Skálmarnesi is both expressied in the phrases *lygisaga*, 'untrue story', and 'but still people can trace their family back to Hrómundr Gripsson' ('Ok þó kunna menn að telja ættir sínar til Hrómundar Gripssonar') on the other. By using the phrase *lygisaga* the author underlines that these stories are not meant to be reliable; they are made up. At the same time he admits that people mentioned in such stories may actually have lived, but what is told about them cannot be trusted. Such stories can be placed in a grey area between history and fiction, including many *fornaldarsǫgur*.

The word *lygisaga* is in fact interesting – referring to stories that are lies. The relationship between history and fiction is equated with the relationship between truth and lies, and fiction is defined in a negative way as 'not true'. This is perhaps typical of fiction in an embryonic form. It may also be typical of the early stages in the development of fiction that the author offers the audience the opportunity to interpret the stories in a more traditional way, as some sort of history. However, by doing so, he simultaneously draws the audience's attention to the fictional elements of the story.

As we have seen, the authors of sagas that presented themselves as true stories – or history – could signal their intention to tell the truth in different ways. What signals do the authors who tell stories without the intention of being trusted give?

Hrólfr af Skálmarnesi probably told stories about the distant past. The *fornaldarsǫgur* usually deal with the time before the settlement of Iceland during the reign of King Haraldr Finehair. The very long span of time, as well as a vague and unclear indication of both time and space, may in itself be a signal that these stories were not meant to be trusted. In our era the formula 'once upon a time' is a clear indication that the story which follows is fictional. The heroic Eddic poetry, which should be seen in connection with the *fornaldarsǫgur*, uses a formula several times: *Ár var alda* (*Helgakviða Hundings-*

bana I),[30] or *Ár var* (*Guðrúnarkviða* I, *Sigurðarkviða hin skamma*). This denotes that the following story happened in the olden days. In an article about formulas in Old Norse Eddic poetry, Lars Lönnroth writes that '*Ár var alda* is a formula used to begin a new story, much like "once upon a time"' (Lönnroth 1981). If *ár var* (*alda*) functions like 'once upon a time', this clearly entails fictionality. The formula signals that these events happened so long ago that no one can guarantee their factuality. However, this does not necessarily mean that people in Old Norse culture did not believe in anything that was told in the Eddic poems. In his pilgrim's guide to Rome and Jerusalem, *Leiðarvísir* from the 1150s, the Icelandic abbot Nikulás of Munkaþverá described the pilgrim's road through the German landscape and over the Alps and pointed out the place where Gunnarr was thrown into the snake pit – according to what some men said.[31] As we have seen, people in Old Norse society believed that the heroes of the *fornaldarsǫgur* could be real people who had lived a long time ago, and their attitude to the heroes and heroines of the Eddic poems was probably the same.

In addition to the span of time – including formulas emphasizing this distance – the use of fantastic elements can also be a marker of fictionality. Fantastic elements are found in all the saga genres, and it is impossible to draw clear boundaries between the mainly realistic sagas of Icelanders, which presented themselves as history, and the *fornaldarsǫgur* on the basis of how the two groups of sagas use fantastic and supernatural elements. However, there is a clear tendency towards a much more extensive use of fantastic and supernatural elements in the *fornaldarsǫgur* – and in the heroic Eddic poetry – than in the realistic saga literature. A wider variety of fantastic motifs is also used, such as talking animals or birds, metamorphoses, visits to the world of trolls, people living for several hundred years, and so on. It is, however, the *attitude* to the fantastic which most clearly shows that we are no longer governed by the laws of the real world. In the realistic saga genres, which are presented as true stories, the fantastic and the supernatural are clearly defined as such. In Eddic poetry and in the *fornaldarsǫgur* the borderline between the real and the supernatural or fantastic is no longer marked. To talk with birds is con-

30 This formula is also used in the mythological poem *Vǫluspá*, here meaning 'early in mythic time'.
31 See *Sturlunga saga* III: 56.

sidered nothing out of the ordinary, metamorphoses are almost as normal as changing clothes, the hero can sail away to the land of trolls or giants, and *valkyrjur*, who are daughters of legendary kings, ride on horses through the air. The acceptance of the fantastic and supernatural as 'normal' gives a very clear signal that we are no longer in the real world, but in a world of fantasy.[32] At the same time, the stories in the *fornaldarsǫgur*, and to some extent in Eddic poetry as well, are in many ways rooted in the real world. Some of the principal characters are assumed to have lived in the distant past, sometimes place names known to the Old Norse audience are mentioned, and long passages are told in the realistic mode.

Some authors of *fornaldarsǫgur* do in fact lay claim to historical accuracy.[33] A good example of this is found in *Gǫngu-Hrólfs saga*, chapter 25, where the hero, Hrólfr, is out in the wilderness together with his bride-to-be and a deceitful man. While sleeping, Hrólfr has both his feet cut off by this man and is then abandoned. He manages, however, to mount his horse. On his way he rescues a friend, and he finally finds the place where both his feet and his bride-to-be were left by his enemy; a dwarf who is a very good doctor happened to stay at the same place, and when Hrólfr arrives, the dwarf tells him to lay down by the fire and warm the stumps. The story continues:

> Hrólfr did so, and he [the dwarf] put salve onto the wounds and placed the feet against them, bound them with splints and let Hrólfr lie like that for three nights. Then he took off the bandages and asked Hrólfr to stand up and test himself. Hrólfr did so, and his feet were then as good and nimble as if they had never been wounded.[34]

This story is unbelievable, and the author admits that many people may find it difficult to believe that this event had taken place. Therefore he finds it necessary to interrupt his own story to assure the audience that he tells the truth:

> Now even if people may find such things unbelievable, everyone still has to

32 For more on this topic, see Mundal (2006).

33 A list of truth claims that also includes truth claims in the *fornaldarsǫgur* are found in O'Connor (2005: 126 f.).

34 'Hrólfr gerði svá. Smurði hann þá smyrslunum í sárin ok setti við fætrna ok batt við spelkur ok lét Hrólf svá liggja þrjár nætr, leysti þá af umbönd ok bað Hrólf upp standa ok reyna sik. Hrólfr gerði svá. Váru honum fætrnir þá svá hægir og mjúkir sem hann hefði á þeim aldri sárr verit' (*Göngu-Hrólfs saga*: 230–1).

> tell what he has seen or heard. It is also difficult to contradict what learned people in former times have put together.[35]

Most scholars have taken such assurances of the truth in unbelievable stories as a sign that the authors mean the opposite of what they say and are playing games with their audience.[36] However, some scholars have argued that the matter is more complicated and that the authors may at least have wanted their audience to believe that their stories were true because they knew that the audience expected to be told the truth.[37] Recently Ralph O'Connor has argued that the concept of literary fiction was too problematic to be fully acceptable within the social practice of saga entertainment. Learned people may have accepted that a story was literary fiction and perhaps flirted with the new mode, but not the common audience. They expected to be entertained by stories that purported to be true, and the guarantees from the authors or sagatellers must be seen in terms of this (O'Connor: 2005).

A text like *Gǫngu-Hrólfs saga* sends out mixed signals. Authors/narrators who express the will to tell the truth – or even guarantee that they tell the truth – may mean what they say. But I think we have to evaluate the individual cases. When the narrator affirms the truth of the unbelievable, as in the case of *Gǫngu-Hrólfs saga* and some other texts of the same type, he sends out signals of such an ambivalent character that the guarantee of truth increases the scepticism. The narrator dwells on the unbelievable and wins the full attention of the audience, who has time to reflect on truth and lies. In any case, assurances of the truth of the kind that we have in *Gǫngu-Hrólfs saga* tell us that there was a limit to what people in an Old Norse audience would believe. In this particular case, the author, after having guaranteed the truth, says that no man need to place much confidence in what he says, but should be delighted while listening ('Þarf ok engi meira trúnað á at leggja, en hafa þó gleði af, á meðan hann heyrir').

The guarantees of truth in the *fornaldarsǫgur*, in my opinion, reveal more about the authors' interests in playing with the borderline between the believable and the unbelievable – and with their audience – than their interest in truth. This is a characteristic of saga literature which can also be observed in

35 'Nú þótt mönnum þykki slíkir hlutir ótrúligir, þá verðr þat þó hverr at segja, er hann hefir sét eða heyrt. Þar er ok vant móti at mæla, er inir fyrri fræðimenn hafa samsett' (*Göngu-Hrólfs saga*: 231).

36 See, for instance, Sverrir Tómasson (1988: 250 f.) where these defensive statements are seen in the context of prologues in medieval literature.

37 See Hallberg (1982: 6 ff.); Kalinke (1985: 318 ff.).

the sagas of Icelanders (see p. 175). However, while the authors in the realistic saga literature are playing with the borderline between the believable and the unbelievable, in the *fornaldarsǫgur* this boundary has been moved far into the fantastic world towards the absolutely unbelievable.

'HISTORICAL TRUTH' IN DIFFERENT SAGA GENRES

It seems that the borderline between history and fiction – in its embryonic form – was not clear-cut in Old Norse society. We have 'history' or 'historical truth' in a rather narrow sense in the writings of authors like Ari fróði and Theodoricus, and the skaldic poetry, which, with the exception of a few mythic poems, in the early Old Norse era told about contemporary events, was probably also regarded as 'historical truth' in a narrow sense.

In the realistic saga genres we find the concept of 'historical truth' in a much wider sense. It is, however, possible that the authors give slightly different signals in different groups of sagas, signals that indicate that some groups of sagas aim at presenting historical truth in a more narrow sense than other groups of sagas.

Sagas of kings constitute a very heterogeneous group of sagas. Some of them tell about the distant past and some are contemporary sagas. However, in sagas of kings, even in sagas about the relatively distant past, such as in Snorri's *Heimskringla*, we can observe a critical attitude that also functions as an indication to the readers and listeners that the author aims at telling the historical truth. Such signals include the mentioning and evaluation of sources.[38] In sagas of kings the typical use of skaldic poetry is different than its use in sagas of Icelanders. In sagas of Icelanders, skaldic stanzas will typically be part of the flow of the story, whereas in sagas of kings the most typical use of skaldic stanzas is as documentation: the stanzas document something that is already told in prose. Both ways of using skaldic stanzas probably strengthened the impression of reliability, but the use of skaldic stanzas as documentation emphasized the historical nature of the text and signalled 'history' as probably defined in a more narrow sense than in the other function of skaldic stanzas. If that is correct, the different function of skaldic stanzas in the two groups of sagas signals a slightly narrower meaning of historical truth in sagas

38 Meulengracht Sørensen (1993: 60 ff.) argues that the critical attitude towards the sources in sagas of kings has nothing to do with the more narrow meaning of truth in sagas of kings as compared to sagas of Icelanders. The reason for the difference is conventional rhethoric.

of kings than in sagas of Icelanders. It may also be worth mentioning that skaldic stanzas are combined with the saga genres that present themselves as history of some sort. The *fornaldarsǫgur*, which normally do not lay claim on telling the truth, may quote stanzas of the Eddic type. Quotations of stanzas in skaldic metres in this genre should be seen as exceptions.

Another difference between sagas of kings and contemporary sagas (the sagas in the *Sturlunga saga* cycle) on the one hand and sagas of Icelanders on the other, which may indicate somewhat different attitudes towards historicity, is found in the use of supernatural and fantastic elements. In the *fornaldarsǫgur* the use of such elements was one of the strongest signals of fiction. The saga genres that claim to tell historical truth do not completely abstain from using such elements, but there are differences between the genres. The fantastic is very rarely found in contemporary sagas and rarely in sagas of kings, but more so in sagas of Icelanders. Within the realistic saga genres, which all present themselves as historical, the sagas of Icelanders are closer to the *fornaldarsǫgur* in this respect than the other saga genres. It is of course difficult to know whether a supernatural or fantastic element in a saga text was considered to be unbelievable or not by an Old Norse audience, and the differences between the genres in this field can be explained in many ways. Distance in time or space allows for more fantastic elements than a text describing the recent past. The issue is related to different functions, different genre expectations and so on. It is plausible, however, that the less extensive use of supernatural and fantastic elements in contemporary sagas and in sagas of kings as compared to the sagas of Icelanders may indicate that the authors of the first two genres presented a stronger truth claim than the authors of the latter.

There are also differences between the saga genres in their use of dialogue. As stated above, the authors who composed the written sagas and made up dialogues were very well aware that these dialogues were not historical, and there is no reason to believe that the audience held them to be genuine either. Within sagas of kings the extent to which dialogues are used varies greatly from one saga to another, but the average use of dialogues both in sagas of kings and in contemporary sagas is limited compared to their presence in sagas of Icelanders.

How the authors of different genres refer to their sources may also be revealing. The authors of the *fornaldarsǫgur* do not usually mention sources. Exceptions are references to learned people in the past such as in the quotation from *Gǫngu-Hrólfs saga* (see p. 185), which does not seem to be very trustworthy. There is, however, an interesting difference between sagas of kings and sagas of Icelanders. In sagas of kings we find – admittedly not very often – references to authorities or informants by name and references to books. In sagas of Icelanders there are a few references of this type, but much more frequently the references point to an anonymous tradition in the form of the phrase 'people say...'. References to named persons and books probably signal 'historical truth' in a more narrow sense than references to anonymous tradition.

Concerning the question of fiction, the borderline between literature that can be characterized as *lygisǫgur* (the *fornaldarsǫgur*) and sagas that are presented as true stories is, in principle, a more important boundary than the other borderlines between the different saga genres. But it seems wrong to draw a sharp borderline between 'history' and 'fiction' in early Old Norse society. There is a gradual transition from history in a narrow sense to history in a broad sense – which could include many elements which were the authors' or the storytellers' inventions – to sagas that were looked upon as untrue, or fictional, but still claimed to be partially rooted in history.

NEW FICTIONAL GENRES

During the Middle Ages, partly as a result of Christianization, new forms of literature were introduced which may have speeded up the development of fiction within Old Norse culture. Biblical parables and the *exempla* used in preaching to illustrate main points in the teaching of the Church could in fact be presented as invented stories. In Old Norse the term *ævintýr*, which also became the term for fairytales, was used for *exemplum* and clearly shows that people were aware of the fictional characters of these stories. The use of fiction within the Church might have given some 'moral support' to the use of fiction. Christian and European literature offered new ways to interpret fantastic elements and fictional texts. They could be understood in a metaphorical way and contain truth on a 'higher level'. In connection with the unbelievable story quoted from *Gǫngu-Hrólfs saga* (see p. 184), the author says:

> There have also been some wise men who have often talked figuratively about some subjects, as for example master Galterus in *Alexanders saga*

> and the poet Umeris in *Trójumanna saga,* and later masters have taken that to be true rather than arguing that it could not be so.[39]

Another way of including the unbelievable in stories that were presented as true history, especially in Christian literature, was to present the unbelievable as the work of the Devil. This is the strategy chosen by Oddr munkr in his saga (from around 1200) about King Óláfr Tryggvason. Oddr tells the story about the Christianization of northern Norway. The king's men witnessed many strange things, for example metamorphoses. Oddr admitts that the story is less than credible, but he can explain what happened:

> The matters that we have related with respect to such tales and examples we do not judge to be true in the sense that they happened, but rather we believe that they appeared to happen because the devil is full of deceit and evil. (Andersson (ed.) 2003: 97)[40]

These strategies made it possible to include unbelievable elements in all kinds of texts.

The Old Norse myths, both in the form of prose and poems, that were accepted as truth – but not historical truth – became untrue after Christianization, and were probably regarded as some kind of fiction.

From the twelfth century onwards a large number of continental and insular texts were translated into Old Norse. Most influential for the development of fictional literature in the North were the translations of Old French verse epic into Old Norse prose in the circles around King Hákon Hákonarson – the first translation that we know of was made in the year 1226. The new prose genre was called *riddarasǫgur* (sagas of chivalry). Like the *fornaldarsǫgur,* which probably existed only as oral tradition at the time the first French texts were translated, the new genre dealt with events that had taken place a long time ago, and from a Nordic point of view, they had also taken place far away. The *riddarasǫgur* shared some of its characteristics with the native

39 'Hafa þeir ok sumir spekingar verit, er mjök hafa talat í fígúru um suma hluti, svá sem meistari Galterus í Alexandrí sögu eða Umeris skáld í Trójumanna sögu, ok hafa eftirkomandi meistarar þat heldr til sannenda fært en í móti mælt, at svá mætti vera' (*Göngu-Hrólfs saga*: 231).

40 'En þessa luti er ver segiom fra slicum lutum oc dœmisogum. þa dœmum ver þat eigi sannleik at sua hafi verit. helldr hyggiom ver at sua hafi synnz þui at fiandinn er fullr up flærðar oc illzku' (Finnur Jónsson (ed.) 1932: 142–3).

fornaldarsǫgur, for example, a rather frequent use of fantastic elements, even though the motifs were often slightly different. Sharing characteristics with a native tradition that could be characterized as *lygisǫgur*, the *riddarasǫgur* were probably regarded as mainly fictional literature. The fact that they were rooted in foreign soil made the possibility that these sagas could in some cases contain small fragments of historical truth a matter of less importance in the North. Judging the importance of these texts in the development of fiction – or the consciousness of fiction – in Old Norse culture, Jürg Glauser draws attention to what he calls 'the awareness of writtenness', which includes a metafictional self-reflection in these sagas. The translated *riddarasǫgur* contributed to the broadening of narrative and fictional possibilities. In writing, as opposed to exclusively oral narration, different fictional possibilities could be tried out.[41]

The new genre soon became popular in Iceland, and here the translated *riddarasǫgur* gave birth to a new genre, the indigenous *riddarasǫgur*. In these sagas historicity is not the issue. The milieu is more foreign and exotic than in any other genre. The events are set in an undefined period in the past, and some sagas are located in places as far away as India or Africa. The authors signal that these stories are meant for amusement; they are invented stories, and in some cases the author says clearly that he has made up, or written, the story himself. This is, for instance, the case in *Victors saga ok Blávus* where the author begins by mentioning King Hákon Magnússon of Norway who had sagas translated to amuse people. The author then continues:

> [A]nd therefore I know that good old men will wish to pattern themselves and their entertainment after his fair custom and put aside laughter and leaping, dancing and dizziness, and all vain vileness. But lest one after another remain silent, we here begin a written tale for the amusement of children and unlearned people...[42]

If we compare different sagas in the group of indigenous *riddarasǫgur*, we can, in many cases, see how the authors have borrowed motifs from older texts, changed them and arranged them in new ways to form new stories. In some cases we find prologues and references to learned literature. It may be that this

41 Glauser (2005: 382 ff.).

42 'ok þui weit ek at goder gamler menn uilia likia sig ok sina skemtan epter hans fogrum haatum enn af leggia hlaatur ok hopp danzs ok dáraskap ok hégomligt herianskit. Enn til þess at eigi þegi huer at audrum byrium wer eina boguliga fra sogn bornum ok ofrodum monnum til skemtanar...' (*Viktors saga ok Blávus*, p. 3).

is some sort of playing with the more 'serious' literature. A parodic or ironic attitude is also found in some of the *fornaldarsǫgur* proper from the late Middle Ages.[43] The growing use of parodical elements in the texts, the 'awareness of writtenness' and the use of metafictional comments of different kinds indicate that a consciousness of fiction was growing.

In the late Middle Ages fictional literature seems to have gained ground in Old Norse culture. Even the late sagas of Icelanders were influenced by the new fictional literature, and a new kind of sagas of Icelanders came into being. Sagas like *Bárðar saga Snæfellsás, Víglundar saga, Kjalnesinga saga* and a few others tell about saga heroes who probably never existed, even though the stories are rooted in Icelandic soil. The realism in sagas of Icelanders here gives way to the non-realistic style of the *fornaldarsǫgur* and the *riddarasǫgur* with their extensive use of fantastic elements.

It is of course difficult to say how these young sagas of Icelanders were assessed by the Icelandic society in the late Middle Ages. As in the folklore of later times, the distance in time and space made room for more fantastic elements within a realistic framework. Ármann Jakobsson has argued that *Bárðar saga Snæfellsás,* where even trolls appear, must be read as a kind of historical narrative, in which the trolls and related beings belong to the past (Ármann Jakobsson 1998 and 2006). Vésteinn Ólason (2007) has investigated the fantastic and supernatural elements in all the late sagas of Icelanders from the fourteenth century, and he argues that such elements are given a different and more important function than in the older sagas. However, in spite of their proximity to the *fornaldarsǫgur,* these late sagas of Icelanders – according to Vésteinn Ólason – still have the generic indicators that show that they pretend to be history. As I see it, these sagas send out such mixed signals that the author undermines his trustworthiness. The strong influence on the late sagas of Icelanders from literature of a mainly fictional character demonstrates that fiction gains ground.

In Iceland many of the fictional sagas were transformed into *rímur* ('rhymes'), and motifs and subject matter known from *fornaldarsǫgur* and *riddarasǫgur* found their way into the Scandinavian ballads. The oral ballads seem to have followed the same path as the *riddarasǫgur,* from France and Anglo-Norman England to western Norway, from where they spread to the

43 On this matter, see Viðar Hreinsson (1990); Vésteinn Ólason (1994); Jørgensen (1997 /1996); Barnes (2000); Kramarz-Bein (2000); Mundal (2003).

rest of the northern regions.[44] The *rímur*, and especially the Scandinavian ballads, in many cases rooted in fictional prose texts, were oral genres which spread to all social layers of the society and bear witness to the great popularity of fiction in the late Middle Ages.

HOW DID FICTION IN OLD NORSE CULTURE DEVELOP?

Finally, is it possible to say anything about how, and from where, the development of fiction began in Old Norse culture? Dennis Green has argued that fiction in the Middle Ages arose when authors started to fill in lacunas or gaps in the works of historians.[45] If *Hrafnkels saga* came into being in the way Sigurður Nordal suggested, it would be a good example of how a saga filled in a lacuna in *Landnámabók*. But, as already stated, it is difficult to find clear signals of fictionality in sagas of Icelanders – with the exception of the group of late sagas mentioned above that occupy a position between sagas of Icelanders and *fornaldarsǫgur/riddarasǫgur.* As regards the sagas of Icelanders, the contract between author and audience was rather that texts of this kind were some sort of history. And the sagas of Icelanders did not develop into fiction by authors filling in older texts, but rather by changing literary mode – from realistic to fantastic stories – as in the late sagas of Icelanders, which at least developed in the direction of fiction. The *fornaldarsǫgur,* which seem to have been regarded as fiction of some kind even at the oral stage, could not – except in a few cases – have developed according to Green's theory, since extremely few historical works which mentioned heroes from the *fornaldarsǫgur* were available to be filled in.

In a paper presented at the Saga Conference in 2006, Marianne Kalinke discussed the genesis of fiction in the North, and pointed out one clear example in which an author could have generated fiction as a means of filling in the gaps of history. This *fornaldarsaga* is *Hrólfs saga kraka,* the main character of which is mentioned in *Skjǫldunga saga,* in Saxo's *Gesta Danorum* and by Snorri.[46] Kalinke does not, however, see this development as a common occurrence in Old Norse culture, and she also points to examples of when a fictional text has developed from another fictional text.

In Old Norse society, as in the rest of Europe, creating new texts by fill-

44 See Jonsson (1991).
45 Green (2002).
46 Kalinke (2006: 468).

ing in gaps in older texts was a very common process throughout the Middle Ages. This development from shorter texts in the early Middle Ages to the very long interpolated texts in the late Middle Ages is clearly demonstrated by Carol Clover in her book *The Medieval Saga* (1982). Normally this textual growth took place within one and the same genre, but not always. The emergence of fiction from historiography should be seen in this wider connection of increased textualization and the expanding functions of writing in books. However, it does not seem that Green's theory alone can account for the rise of fiction in the North, but perhaps the 'filling-in process' is one factor among others.

In Old Norse culture both heroic poems and tradition of the same type as is found later in the written *fornaldarsǫgur* were, in all likelihood, regarded as some kind of fiction even before continental and insular fictional literature was translated into Old Norse. But the translated literature probably strengthened the fictional trends of Old Norse literature by introducing fictional genres and new fantastic motifs. The translated stories had not only taken place long ago, but also far away, which made the question of historical accuracy less important. A decisive step in the development of Old Norse fiction was taken when authors started writing stories that were not rooted in Old Norse soil at all.

RESTRICTIONS ON OLD NORSE FICTION

However, in spite of the popularity of fiction in Iceland and Scandinavia in the late Middle Ages, the question remains as to whether it was possible to write fictional literature in any mode of writing, about any subject, and place the events in any period of time? Would it, for instance, be possible to write a fictional text in the realistic mode and place the story in the author's own time and environment? – and if an author tried to do so, would his audience understand that the text was meant to be fictional?

If Sigurður Nordal's hypothesis that *Hrafnkels saga* is to be regarded as fiction written by an author who had found some names and a few facts in *Landnámabók,* but apart from that had invented the whole story himself, we would have an example of a fictional saga of Icelanders written in the realistic mode, telling a story similar to other sagas of Icelanders, placing the story in the author's own environment, but not in his own time. Perhaps many sagas of Icelanders are what we would like to define as fiction, but the signals given by the authors denote them as history. In Old Norse saga literature the combination of realism and fiction seems to be an impossibility, and there is no fictional saga that tells about events in the author's own time. The Old Norse concept of 'fiction' seems to be connected only to what is defined as *fabula* in the classical division of texts, not to *argumentum*, or at least not to *argumentum* alone. Fictional literature and a consciousness of fiction did develop in Old Norse culture, but the framework within which fiction flourished was still very narrow.

References

TEXTS

There are great differences between the saga genres as to how many sagas are available in English translations. All sagas of Icelanders have been published in English translation by Leifur Eiríksson Publishing in *The Complete Sagas of Icelanders*, vol. I–V, ed. Viðar Hreinsson (Reykjavík, 1997).

Most of the sagas of kings have been translated into English as well. The most renowned of these sagas, Snorri Sturluson's *Heimskringla*, has been translated by Samuel Laing, *Heimskringla: The Norse King Sagas* (London, 1951) and by Lee M. Hollander, *Heimskringla. History of the kings of Norway* (Austin, 1964). *Sverris saga* was translated by J. Sephton, *Sverrissaga: The Saga of King Sverri of Norway* (Felinfach, 1994). *Ágrip* has been translated by M. J. Driscoll, *Ágrip af Nóregskonungasǫgum: A Twelfth-Century History of the Kings of Norway* (London, 1995). In addition to *The Saga of Olaf Tryggvason* by Oddr Snorrason (mentioned in the bibliography below) Theodore M. Anderson has translated *Morkinskinna* – together with Kari Ellen Gade. The title of the translation is *Morkinskinna: The Earliest Icelandic Chronicle of the Norwegian Kings (1030–1157)*. *Fagrskinna* has been translated by Alison Finlay, *Fagrskinna: A Catalogue of the Kings of Norway* (Leiden, 2004).

The *Sturlunga saga* collection was translated by Julia McGrev, *Sturlunga Saga*, vol. 9 and 10 in The Library of Scandinavian Literature (New York, 1970–74).

A number of the more renowned *fornaldarsǫgur* have been translated into English. For example, a collection of such sagas are available in *Seven Viking Romances*, translated by Herman Pálsson and Paul Edvards (Harmondsworth: Penguin Classics, 1985). The same translators have published a translation of *Hrólfs saga Gautrekssonar*: *Hrolf Gautreksson: A Viking Romance* (Toronto, 1972) and of *Gǫngu-Hrólfs saga*: *Göngu-Hrolfs Saga* (Toronto, 1980). *Hrólfs saga kraka* has been translated by Jesse

L. Byock, *The Saga of King Hrolf Kraki* (1990), and *Vǫlsunga saga*, also by Byock, *The Saga of the Vǫlsungs* (1999), both in Penguin Classics.

Some of the translated *riddarasǫgur* (the translations from French verse epic into Old Norse prose) have been publised in English translation in *Norse Romance*, vol. I–III, ed. Marianne E. Kalinke (Cambridge, 1999).

The Icelandic indigenous *riddarasǫgur* are nearly unknown outside the circles of Old Norse philologists. A sample of the genre can be found in Rudolf Simek's translation into German of *Samsons saga fagra* in *Die Saga vom Mantel und die Saga vom Schönen Samson* (Vienna, 1982).

Andersson, Theodore M. (ed.) (2003) *The Saga of Olaf Tryggvason* (Oddr Snorrason. Translated from the Icelandic with Introduction and Notes by Theodore M. Andersson), Ithaca and London: Cornell University Press.

Finnur Jónsson (ed.) (1911) *Snorri Sturluson. Heimskringla. Nóregs konunga sǫgur,* Copenhagen: Gad.

Finnur Jónsson (ed.) (1932) *Saga Óláfs Tryggvasonar af Oddr Snorrason munk,* Copenhagen: Gad.

Göngu-Hrólfs saga, in Guðni Jónsson (ed.), *Fornaldar Sögur Norðurlanda* III, Reykjavík: Íslendingasagnaútgáfan, 1976. [First published 1954.]

Íslendingabók, in Jakob Benediktsson (ed.), *Íslenzk fornrit* I:1, Reykjavík: Hið íslenzka fornritafélag, 1968.

Storm, Gustav (ed.) (1880) *Monumenta Historica Norvegiæ. Latinske kildeskrifter til Norges historie i middelalderen,* Kristiania (Oslo): Brøgger.

Sturlunga saga I and III, Örnólfur Thorsson (ed.), Reykjavík: Svart á hvítu, 1988.

Viktors saga ok Blávus, in Jónas Kristjánsson (ed.), *Riddarasögur* II. *Viktors saga ok Blávus,* Reykjavík: Íslendingasagnaútgáfan, 1964.

STUDIES

Ármann Jakobsson (1998) 'History of the Trolls? *Bárðar saga* as an Historical Narrative', *Saga-Book* 25: 53–71.

Ármann Jakobsson (2006) 'The Good, the Bad and the Ugly: *Bárðar saga* and Its Giants', in John McKinnell, David Ashurst and Donata Kick (eds.), *The Fantastic in Old Norse/Icelandic Literature: Sagas and the British Isles* (Preprint papers of The Thirteenth International Saga Conference, Durham and York, 6th–12th August 2006), Durham University, pp. 54–62.

Barnes, Geraldine (2000) 'Romance in Iceland', in Margaret Clunies Ross (ed.),

Old Icelandic Literature and Society (Cambridge Studies in Medieval Literature, 42), Cambridge: Cambridge University Press, pp. 266–86.

Bjarni Einarsson (1975) *Litterære forudsætninger for Egils saga* (Rit Stofnun Árna Magnússonar á Íslendi), Reykjavík: Stofnun Árna Magnússonar.

Bjarni Guðnason (1979) 'Frásagnalist Snorra Sturlusonar', in *Snorri. Átta alda minning*, Reykjavík: Sögufélag, pp. 139–59.

Clover, Carol J. (1982) *The Medieval Saga*, Ithaca and London: Cornell University Press.

Glauser, Jürg (2005) 'Romance (Translated *riddarasögur*)', in Rory McTurk (ed.), *A Companion to Old Norse-Icelandic Literature and Culture*, Malden, Oxford and Victoria: Blackwell Publishing, pp. 372–87.

Green, Dennis H. (2002) *The Beginnings of Medieval Romance: Fact or Fiction, 1150–1220*, Cambridge University Press.

Hallberg, Peter (1974) 'The Syncretic Saga Mind: A Discussion of a New Approach to the Icelandic Sagas', *Medieval Scandinavia* 7: 102–17.

Hallberg, Peter (1982) 'Some Aspects of the Fornaldarsögur as a Corpus', *Arkiv för nordisk filologi* 97: 1–35.

Halldórsson, Óskar (1976) *Uppruni og þema Hrafnkels sögu*, Reykjavík: Hið íslenzka bókmenntafélag.

Hauch, Carsten (1855) 'Indledning til Forelæsning over Njalssaga og flere med den beslægtede sagaer', in *Afhandlinger og æsthetiske Betragtninger*, Copenhagen: Reitzel, pp. 411–67.

Heusler, Andreas (1914) *Die Anfänge der isländischen Saga* (Abhandl. der königl. preuss. Akademie der Wissenschaft, philos.-hist. Cl. 1913), Berlin.

Hreinsson, Viðar (1990) 'Hetjur og fífl úr Hrafnistu', *Tímarit Máls og menningar* 4: 41–52.

Johnsen, Oskar Albert, and Jón Helgason (eds.) (1941) *Saga Óláfs konungs hins helga. Den store saga om Olav den hellige*, Oslo: Kjeldeskriftfondet.

Jonsson, Bengt R. (1991) 'Oral Literature, Written Literature: The Ballad and the Old Norse Genres', in Joseph Harris (ed.), *The Ballad and Oral Literature* (Harvard English Studies, 17), Cambridge, Mass. and London: Harvard University Press, pp. 139–70.

Jørgensen, Jon Gunnar (1997/1996) 'Bósi hét annarr son þeirra', in Bergljót S. Kristjánsdóttir and Peter Springborg (ed.), *Frejas Psalter: En psalter i 40 afdelinger til brug for Jonna Louis-Jensen*. Det arnamagnæanske Institut, Copenhagen, pp. 101–5.

Kalinke, Marianne (1985) 'Norse Romance (*Riddarasögur*)', in Carol J. Clover and

John Lindow (eds.), *Old Norse-Icelandic Literature: A Critical Guide*. Ithaca and New York: Cornell University Press, pp. 316–63.

Kalinke, Marianne (2006) 'The Genesis of Fiction in the North', in John McKinnell, David Ashurst and Donata Kick (eds.), *The Fantastic in Old Norse/Icelandic Literature: Sagas and the British Isles* (Preprint papers of The 13th International Saga Conference, Durham and York 6th–12th August 2006), Durham University, pp. 464–78.

Kramarz-Bein, Susanne (2000) 'Die jüngere altisländische *Tristrams saga ok Ísondar* und ihre literarische Tradition', in Robert Nedoma, Hermann Reichert and Günter Zimmermann (eds.), *Erzählen im mittelalterlichen Skandinavien* (Wiener Studien zur Skandinavistik, 3), Vienna, pp. 21–45.

Lönnroth, Lars (1981) '*Iǫrð fannz æva né upphiminnk*: A Formula Analysis', in Ursula Dronke, Guðrún P. Helgadóttir, Gerd Wolfgang Weber and Hans Bekker-Nielsen (eds.), *Speculum Norroenvm: Norse Studies in Memory of Gabriel Turville-Petre*, Odense: Odense University Press, pp. 310–27.

Lie, Hallvard (1937) *Studier i Heimskringlas stil. Dialogene og talene* (Skrifter utgitt av Det norske Videnskaps-Akademi i Oslo, II. Hist.-Filos. Klasse 1936, No. 5), Oslo.

Meulengracht Sørensen, Preben (1993), *Fortælling og ære. Studier i islendingesagaerne*, Aarhus Universitetsforlaget.

Mundal, Else (1977) *Sagadebatt*, Oslo, Bergen and Tromsø: Universitetsforlaget.

Mundal, Else (1994) 'Snorre som forfattar – kjelde i forskinga', in Turid Brandstad and Jan E. G. Eriksson (eds.), *Seminaret 'Snorre – litterat og historiker', 24.–26. November 1993*, Tønsberg bibliotek og Riksantikvaren, Utgravingskontort for Tønsberg, pp. 29–37.

Mundal, Else (2003) 'Fornaldarsogene – vurderinga og vurderingskriteria', in Ármann Jakobsson, Annette Lassen and Agneta Ney (eds.), *Fornaldarsagornas struktur och ideologi. Handlingar från ett symposium i Uppsaga 31.8–2.9 2001* (Nordiska texter och undersökningar 28), Uppsala, pp. 25–35.

Mundal, Else (2006) 'The Treatment of the Supernatural and the Fantastic in Different Saga Genres', in John McKinnell, David Ashurst and Donata Kick (eds.), *The Fantastic in Old Norse/Icelandic Literature: Sagas and the Britich Isles* (Preprint Papers of The Thirteenth International Saga Conference. Durham and York, 6th–12th August 2006), Durham University, pp. 718–26.

Müller, Peter Erasmus (1832) 'Om den islandske Historieskrivnings Oprindelse, Flor og Undergang', *Nordisk Tidsskrift for Oldkyndighed* I: 1–54.

O'Connor, Ralph (2005) 'History or Fiction? Truth-Claims and Defensive Narrators in Icelandic Romance-Sagas', *Medieval Scandinavia* 15: 1–69.

Ólason, Vésteinn (1994) 'The Marvellous North and Authorial Presence in the Icelandic Fornaldarsaga', in Roy Eriksen (ed.), *Contexts of Pre-Novel Narrative: The European Tradition*, Berlin and New York: Mouton de Gruyter, pp. 101–34.

Ólason, Vésteinn (2007) 'The Fantastic Element in Fourteenth Century *íslendingasögur*: A Survey', *Gripla* XVIII: 7–22.

Paul, Fritz (1971) 'Zur Poetik der Isländersagas. Eine Bestandsaufnahme', *Zeitschrift für deutsches Altertum* 100: 166–78.

Paul, Fritz (1982) 'Das Fiktionalitätsproblem in der altnordischen Prosaliteratur', *Arkiv för nordisk filologi* 97: 52–66.

Petersen, Niels Matthias (1866) *Bidrag til den oldnordiske Literaturs Historie*, Copenhagen: Berlingske Bogtrykkeri.

Rubow, Paul V. (1936) 'Den islandske familieroman', in *Små kritiske breve*, Copenhagen: Munksgaard, pp. 7–33.

Rühs, Friedrich (1812) *Die Edda*, Berlin: Realschulbuchhandlung.

Schlözer, August L. (1771) *Allgemeine nordische Geschichte*, Halle: Johann Justinus Gebauer.

Sigurður Nordal (1940) *Hrafnkatla* (*Studia Islandica*, 7), Reykjavík: Ísafoldarprentsmiðja H.F.

Steblin-Kamenskij, M. I. (1967) 'On the Nature of Fiction in the Sagas of Icelanders', *Scandinavica* 6: 77–84.

Steblin-Kamenskij, M. I. (1973) *The Saga Mind*. Translated by Kenneth H. Ober, Odense: Odense University Press.

Tómasson, Sverrir (1988) *Formálar íslenskra sagnaritara á miðöldum*, Reykjavík: Stofnun Árna Magnússonar.

Tulinius, Torfi H. (2002) *The Matter of the North: The Rise of Literary Fiction in Thirteenth-Century Iceland*. Translated by Randi C. Eldevik, Odense: Odense University Press. [Originally published as *La Matière du Nord. Sagas Légendaires et fiction dans l'Islande du XIIIe siècle*, Paris, 1995.]

Tulinius, Torfi H. (2004) *Skáldið í skriftinni. Snorri Sturluson og Egils saga*, Reykjavík: Hið íslenska bókmenntafélag.

Authentication and Authenticity in the Sagas of Icelanders and Serbian Epic Poetry

Slavica Ranković

On the face of it, the two literatures to be examined comparatively in this essay could hardly be more different. On the one hand we have the thirteenth- and fourteenth-century literary narratives in some cases the length of a decent novel, and, on the other, short heroic poetry orally composed and systematically collected by the nineteenth-century scholar Vuk Stefanović Karadžić.[1] The sagas of Icelanders (*Íslendingasögur*) and Serbian epic songs (*srpske junačke pesme*) were produced by societies geographically, historically and culturally far apart, yet in response to the pressures and opportunities afforded by their respective socio-historical environments, in the 'analogous function' (cf. Tynjanov 1971: 76) they performed, the two literatures are extraordinarily similar. Created by two small peoples facing the threat of cultural assimilation, produced multi-locally, within decentralized social structures, and catering for the tastes of a diverse audience, the Icelandic sagas and Serbian epics converged upon a similar kind of representational complexity. The nature of this complexity (the two literatures' famous 'realism'), as well as the unlikely parallels in the two societies' political, economic and belief systems, are discussed at length elsewhere (Ranković 2006a). The present paper, however, will concentrate on one particular aspect of the two literatures' representational similarity: the role of authentication in their constructions of the past.

1 Vuk Stefanović Karadžić (1787–1864) was the reformer of the Serbian language, an ethnographer, lexicographer and folklorist. This self-taught scholar was the first to systematically collect Serbian folk literature, and even the fiercest critics of some of his linguistic reforms, such as Jovan Skerlić, still highly praise this aspect of his activity. Among the many of the admirers of Karadžić's work were Johann Wolfgang Goethe and Jakob Grimm. Goethe had even learned the language in order to enjoy the literature in the original and translate it, while the brothers Grimm advised Vuk concerning the way of collecting and editing the material.

THE SAGAS OF ICELANDERS AND SERBIAN EPIC SONGS AS COMMUNAL HISTORIES

Infuriated by the publication of *The Battle of Čačak* (1823), a poem which, he felt, downplayed his role in the eponymous battle, Serbian prince (*knez*) Miloš Obrenović wrote to Vuk Karadžić: 'I will not allow you to disseminate lies about my deeds among our kind'. Karadžić's response that 'a song is not history' (Nedić 1990: 103)[2] did little to pacify the illiterate prince: for him, as for the most of his people, the song *was* history (even if, as we shall see later, a history of a very special kind). And it seems that Prince Miloš was not the only one worried about the representation of his deeds before his peers and posterity: Jovan Deretić writes that in the 'epic cultures', such as Montenegro at the time, 'there were noted cases when charges against singers were raised in court because they failed to mention someone's heroism or had downgraded it' (2000: 59; see also Kilibarda 1970: 94).

Unlike other traditional genres such as a folktale or a fairytale, a lullaby or a charm, a wedding song or a work song, an epic poem or a traditional heroic narrative such as an *Íslendingasaga* is 'a tale of the tribe' (cf. Downes 1997: x) and therefore has a responsibility to tell the truth about the past of the community. The writer of *Þórðar saga hreðu* appears to be well aware of this when he ends his story with the words 'Thord Menace died in his bed. We have not heard any more *true* stories about him' (CSI III: 396, my emphasis).[3] This statement has at least two important implications. The first one is of a general kind: as in the famous passage of *Þorgils saga ok Hafliða*, a distinction between two types of sagas can be inferred – those that are 'true' or trustworthy, and those that are 'untrue' or even 'lying' (*lygisögur*).[4] The second implication is more specific and points to the selection principle that the saga writer employs: out of a number of stories that were presumably circling about Þórðr, he is making his audience aware that he has chosen to concentrate only on those that were true (or rather, considered true by him and his community). Just how careful one is expected to be with the kinds of stories that can circulate is powerfully illustrated by the episode in *Grettis saga* in which the hero is accused of caus-

2 The above quotations (originally published in vol. II of Karadžić's correspondence) are here taken from the book of essays about Vuk's singers by Vladan Nedić (*Vukovi pevači*). Please note that, unless otherwise stated, all translations from Serbian are mine, and that, wherever original quotations appear in this text, they are, for readers' convenience, given in Latin rather than Cyrillic script.

3 'Þórður hreða varð sóttdauðr. Höfum vér ekki fleira heyrt með sannleik af honum sagt' (ÍS III: 2043).

4 The passage is quoted and considered in more detail in this volume by Else Mundal.

ing the death of some of his fellow Icelanders through a fire on his way to Norway (Ch. 46). Refusing to condemn Grettir in his absence and solely on the basis of a dubious report presented by his ill-wishers, Skapti the Lawspeaker elucidates his decision as follows: '[O]ne man only tells half a tale, and more people prefer the worse side of a story which has two versions' (CSI II: 119).[5] Even if we take this as Skapti's cunning ploy to make people at the Assembly more sympathetic to Grettir (or as the writer's/saga-teller's ploy to affect his reader/listener in the same way), we must assume that for any such ploy to actually work, the attitudes expressed need to have some general currency. In weighing their 'evidence' and discriminating between what is reliable information and what is not – and in treating, what is more, one's own motivations in deciding the plausibility of an account as suspect – saga writers do not differ much from historiographers. Indeed, the preserved redactions of the early Icelandic piece of historiography *Landnámabók* make free use of the material from the written sagas (cf. Mundal's contribution to this volume) and also refer to oral tradition as their source.[6] This is perhaps not so surprising considering that, as Judith Jesch notes (1984: 116), saga writers and the redactors of *Landnámabók* 'may often have been the same people'.

A singer of oral epics also exhibits the kind of concern with truth and facts that we commonly associate with historians. This concern becomes most prominent when he is faced with the task of composing a song about events that have taken place recently, a song that is yet to face the 'preliminary censorship by the community' (Jakobson and Bogatyrev 1971: 91). The case of the famous blind singer Filip Višnjić illustrates this very well. As a favour to Vuk Karadžić and Jernej Kopitar, the learned poet and archimandrite Lukijan Mušicki invited Višnjić to his monastery of Šišatovac in order to collect some biographical information from the singer. Among other things Mušicki asked Višnjić about the way he composed his Uprising songs. Višnjić explained that he started by interviewing the participants, asking '"who was their leader", "where did they fight", "who was killed, against whom they advanced"' (Nedić 1990: 52).[7] Following the rebel army and being a most welcome guest and

5 'jafnan er hálfsögð saga, ef einn segir, því at fleiri eru þess fúsari, at fœra þangat, sem eigi berr betr, ef tvennt er til' (ÍF VII: 146).

6 It may be of interest to note here that both Miodrag Maticki (1989: 107) and Jovan Delić (1990: 385) find in the works of the nineteenth-century chroniclers of the Serbian Uprisings (1804 and 1815), Vuk Karadžić, Matija Nenadović and Jovan Hadžić, typical expressions of epic poetry, sometimes even a hidden decasyllabic verse. In both cultures, historiography and epic narrative have close encounters both in terms of style and structure.

7 We can easily imagine a war correspondent or an oral historian asking these same questions.

entertainer at the houses and encampments of their noted leaders, Višnjić was in a very good position to gather the information he needed.[8] Furthermore, he had his own personal experiences to draw from, as the traces of sabre cuts on one of his cheeks and ear seemed to testify (cf. Nedić 1990: 45). He had also shared the destiny of the insurgents during the twelve-day siege of the town of Loznica, enduring with them the constant shelling, gunfire and water deprivation (the local river was poisoned), while raising their spirits and battle morale with his singing (cf. Nedić 1990: 43–4).

Taking care with the sources of information, however, has nothing to do with the honesty of any particular singer, or with what the famous portrait of our Višnjić seems to suggest:[9] the towering personality of the singer-seer whose authority and righteousness one should not doubt. Rather, it has to do with the medium of an epic song as a vehicle of communal memory on the one hand, and, on the other, with the proximity of the events related, and thus (as the above anecdote about Prince Miloš suggests) the liability to censure by the people who took part in them. In fact, once outside an epic poem, Višnjić is known to have related to his villagers stories such as the one in which he, supposedly before he lost his eyesight, pretended to be blind and spied on the Turks for the insurgents; or the one in which he heroically manages to escape, his eyes freshly pierced by the Turks, by swimming in such a state over the river Drina, leaving his native Bosnia for the relative safety of rebel Serbia. While this might bear witness to the singers' imaginative capabilities, it has nothing to do with some inherent, elevated sense of personal honesty or faithfulness: at the time of the First Serbian Uprising Višnjić was a man of fifty, his blindness was caused by chicken pox at the age of eight, which makes his first story of 'spying on Turks' improbable and his second story an outright falsehood, exhilarating though it is. Relating personal anecdotes leaves the singer with considerable freedom; relating events of wider social importance, and that within the solemn medium of the epic song, is quite another matter.

8 Stojan Čupić was particularly fond of Višnjić and had famously presented the singer with a white horse for the song *Battle of Salaš* in which his deeds were celebrated. This case is, however, noted by its rarity. Unlike their Muslim counterparts ('beys' singers') who entertained local noblemen (agas and beys), Christian singers of Serbian epics did not enjoy any sustained or substantial form of patronage as there were no distinct upper classes that would promote the production of epic. For more on differences between these two cognate oral traditions, see Foley (1991); for more on patronage in Serbo-Croatian Muslim epics, see Šmaus (1972).

9 What I have in mind is the work by Josip Danilović from 1901. The portrait can be seen online at: <http://www.rastko.org.yu/likovne/img/sl008.jpg>. This image is also used as a logo of the journal *Oral Tradition* edited by John Miles Foley <http://journal.oraltradition.org>.

This being said, we hardly regard traditional heroic narratives nowadays as factually accurate accounts of the past events to which they refer.[10] We are, however, equally weary of the 'gullibility of disbelief' (Jones 1986: 14) and have stopped dismissing these works as important sources for learning both about the times of which they tell, and, even more so, of the times in which they are told/written. Between an uncritical acceptance and a wholesale rejection, we are now navigating with more precision towards what kind of knowledge to expect from them. The relatively recent recognition of the value of oral history[11] and the general shift of interest from political to social history have cast a new light on traditional heroic narratives, and so the sagas are now perceived as 'a medium of cultural memory' (Glauser 2000: 211) or 'ethnographic documents' (Whaley 2000: 166; see also Byock 2001: 21). Influenced by the French Annales School's idea of a *longue durée* history, Jovan Deretić considers Serbian epics as vehicles of 'historical memory' (1994: 93), the kind that may not preserve precise facts about important events, but is nevertheless a very accurate indication of the impact they had (and continued to have) on a community. In other words, historical/social/cultural/communal memory documents 'coming to terms with the past' (Glauser 2000: 204) and hence coming to terms with the present too.

THE SAGAS OF ICELANDERS AND SERBIAN EPIC SONGS AS FICTIONS

If singers, saga-tellers/-writers and their audiences were all aware that traditional heroic songs or sagas were their histories, they were also aware that they were (and demanded of them to be) just that – songs and sagas. Apart from preserving the past of the community and reinterpreting it so as to make sense of the present,[12] these genres were also charged with other functions: to instruct and entertain, to comfort and challenge, to mystify and astonish, to

10 It is the ever-suspicious historians of the Enlightenment who had begun casting doubt on traditional epic narratives most relentlessly. Jovan Rajić (1726–1801) treated the idea of Serbian epics as histories with contempt, although he relied on them indirectly, by using the 'historical documents' that were actually based on traditional lore (cf. Deretić 2000: 61). One of Rajić's Icelandic contemporaries has similarly dismissed the sagas as stories about 'farmers at fisticuffs' (cf. Byock 2001: 154).

11 On oral history as an established genre within the historical canon, see Vansina (1988). Also see Prins (2001: 120–52).

12 Reinterpretation of the past for the purposes and interests of the present is, of course, what historiography does as well. If new times, different cultures and social groups did not require interpretations that bring past and present to bear upon each other, it would be hard to account for such an astonishing number of histories that spring up every year and that, in various languages and from various perspectives, all treat Tudors, for example, or the French Revolution, or the Golden Horde.

excite and enlighten, to procure catharsis or, as it sometimes happens, frustrate further the recipients' need for it. In other words, they needed to do what good stories normally do.

While granting the *Íslendingasögur* 'a genuinely historical sensibility', Diana Whaley still finds it significant that the titles of two early Icelandic historiographies (*Íslendingabók* and *Landnámabók*) both end in *bók* rather than *saga* (Whaley 2000: 166–7). The former ending decidedly links historiography to literacy, while, derived from the verb *segja* ('to say'), the latter carries the inevitable connotation of orality, regardless of the fact that *saga* could refer to both an oral and a written story. This indicates that the difference between the two genres was felt to some degree, even if it was not perceived as too sharp[13] to prevent their encroachment upon one another.[14] If there was a strong pull in traditional epic singing and storytelling towards giving a true account of the community's past, there was an equally strong pull in another direction, a pull towards translating the facts about that past into the medium of an epic song or a saga with its pre-existing narrative structures, formulaic idioms and universalizing tendencies that Aristotle already identified in his *Poetics* (51.b) as the distinguishing feature of poetry (i.e. literature) in respect to history. Scholars nowadays generally refer to this process as 'fictionalization of history/ facts' (e.g. Deretić 2000: 71), or 'mythologization of history' (e.g. Hainsworth 1991: 63), regardless of whether they deem the first (in respect to the second) part of the syntagm a conquest or a corruption of sorts.

While appreciating the appeal that stems from their apparent explanatory power, I still find these expressions inadequate and imprecise. The fictionalization or mythologization has a role to play in any kind of discourse, whether literary or factual, although the prominence and the exact nature of that role has been a matter of heated debate in the past decades (cf. Ankersmit 1994). The representational character of historiography, the necessity for selection, ordering and interpretation of data, evidence and such, require from a historian to reach for the available narrative/fictional

13 In fact, in his effort to reconstruct parts of the *Heiðarvíga saga* that perished in the infamous Copenhagen fire (1728), Jón Ólafsson, the eighteenth-century scribe and an associate of Árni Magnússon, refers to *Landnámabók* as *Landnámasaga* on at least one occasion (cf. ÍS II: 1352; CSI IV: 83). Taking into account the emphasis that scholars of the Enlightenment used to place on divisions between genres and styles, one can only assume that such interchangeable use was more frequent in medieval Iceland.

14 Some overlaps between *Laxdæla saga* and Sturla Þórðarson's version of *Landnámabók* are discussed in Ranković (2006b: 46–7).

structures and patterns. This, as Ludmilla Jordanova notes (2000: 156), does not mean that historians 'make things up',[15] but that 'their accounts of the past are structured and gain plausibility in the same manner as other narratives'. The question that inevitably follows such a recognition – what it is that distinguishes history from 'other narratives'/fiction – has also much occupied philosophers of history and literary historians alike. As opposed to Hayden White who considers the relationship between history and fiction as generic (e.g. White 1978), Dennis Green sees it as 'genetic', since fiction arises from the supposed 'gaps in real history' (Green 2002: 134, 152; also see Green's contribution to this volume).[16] For Green, the main difference between the two is that history is 'externally referential' (i.e. it seeks consistency with the 'real world'), while fiction, even when it treats historical subjects, is 'fundamentally self-referential, it remains true to its own fabricated world and seeks consistency within its limits' (2002: 142). David Perkins (1993: 34) similarly emphasizes the self-sufficiency of the fabricated fictional world and goes on to say: 'Narrative history differs fundamentally from fiction because, in constructing a novel, the "plot" takes precedence over "story"'. In other words, the *way* the story is told becomes infinitely more important than its particulars, its 'facts', or their relationship to the real world. Vuk Karadžić seems to anticipate Perkins's stance on the primacy of plot in fiction when he comments: '[I]n history one looks for the truth, and in the song one looks at how things are made up (*izmišljeno*) and arranged (*namješteno*)' (in Deretić 2000: 62). In his 1833 preface to the Viennese edition of the fourth book of Serbian folk songs (*srpske narodne pjesme*), Karadžić also notes:

> It is true that in folk songs (as in nearly any [song]) one should not look for *true history*; but the *story*, which is in heroic songs the most important thing, is in songs of good singers never completely at odds with common folk … sense. (1976 IV: 378, Vuk's emphases)

This stance resonates with the Aristotelian (and modern) emphasis on plausibility rather than factual veracity of fiction.

15 At the same time, the fact that in fiction things *are* made up does not make them untrue. Friedrich Engels famously stated that he learned more from Balzac than from all the professional historians, economists and statisticians put together.

16 In *The Dialogic Imagination* (1981) Mikhail Bakhtin argues that these gaps in historical writing gave rise to the novel.

The 'one' Karadžić has in mind in the above quotation, however, is not a member of the audience gathered to listen to Višnjić, for example, but the nineteenth-century European reader of his poems, the kind of reader he wishes his average semi-literate compatriot to become.[17] And while Perkins's and Green's distinctions may well work for novels and the twelfth-century romance (and Green at least does not claim anything else[18]), in traditional (oral and orally derived) epic narratives the precedence of either plot or story, or the precedence of either its function as the vehicle of communal memory or its 'literary function' (as the Formalists would call it), is never so clearly decided. This, rather, remains a matter of tension in which neither aspect, neither function, is consciously or willingly sacrificed. In oral cultures, the very survival of epic narratives depends on their being considered true (and thus relevant), on the one hand, and on their being well told (and thus entertaining), on the other. It is both of these aspects that make the narratives memorable and that, with the support of the traditional idiomatic structures, ensure their continued existence. When it comes to the early manuscript cultures such as that of medieval Iceland, the same principles of memorability apply as in oral societies, since the early literates in many ways retain and perpetuate oral 'habits of mind' (cf. Ong 1982) and carry the oral poetics over to the new medium (e.g. Doane 1991). During this period, books were still precious and expensive to make, and whatever gets preserved or recreated from the oral tradition has to be well worth the effort. Moreover, even after such material is put down on parchment, if it stops fulfilling its purpose, the text will not be copied further and can also easily be scraped and written over. Or, it can be put to an entirely new use, say, it can become a sawing pattern for some industrious Icelandic woman, as was, at some point, the case with page IX, 16 of *Reykjarfjarðarbók Sturlungu* AM 122 b fol. In short, at no point is the singer/saga-writer/-teller or their audiences ready to compromise either the veracity of their narrative or its beauty. Ideally, they should both always be maximal, but of course this would in given circumstances mean something different, just as strength and agility are both equally important and yet differently distributed in antelopes and lions, boxers and ballerinas.

17 It is the common and uncritical belief of most of his fellow Serbs in historical accuracy of their epics that elicits Vuk's need to educate them about the fictional character of these stories. This has also, most likely, necessitated that he overstate the issue.

18 Green in fact acknowledges that 'the changing nature of fictionality over time' (Green 2002: 26) poses immense problems to a unified definition. He thus insists on the relevance of his own definitions only to the period 1150–1220 and locality under scrutiny.

NEGOTIATING FACTUAL AND FICTIONAL ATTRACTORS[19]

'The fictional' and 'the factual' could be usefully conceived of as different pulls or attractors that both act on tradition as it evolves, and in every particular realization (oral or textual performance) of a narrative their relationship is negotiated according to the specificities of the circumstances in which such a realization takes place. While to the singer/saga-teller/-writer and their audiences it is, at any one time, *equally* important that a song/saga is both factually true and well told, the varying constraints and opportunities of the cultural environment will inevitably be nudging the narrative as it unfolds towards one or the other attractor. The temporal proximity to the events portrayed often plays a crucial part when it comes to which of the attractors will (on the whole) exert more force on traditional narratives. Namely, the closer the saga/song is to the events it relates, the stronger the pull of the factual attractor tends to be, and vice versa.

While praising the subtle artistry and the heightened sense for drama that the singer Old Raško exhibits in the songs depicting the demise of Serbian medieval splendour, Svetozar Koljević (rather harshly, if not unjustifiably) charges Raško's contemporary song *The Battle of Deligrad* with 'maniacal monotony' (1980: 281), as the singer seems compelled to mention nearly every person who took part in the battle. Similarly, considering the songs that treat the contemporary theme of the liberation of Montenegro, Novak Kilibarda argues that these rarely 'develop into poetry' (1991: 281) but more often tend to remain epic chronicles, and the reason for this, he insists, is the fact that the audience consists of the participants in the events related. According to Kilibarda, the tribal pride of 'the ambitious warriors [...] clipped the wings of the imagination of the Montenegrin bards' (1991: 283). Theodore M. Andersson (2002) sees such dynamics as characteristic of all 'short term traditions', in his particular example, the contemporary sagas. As opposed to the 'classical sagas' (*Íslendingasögur*), he considers the conflicts represented in the contemporary ones 'disconnected and repetitive' (394), the materials 'arranged serially rather than dramatically' (395), given

19 In mathematics and the sciences that deal with dynamical (i.e. changing) systems, an attractor is a point or a set of points (in some space) towards which a system tends and would eventually settle upon (cf. Stewart 1997). The dynamical systems range from the abstract mathematical models to natural and cultural phenomena such as the weather, economic markets, living organisms, or, in our case, tradition.

in 'superabundant detail' (411) and generally finds that these sagas lack the refinement in the oral tradition through which they would acquire 'a leaner, simpler, more dramatic style' (411).

This way of looking, of course, makes sense only from the contingency of our perspective in time. The original audiences would not have felt that their enjoyment was being compromised by a performer/writer who lacked imagination and was drowning them in detail and monotony. Unlike for us, the entertainment factor was for them a given, since they had an advantage of a shared referentiality that gave a special resonance to each name and imbued with special interest each particular mentioned. However, as with the Cold War jokes that either had to keep their Russian and American anonymous, or to keep giving them names of the current presidents in order to remain funny, the resonance of the particulars about an event will start waning within a generation, and if it is to survive, the song/saga will imperceptibly (and yet in many ways and on various levels) start adapting to the changing needs and interests of the audience. This is also the point at which our perspective of a hindsight and recognition of the regularities of change become valid again.

That the pull of the factual attractor in short-term traditions will be generally stronger does not mean that the fictional pull is not also felt. As Jovan Deretić rightly points out (2000: 68–9):

> Events precede songs, but so do songs precede events... [Songs about contemporary events] show a great accuracy in recounting the facts, but also a tendency to adjust themselves to the demands of the traditional epic poetics ...

Indeed, as he lists the aesthetic weaknesses of the contemporary sagas, Andersson finds the depiction of the battles on Sælingsdalsheiðr and of Staðhyltinegar against the Búðdœlir in *Sturlu saga* to be exceptions, as they 'approach the scenic articulation characteristic of the classical sagas' (2002: 395). In other words, the depictions of these battles show a greater tendency to adjust themselves to the traditional saga poetics. The degree to which such adjustments will be made, and the exact shape they will take, will vary from one tradition to another, from one social environment to another, from one singer/storyteller to another, and from an intractable number of factors pertaining to the specific circumstances in which a concretization (oral or textual) of an ever immanent epic song/saga takes place.[20]

If we compare Serbian and Montenegrin songs about the contemporary (nineteenth-century) struggles with the Turks, we can say that, on the whole, Serbian epic songs show a greater degree of such adjustments to the traditional epic poetics (i.e. the fictional attractor exerts a slightly stronger pull) than do their Montenegrin counterparts. The differences can be felt regardless of whether they are due to the fact that we are indeed dealing with the peculiarly 'truth-loving Montenegrins' (Kilibarda 1991: 281), or because the strong inter-tribal competition in Montenegro (sometimes even an animosity, suspended only during the fight against the common and stronger enemy) placed an extra pressure for factual veracity on Montenegrin singers (cf. Kilibarda 1970: 88–9, 102). Such variations in adherence to fictional/factual attractors are also discernable in the songs of different singers, and so Višnjić's *Battle of Salaš* and *The Beginning of the Revolt against the Dahijas* show closer adjustment to the traditional idiom and escape some of the tedium of the mentioned contemporary song by Old Raško (*The Battle of Deligrad*), or indeed, another song by Višnjić himself, *The Battle of Čokešina*.[21] In this, as in many other of his Uprising songs, Višnjić is more of a 'chronicler – dry, diffuse, uniform' (Nedić 1990: 60). The difference in the pull of the fictional and factual attractors can thus be detected in the repertoire of one and the same singer and, what is more, in the different deliveries of the same song. As his case is better documented than that of most other singers, I turn again to Filip Višnjić for an example. According to Nedić (1990: 60), both the 1814 and 1833 published versions of *The Battle of Mišar* were recorded from Višnjić, yet the latter shows a far better command of the traditional idiom and escapes the triumphalist perspective of the former by including verses that mourn the wasted lives of the fallen Muslim warriors, their youth and beauty, their bereaved families – the mother of Ostroč-captain deprived of her only son, the young fiancée ('betrothed treasure') of the handsome Bešir's Aso, widowed before she even got married, etc.[22]

20 On the immanent nature of traditional narratives, see Clover (1986) and Foley (1991). Also see Ranković (2006a).

21 Note that we are still talking about 'short-term traditions'. If all four contemporary songs were compared to one that treats a more distant past (e.g. *Banović Strahinja* by Old Milija, with his peculiarly individualistic style), then all four would lean closer to the factual rather than the fictional attractor.

22 These verses are indeed put into the mouth of Kulin-captain's (the leader of the Turkish forces) widow, but could not have been conceived without some empathy on the part of the singer.

These, of course, are general observations of large-scale features of the negotiation dynamics between the fictional and factual attractors acting on short-term traditions. If we could observe these narratives through a finer grain filter, the picture that would emerge is likely to be even more complex, as the various parts and instances of either version of *The Battle of Mišar*, or *Sturlu saga* for that matter, would themselves twist and turn towards one or the other attractor as the narrative develops, creating an intertwined, enmeshed pattern. This meshing and intertwining also renders the separation of the factual and fictional impossible.

While the temporal proximity to the events related proves an important parameter when it comes to the stronger adherence of the narrative towards one or the other attractor, it is so by implication only. At no point, as time goes by, do traditional singers or saga-tellers/-writers make a conscious decision to sacrifice a factual detail to narrative expediency, dramatic arrangement of events, or to a more polished turn of phrase, and yet they inadvertently do so, all the time responding to the subtle pressures and opportunities of the specific environment in which they create. An analogy can be offered here from another, still living tradition – that of fashion. Most of us today are not likely to remember when exactly we decided to stop wearing platform shoes,[23] and the reason for this need not solely be our feeble memories. It is rather the case, I think, that we never really made the decision in the first place: we simply kept opting for something else to wear. By the time the next spring cleaning came, the cumulative effect of our choices will have *amounted* to a decision to discard the platforms (or perhaps turn them into something entirely different – a relic, a memento). In very much the same manner (i.e. by the cumulative selectivity of narrational commitments) traditional epic songs/sagas depicting events that took place further in the past will tend more strongly towards the fictional attractor. At the same time, this process is not inexorable, and the factual attractor exerts its pull as well. Traditional singers and storytellers may not have the exact equivalent to 'spring cleaning' when it comes to songs/sagas covering events set in far past, but they are nevertheless aware of their lack of control over such material in terms of factual veracity, which always remains an important parameter. Not being themselves (or not having an access to) eyewitnesses of the events which they relate, yet well aware of the

23 That is presuming that 'we' wore them in the first place (in either the 1970s or the 1990s when they were 'in' again, at least when it comes to the fashion of women). But the reader can either indulge me, or imagine an outdated garment of his or her choice.

gravity of their role as 'stewards of tradition' (Meulengracht Sørensen 1993: 76), singers and saga-tellers/-writers resort to a certain corrective mechanism that they have at their disposal, the mechanism that will re-inaugurate the subtle negotiations of the two attractors, that is, authentication. While in the narratives depicting recent events authentication is a part of these narratives' bid for admission in the traditional canon, in the narratives that refer to the far past it functions as a kind of truth-checking, or rather, truth-calibrating mechanism, given that 'truth-checking' also always involves truth-making.

AUTHENTICATION IN THE *ÍSLENDINGASÖGUR AND SRPSKE JUNAČKE PESME*

When it comes to the material for which no eyewitnesses exist (and the majority of traditional heroic narratives deal with such material, of course), the most common way of establishing a relationship of trust between the singers/storytellers and their audience is for the former to evade direct responsibility for their story by stating that they are giving us an account as they heard it themselves. In this way the responsibility for the truth is referred to a far greater authority – that of the collective and the tradition as a whole – and, in turn, the believability of the account becomes enhanced.[24] While this device originates with oral epics, it is also exploited in the orally derived epics and adopted by the literary ones. Thus, *Beowulf* opens with the announcement that the story will be about the Spear-Danes and their princes of whose heroic campaigns 'we have heard' (2002: 3), while the *Chanson de Roland* finishes in the like manner, with the scribe Turoldus asserting, and in the same breath conditioning, his authority by signing his name yet informing us that he 'heard this history' (1983: 135). A number of events related in the *Nibelungenlied* are similarly conditioned and affirmed by the phrase, 'so we are told' (e.g. 1969: 58, 85).

I have elsewhere (Ranković 2006a) already pointed out that, despite the fact that they are historically and culturally unrelated, and despite their all too apparent formal differences, *Íslendingasögur* and *srpske junačke pesme* are very similar in the ways in which they diverge from the earlier European epics. One of those similarities concerns the range and usage of authenticating devices.

24 This gesture that, on the one hand, places the authority of the whole community behind the account and acts as an advertisement, on the other (i.e. only a good story survives the censure of the collective), is so powerful that Serbian singers who composed new songs also often claimed that they heard them from others (cf. Karadžić 1976 I: 536; also see Ranković 2006b: 44).

In comparison to the epics mentioned above where the stress lies on the narrator hearing or being told a story, the *Íslendingasögur* and *srpske junačke pesme* exhibit a far greater number of finely gradated devices that not only confirm but also profess uncertainty (e.g. due to conflicting information, or its lack) and cast doubt over the events related. Although very rarely, the whole story or its parts can even be dismissed as unlikely or untrue. Without pretensions to a comprehensive coverage,[25] this second part of the chapter will attempt to illustrate the range and employment of authenticating devices in our two literatures. The aim of the analysis is to suggest that the presence of such a wide variety of authenticating tools and techniques is an index of an 'arms race' between the audience demanding veracity of the accounts related on the one hand and, on the other, the traditional singers/saga-tellers/-writers coming up with ever fresher ways of either guaranteeing the truth of the narrative, or delineating its limits, specifying the degree to which they can be believed. This truth-calibration (regardless of whether it was always genuinely exercised or applied by sheer narrative inertia) testifies, I think, to the pull that the factual attractor exerts on the stories set in the near, but also those set in the distant past.

AUTHENTICATION BY AFFIRMATION

I have mentioned earlier how the sagas and historiography of the time (e.g. versions of *Landnámabók*, 'kings' sagas', etc.) interpenetrate. One of the ways in which this becomes most apparent is the sagas' concern with dates, numbers and 'evidence' – the specifics. Every important character that is introduced is located within a more or less extensive genealogy and each saga is set against the backdrop of the rule of a particular Norwegian king.[26] Furthermore, many an event is set in even more concrete terms, with the saga writer giving us a specific number of years that divides that from another, historically more sig-

25 In the appendix of her book on the poetics of epic formulae (*Urok i nevesta: poetika epske formule*, 1996: 167–72), Mirjana Detelić provides, among other types of formulae, a comprehensive list of those that deal with the veracity of the story related. She divides these into further nine subgroups (1996: 28) of a spectrum that starts from those that affirm the story with confidence over those that profess uncertainty, to those that negate the authenticity of the account. However, while Detelić's goal was the typology and poetics of the epic formulae, my aim is to point to the ways in which they function as authenticating devices.

26 Kings and nobles of other countries are also often mentioned and their lineage and rule discussed in some detail (consider for example the introduction of the English king Athelstan in Ch. 50 of *Egils saga*).

nificant and widely known event. So, in *Eyrbyggja saga* we are told that Þórólfr Moster-beard incurred king Haraldr's anger for sheltering an outlaw 'ten years after Ingolf Arnarson had left to settle in Iceland…' (CSI V: 133),[27] while Eiríkr the Red went back to settle Greenland (which he discovered four years prior to this) 'fourteen years before Christianity was adopted by law in Iceland' (CSI V: 157).[28] *Laxdæla saga* similarly places the death of the famous Icelandic chieftain Snorri goði 'one year after the fall of King Olaf the Saint' (CSI V: 118),[29] and corroborates it further by invoking the authority of the famous cleric-historian Ari Þorgilsson the Learned (*inn fróði*) with the characteristic phrase *svá sagði* ('so said').[30] Regardless of whether they prove ultimately accurate or not, these and similar specifics (e.g. in *Eyrbyggja saga* we are told not only that Þórir's leg was cut off by Þórarinn, but that it was cut 'at the thickest part of the calf' (CSI V: 146)[31]), details that are not necessary for the progress of the narrative, give the account an aura of objectivity.

The example above from *Laxdæla saga* leads us to another category of authenticating tools, the one that involves summoning an authoritative figure to vouch for the trustworthiness of the account. Apart from Ari the Learned (e.g. *Laxdæla saga*, Ch. 4; *Eyrbyggja saga*, Ch. 7; *Njáls saga*, Ch. 114), sagas also refer to another famous historian and lawspeaker – Sturla Þórðarson. For example, in Ch. 69 of *Grettis saga* the narrator turns to Sturla in order to establish the number of years of Grettir's outlawry at the time he settled on the island of Drangey, as is the case with the concluding chapter (93), in which Sturla is invoked in the final assessment of Grettir's character. In addition to historians and lawspeakers, other people of authority are also called upon to testify to the veracity of an account. Among them are skalds[32] (e.g. Þormóðr Trefilsson[33] in *Eyrbyggja saga*, Chs. 26, 37, 44, 56 and 62), bishops (e.g. Egill Eyjólfsson in Ch. 9 of *Þórðar saga hreðu*) and priests (e.g. Rúnólfr Daggson in *Bjarnar saga Hítdælakappa*, Ch. 19). Other eminent personages are invoked

27 'tíu vetrum síðar en Ingólfr Arnarson hafði farit at byggja Ísland' (ÍF IV: 7).

28 'fjórtán vetrum fyrir kristni lögtekna á Íslandi' (ÍF IV: 60).

29 'einum vetri eptir fall Óláfs konungs ins Helga' (ÍF V: 226).

30 The present tense variant of this phrase, *svá segir* ('so says'), is also very common.

31 'þar er kálfi var digrastr' (ÍF IV: 37).

32 On how reliable a witness skaldic poetry was considered to be, see the famous Prologue to the *Heimskringla* (ÍF XXVI) by Snorri Sturluson.

33 Þormóðr Trefilsson is particularly interesting because he acts here as an 'independent' witness. Otherwise, we could assert that, apart from its other important functions (e.g. revealing the innermost thoughts, feelings and dilemmas of heroes), skaldic poetry that appears in the sagas of warrior poets and is attributed to the heroes themselves (e.g. Egill, Grettir, Gísli, Gunnlaugr, etc.) also serves as a means of corroborating the events related.

too, for example Guðný Böðvarsdóttir (the mother of the famous historian and statesman Snorri Sturluson), who is reported to have witnessed the exhumation and transfer of the bones of Snorri goði, his uncle and mother, as well as giving an account of the size and state of each skeleton (*Eyrbyggja saga*, Ch. 65). The social position, character and widely acknowledged wisdom of these authorities provide a solid guarantee for the stories narrated.

A further category of authenticating tools refers not to people, but objects, i.e. 'the material evidence' whose present tangibility places an account beyond question. ('If the goat lies, its horn does not', goes an old Serbian saying.) These can be weapons such as Grettir's spear which he threw at one of his enemies and which was, we are duly informed, found in Sturla Þórðarsson's time, in the field in which the clash is just reported to have taken place (*Grettis saga*, Ch. 49). They can also be valuable items, such as the garter with which the saintly king Óláfr Haraldsson presented Björn the Champion of the Hitardal people (*Hítdælakappi*) and which Björn apparently always wore around his leg. It was, many years later, found during the exhumation of Björn's skeleton. Even though everything else had decayed, the garter was uncorrupted, we are told, and 'it is now the cincture of a set of mass vestments at Gardar on Akarnes' (CSI I: 267).[34]

The material evidence can also include parts of the landscape. I do not merely have in mind legends about place names in which the sagas abound (e.g. Ch. 5 of *Laxdæla saga* depicting the exploration of Iceland by Auðr the Deep-minded and place-naming according to the events of the journey), but more concrete references. After settling a dispute regarding the defilement of the Þórsness assembly site, we are told that Þórðr Bellower (*Eyrbyggja saga*, Ch. 10) decided to move the assembly further up the headland. The saga writer offers in addition the following curiosity:

> It is still possible to see the judgement circle in which men were sentenced to be sacrificed. Within the ring stands Thor's stone, across which men's backs were broken when they were sacrificed, and the stain of blood can still be seen on the stone.[35] (CSI V: 138)

34 'er þat nú messufatalindi í Görðum á Akranesi' (ÍF III: 134).

35 'Þar sér enn dómhring þann, er menn váru dœmðir í til blóts; í þeim hring stendr Þórs steinn, er þeir menn váru brotnir um, er til blóta váru hafðir, ok sér enn blóðslitinn á steininum' (ÍF IV: 18).

Similarly, according to *Egils saga*, the stone on which Skalla-Grímr forged his iron can still be seen and identified further by the fact that its surface is marked with hammer strokes (Ch. 30) – recognizable as was one of the halls that Þórðr the Menace built, Skeggi of Miðfjörðr's cairn (*Þórðar saga hreðu*, Ch. 14) and the handiwork of the two berserk brothers, Halli and Leiknir. Both *Eyrbyggja* and *Heiðarvíga saga* mention this handiwork, with the former stating that it is the remnants of the wall they built that can still be seen (Ch. 28), and the latter claiming verifiability of the lava road that the brothers cleared on Víga Styrr's request (Ch. 4).

It is not always objects, but also a current custom or a state of affairs that acts as evidence. Chapter 38 of *Eyrbyggja saga* provides a particularly illuminating example. That the settlement for the killing of Arnkell goði was utterly unfitting for such a great chieftain is blamed on the fact that he did not have male heirs and that his case was prosecuted poorly and with less vigour by the female relatives. This, we are told, is why

> the leading men of the land made a law that a woman or a young man under the age of sixteen could never prosecute a manslaughter case, and this has been the law ever since.[36] (CSI V: 179)

Albeit differently (and having to deal with the constraints of verse), Serbian singers also use landmarks as well as the present state of affairs to validate an event that was supposed to have taken place in the past. After relating the story about the wedding of the Ban of Kruševo (Vuk VI 40[37]) – with the usual obstacles and the compulsory menacing Arab – the singer does not seem entirely confident about its veracity. However, he still refers his audience to two facts that speak in its favour: one has to do with the authority of the collective ('People say this happened in earnest'[38]), and the other with the fact that in the places mentioned there still are people that bear the same surnames as the characters from the song: 'There is a lot of Zotović's today / In Dubrovnik a lot of Červos and Červićes'.[39] Unlike the songs which merely state that something 'really happened' (e.g. 'This happened, it happened indeed' (Vuk VIII

36 'þá fœrðu landsstjórnarmenn lög á því, at aldri síðan skyldi kona vera vígsakaraðili né yngri karlmaðr en sextán vetra, ok hefir þat haldizk jafnan síðan' (ÍF IV: 104).

37 Here and elsewhere in this chapter, the number corresponds to the song (rather than the page) number in the collection.

38 'Ljudi vele istina je bilo'.

39 'Eto danas dosta Zotovića / U Dubrovnik Červa i Červića'.

21)[40] or, 'This is not a jest or trickery, but the truth, just as it happened!' (SM 140),[41] the singer of the above song endeavours to provide some proof for his account.

In a number of poems about the contest between Christian and Muslim priests, the current situation is similarly exploited. A Turkish sultan (Suleiman the Magnificent in one of the variants) sets off to Islamize his Christian subjects by trying to bribe (or threaten) the patriarch (a Niko or, more often, a Savo[42]). The contest in performing miracles between Islamic and Christian priests ensues, and, impressed by the Christian superiority in these, the Sultan nearly ends up a Christian himself. It is his vizier Ćuprilić (an Islamized Slav, as his name suggests) that lends him some sobriety and manages to channel the Sultan away from baptism and into a happy substitute: a yearly tribute in candle-wax and incense is to be given to the Church.[43] The poems end thus: 'So it was then, and so it is now' (Vuk III 50 and 54).[44] The common knowledge that the Orthodox Church occasionally received such contributions from the Porte but also from the Islamized Slavs, some of whom retained the habit of presenting churches with wax and incense at times of great Christian festivities (most notably Christmas and Easter),[45] is called upon to testify to the story about the contest between the religions. The same concluding formula is applied in the song *The Wedding Guests of Nuko Novljanin*, only this time it is the fact that the city of Novi is free from Turkish rule that is used to vouch for the story. The concealed animosities between Christian and Muslim guests forming the wedding party of Nuko are stirred and eventually boil over when the beautiful Turkish bride is taken from her groom and nominated as the prize for the warrior who wins her in a contest. What was supposed to be a happy event is turned into a bloody affair instead, and as a result of the Christians' victory the city of Novi changes hands: 'It was then that Novi fell to the giaours,[46] / So it was then, and so it is now' (Vuk III 33).[47]

40 'To je bilo, istina je bilo'.

41 'Nije ovo šala ni prevara, / No istina sve kako je bilo!'

42 This is no doubt due to the fact that this was the name of the national saint, St Sava, the youngest son of Stefan Nemanja (the twelfth-century progenitor of the first Serbian royal dynasty, the Nemanjićs) and founder of the Serbian autocephalous church.

43 In another variant he allows the existence of a Christian church in his capital.

44 'Kako tade, tako i danaske'.

45 See Stavrianos (1965). Also see Đorđević (1984 II: 258).

46 This was a derogatory term Turks used for 'infidels' generally, but in Serbian epic poems heroes wear this label with pride and in defiance of their overlords (i.e. 'if being a giaour means not being a Turk/ Muslim, then I am proud to be one').

47 'Tad je Novi pod kaure pao, / Kako tada, tako i danaske'.

The authenticating mechanisms in the above examples resemble those circular arguments upon which legends rest: the story of a place-name (in our case a state of affairs) validates the place-name, while the existence of such a place-name validates the story. In this respect, the example from *The Building of Ravanica, Again*[48] is especially telling. The splendour of a newly built church dazzles the eyes of Tsar Lazar's horse who jumps in fear, tumbling the tsar. The singer informs us: 'That place is called "The Tsar's Great Bruise"[49] / So it was then, and so it is now' (Vuk II 36).[50] At this point Vuk Karadžić conscientiously notes that he could not find out whether there is such a place around the monastery of Ravanica.[51] What makes this example particularly interesting is the fact that it is not necessarily the existence of a place (or a custom, or a state of affairs) in the present that validates an event, but that, as though by metonymic extension, the idiomatic expression 'so it was then, so it is now' has acquired a validating power in its own right.

There are, of course, concrete landmarks that are occasionally evoked too. Such can, for instance, be found in the two variants (one recorded from Blind Stepanija, the other from Filip Višnjić) of the song *Saint Savo*. Both variants open with Serbian nobles gathering after a liturgy and speculating on the whereabouts of Stefan Nemanja's immense wealth (was it spent on majestic palaces? wars to further his earthly glory?). Nemanja's youngest son Sava overhears the speculations and is thus provoked to defend the wisdom of his family's investments, which prompts the two singers to offer a catalogue of monasteries and churches that the Nemanjićes built as their memorials (and, in Višnjić's case, some that they did not!), offering for each specific and largely accurate geographical references. This is perhaps not so surprising considering that the two blind singers are likely to have visited some of the places they mention. Their very livelihood depended on travels from one monastery to another where they would receive alms or, during the festivities and fairs organized on church premises, earn their keep from the gathered populace. Their disability may have also made them especially sensitive to the landscape they were crossing, particularly the things they could hear, such as rivers, which feature strongly in the variant of the exceptionally well-travelled Filip Višnjić (cf. Nedić 1990: 47).

48 'Again' marks that this is the second of the two variants of the song.

49 'The Tsar's Great Bruise' is Locke's translation of *Carevo Bupilo* (1997: 113). The rest of the translation is mine.

50 'Tu se zove Carevo Bupilo, / Kako tadaj, tako i danaske'.

51 Vuk II: 156, n. 29.

Unsurprisingly perhaps, the immediacy of personal experience – 'I've been there, seen it with my eyes' (Vuk VIII 61; SANU III 19)[52] – and the tactile quality of the evidence available is exploited to the full in the songs depicting more recent events. In *The Battle of Salaš* (Vuk IV 28), Višnjić describes how a handful of Serbian rebels managed to recapture Mačva, rescue many captives and slaughter hosts of enemies.[53] For all the unlikelihood of the feat related, Višnjić is confident of its veracity and ends his poem by inviting the audience to check his account by visiting the site of the battle:

If there is someone who will not believe,
Let him go and see with his eyes:
The place where the Turks shed their bones
Will be known till there is sun and Salaš.[54]

The recommendation to use the eyes as main witnesses comes across especially forcefully as it is made by a blind singer, someone who does not have the use of his eyes, but in this case, it seems, does not need them to believe. Similar in this respect is the song depicting another rare feat, the 1858 battle of Grahovac (Vuk IX 14). The singer is so confident of the truth of his account that he apparently does not even care whether he is believed or not:

Now believe, brother Slav,
This truthful song of mine.
Either believe, or do as you please,
But the Turks will believe this,
As will our neighbour who was watching
From the top of Vršnik, the high mountain.[55]

52 'Tu sam bio, očima vidio.'

53 This event took place in 1806 in the north-west of Mačva, near the border with Bosnia. For more details, see Koljević (1980: 286).

54 'Ako li tko vjerovati ne će
Neka ide i očima vidi:
Znati će se Turska košturnica
Dokle teče sunca i Salaša.'

55 'Sada vjeruj, brate Slavjanine!
Ovu moju pjesmu od istine,
Ali vjeruj, al' kako ti drago,
Al' će Turci ovo vjerovati,
I naš susjed, koji je gledao
Svrh Vršnika, visoke planine.'

Paradoxically, it is precisely this professed lack of care, but also the reference to witnesses (one of them being the defeated enemy), that in effect enhance the believability of the story. Furthermore, like in the above example with Þórir's leg (*Eyrbyggja saga*), here too the reference to the specifics pertaining to the relation of the witness to the singer (neighbour, even if unnamed) and his observation spot (mountain Vršnik) produce the feeling that the account 'can't be fake', or, as Roland Barthes (1989) would say, they produce *l'effet de réel*.

In terms of the specifics, the following example is very interesting. Its freshness and uniqueness point to the importance of the performative context and the opportunistic attitude of the singers in authenticating an account. In *A Heroic Deed of Old Novak* the outlaw Radivoj is envious of the fame his older brother (Old Novak) enjoys and suggests a duel to ascertain who is the better warrior. To avoid fratricide, Novak suggests that they have a contest instead and that they both challenge the three-headed monster of the lake on the mountain Zvijezda. As soon as he catches a glimpse of the monster, Radivoj takes to his heels, but Novak defeats it. Like in the example with Grettir and the trollwoman that we shall soon discuss, the singer seems to (over) compensate for the unlikelihood of the event by combining two authenticating techniques – the invocation of a witness, on the one hand, and reference to local landmarks on the other:

> The one who's been writing knows this well,
> His house is even closer
> By Zvijezda, the high mountain,
> Wild goats leap all over it,
> There is a lake there even now.[56] (Vuk VII 35)

However, what makes this example exceptional is that the singer calls upon the person writing down his song to corroborate the story, the person who, given his likely prestigious status within a largely illiterate community, makes a particularly strong witness.[57]

56 'Koji piso o tom dobro znade,
Jošte bliže on kuću imade
Kod Zvijezde visoke planine,
Sve po njojzi divokoze skaču,
Tu jezero i sada imade.'

57 Including remarks on the act of recording during performance is something that singers often do,

AUTHENTICATION BY DOUBT AND UNCERTAINTY – NEGATIVE AUTHENTICATION

Expressions of doubt and uncertainty about events narrated in our two literatures seem to afford even more opportunity for diversifying, grading and qualifying the information than do those that assert its truth. One of the most common ways in which uncertainty is expressed in the sagas of Icelanders is to point to different, or even conflicting, traditions about an event related or a fact stated.[58] So, when the marriage of Þórólfr Moster-beard to Unnr is mentioned in *Eyrbyggja saga*, we are told that 'some people say that she [Unnr] was the daughter of Thorstein the Red, but Ari Thorgilson the Learned does not count her among his children' (CSI V: 135).[59] In *Njáls saga* Þórólfr Moster-beard is the cause of yet another uncertainty, this time regarding his father, rather than his wife.[60] Ari's testimony is invoked here too, but while in *Eyrbyggja saga* his authority seems to slightly outweigh that of the anonymous *sumir*, in *Njáls saga* something different is happening. The writer informs us in positive terms that Þórólfr Moster-beard was the son of Örnólfr the Fish-driver (i.e. he does not relativize the information by reference to 'some people'). He nevertheless adds, in the characteristically cool, detached manner: 'Ari the Learned, however, says that Thorolf was the son of Thorgils Whaleside' (CSI III: 135).[61] For all the authority Ari the Learned enjoys in saga tradition, it is interesting that his reckoning is here not given precedence over the one the saga writer offered first. Rather, the two are left poised in perfect balance, unresolved, with the audience having to decide to which account to adhere (if any). It is precisely by refusing to do their thinking for them (i.e. his readers and listeners) that the saga writer achieves the strong sense of credibility.

Another important function of the above 'some say this, while others say

even though these metatextual comments often get edited out when the song is published (cf. Kleut 1991: 267–8). Mirjana Detelić (1996: 169) provides a list of formulas that include such references.

58 Theodore M. Andersson (1966) offers a rather comprehensive survey of the phrase *segja sumir* ('some say') and its cognates (e.g. *þat mæltu sumir*), including the instances of conflicting tradition and the professed lack of information. The purpose of his inquiry, however, was not the authentication per se, but establishing to what extent these phrases evidence the existence of an oral tradition behind the sagas.

59 '... segja sumir, at hon [Unnr] væri dóttir Þorsteins rauðs, en Ari Þorgilsson inn fróði telr hana eigi með hans börnum' (ÍF IV: 12).

60 The wife's name is here given as Ósk, which is in agreement with Ari's *Íslendingabók* (cf. Einar Ól. Sveinsson's note 9, ÍF XII: 286). In *Gull-Þóris saga* (ÍS II: 1120) Ósk the daughter of Þorsteinn the Red is also mentioned – not as the wife of Þórólfr Moster-beard, but rather as his daughter-in-law, the wife of his son Hallsteinn.

61 'en Ari inn fróði segir hann vera son Þorgils reyðarsíðu' (ÍF XII: 286).

that' formula (cf. Kellogg 1991) is well illustrated by the following example from *Grettis saga*. The hero's own testimony, which is often called upon and treated as reliable (e.g. Chs. 21 and 36; see also Ranković 2006b: 50), is on the occasion involving his struggle with the trollwoman pitted against that of the people of Bárðardalur:

> According to Grettir, the trollwoman plunged into the chasm when she received her wound, but the people of Bardardal claim she turned to stone at daybreak while they were wrestling and died when he chopped off her arm, and is still standing there on the cliff, as a rock in the shape of a woman.[62] (CSI II: 153)

Whether or not the audience really believed in trolls – we must assume that, as John Lindow notes (1986: 274), 'every society has its skeptics' – the employed authenticating form itself aids the writer in maintaining the sense of the documentary. As to his own attitude, it is perhaps discernable from the fact that he chooses to combine two types of authenticating devices (the conflicting report and the offer of 'tangible' evidence): he felt, it seems, that the material was in need of some extra backing. Whatever is ultimately the case, the way in which the sagas deal with what we deem fantastic (or 'marvellous', according to Todorov (1973)) is markedly different from the way this is done in *fornaldarsögur* and romances where 'the marvelous seems taken for granted and the supernatural attaches rather to it than to reality' (Lindow 1986: 280).[63] Hence Lindow speaks of the fantastic in the *Íslendingasögur* in terms of 'the verisimilitude of supernatural experience' (264) and 'the empirical supernatural' (280).

A couple of examples that follow are interesting because they maintain the basic structure of the 'some say this, while others say that' formula, but add a certain twist at the end. Namely, after the reader is presented with the dilemma between conflicting reports about the same event, the writer steps in and points to some important certainty amidst all the uncertainty, thus (effectively) brushing the relevance of the discrepant versions aside. When the maternal uncle of the infamous Hallgerðr, Svanr, goes missing, the writer of *Njáls saga* duly reports:

62 'Þetta er sögn Grettis, at trollkonan steypðisk í gljúfrin við, er hon fekk sárit, en Bárðardalsmenn segja, at hana dagaði uppi, þá er þau glímðu, ok sprungit, þá er hann hjó af henni höndina, ok standi þar enn í konulíking á bjarginu' (ÍF VII: 213).

63 This is also the case of Serbian epics in respect to other genres from the same tradition, e.g. fairytales.

> Fishermen who were at Kaldbak thought they saw Svan enter the mountain Kaldbakshorn and get a warm welcome there. Some denied this and said that there was nothing to it. *Everyone was certain however that he was never found, alive or dead.*[64] (CSI III: 21, my emphasis)

A similar dismissal of the relevance of discrepancy can be found in *Reykdæla saga ok Víga-Skútu* and it concerns Fly, the favourite weapon of Víga-Skúta:

> On this matter, people do not tell the same story. Some people say, as it says here, that it was an axe and was called Fly, but some that it was a sword and was called Fly. *But whichever it was, Skuta always had that weapon in hand and so it was at this time.*[65] (CSI IV: 297, my emphasis)

What makes this example particularly interesting is the fact that the saga writer, even when he seems to give credence to one version over the other (or simply decides to stick with the one he knows better), still feels compelled to offer the account of the other version.

While in the above passage the writer of *Reykdæla saga ok Víga-Skútu* finds some certainty to cling to, on another occasion he seems almost annoyed, as the apparent abundance of conflicting information does not make him any wiser as to what actually happened to the scheming Eysteinn Mánason (Ch. 3). Again we have two groups of people with different opinions on the score: one group claims that he went to Denmark, and the other that he burned together with his family and livestock whom, as all his machinations failed, he decided to destroy in the final act of bitter defiance. Amidst the possibilities, the writer, however, feels forced to admit defeat: 'But for all that, we do not know for sure if that was the cause of his death' (CSI IV: 261).[66] One of life's paradoxes, however, is that admission of defeat often turns it into a victory of sorts, and this is the case here. Acknowledging the limitations of one's knowledge, or carefully delineating its extent, selecting the bits of information for which one is and is not prepared to vouch, is one of the most economical and

64 'En fiskimenn þeir, er váru at Kaldbak, þóttusk sjá Svan ganga inn í fjallit Kaldbakshorn, ok var honum þar vel fagnat; en sumir mæltu því í móti ok kváðu engu gegna, *en þat vissu allir, at hann fannsk hvárki lífs né dauðr*' (ÍF XII: 46, my emphasis).

65 'Þar segja menn eigi einn veg frá. Sumir segja svá sem hér er sagt, at þat væri øx ok héti Fluga, en sumir segja, at þat væri sverð ok héti Fluga. *En hvárt [sem] heldr var, þá hafði Skúta þat vápn jafnan í hendi, ok svá var nú þetta sinn*' (ÍF X: 233, my emphasis).

66 'Ok vitu vér þó eigi, hvárt honum hefir heldr at bana orðit' (ÍF X: 159).

most powerful methods for establishing believability, as it leads the reader to assume that the rest of the narrative must be reliable.

The sagas of Icelanders make ample use of this authenticating device. To satisfy his younger brother's desire for brave deeds and to show that he himself does not lack the skills of a warrior, the otherwise temperate and wise Þórolfr (*Svarfdæla saga*) decides to sell their trading vessel (a *knorr*), buy two longships and go raiding. As to where the brothers went from there, we are told that 'it is not recorded where they raided' (CSI IV: 152).[67] The writer of *Eyrbyggja saga* similarly informs us that 'it is not mentioned' whether Snorri goði and Arnkell exchanged any words upon their fateful encounter at the haystack (CSI V: 178),[68] and indeed, we come across similar examples in many other sagas: Skalla-Grímr (*Egils saga*) is buried with his horse, weapons and tools, but 'it is not mentioned' (CSI I: 153) whether any money was put in his tomb;[69] in *Reykdæla saga ok Víga-Skútu* it is not known what the dealings between the feuding parties led by Áskell goði and Steingrímr Örnólfsson were until after three years had past (ÍF X: 187; CSI IV: 275); and after the final clash in which Steingrímr gets killed, we are told in regard to Áskell that 'it is not reported that he lost any people in the battle' (CSI IV: 281).[70] In the above examples saga writers lack the information they feel should be available, since details concerning places where people went raiding, last words they uttered before they died, treasures with which they were buried and such are abundant in the saga tradition. They know that their audience will expect these too, but they counter this by owning up to the lack of information, rather than inventing it. Of course, professing the lack of information (as well as giving an account of conflicting traditions that we discussed above) can itself be an invention. Yet even if this was the case in at least some examples, the very effort still indicates the importance that is placed on veracity of the sagas. I thus agree with Theodore Andersson (1966: 14–15) who thinks that 'such deception would have been transparent to the thirteenth-century audience', and contends that when saga writers refer to either conflicting traditions or declare their lack 'they are serious. They are informing the reader that the tradition goes no further, though it might reasonably have done so'.

In an admittedly more stylized form (as fits the verse), Serbian epic songs

67 'ekki er getit, hvar þeir herjuðu' (ÍF IX: 134).
68 'þá er eigi getit' (ÍF IV: 101).
69 'ekki er þess getit' (ÍF II: 175).
70 'Ekki er þess getit, at hann týndi neinum manni í bardaganum' (ÍF X: 200).

show a similar fine grading of uncertainty, and sometimes even dismiss the whole narrative (or its parts) as false. Inflamed by patriotic zeal and hungry to hear about the defeat of the notorious dahijas of Belgrade Pashalik (Serbia), the Montenegrin audience might have not been so shrewd and discerning for their singer to need to volunteer the following caution: 'Neither was I there, nor have witnessed it with my eye, / But I heard, others told me' (Vuk IV: 25).[71] Away from contemporary struggles in neighbouring Serbia, however, this seems as far as the Montenegrin singer is prepared to go to vouch for his account.

An interesting variation of this ending is found in the song *Taking of Drežnik* (Vuk VIII: 36). The singer also distances himself from the account by pointing out that he is no witness to the event, but rather than invoke the authority of the collective to counterbalance this, he is self-critical to the full: 'Neither was I there, nor did I tell it right'.[72] At the same time, it is precisely this strong self-censure that anticipates and renders obsolete any possible reproach from the audience. By placing doubt on his ability to relate the event with utmost precision (hence pointing to the high standard of veracity he demands of himself), the singer simultaneously draws the doubt away from the event itself, i.e., it has for sure taken place. By asking less, the singer in fact gets more: the audience not only accepts that the event really happened but is likely to grant the singer that it happened in some such manner too.

Even if relativized, credibility of the information offered in the examples above is at least suggested as possibly being true; in the ones to follow, however, the uncertainty is further heightened. In *Staniša of Kotari and Pasha of Pazar* (Vuk VI 73) we are told about an exceptional act of mercy by a Turkish pasha who, moved by the sacrifice that the mother and the young bride of his outlaw captive are prepared to make in exchange for his freedom, decides to release the outlaw. The singer comments: 'This happened, I don't know whether it did / Good health to us and our company'.[73] The songs that recount similarly extraordinary or unlikely events, for example chivalric and merciful conduct of Christian and Muslim warriors towards one another, bold rescue operations and daring enterprises involving dying heroes or disguised weapon-wielding women (the warrior-maiden motif), also tend to end with a cheerful dismissal: 'That happened when it took place, / I have no idea if in

71 'Nit' tu bio nit' okom vidio, / No sam čuo đe mi drugi kažu'.

72 'Ni tu bio, ni pravo kazao'.

73 'To je bilo, ne znam je li bilo, / Nam i društvu dobro zdravlje bilo'.

truth it did' (SANU II: 44, 63);[74] 'God alone knows whether this happened so, / As to us, brothers, let us be merry!' (Vuk III: 71, 72);[75] 'It happened when it took place, / To us, brothers, good health and mirth!' (Vuk III: 81).[76] While some comments leave the truth as an open question, others play with the very notion of the documentary, the form of the verse promising information, but the content eluding us with its mischievous pleonasm: 'It happened when it took place'. All singers, however, end their songs by inviting the audience to be merry and/or wishing them good health, the invitation within this particular context emphasizing the fact that the song is not intended to be taken too seriously. This, in fact, is as close as one gets to a fictional contract (cf. Green 2002) in traditional heroic literature. Yet, this is so only on the level of a particular song. On the level of epic tradition as a whole, questioning or dismissal of veracity of the particular piece enhances the credibility of the whole.

It is also interesting to note that merely wishing the audience good health and mirth does not always function as a merry dismissal of the events related. The poem about the death of the famous *uskok* (border-raider) Ivan Senjanin (Vuk III: 31) ends thus: 'And he died, woe to his mother! Let God grant him a place in heaven! / To us, brothers, good health and mirth!'[77] While in the previous instances these wishes act as a bridge over which to slip smoothly from the world of the story back into the immediate present, in this last example they make a sharper break and the tone is more solemn. In the songs about warrior maidens/wives we are dealing with the stuff romances are made of, the main characters (anonymous or arbitrary) survive, and the time is perceived as one long tract of uninterrupted all-time, stretching to the present of the audience. In the last example, however, we are dealing with a well-known hero whose death marks a break in a seemingly concrete time in history. Wishes of good health and mirth to the audience, on the one hand, and a plea for the hero's place in heaven, on the other, act to separate the past and present, the world of the living and that of the dead, the world of ordinary people in pursuit of simple pleasures and comforts and that of heroes in pursuit of great deeds and glory. To each God is asked to grant its own. Rather than being dismissive, these wishes act in affirmation of the story set in Senj and Italy, relating the exploits and fatal wounding of Ivan Senjanin. This example bears witness to a

74 'To je bilo kad se je činilo, / ništa ne znam je li istina bila'.
75 'Bog sam znade je li tako bilo, / A mi braćo, da se veselimo!'
76 'To je bilo kad se i činilo, Nama, družbo, zdravlje i veselje!'
77 'I umrije, žalosna mu majka! Bog mu dao u raju naselje! / Nama, braćo, zdravlje i veselje!'

remarkable flexibility of formulae, their ability to mean different (even completely opposite) things, depending on the context in which they are used. It is this malleability and creative potential that distinguishes traditional formulae from literary clichés with which they are sometimes confused.[78]

If in the songs discussed above truth is not known, or is questioned, in others the events related are straightforwardly dismissed as lies. For example, in *The Serpent Bridegroom* (Vuk II: 12) the legendary and folk-tale material is cast into the form of an epic poem, and so the singer finds it necessary to caution his audience about this experiment, aware of their expectations as regards epic songs and their truthfulness. Before he starts his account, he prepares them with the words: 'Wait, brothers, till I tell you a wonder'.[79] He forewarns them that what they are about to hear is something miraculous, extraordinary, something that requires from them to adjust their sensibilities. At the same time, he reveals his own position: he too regards this material as fantastic. And, in case they all got a bit carried away during the course of the poem, at the very end the singer reinforces his assessment of the material: 'They lied to us, we lie to you'.[80] In addition, Vuk Karadžić offers a variation on this line used by other singers: 'That one lied, who told me of this, / that one lied, and I'm repeating the lie',[81] noting that: 'With this the singer shows that he himself does not hold everything he sings about for *utter truth*' (Karadžić 1976 II: 52 n. 9, Vuk's emphasis). This note seems significant in two ways. Firstly, as Vuk says, it shows the singer's own awareness of his material, awareness which he deems important to share with his listeners since he might want to relate another epic song at some point, and the trust of the audience is something he will want to take for granted. And secondly, the fact that different singers use different variations of this ending shows that the version we have before us is not an isolated move of a particular singer, but rather a more widespread occurrence. As with the previous group of poems, negation of truth (negative authentication) in a particular song acts as a powerful authenticating device for the epic tradition in general.

It is important to note, however, that negative authentication of a particular song/heroic story works as a positive authentication of the whole epic tradition only when it is made from *within* that tradition. How differently a

78 The above discussion of the sagas' 'some say this, while others say that' formula illustrates this point equally well.

79 'Stan'te, braćo, da vi čudo kažem'.

80 'Nas lagali, mi polagujemo'.

81 'Onaj laže koji meni kaže, / Onaj laže a ja polagujem'.

negative authentication sounds and functions when it is made from outside the tradition is well illustrated by the *Book of Leinster* ending of the famous Irish saga *The Cattle Raid of Cooley* (*Táin Bó Cúalnge*, 1967: 272):

> But I who have written this story, or rather this fable, give no credence to the various incidents related in it. For some things in it are the deceptions of demons, other poetic figments; some are probable, others improbable; while still others are intended for the delectation of foolish men.

What we have here is a member (a cleric) of one culture (literate) passing moral and aesthetic judgement on, and perhaps also giving an apology for, another (oral tradition).

BY WAY OF CONCLUSION

There are probably many reasons as to why we encounter such a broad and fine range of authenticating tools and techniques in the sagas of Icelanders and Serbian epic songs, but not in the classical medieval European epics referred to above (*Beowulf, La Chanson de Roland, Das Nibelungenlied*). I will mention here a few that I deem most likely. To start with, the sheer number of preserved saga manuscripts (that 'Icelandic miracle', cf. Tulinius 2002: 11) and of recorded Serbian epic songs (collected on an unprecedented scale in the nineteenth century) immediately renders our comparison problematic, as other traditions considered are obviously not as well represented and are therefore at a disadvantage. Furthermore, the metatextual character of commentaries pertaining to authentication as well as their strong connection to the performative context are likely to have led to their being edited out once that context was removed or rendered obsolete.[82] At the same time, the number of recorded/preserved texts may not be all down to chance. The fact that (once presumably rich) heroic traditions were scaled down to a comparatively limited number of representative texts in Anglo-Saxon England and medieval France and Germany is perhaps telling of the place traditional heroic genres occupy in the literary canon of these societies. The letters of the Anglo-Saxon abbot and scholar Alcuin (eighth century) are indicative of the contemporary derogatory attitude of those in charge of writing (and hence the preservation

82 See footnote 45 above.

of the lore) towards the 'pagan songs' celebrating heathen heroes (in Donoghue 2002: 91–2). On the other hand, at the time from which the earliest surviving manuscripts of the *Chanson de Roland* and the *Nibelungenlied* date (twelfth and late twelfth, early thirteenth century respectively), the literary canon in both countries appears more receptive to the romance rather than the epic. According to Arthur T. Hatto (1969: 293–347) the *Nibelungenlied* is in fact an attempt to recast the traditionally epic material into the form of romance.

If we look beyond the number of texts, another possible reason for the less varied authenticating devices in the major medieval European epics emerges. Namely, the fact that authenticating devices are not as diverse as in the two literatures examined is probably indicative of these epics' diminishing role as central means of preservation of their community's history, the role in which they were superseded by the contemporary historiography. Unlike in medieval Iceland, the strong culturally centralizing institutions that we find in medieval France, for example (i.e. state, Church – Bakhtinian 'centripetal forces'[83]), will have effected a more rigorous division of genres and more sharply delineated their function. In other words, instead of remaining a matter of tension and constant negotiation, the fiction-fact relationship is in the epics of European centres resolved: they had eventually gravitated more decidedly towards the fictional attractor. This is not to say that the audience did not believe the accounts related (they might have, in fact, taken the truth for granted[84]), but that in these epics the authentication is no longer an active truth-calibrating mechanism, and its few crystallized remnants are there mainly to evoke the immediacy of oral address (fictionalized orality). By contrast, at the time the *Íslendingasögur* and *srpske junačke pesme* were written/recorded, authentication still seems to have been a live force. Even when the singers and saga-tellers/-writers are fully aware of the rhetorical power of the devices they use, they are on the whole never solely employed in order to achieve particular rhetorical effects. Rather, they seem to be a complex response to a complex set of demands and expectations by the two communities in terms of the trustworthiness of the accounts on offer. While undoubtedly the source of great entertainment, the two literatures still play the central (or, in the case of the sagas, at least as central as that of the contemporary historiography) role in preserving the past of their respective communities. As

83 See Bakhtin (1981: 271–2).

84 See Agapitos's contribution to this volume.

a live truth-calibrating mechanism, authentication in the sagas of Icelanders and Serbian epic songs keeps the factual and fictional attractors at constant negotiation and imbalance.

References

ABBREVIATIONS

CSI – *The Complete Sagas of Icelanders.*

ÍF – Íslenzk fornrit edition.

ÍS – Íslendinga sögur edition.

SANU – Sebian epic songs published by Srpska akademija nauka i umetnosti (Serbian Academy of Sciences and Arts), here quoted from the CD-ROM *Gradovi u hrišćanskoj i muslimanskoj usmenoj epici.*

SM – Sebian epic songs collected and published by Sima Milutinović Sarajlija, here quoted from the CD-ROM *Gradovi u hrišćanskoj i muslimanskoj usmenoj epici.*

Vuk – Sebian epic songs collected by Vuk Stefanović Karadžić (vols. I–IV are from printed collections, vols. VI–IX refer to the CD-ROM *Gradovi u hrišćanskoj i muslimanskoj usmenoj epici*).

TEXTS

Beowulf, trans. Seamus Heaney, London: Norton, 2002.

Bjarnar saga Hítdælakappa in *Borgfirðinga sögur*, ed. Sigurður Nordal and Guðni Jónsson, Reykjavík: Íslenzk fornrit, 1938, vol. III, pp. 111–211.

Brennu-Njáls saga, ed. Einar Ól. Sveinsson, Reykjavík: Íslenzk fornrit, 1954, vol. XII.

The Complete Sagas of Icelanders, ed. Viðar Hreinsson, Reykjavík: Leifur Eiríksson Publishing, 1997, vols. I–V.

Egils saga Skalla-Grímssonar, ed. Sigurður Nordal, Reykjavík: Íslenzk fornrit, 1933, vol. II.

Eyrbyggja saga, ed. Einar Ól. Sveinsson and Matthías Þórarson, Reykjavík: Íslenzk fornrit, 1935, vol. IV.

Gradovi u hrišćanskoj i muslimanskoj usmenoj epici [CD-ROM], Belgrade: Balkanološki institut SANU.

Grettis saga Ásmundarsonar, ed. Guðni Jónsson, Reykjavík: Íslenzk fornrit, 1936, vol. VII.

Heiðarvíga saga in *Íslendinga sögur og þættir*, ed. Bragi Háldorsson et al., Reykjavík: Svart á hvítu, 1987, vol. II, pp. 1336–96.

Laxdæla saga, ed. Einar Ól. Sveinnson, Reykjavík: Íslenzk fornrit, 1934, vol. V.

Nibelungenlied, trans. Arthur H. Hatto, London: Penguin, 1969.

The Serbian Epic Ballads, trans. Geoffrey N. W. Locke, Belgrade: Nolit, 1997.

The Song of Roland, trans. C. H. Sisson, Manchester: Carcanet Press Limited, 1983.

Srpske narodne pjesme. ed. Vuk Stefanović Karadžić, Belgrade: Prosveta, 1976, vols. I–IV.

Svarfdæla saga in *Eyfirðinga sögur*, ed. Jónas Kristjánsson, Reykjavík: Íslenzk fornrit, 1956, vol. IX, pp. 129–208.

Táin Bó Cúalnge from the Book of Leinster, trans. Cecile O'Rahilly, Dublin: Dublin Institute for Advanced Study, 1967.

Þórðar saga Hreðu in *Íslendinga sögur og þættir*, ed. Bragi Háldorsson et al., Reykjavík: Svart á hvítu, 1987, vol. III, pp. 208–52.

STUDIES

Alcuin (2002) 'What Has Ingeld to Do with Christ?' in *Beowulf. A Verse Translation*, ed. Daniel Donoghue, London: Norton, pp. 91–2.

Andersson, Theodore M. (1966) 'The Textual Evidence for an Oral Family Saga', *Arkiv för nordisk filologi*, 81: 1–23.

Andersson, Theodore M. (2002) 'The Long Prose Form in Medieval Iceland', *Journal of English and Germanic Philology* 101: 380–411.

Ankersmit, F. R. (1994) *History and Tropology: The Rise and Fall of Metaphor*, Berkeley: University of California Press.

Aristotle (1996) *Poetics*, trans. Malcolm Heath, London: Penguin.

Bakhtin, Mikhail M. (1981) *The Dialogic Imagination*. Translated by Caryl Emerson and Michael Holquist, Austin and London: University of Texas Press.

Barthes, Roland (1989) 'The Reality Effect', in *The Rustle of Language*, trans. Richard Howard, Berkeley: University of California Press, pp. 141–8.

Byock, Jesse L. (2001) *Viking Age Iceland*, London: Penguin.

Clover, Carol J. (1986) 'The Long Prose Form', *Arkiv för Nordisk Filologi* 101: 10–39.

Clunies Ross, Margaret (2000) *Old Icelandic Literature and Society*, Cambridge: Cambridge University Press.

Delić, Jovan (1990) *Tradicija i Vuk Stefanović Karadžić*, Belgrade: BIGZ.

Deretić, Jovan (1994) 'Poems and Events: Historicity in Serbo-Croat Oral Epics', in Michael Branch and Celia Hawkesworth (eds.), *The Uses of Tradition: A Com-*

parative Enquiry into the Nature, Uses and Functions of Oral Poetry in the Balkans, the Baltic, and Africa, London: Quorn Selective Repro, pp. 83–94.

Deretić, Jovan (2000) *Srpska narodna epika*, Belgrade: Filip Višnjić.

Detelić, Mirjana (1996) *Urok i nevesta: poetika epske formule*, Belgrade: Čigoja.

Doane, A. N. (1991) 'Oral Texts, Intertexts, and Intratexts: Editing Old English', in Jay Clayton and Eric Rothstein (eds.), *Influence and Intertextuality in Literary History*, Madison, WI: University of Wisconsin Press, pp. 75–108.

Downes, Jeremy M. (1997) *Recursive Desire: Rereading Epic Tradition*, Tuscaloosa, AL: University of Alabama Press.

Đorđević, Tihomir (1984) *Naš narodni život*, Belgrade: Prosveta, vols. I–IV.

Foley, John Miles (1991) *Immanent Art: From Structure to Meaning in Traditional Oral Epic*, Bloomington and Indianapolis: Indiana University Press.

Glauser, Jürg (2000) 'Sagas of the Icelanders (*Íslendinga sögur*) and *þættir* as a Literary Representation of a New Social Space', in Margaret Clunies Ross, *Old Icelandic Literature and Society*, Cambridge: Cambridge University Press, pp. 203–20.

Green, Dennis H. (2002) *The Beginnings of Medieval Romance: Fact and Fiction, 1150–1220*, Cambridge: Cambridge University Press.

Hainsworth, J. B. (1991) *The Idea of Epic*, Berkeley and Los Angeles: University of California Press.

Jakobson, Roman, and Petr Bogatyrev (1971) 'On the Boundary between Studies of Folklore and Literature', in Ladislav Matejka and Krystyna Pomorska (eds.), *Readings in Russian Poetics: Formalist and Structuralist Views*, Cambridge, MA: The MIT Press, pp. 91–3.

Jesch, Judith (1984) *The Lost Literature of Medieval Iceland: Sagas of Icelanders*, Unpublished Ph.D. thesis, London: University College London.

Jones, Gwyn (1986) *The Norse Atlantic Saga*, Oxford: Oxford University Press.

Jordanova, Ludmilla (2000) *History in Practice*, London: Arnold.

Katalog over den Arnamagnæanske Håndskriftsamling, vol. I (1889), Copenhagen: Gyldendalske Boghandel.

Kellogg, Robert (1991) 'Literacy and Orality in the Poetic Edda', in A. N. Doane and C. B. Pasternack (eds.), *Vox Intexta: Orality and Textuality in the Middle Ages*, London: The University of Wisconsin Press, pp. 89–101.

Kilibarda, Novak (1970) 'Specifičnost crnogorske narodne epike', in Novak Kilibarda (n.d.), *Poezija i istorija u narodnoj književnosti*, Belgrade: Slovo Ljubve, pp. 85–103.

Kilibarda, Novak (1991) 'The Montenegrin Oral Epic in a New Perspective', *Oral Tradition* 6, nos. 2–3: 279–83.

Kleut, Marija (1991) 'Concluding Formulas of Audience Address in Serbo-Croatian Oral Epic', *Oral Tradition* 6, nos. 2–3: 266–78.

Koljević, Svetozar (1980) *The Epic in the Making*, Oxford: Clarendon Press.

Lindow, John (1986) '*Þorsteins þáttr skelks* and the Verisimilitude of Supernatural Experience in Saga Literature', in John Lindow, Lars Lönnroth and Gerd Wolfgang Weber (eds.), *Structure and Meaning in Old Norse Literature: New Approaches to Textual Analysis and Literary Criticism*, Odense: Odense University Press, pp. 264–80.

Maticki, Miodrag (1989) *Ponovnice: Tipovi odnosa usmene i pisane književnosti*, Novi Sad: Književna zajednica Novog Sada.

Meulengracht Sørensen, Preben (1993) *Saga and Society: An Introduction to Old Norse Literature*. Translated by John Tucker, Odense: Odense University Press.

Nedić, Vladan (1990) *Vukovi pevači*, Belgrade: Rad.

Ong, Walter J. (1982) *Orality and Literacy: The Technologizing of the Word*, London: Routledge.

Perkins, David (1993) *Is Literary History Possible?* Baltimore: The Johns Hopkins University Press.

Prins, Gwyn (2001) 'Oral History', in Peter Burke (ed.), *New Perspectives on Historical Writing*, Cambridge: Polity, pp. 120–52.

Ranković, Slavica (2006a) *The Distributed Author and the Poetics of Complexity: A Comparative Study of the Sagas of Icelanders and Serbian Epic Poetry*, Unpublished Ph.D. thesis, Nottingham: University of Nottingham, http://etheses.nottingham.ac.ku/2098/.

Ranković, Slavica (2006b) 'Golden Ages and Fishing Grounds: The Emergent Past in the *Íslendingasögur*', *Saga-Book* 30: 39–64.

Šmaus, Alojz (1972) 'Studije o krajinskoj epici', in Vladan Nedić (ed.), *Narodna književnost*, Belgrade: Nolit, pp. 287–309.

Stavrianos, L. S. (1965) *The Balkans Since 1453*, New York: Holt, Rinehart and Winston.

Stewart, Ian (1997/1989) *Does God Play Dice? The New Mathematics of Chaos*, Oxford: Blackwell Publishing.

Todorov, Tzvetan (1973) *The Fantastic: A Structural Approach to a Literary Genre*. Translated by Richard Howard, Cleveland: The Press of Case Western Reserve University.

Tulinius, Torfi H. (2002) *The Matter of the North: The Rise of Literary Fiction in Thirteenth-Century Iceland*. Translated by Randi C. Eldevik, Odense: Odense University Press. [Originally published as *La Matière du Nord. Sagas Légendaires et fiction dans l'Islande du XIIIe siècle*, Paris, 1995.]

Tynjanov, Jurij (1971) 'On Literary Evolution', in Ladislav Matejka and Krystyna Pomorska (eds.), *Readings in Russian Poetics: Formalist and Structuralist Views*, Cambridge, MA and London: The MIT Press, 1971), pp. 66–78.

Vansina, Jan (1988) *Oral Tradition as History*, London: James Currey.

Whaley, Diana (2000) 'A Useful Past: Historical Writing in Medieval Iceland', in Margaret Clunies Ross (ed.), *Old Icelandic Literature and Society*, Cambridge: Cambridge University Press, pp. 161–202.

White, Hayden (1978) *Tropics of Discourse*, Baltimore: The Johns Hopkins University Press.

In Rhomaian, Frankish and Persian Lands: Fiction and Fictionality in Byzantium and Beyond

Panagiotis A. Agapitos

It could be argued that Byzantium as a historical and cultural phenomenon has not been viewed as peripheral to the rest of medieval European culture. However, since the seventeenth century, when scholarly interest in the history of the novel emerged, Byzantine fiction has been judged as utterly marginal and unworthy of serious study.[1] Despite the substantial quantitative growth of scholarly output within the field of Byzantine studies in the last forty years on a group of texts sometimes referred to as 'medieval Greek romance', these fictional narratives are still omitted from any discussion of Western medieval romance,[2] even though the composition of such narratives in Byzantium began approximately twenty years before the date assigned to the *Roman de Thèbes* (c. 1150–55), the oldest of the three French *romans d'antiquité*.

Byzantine authors and readers of fiction signalled such narrative compositions as a 'plot of fate', a 'fantastic tale' or even a 'figment', thus employing a variegated poetical metalanguage about narrative fictionality. Despite this fact, no study of the concept of fictionality, and much less of the notion of the fictive, has been attempted for Byzantine fiction. The present paper cannot fill this gap in any kind of exhaustive way; its main aim is two-fold. On the one hand, it examines fictionality as a theoretical question and a compositional

* My thanks extend to all participants of the Bergen-Nicosia workshop for our stimulating conversations. Furthermore, I wish to thank Stavroula Constantinou, Martin Hinterberger and Tomas Hägg for their insightful comments; Megan Moore, Anthony Kaldellis, Tasos Kaplanis and Stratis Papaioannou for allowing me to use their papers prior to publication; Diether Roderich Reinsch for providing me with copies of various bibliographical items. I am particularly indebted to David Jacoby for his incisive criticism on historical and cultural matters. The paper could not have been written without the financial support of the Research Committee of the University of Cyprus and the A.G. Leventis Foundation.

1 For a critical assessment of this perspective, see Agapitos (1991: 3–10; 1992: 239–51; 2000a).

2 One might indicatively point to the absence of a respective chapter in the recent *Cambridge Companion to Medieval Romance* (Krueger 2000).

practice in Byzantine culture, with particular emphasis on such key issues as historicity and authorial contracts with the audience. On the other hand, the paper attempts to place Byzantine fictional narratives within the broader context of Western and Eastern fiction in medieval times. Through this twofold and parallel analysis a number of clearer conclusions will be drawn about whether and how three distinct and yet interrelated contemporary cultures converge and/or diverge in their handling of narrative between the poles of history and fiction over the same period of approximately four centuries (c. 1100–1500).

The title of the paper suggests a Byzantine geographical point of view: Rhomania (Ρωμανία), the 'land of the Rhomaioi', was the name the Byzantines themselves gave to their country, while Frangia (Φραγγία) and Persia (Περσία) were the generic appelations for the Near West (including Italians, French and Germans) and the Near East (including Arabs, Persians and Turks) respectively. The analysis is accordingly based on a fairly large number of Byzantine, French, German, Arab and Persian narrative texts. In the first part of the paper these texts will be comparatively grouped into four categories and briefly introduced. The second part will present the historical context of textual production in Byzantium from the late eleventh to the fifteenth centuries, drawing attention to the parallel but not necessarily similar developments in the European West and the Middle East.

Parts three to seven form the paper's core of literary analysis. The third part explains the linguistic and literary situation in Byzantium, where Greek was not seen as divided into distinct linguistic realms; this, initially at least, stands in contrast to Latin as a language of authority and to French or German as vernaculars that first developed as literary media in the context of translation from Latin. In the fourth part the system of education in Byzantium, the availability of manuscripts, the presence of ancient canonical texts of fiction, and the role of readers in evaluating such texts and defining the genre of the 'novel' are presented. The fifth part examines narrative between history and fiction: on the one hand, it explores how texts of fiction use a historiographic model to buttress the authority of their subject matter and texts of historiography employ devices deriving from fiction to enhance their respective subject matter; on the other hand, it investigates how this conjunction of literary conventions affects the composition of epic discourse. The sixth part shows that the Western tradition of defending or excusing fiction is not even remotely applicable to Byzantine romance or other fictive texts, such as dramatic or satirical performative monologues; fictionality in Byzantine romance is absorbed into a variety of plot settings (occidentalist, historicist, antiquarian, utopianist) that underline the fictive character of romance without problematizing the issue in theoretical terms. Finally, the seventh and longest part of the paper examines (in comparison with French, German and Persian romances) authorial contracts with the audience by looking (i) at the prologues and epilogues of Byzantine romantic and allegorical narratives of fiction, and (ii) at the intratextual devices employed in order to establish the notion of make-believe for the intended audience of listeners or readers.

Obviously, it is impossible to discuss every issue of so diverse a material and through so broad a perspective. As Thomas d'Angleterre succintly put it in his *Roman de Tristan* (c. 1170–73): 'I do not wish to overcrowd my verse: the subject matter is indeed diverse' (frg. Douce 841–842).[3] Selection, variety and brevity are therefore called for. However, what I more generally hope to show is that the study of romance in Rhomaian, Frankish and Persian lands can indeed profit immensely from a comparative mapping of its textual and cultural geography, especially if such a cartographic project is set within an interdisciplinary context and supported by an appropriate literary and historical method.

I. A PERFUMED GARDEN OF TEXTS

Having walked in late May for a couple of hours through the dusty streets of a medieval Mediterranean town – let us say, Palermo in the middle of the thirteenth century – a group of pleasantly tired visitors has been invited by their noble host to rest in the garden of her spacious mansion. While refreshments were being served, the visitors, who had arrived from lands north of the Alps, strolled through the garden. The rectangular yard was enclosed on its two sides by covered colonades in a style that the lady described as Rhomaian. The front of the house, with pointed arches framing doors and windows, was familiar to them from their own Latin countries. The garden itself was a series of four flowerbeds divided by paths of pinkish gravel stone. At each of the four corners a fruit-bearing tree threw its shadow over the flower beds. The garden was dominated by a large water basin with a marble fountain in its centre constructed in a style that one of the visitors recognized as Sara-

3 'Ne vol pas trop en uni dire: | Ici diverse la matyre' (Lacroix and Walter 1995: 434; Mölk 1969: 30).

cen. The noble lady explained that her house belonged once to a Greek lord and was later bought by an Arab doctor, until her grandfather took it over and rebuilt it some forty years ago. The coolness in the garden and the soft odours emanating from the flowers and the blossoming trees delighted the visitors who started examining more carefully what kinds of flowers were arranged in the four flowerbeds. It might be useful to follow their example and look at the fragrant texts examined in the present paper. Despite their richly colourful variety and their different provenance, the texts under consideration have also been arranged in four broader categories that do not necessarily reflect groupings according to language or (sub)genre.[4]

(i) ROMANCES SET IN A REMOTE PAST. This is a past that was consciously and explicitly perceived as 'ancient' by each of the three cultures under consideration, in this case, Greek, Roman and pre-Islamic Iranian or Arabic antiquity respectively. In Rhomania we find four novels (set in a somewhat vague Hellenistic age and composed in a learned idiom), written in the second quarter of the twelfth century by well-known authors: Eumathios Makrembolites's *Hysmine and Hysminias,* Theodore Prodromos's *Rhodanthe and Dosikles,* Niketas Eugeneianos's *Drosilla and Charikles,* and Constantine Manasses's *Aristandros and Kallithea.* Furthermore, we have four anonymous vernacular romances that are set in Homeric or classical times: *The War of Troy,* late thirteenth to early fourteenth century; *The Tale of Achilles,* first half of fourteenth century; *The Tale of Troy,* late fourteenth to early fifteenth century; *Alexander and Semiramis,* first half of fifteenth century. Frangia is represented by four works set in Graeco-Roman mythical times, three in French and one in Ger-

4 The standard handbook treatments of Byzantine fiction are to be found in Hunger (1978: II, 119–42, Komnenian learned novels) and Beck (1971: 117–53, Palaiologan vernacular romances and allegorical poems). The only broader treatment of the totality of 'Medieval Greek Romance' remains Beaton (1996, originally published in 1989), on which see the extensive criticism by Agapitos and Smith (1992). For a more balanced survey of the same texts see now Cupane (2004). Two points of clarification: (a) the terms 'novel' and 'romance' are used here in order to distinguish the twelfth-century texts, feigning a 'bourgeois antique' setting, from the later ones which are placed in a 'contemporary aristocratic' environment; (b) the terms 'learned' and 'vernacular' for Medieval Greek refer to the idiom of the texts and are not comparable to a distinction of the type Latin vs. Old French/High Middle German (on this see below, pp. 245–8). As far as French romance is concerned, volume I of Frappier and Grimm (1978–84) remains the most complete overview, while for German romance one might consult Bumke (2004), Brunner (2004a) and Wehrli (1997: 237–325). As far as Persian heroic and romantic epics are concerned, Bürgel (1990) offers the most recent survey. For abbreviations of the most often quoted works, as well as references to editions and translations, see the first section of the references ('Texts'). Because of the complexity of the textual situation for most of medieval literature, references include more than one edition, and often translations in more than one language. The English ones used in the present study are indicated by an asterisk. In those cases where no asterisk is to be found in the reference translations are my own.

man: *Roman de Thèbes* (c. 1150–55), *Roman d'Enéas* (c. 1155–60), Benoît's de Saint-Maure *Roman de Troie* (c. 1160–65), and Heinrich's von Veldeke *Eneasroman* (c. 1170–84). In Persia we find three verse romances set in a hazily drawn Arab, Hellenic or Sasanian past with no or minimal reference to Islam; they were all composed during the first half of the eleventh century in the following sequence: Ayyuqi, *Varqeh and his cousin Gulshah*; Abulqasim Unsuri, *Vamiq and Adhra* ('The Lover and the Virgin'); Fakhruddin Gurgani, *Queen Vis and Prince Ramin.*

(ii) ROMANCES OF LOVE AND ADVENTURE. These are set in seemingly recognizable historical periods or in times apparently contemporary with their actual composition. In Rhomania we have the following five Palaiologan romances: *Livistros and Rhodamne,* middle of thirteenth century; *Velthandros and Chrysantza,* late thirteenth century; *Kallimachos and Chrysorrhoe,* second quarter of fourteenth century; *Florios and Platziaflore,* second half of fourteenth century; the unrhymed redaction of *Imperios and Margarona,* third quarter of fifteenth century. In Frangia we find, on the one hand, the five romances of Chrétien de Troyes, composed between c. 1165 and 1191 in the following sequence: *Erec and Enide, Cligès, The Knight of the Cart* (or *Lancelot*), *The Knight with the Lion* (or *Yvain*) and *The Tale of the Graal* (or *Perceval*). On the other hand, we have the German romance production: Hartmann's von Aue, *Erec* (c. 1185) and *Iwein* (c. 1200), Wolfram's von Eschenbach *Parzival* (c. 1200–10) and Gottfried's von Straßburg unfinished *Tristan* (c. 1200–10). Persia is represented by three works of the Persian poet Ilyas ibn-Yusuf Nizami, all of them composed in the last quarter of the twelfth century and in the following sequence: *Khosrow and Shirin, The Seven Images* and *The Book of Alexander.*

(iii) EPIC AND HISTORICAL NARRATIVES. Here belong texts that focus on some legendary moment in history or that deal with a longer span of historical time. In Rhomania we find: *Digenis Akritis,* third quarter of twelfth century; Constantine Manasses's *Annalistic Compendium* (c. 1140–42); *The Tale of Belisarios* (redaction χ), late fourteenth century. In Frangia we have: the *Chanson de Roland* (c. 1100), Master Wace's *Roman de Brut* (c. 1150–55), the *Poema de mio Cid* (c. 1200), Konrad's *Rolandslied* (c. 1170–72), and Wolfram's unfinished *Willehalm* (c. 1212–17). In Persia we find, on the one hand, the anonymous Arab prose epic *Tale of the Holy Warriors* (thirteenth–fourteenth century) and its romance-like adaptation *The Tale of Umar al-Numân* (seventeenth–eighteenth century), while, on the other hand, Persian literature is represented by Abulqasim Firdowsi's vast historical epic *The Book of Kings*, completed in the first decade of the eleventh century.

(iv) ALLEGORICAL/FABULISTIC NARRATIVES. These are texts that include both human and personified allegorical characters, or different groups of animals. In this category we are going to include only two Byzantine vernacular texts: *A Consolatory Fable about Good and Bad Fortune*, second quarter of fourteenth century, and *The Entertaining Tale of the Quadrupeds*, late fourteenth century.

II. THE HISTORICAL CONTEXT

One of the most important socio-cultural factors in the rise of vernacular fiction in twelfth-century France and Germany was the gradual formation of new cultural manifestations of feudal aristocracy. The Anglo-Norman court of King Henry II Plantagenet (1154–89) and of his second wife Eleanor of Aquitaine (*1122–†1204), the French court of Countess Mary of Champagne (*1145–†98), daughter of Eleanor from her first husband King Louis VII of France (1137–80), or the German court of Hermann I, Pfalzgraf of Sachsen (1181–90) and Landgraf of Thüringen (1190–1217) promoted a distinctly lay culture where the composition of romances by poets financially supported by the patron fulfilled an important political and social function.[5] Master Wace, Thomas d'Angleterre, Chrétien de Troyes, Gautier d'Arras, Heinrich von Veldeke, Hartmann von Aue and Wolfram von Eschenbach lived, wrote and recited their works at the courts of such ambitious patrons. Whatever one might say about the 'discovery of fiction' before the time of the *romans d'antiquité* and of Chrétien,[6] it is the verse vernacular narratives 'in French' (*Cligès* 3: *en romanz*)[7] and 'in the German language' (*Tristan* 4739: *in tiutischer*

5 See the monumental study by Bezzola (1963: 3–247, Henry, and 247–312, Eleanor), in combination with Türk (1977); on Mary and Eleanor, see the diverging assessments of Benton (1961) and McCash (1979), in combination with the cautionary remarks by Krueger (1993: 1–11); on Hermann, see the detailed study by Peters (1981). The issue of literary patronage at the German courts has been extensively discussed by Bumke (1979); see also the collection of older studies in Bumke (1982), as well as the succinct overview in Bumke (1986: 638–77).

6 See Dennis Green's contribution in the present volume and more broadly Green (2002: 187–201).

7 Although Chrétien's works are quoted from the Lettres gothiques series, I have also consulted the Pléiade edition (Poirion 1994). Despite the criticism it has received as to constitution of the text and the critical apparatus (see the summary of the debate in Busby 1998: xv–xx), it offers a 'uniform' textual image through its use of the Guiot manuscript (codex **A** = Paris, B.N. fr. 794, c. 1230–35), while it includes very good introductions and commentaries to the individual romances. All technical issues concerning Chrétien's romances have been dealt with in Frappier and Grimm (1978–84: II, 95–107 (nos. 108, 112, 116, 120, 124)).

zungen) that decisively shaped the literary image of aristocratic/chivalric lay culture from c. 1150 to 1220 in medieval France and Germany. In their turn, these works became the canonical starting point for the generation of poets after Chrétien, Hartmann and Wolfram.[8]

This political and socio-cultural context of independent feudal courts spread out in different geographic areas and with different languages was completely foreign to the medieval Greek world of the eleventh and twelfth centuries.[9] There existed only one centralized state, the 'Empire of the Rhomaioi' (βασιλεία 'Ρωμαίων), run by the rulers of the Komnenian family (1081–85) through an extended bureaucratic apparatus and supported by means of a fairly developed system of primary and secondary education (see below, pp. 251–3). Above all, there existed only one city where patronage was actively undertaken, namely, the 'Eye of the terrestrial world' (ὀφθαλμὸς τῆς οἰκουμένης) as the Byzantines called it, or 'Great castle' (*mikligardhr*) as it was known in the Icelandic sagas. Constantinople was the largest and wealthiest city medieval Europe had known until the end of the twelfth century. Literary patronage, of which there was plenty in the capital, functioned not within distinct courts but within individual households of an urban aristocracy and for a very small number of participants. Recitation of texts, literary criticism of older and contemporary works, philosophical and theological discussions were all conducted in a loose form of gathering called 'theatre of discourse' (θέατρον τῶν λόγων). We know of at least four such *theatra* in the first half of the twelfth century.[10] Interestingly enough, the patrons of three of these literary salons were high-born women whose husbands supported in one way or another the interests of their educated wives: Eirene Doukaina (1066–c. 1123), widow of Emperor Alexios I Komnenos (1081–1118); Anna Komnene (1083–c. 1154), daughter of Emperor Alexios and wife of *kaisar* Nikephoros Bryennios (†1138); Eirene Komnene († c. 1153), wife of the *sebastokrator* Andronikos Komnenos. The fourth salon was held for a short time by Stephanos Komnenos (c. 1127–c. 1156), a less exalted member of the reigning family.[11]

8 On the French side of their reception, see Schmolke-Hasselmann (1998), on the German side, see Mertens (1998).

9 On Byzantine political history during these two centuries, see the broad treatment by Angold (1997), as well as the overviews by Angold (2004) and Magdalino (2004); Stephenson (2005) offers a succinct overview of the state of historical research. On Constantinopolitan 'court culture' in the Middle Byzantine period, see the collection of essays in Maguire (1997).

10 On these, see Mullett (1984) and MacAlister (1996: 155–6).

11 On prosopographical data of these three women, see respectively Polemis (1968: 70–84); Barzos (1984: I, 176–97); Jeffreys and Jeffreys (1994). On Stephanos Komnenos, see Sideras (1994: 168–71).

When Constantinople fell to the knights of the Fourth Crusade and Venice in April of 1204, a political, social and cultural break took place in the eyes of the Byzantines.[12] The Roman Empire and the Ecumenical Patriarchate found themselves exiled in the Bithynian town of Nicaea. The new emperor, Theodore I Laskaris (1205–21), a descendant of a secondary branch of the Komnenoi, was forced to establish as quickly as possible a flexible and efficient administrative system so as to restore order in western Asia Minor (Angold 1975). At the same time, two other families, offshoots of the Komnenoi, established Greek principalities in Trebizond of the Pontos and Arta in Epirus, fighting against the Frankish states in Greece, the Venetian dominions in the southern Aegean, and the Seljuq Turks in central Anatolia.[13] Theodore's son-in-law and successor, John III Batatzes (1221–54), raised the empire of Nicaea to a prosperous military power that played an important role on the international political and diplomatic stage.[14] John, who entertained personal relations with the German emperor Frederick II of Hohenstaufen (1220–50), and actively involved himself in the affairs of the Armenian Kingdom of Cilicia, the Lusignan Kingdom of Cyprus, and the Seljuq Sultanate of Konya, promoted the creation of a 'new' imperial court culture, both at Nicaea and at Nymphaion, the imperial summer residence close to Smyrna. However, all of these efforts served only one ultimate purpose: to regain Constantinople from the Latins and to restore the Empire back to its ancient seat. This, indeed, happened almost by coincidence in the summer of 1261, and Emperor Michael VIII Palaiologos (1259–82) moved into a despoiled and depopulated city.

The Palaiologan government consolidated its power and, while the Frankish principalities in Greece were beginning to diminish in military power and political influence, succeeded in restoring a new system of education and in reviving certain aspects of court culture, albeit on a very restricted scale. By the middle of the fourteenth century even these remnants of court culture had vanished. The long-lasting civil wars between the factions of the Palaiologan family and their supporters exhausted the resources of the state[15] that

12 On the Fourth Crusade, see now Angold (2003). For a good overview of late Byzantine history, see Nicol (1993), in combination with the report on the state of research by Harris (2005).

13 On Epirus, see Nicol (1957 and 1984); on the antagonism between Nicaea and Epirus, see Stavridou-Zafraka (1990); on Trebizond, see Bryer (1980); on the Frankish states, see Lock (1995), and on the Seljuqs, see Cahen (1991).

14 No monograph on John III exists; for a brief presentation with the older bibliography, see the relevant entry in *Oxford Dictionary of Byzantium* 2 (1991), pp. 1047–8 (Michael J. Angold).

15 See Laiou (1972: 284–300) and Matschke (1971).

had shrunk to a small kingdom, vassal to the Ottoman Sultan.[16] A growing number of Greek-speaking areas of western Asia Minor, Thrace, Macedonia and the Aegean Archipelago had completely separated themselves from the central Byzantine government. In the Latin principalities of southern Greece some of the local Byzantine magnates sought to incorporate themselves into the Frankish feudal system, while in the Lusignan Kingdom of Cyprus a process of acculturation was taking place, where the French aristocracy was to a certain extent merging with the upper social strata of the Greek population.[17] It is in this fragmented context of the late fourteenth century that Greek landlords and merchants expanded their business involvement and, while retaining their Orthodox creed, probably moved more freely within the other major vernacular languages spoken in the eastern Mediterranean (French, Italian, Turkish).[18]

III. BYZANTINE POETS AND THEIR LINGUISTIC MEDIA

Even this cursory glance at the historical context in which fiction emerged and was produced in Byzantium clearly shows the vast differences between the Greek world and France, England and Germany of the twelfth and thirteenth centuries. These differences are not only to be gleaned from the broader historical phenomena, they are also reflected in the surviving texts themselves. In the first place, there was no canonically recognizable Latin 'novel' in the West that scholars or authors could refer to as a paradigmatic text. The *Historia Apollonii Regis Tyri* was unquestionably popular but rather idiosyncratic, while the partly humorous *Metamorphoses* of Apuleius and the highly parodic *Satyrica* of Petronius never moved outside a restricted readership. The romantic story of two lovers and their adventures in the style of Hellenistic fiction

16 On Byzantine–Ottoman relations after the middle of the fourteenth century, see indicatively Barker (1969); on the Western travellers' impressions of Constantinople's destitute state, see Angold (2002).

17 On this situation in the Latin principalities of Greece, see Jacoby (1986: 177–9) and, more broadly, Ilieva (1991: 155–239); on Cyprus, see the relevant chapters in Nicolaou-Konnari and Schabel (2005).

18 On Greek merchants and their interaction with Italians and Ottomans, see Necipoglou (2000), the volume edited by Maltezou and Schreiner (2002), as well as Jacoby (2005, nos. VII–IX, XII). On the decline of learned 'secular' culture in the second half of the fourteenth century and the changes in patronage and education, see Kyritses (2005, with the older bibliography). On linguistic interaction in the late medieval eastern Mediterrenean, see Kahane, Kahane and Tietze (1958) and Kahane and Kahane (1982) (as well as Cupane 1999: 48 n. 74 for further bibliography), while on Greek literature in the Frankish and Italian dominated regions of Greece, see Cupane (1995b) and Panagiotakes (1995) respectively.

was unknown.[19] In this sense, the 'discovery of fiction' before the appearance of the *romans d'antiquité* was indeed a matter of novelty, joining together very different strands of narrative traditions. It is therefore quite indicative that the three medieval Latin texts seen as forming this 'discovery of fiction', namely *Ecbasis captivi, Ruodlieb* and *Ysengrimus*,[20] do not in the least resemble what is conventionally taken to be the 'form' of the ancient Greek romantic novel.[21] Moreover, except for the popular twelfth-century *Ysengrimus* and its importance for vernacular beast tales,[22] the early eleventh-century *Ecbasis captivi* has survived in only one manuscript of the twelfth century,[23] and the late eleventh-century *Ruodlieb* in the fragmentary author's copy and one further fragment, also of the late eleventh century.[24] In my opinion, their possible influence on the formation of vernacular fiction can be accepted only in a very vague kind of way.

However, the consistent use of the vernacular as a literary medium in the West allowed for the creation of a self-referential semiotic code of fictionality in Arthurian romance across linguistic boundaries; the comparison between Chrétien's *Yvain* and Hartmann's *Ywein* is quite instructive in this respect.[25] At the same time, Chrétien did refer to his activity as translator of Ovid into French (*Cligès* 2–3) and Hartmann did point to his knowledge of Latin (*Ywein* 21–25 and *Heinrich* 1–3). Such knowledge gave both of them credibility as narrators of fiction while it also pointed to a new and differentiated distinction between Latin and the vernaculars (Haug 1992: 25–74). Despite these references to their knowledge of Latin, neither Chrétien nor Hartmann presented their patrons with a Latin narrative text; the voice of their authorial

19 It is indicative that Macrobius's reference (*In Somnium Scipionis* 1.2.7–8) to *fabulae* ('stories') includes only Petronius and Apuleius headed under the category *argumenta fictis casibus amatorum repleta* ('verisimilar tales full of the fictitious adventures of lovers'), which, however, barely fits the two Roman novels (see Morgan 1993: 176–8).

20 Green (2002: 7–8, 18–26), but see Paul Gerhard Schmidt's justified objections in the present volume.

21 For an eloquent exposition of the conventional concept, see Reardon (1991), along with the concise presentation by Holzberg (1995); this conventional generic 'form' has been now convincingly questioned by Hägg (2006).

22 See briefly Mann (1987: 188–9) on the textual history of *Ysengrimus*; Mann (1987: 10–77) on the poem's literary structure and Knapp (1979) for the broader context of medieval Latin beast epics.

23 See Trillitzsch (1964) with German translation and Zeydel (1964) with English translation; German translation in Haug and Vollmann (1991: 300–87).

24 See Haug and Vollmann (1974–85) for a facsimile publication of the surviving fragments along with the most recent critical edition; German translations by Knapp (1977) and Haug and Vollmann (1991: 387–551). For a broad interpretative synthesis of the poem, see Vollmann (1993).

25 On the 'Arthurian code' as a semiotic constituent of the *matière de Bretagne*, see Schmolke-Hasselmann (1998: 41–55) and Haug (1992: 91–107); on the common self-referential code underlying *Yvain* and *Ywein*, see Mertens (1998: 63–87) and Brunner (2004b: 117–26).

personae remained consistently vernacular. In fact, the growing self-esteem of such poets, backed by the support of their influential patrons and the successful acceptance of their works by their primary recipients, gradually widened the distance from Latin clerical education, so much so that Wolfram could polemically declare that 'I know not even one letter' (*Parzival* 115,27: *ine kan decheinen buochstap*). On account of their social status and artistic distinction, poets like Chrétien, Hartmann, Gottfried and Wolfram staged themselves as narrating authorial *personae* in their works, offering supposedly autobiographical information, expressing opinions on poetry and language, attacking their colleagues, praising their patrons and, lastly, guiding their audiences through their novel tales.[26]

The situation in Byzantium is very different because no such conscious linguistic break ever took place and no poet ever needed to excuse his choice of linguistic idiom. Obviously, differences between a higher and a lower stylistic level were very much perceived and even discussed by Byzantine authors and teachers of rhetoric, but high and low style (Ševčenko 1981–82) is not to be equated with what is defined today as 'learned' and 'vernacular' idiom. The marked division between a supposedly learned and a supposedly vernacular Greek language is a sixteenth-century humanist construct, fully developed and ideologically bolstered by amateur scholars in the late eighteenth century and professional philologists in the nineteenth.[27] Crucial binary oppositions such as *literatus-illiteratus*, on which Wolfram could play (Green 1994: 190–4), were almost unknown to Byzantine intellectuals who to a substantial extent were not monastic or ecclesiastic clerics but laymen educated in lay private schools, and who often shared this education with the aristocracy in the capital. Admittedly, a change in education did take place at the beginning of the eleventh century, but it was a change in the social provenance of intellectuals and the resulting relations between teachers and imperial power. It was decidedly not some form of expressly stated rupture with an idealized past, a canonical set of texts, or a linguistic idiom of the ecclesiastical elite.[28]

26 On the French poets, see Kelly (1992); on the German poets, see Haug (1992: 119–227); on Wolfram as a deviating authorial *persona* in *Parzival* and *Willehalm*, see Bumke (2004: 203–23, 358–75).

27 On this issue, see Agapitos (1992: 244–51) and Mackridge (1998).

28 On the changes in the system of education from the tenth to the eleventh centuries, see Agapitos (1998a); on education in the twelfth century, see Katsaros (1988: 163–209) and Katsaros (2003), as well as the differing views of Loukaki (2002 and 2005). The relation of the Church to education in the second half of the twelfth century has been also discussed by Angold (1995: 89–98).

Thus, a scholar and writer like Theodore Prodromos (c. 1100–c. 1175)[29] composed a subversively humorous poem around 1140, addressed to the *kaisarissa* Anna Komnene. Therein he regretted having become a man of letters instead of a shoemaker and asked his patroness for financial assistance (*Carmina Historica* no. 38; Hörandner 1974: 377–81). Many years later Theodore addressed a highly burlesque poem on the same topic and with a very similar structure (*Ptochoprodromika* no. 3; Eideneier 1991: 117–36) to Anna's nephew, Emperor Manuel I Komnenos (1143–80).[30] The poem to Anna is composed in dactylic hexameters and the appropriate Homeric diction, while the poem to Manuel is written in *politikos stichos* ('city verse')[31] and in a vernacular idiom. Superficially viewed, the two poems are stylistically and metrically so different[32] that older scholarship thought they were written by different poets, this being decidedly not the case.[33] In neither poem is the issue of language raised because for poets and audiences in the twelfth century, variance of stylistic register or of linguistic idiom, and change of authorial voice was related to literary genre and performance context rather than to the poet's or the audience's education. The same attitude towards choice of stylistic register characterizes, for example, Prince Andronikos Palaiologos (first half of fourteenth century), who wrote a series of prose theological treatises in a 'learned' idiom, as well as a verse romance in the 'vernacular'.[34] Thus, the traditional view that vernacular medieval Greek literature is in its totality 'popular' literature proves to be yet another construct of nineteenth-century philology (Cupane 2003).

This linguistic and/or stylistic variety of Byzantine literature[35] can be found even within the closely related group of the Komnenian novels. One might compare, for example, the 'higher-level' tragic diction of Prodromos's *Rhodanthe and Dosikles* to the rhythmically flowing 'middle-level' prose of

29 No consensus has been reached on the dates of Prodromos's life; see the diverging views of Hörandner (1974: 21–32) and Kazhdan and Franklin (1984: 87–114), as well as the entry in the *Oxford Dictionary of Byzantium* 3 (1991), pp. 1726–7 (Alexander Kazhdan).

30 Reinsch (2001: 221–2) has now convincingly dated the poem to c. 1170 on the basis of a clear reference to Manuel's recently born son Alexios.

31 On the accentuated fifteen-syllable verse – the non-quantitative metre *par excellence* of medieval Greek poetry – see Lauxtermann (1999) with full bibliography.

32 The effect is something like having two hundred rhyming couplets of Chrétien (e.g. *Yvain* 745–959, describing the hero's combat with the knight protecting the wondrous fountain of Barenton) translated into seventy hexameters in the style of Prudentius (e.g. *Psychomachia* 109–77, the combat between Patience and Anger).

33 See the convincing argumentation in Hörandner (1993).

34 Whether Andronikos is the author of the surviving romance *Kallimachos and Chrysorrhoe* is quite another issue (Agapitos 2006a: 157 n. 162).

35 See the excellent analysis by Hinterberger (2001 and 2002).

Eumathios Makrembolites's *Hysmine and Hysminias*. Even more variety is found within the individual redactions of a single Palaiologan romance. Thus, the late fifteenth-century redaction **V** of *Livistros and Rhodamne* differs to such an extent from the fourteenth-century redaction **α** of the same romance (originally composed in the middle of the thirteenth century) that the two texts have to be examined as distinct literary works.[36] In most of the available editions such differences have been removed because the editors arbitrarily and heavy-handedly emended the texts transmitted in the manuscripts by mixing distinct versions, transposing whole passages, cancelling linguistic polymorphy and modernizing the *politikos stichos* (Agapitos 1992: 254–60). However, substantial stylistic variety within the works of a single author or extended linguistic polymorphy within a single vernacular text are part and parcel of Byzantine attitudes to the art of discourse.[37]

The first time the notion of a change to a different linguistic idiom or of a transposition in stylistic level was actually commented upon in Byzantium is in the case of a transposition from a lower to a higher level of style. A vast project of transferring the early Byzantine Lives of Saints to an idiom more appropriate to the literary tastes of the tenth century was set into motion by Symeon the Logothete and his team (Høgel 2002). It was Michael Psellos (1018–c. 1079) who, in the oration *In Praise of Lord Symeon the Metaphrast* (Fisher 1994: 269–88), pointed to Symeon's project and discussed the stylistic and performative issues concerning such a 'transfer'. The shift in the other direction (i.e. from a higher to a lower diction), and explicitly referred to as such, appeared in the fourteenth century. On the one hand, we find the 'translation' (μετάφρασις) of stylistically complex texts to a less complex register, when, for example, Nikephoros Blemmydes's *Imperial Statue* (c. 1250) was transposed in c. 1320 by George Galesiotes and George Oiniaiotes (Hunger and Ševčenko 1986). On the other hand, we detect in some of the vernacular romances references to the 'change' or 'transfer' (μεταβολή, μεταφορά) of a purportedly mythological or historically remote subject, such as the Trojan War or early Byzantine history, to a simpler diction for private readers.[38] Especially the second type of

36 On this question, see Agapitos (2006b: 109–59, 216–19); Lendari (2007).

37 One might consult the detailed metrical and linguistic analysis offered by Hinterberger (1993 and 2005).

38 *Ach* **N** 1908: καὶ μετεβάλομεν αὐτὴν εἰς σαφεστέραν ρῆσιν ('and I changed the story into a clearer diction'), *ByzIl* 1061: εἰς ἰδιώτας πεδινὰ γράφω τὰ τῆς Τρωάδος ('I write the story of Troy for private individuals and in a flat style'), *Belis* **χ** 562: καὶ ἐμετάφερον αὐτὴν λόγου παιδείας χάριν ('and I transformed the story on account of literary education'); on these passages, see Smith (1999: 149–53).

intralinguistic 'translation' forms part of a specific mental attitude to language in the context of Medieval Greek since it refers to the 'transfer' of story matter and not the translation of a specific text. Broadly speaking, these adaptations have nothing to do with the 'translations' from Latin to Old French or from Old French to Middle High German.

IV. MANUSCRIPTS, READERS, SCHOOLS AND AUTHORITATIVE TEXTS

I have already referred to the absence of ancient Latin canonical texts of fiction that would have been viewed as a recognizable genre in the Western lands. This absence resulted in the lack of an appropriate Latin term to designate such a hypothetical genre.[39] In contrast to this situation, such canonical texts did exist in Byzantium. Already in the fourth century, as attested, for example, by remarks on erotic fictional tales made by the physician Theodorus Priscianus[40] or the emperor Julian,[41] a sense for a sub-group of texts similar in subject and structure had been established.[42] Moreover, the 'genre of the novel' was fairly clearly defined around the middle of the ninth century by the learned Patriarch Photios (c. 815–c. 890) in his famous *Bibliotheca*. By using a specific terminology derived from rhetorical school practice, Photios, on the one hand, united the narratives of Heliodorus, Achilles Tatius, Iamblichus, Lucius of Patrae (?) and Antonius Diogenes under one category that he named δρᾶμα ('fiction') or δραματικόν <sc. διήγημα> ('fictional story'). On the other hand, he specifically placed these narrratives close to historiography (e.g., Diodorus, Cassius Dio, Ctesias of Cnidus), hagiography (e.g., St John Chrysostom) and paradoxography (e.g., Damascius). Thus, for example, his extensive summaries of Heliodorus's *Aithiopika* and Iamblichus's *Babyloniaka* reflect his strong interest in historical and paradoxographical information, such as the 'cowherd' bandits, necromancy, killer bees, false ghosts, the rivers Tigris and Euphrates. However, these summaries also show his complete disinterest in such narrative devices like *in medias res* or *ab ovo* openings, and first-person or third-person perspective (Agapitos 1998b: 128–32).[43] On

39 *Historia, fabula* and *argumentum* (as discussed by Green 2002: 1–17) are modes of narration within fiction but they do not constitute independent genres recognized as such by medieval theoreticians. On this notional triad, see the exhaustive treatment by Mehtonen (1996).

40 Quoted in Rohde (1914: 241 n. 1: *amatorias fabulas*).

41 *Ep.* 89b (I.2, 169.11 Bidez): ἐρωτικὰς ὑποθέσεις ('amorous plots'); also in Rohde (1914: 375 n. 4).

42 On the lack of ancient Greek theoretical treatments of the 'novel', see Morgan (1993: 175–93); on the notion of a certain generic cohesion, see Hägg (2006).

43 Morgan (1993: 193–7) discusses Photios as a reader of the Greek novel; however, I do not consider

account of Photios's importance for the formation of school curricula in the tenth century, promoted through the efforts of his influential students such as Arethas (c. 850–928), archbishop of Caesarea, the novel became part of the 'reading list'. It is therefore no coincidence that Heliodorus was excerpted afresh for the compilation of new *gnomologia* in the tenth century (Gärtner 1969: 54–6).

In the mid-eleventh century Michael Psellos compared Heliodorus to Tatius in an essay with the title *What Is the Difference between the Books Whose Plots Concern Charikleia and Leukippe?* (Dyck 1986: 90–9), probably delivered as a lecture for his own school. In contrast to Photios, Psellos focused on the most prominent literary devices of the two novels, as he saw them: Heliodorus's 'serpentine' opening as opposed to Tatius's 'natural' sequence, episodic narrative structure (ἐπεισόδια διηγήματα) in the *Aithiopika*, theatrical first-person perspective (θεατρικόν) in Tatius, Heliodorus's grandiloquent rhetoric of display (μεγαλοπρεπές) and Tatius's seductively sweet style (γλυκύτης). Furthermore, he emphasized literary novelty (καινότης) as a positive quality for both books.[44] These are all devices that Psellos used, for example, in his justly famous *Chronographia* (Books I–VII.91, written c. 1060–65), wherein he combines historiography, *drama*, episodic structure, alteration of first- and third-person perspective, rhetoric of (self-)display, and overall novelty to a degree never seen before in Byzantine historiographical discourse.[45]

It is also in the middle of the eleventh century that we meet the *protospatharios* Eustathios Boilas who, after having served for a long time as judge in the capital, retired to his family estates in Asia Minor, where he passed the remaining years of his life together with his two daughters and their families. Eustathios was a typical middle-level bureaucrat of his time: affluent but not vastly rich, educated but no scholar or writer, well-situated in society but no man of power. He owned a private library, the contents of which he duly listed in his testament, dated April 1059.[46] There is no reason to assume that such a

this discussion appropriate to Photios or the ancient texts because it masks the completely different socio-cultural contexts in which the novels were written and in which Photios read them. As I have argued in my study quoted above, Photios's comments reveal nothing about the reader response of the Greek novel's primary recipients.

44 Praise of the two novels, however, is not unconditional for Psellos. In his lecture *On the Style of Certain Books*, he criticizes inexperienced authors who mistakenly use *Leukippe* and *Charikleia*, alongside with Philostratus and Lucian, for the purpose of building a house solely out of decorative mosaics rather than with solid floors and walls (Boissonade 1838: 48–9).

45 On Psellos's essay, see Agapitos (1998b: 132–9); on some of his literary achievements in the *Chronographia*, see now Pietsch (2005) (with the older bibliography).

46 The original document is lost, but a copy, signed by Eustathios himself, was included at his behest in

library was particularly extravagant for a person of Eustathios's standing. The library consists of eighty volumes, from illuminated manuscripts of the Gospels to various chronicles, from secular law books and collections of canon law to hymnographic collections, from lives of saints and homiletic works to handbooks of grammar and the poetry of Gregory of Nazianzus. Among these volumes we find the following five items: 'Alexander, Leukippe, Judge of Dreams, Of the Twelve Patriarchs, Aesop, Pisides' (Lemerle 1977: 25.160–1).[47] Thus, Eustathios kept in his library a copy of *The Alexander Romance*,[48] Achilles Tatius (considered the more salacious among the surviving ancient novels), a Dream-book (probably of the more recent production rather than a copy of Artemidorus),[49] the apocryphal *Testament of the Twelve Patriarchs*, some Byzantine version of the *Vita Aesopi*,[50] and the poems of George Pisides (first half of seventh century). Here we can easily see the difference with the French and German West concerning the social status of lay education, the role of state bureaucracy and the availability of manuscripts in Byzantium. No layman like Eustathios Boilas with a similar private library could be found serving as judge at some royal western court of the eleventh century, seven years before England was conquered by Duke William of Normandy and eighteen years before the German emperor Henry IV undertook his momentous winter journey to Canossa.

These three instances of historically attested Byzantine readers of the ancient novels form part of a broader interest (i) in collecting and defining ancient Greek novelistic, specifically erotic, narrative in some sort of systematic way (Photios), (ii) in using such texts for private entertainment (Boilas), and (iii) in teaching erotic fiction in school, while profiting from its literary devices (Psellos). A tangible result of this interest is that the survival of manuscripts transmitting Heliodorus and Tatius starts in the eleventh century, while, for example, Iamblichus's *Babyloniaka* was lost. In this process from scholarly interest to aesthetic appreciation of the Hellenistic novel an

the last quaternio of the *Par. Coislinianus gr.* 263, ff. 159–65. The main part of the manuscript (dated by the scribe Theodoulos on f. 157v to 4 April 1059) consists of John Sinaites's *Scala Paradisi*, and can be identified with one of the two copies of this famous monastic treatise included in Boilas's list of books. For a critical edition and detailed study of the document, see Lemerle (1977: 15–63); English translation and notes by Vryonis (1957); for a study of Boilas's books as archaeological objects, see Parani, Pitarakis and Spieser (2003: 162–3).

47 Ἀλέξανδρος· Λευκίππη· Ὀνειροκρίτης· τῶν δώδεκα πατριαρχῶν· Αἴσωπος· Πισίδης.

48 Probably one of the older redactions; see briefly Moennig (1992: 13–37).

49 On these Byzantine *oneirocritica*, see now Mavroudi (2002: 1–5) (with the older bibliography).

50 E.g. version BPThSA; see Karla (2001: 1–17, 29) (codex **Th** is a fragment of an eleventh-century manuscript).

important change took place. As the novels became more and more known to and read by a broader group of educated people in the capital, they stepped out of their 'eponymity' and moved into an 'anonymity' shared with other popular narrative texts in Byzantium, such as the fictional/historical biographies of Alexander and Aesop or the Lives of Saints, especially the Passions of Early Christian martyrs (Agapitos 2004a: 63–5). Thus, while Photios refers to Tatius and Heliodorus as 'persons', Boilas and Psellos write only of *Leukippe* and *Charikleia* as 'books'. Similarly, in a late eleventh-century manuscript transmitting Heliodorus and Tatius, the scribe copies on the first page of the book the name of the author and the original title of the work, but (i) adds the Byzantine title in order to make clear to the reader what book this is, and (ii) composes an iambic two-verse epigram playing on the etymology of the heroine's name (*Marc. gr.* 409, f. 1r):

> Heliodorus's *Aethiopian Story* – The *Charikleia*. Certainly it offers joy rather than glory this here very book of *Charikleia*.[51]

The etymology is obviously wrong since the first part of Charikleia's name derives from *charis* ('grace, charm') rather than *chara* ('joy'); however, this etymology points to the aesthetic pleasure that Byzantine readers are to obtain from reading a love story. This shift to anonymity that we detect in the reception of the ancient Greek novel will be of some importance when examining the authorial contracts established by Komnenian and Palaiologan poets with their respective audiences.

The fact that Heliodorus and Tatius were read in school brings us to the broader issue of education and the practice of public rhetoric in eleventh- and twelfth-century Byzantium. As hinted already, the social function of public discourse presents us with one of the major differences between the West and Byzantium. The consistent presence of and continuous need for epideictic oratory at the imperial court for celebrating recurring feasts (e.g. delivery of imperial panegyrics on Epiphany, delivery of patriarchal panegyrics on the Saturday of Lazarus, delivery of orations in honour of Constantinople's 'birthday' on May 11) or special events (e.g. crowning ceremonies, weddings, funerals) necessitated the training of young men to become public speakers.

51 Ἡλιοδώρου αἰθιοπικῶν· ἡ χαρίκλεια | χαράν γε πάντως ἀποδίδει οὐ κλέος· | τῆς χαρικλείας τοῦτο δὴ τὸ βιβλίον (quoted directly from the manuscript, but also to be found in the critical apparatus of the Rattenbury-Lumb edition, vol. I, p. 2 [cod. **Z**]).

On account of their talent, some of these young men, like Michael Psellos or Niketas Choniates (c. 1155/57–1217), became members of the bureaucracy and often rose to the highest ranks of the civil service, while others, especially in the second half of the twelfth century, like Michael Choniates (c. 1138–1222), became high ecclesiastical dignitaries and acclaimed preachers (see above p. 245 n. 28).

The school curriculum therefore included the study of rhetorical theory by means of the handbooks of Hermogenes (second century) and Pseudo-Menander (third century) with the help of commentaries, such as the ones written on Hermogenes by John Geometres in the late tenth century (now surviving only in excerpts) and John Doxapatres in the eleventh.[52] Moreover, model texts from epideictic oratory and philosophy were read and studied as to their content, structure and style.[53] Attic drama, read in school as part of the basic linguistic training (one needs only to recall the Byzantine triads of the three tragedians), was rediscovered as a form of poetry in the late eleventh and the twelfth century: old manuscripts were collected and new ones copied, scholia were compiled and interpretative essays written. It was the rhetorical power of drama – in other words, its perceived theatrics of display – that caught the interest of scholars and authors (Agapitos 1998b: 139–43). This discourse of theatrical display was further cultivated through the teaching of *progymnasmata* (exercises of stylistic/rhetorical composition) and, more specifically, of *ethopoiiai* ('dramatic monologues') that offered students the opportunity to explore the representation of a person's 'character' through his or her own thoughts and words.[54] Some of the *ethopoiiai* composed by the teacher and court orator Nikephoros Basilakes (c. 1115–c. 1185) are rather daring attempts at exploring female sexual desire in the face of a non-human yet distinctly male erotic metamorphosis. One might mention, for example,

52 Only Doxapatres's prolegomena to Hermogenes's treatises have been edited by Rabe (1931: 304–18, (*Staseis*), 360–74 (*Heuresis*), 420–6 (*Ideai*)).

53 I have already refered to Psellos's short essay *On the Style of Some Books* (Boissonade 1838: 48–52), wherein he warned prospective authors that before indulging in the graces of Heliodorus, Tatius, Philostratus and Lucian they should study closely Demosthenes, Isocrates, Aelius Aristides, Thucydides, Plato, Plutarch, Lysias and Gregory of Nazianzus. In the first half of the twelfth century the learned Metropolitan of Corinth Gregory Pardos devoted in his treatise *On the Writing of Speeches* a whole chapter discussing the best writings both for prose and poetry (Donnet 1967: 319–23), most of whom are Roman Imperial or early Byzantine authors (e.g. Aelius Aristides, Lucian, Tatius and Heliodorus, Libanius, Himerius, Gregory of Nazianzus, Greogory of Nyssa, Basil of Caesarea, Themistius, Synesius, Procopius and Choricius of Gaza, George Pisides), but also some of his own contemporaries (e.g. Psellos, Nicolas Kallikles, Theodore Prodromos).

54 On this type of exercise see Hunger (1978: II, 108–16).

What would Danaë say having been deflowered by Zeus transformed into a shower of gold, or *What would Pasiphaë say having fallen in love with the bull*.[55] Thus, the Byzantine authors who 're-invented' the antique novel in the second quarter of the twelfth century had all read their ancient books and, in the broadest sense of *mimesis*, had learned their art from them.[56]

But even in the turbulent thirteenth century, when *The Tale of Livistros and Rhodamne*, the oldest and longest of the vernacular romances, was written at the Laskarid court of Nicaea in c. 1240–60, the anonymous poet had also learned his art from books, in fact, the same books that the novelists of the previous century had used. It is in this Laskarid context that the Komnenian literary heritage was collected in order to support the restoration of the education system and the establishment of a court culture with all the necessary public rituals of display.[57] A number of important manuscripts were copied in Nicaea or Constantinople between the years 1240 and 1280. Some transmit the Hellenistic and the Komnenian novels side by side (*Vat. gr.* 114, *Vat. gr.* 1390), some preserve the novels along with rhetorical and philosophical texts of the twelfth century and ceremonial texts of the thirteenth century (*Laur. Conventi soppressi* 627, *Oxon. Baroccianus* 131), while others unite in one volume the works of a single author, for example Michael Psellos (*Par. gr.* 1182, *Vat. Barber. gr.* 240) or Theodore Prodromos (*Palat. gr.* 43).[58] Moreover, a closer study of *L&R* showed that the stylistic level of the romance's oldest redaction is far higher and rhetorically far more artful than had been hitherto assumed (Agapitos 1993: 101–17). Furthermore, it has also been shown that the anonymous poet employed a number of literary devices taken directly from the novels of Makrembolites and Prodromos, while he even quoted a passage from the now fragmentary novel of Konstantinos Manasses (Agapitos 1999: 112–16). The poet of *Livistros and Rhodamne* was therefore fully justified

55 See *Prog.* 46 and 54; Pignani (1983: 191–3 and 221–4 respectively).

56 The issue of *mimesis* in Byzantine literature still remains to be discussed in depth. For differing assessments see, on the one hand, the remarks of Papaioannou (2004) and Papaioannou (forthcoming), ch. 3 in the case of Psellos and the context of a gradually developing performative understanding of *mimesis* from the middle of the tenth to the middle of the twelfth centuries, and on the other hand, Kaldellis (2007a: 225–76 and 2007b), who unconvincingly argues for a nineteenth-century historicist sense among Komnenian literati. For broader historical overviews and theoretical discussions of *mimesis* (with little reference to the Middle Ages and none to Byzantium), see, indicatively, Melberg (1995: 10–50), Walton (1990: 70–105), the collected essays in Gebauer and Wulf (1992) and Scholz (1998).

57 On education in the thirteenth and fourteenth centuries, see Constantinides (1982) and Mergiali (1996); on Laskarid court culture, see briefly Agapitos (2006b: 51–3).

58 On the Nicaean context of the codices, see Agapitos (1998b: 126–7; 2000b: 173–6; 2002: 207–9).

when, speaking through the *persona* of the romance's first-person narrator, he referred to his novel narrative, simultaneously learned and vernacular, as a 'strangely drawn tale of love' (*L&R* **α** 17: ξενοχάραγον ἀφήγημαν ἀγάπης).

Thus, in a spatiotemporal continuum from the ninth to the early fourteenth century, the ancient Greek novel (primarily represented through *Charikleia* and *Leukippe*) was copied by scribes, read by educated members of Byzantine society, taught at high-level lay schools, and used as an authoritative textual starting point for the literary exploration of fiction in an ever changing socio-cultural context.

V. BETWEEN HISTORY AND FICTION

In the prologue to *The Tale of Erec* (c. 1170),[59] his first Arthurian romance, Chrétien de Troyes makes an important statement about the art of fictional narrative poetry. Among other things, the poet suggests that he has employed all of his 'knowledge' (17: *scïence*) to create a 'beautifully ordered composition' out of a 'tale of adventure' (14–15).[60] He then proceeds to defend his innovative project not by suggesting that it is true but by criticizing professional storytellers who actually disfigured the story they told in front of their aristocratic audiences (19–22):

> This is the tale of Erec, son of Lac, which those who try to live by storytelling customarily mangle and corrupt before kings and counts.[61]

Chrétien did not employ again this critique against oral poetry as a device of defence.[62] When a few years later he composed *Cligès* (c. 1176),[63] a work whose story matter and its treatment differed substantially from *Erec*, he introduced in the prologue to this 'Grecian' romance another strategy for defending fic-

59 On *Erec*, see the introductions in Fritz (1992: 5–26) and Poirion (1994: 1053–74) (Peter F. Dembowski) with the relevant bibliography.

60 'Et trait d'un conte d'aventure | Une mout bele conjuncture.' On the *scïence, aventure* and *conjunture*, and their major significance for Chrétien's poetics, see the exhaustive discussion in Kelly (1992: 15–31, 146–204).

61 'D'Erec, le fil Lac, est li contes, | Que devant rois et devant contes, | Depecier et corrompre suelent | Cil qui de conter vivre vuelent.'

62 What kind of oral poetry supposedly lies behind Chrétien's statement and what was the exact nature of the profession of a *jongleur* has been an issue of great debate; see Green (1994: 237–69) (with the older bibliography) and in a more critical vein Green (2002: 35–54).

63 On *Cligès*, see the introductions in Poirion (1994: 1114–31) (Philippe Walter) and in Méla, Collet and Gérard-Zai (1994: 5–19) (Charles Méla); both include good bibliographies.

tion.[64] Having informed his audience about the written source of his historical tale concerning a young nobleman from Greece, found in a book belonging to the library of the Church of Saint-Pierre à Beauvais, the poet declared and explained (*Cligès* 24–8):

> The book containing the true story is very old, therefore it is all the more worthy of belief. Through the books we have, we learn of the deeds of ancient peoples.[65]

Chrétien thus established for his fictional narrative a code of external referentiality that operated on two distinct levels: (i) an ancient source is produced as a materially existing old book guaranteeing the 'truth' (*voire*) of the story, and (ii) the 'Empire of Greece and Constantinople' is, rather nebulously, presented as a historically existing kingdom at the other end of the Mediterranean during the time of King Arthur (45–9).[66] Obviously, both the old book and the Grecian Empire have been absorbed into the fictive Arthurian world of the story offered to the poet's audience. However, these two guarantors do establish a verisimilar, rather than simply a fantastic, semiotic system for the most deviating and subversive among Chrétien's romances (Knapp 2005: 29–30). The prologues to Chrétien's first two tales of adventure clearly show the ambivalent position of fiction in the medieval West, a position that had to be defended by using devices that approached 'history' as the other end of the pole between 'falsehood' and 'truth'. Parts five to seven of the paper will follow this ongoing movement between history and fiction, as well as the ways in which fiction and authorial contract with the audience were dealt with in Rhomaian, Frankish and Persian lands.

In the prologue to *Cligès*, where history and fiction intertwine in order for the latter to be legitimized by the former, Chrétien has followed an established practice of medieval Latin historiographic writings reporting mythical and archaic *materia* as history, a practice that has been termed the 'historiographic paradigm' (Kelly 1992: 68–93). The author presents a single source

64 On this most often discussed of Chrétien's prologues, see the critical assessment of older scholarship by Lyons (1980–81), as well as the differing interpretations by Freeman (1979) and Kinoshita (1996).

65 'Li livres est molt anciens | Qui tesmoigne l'estoire a voire: | Por ce fet ele meulz a croire. | Par les livres que nos avons | Les faiz des anciens savons.'

66 'Crestiens comence son conte, | Si com l'estoire le reconte, | Qui traite d'un empereor | Poissant de richece et d'ennor | Qui tint Grece et Constantinoble' ('Chrétien begins his tale, following his source, which tells of an emperor, mighty in wealth and glory, who ruled over Greece and Constantinople').

as the authenticating book of true narrative, for example, Geoffrey of Monmouth adduces a 'Breton' book, Saxo Grammaticus refers to an 'oral' book.[67] This practice is also followed in the *romans d'antiquité* where the extant ancient Latin source authenticates the medieval vernacular product of *translatio*.[68] Thus, the anomymous poet of the *Roman de Thèbes*[69] refers to 'the book of Statius' (**S** 8543: *le liver d'Estaisce*) in order to lend weight to an episode actually not found in the *Thebaid*. Heinrich von Veldeke in the epilogue of his adaptation (c. 1170–74 and c. 1180–84) of the *Roman d'Enéas* (c. 1160) first points to everyone's familiarity with the story of Eneas; he then refers to his French model he himself has read and to the Latin source truthfully translated by this model (*EneasRom* 354,16–20):

> This [i.e., the story of Eneas and of his clan] is sufficiently well-known, as it has been composed by Heinrich, who read it from French books in which it had been composed from Latin – all of it according to truth.[70]

The most extended presentation of the historiographic paradigm, however, is to be found in Benoît de Saint-Maure's prologue to his vast *Roman de Troie*, composed in c. 1160–65, probably at the behest of Eleanor of Aquitaine (*Troie* 33–9):[71]

> And for this reason I wish to labour by embarking on a story which – should I have understanding and capability – I would like to translate from Latin, where I found it, into French in such a way that even those who do not comprehend the letter [i.e. Latin], will be able to grasp the French.[72]

Having, then, criticized Homer for not having told the truth in his 'book', Benoît introduces Dares (the Phrygian) as an eyewitness to the Trojan War

67 On these two authors and their 'books', see Lars Boje Mortensen's contribution in the present volume.

68 On the concept of *translatio studii* in the case of the antique romances, see Baswell (2000: 31–4); on the importance of the historiographic paradigm for the authentication of 'historical' vernacular fiction, see Kelly (1992: 206–63).

69 See the comprehensive entry in Frappier and Grimm (1978–84: II, 204–6) (no. 460).

70 'Daz is genûgen kuntlîch, | als ez dâ tihte Heinrîch, | derz ûzer welschen bûchen las, | da ez von latîne getihtet was | al nâch der wârheide.'

71 For all technical data see Frappier and Grimm (1978–84: II, 86–9) (no. 70).

72 'E por ce me vuell travailler | En une estoire conmencer, | Que, de latin ou jo la truis, | Se j'ai le sens e se ge puis, | Le voudrai si en romanz metre | Que cil qui n'entendront la letre | Se puissent deduire el romanz.' The whole prologue can also be found in Mölk (1969: 24–8).

(*Troie* 45–128). Towards the end of the romance Dares is joined by Dictys (the Cretan) as the other eyewitness to the siege of Troy: 'In this way <the city> was betrayed because of malice and envy, as it is told by Dictys and Dares' (24391–3).[73] A few lines later, Benoît draws a brief portrait of the 'mighty knight and wise cleric' Dictys, pointing out that 'he wrote his history against Dares; he was, in fact, in the Grecian army' (24400–1).[74] Both these sources are late antique Latin traslations of Roman Imperial Greek texts.[75] They are wholly fabricated but, on account of their immense popularity in medieval times because of their supposed eyewitness value, they served as 'historical' sources of the Trojan War that was at any rate perceived as a historical event and heavily used in the literary legitimization of monarchic and broader feudal constructions of aristocratic history on both sides of the Channel.[76]

That this strategy of poetic authorization was recognized as such by medieval recipients can be seen in its outright rejection by Nicolas de Senlis who in c. 1202 composed for Countess Yolande of Saint-Pol in Flanders the first Old French prose historical text, being a translation of Pseudo-Turpin's prose narrative *Historia Karoli Magni et Rotholandi*.[77] Nicolas begins his preface with the following statement (Paris, B.N. fr. 124, f. 1r):

> I wish to begin the history of how the good Emperor Charlemagne went to Spain in order to conquer the land under the Saracens. Many people have heard it told and sung, but what these singers and jongleurs sing and tell is nothing but a lie. No rhymed tale is true. Everything they say is lies, for they know nothing about it except through hearsay.[78]

The fact that Pseudo-Turpin is just another fabrication based on the *Chanson de Roland* is of little relevance. It is the veracity of prose against the falsehood

73 '<La cité> cum fu traïe | Par mauvestié et par envie, | Si cum Ditys le dit et Daire.'

74 'Contre Daire rescrit l'estoire. | Cist fu de hors, en l'ost grezeis.'

75 On these, see now Papathomopoulos and Jeffreys (1996: xli–l) and Jung (1997).

76 On the Trojan story matter and its political importance in the Franco-Norman world, see Ingledew (1994) and Jung (1996).

77 On Pseudo-Turpin, see Paul Gerhard Schmidt's contribution in the present volume; on the French translations of Pseudo-Turpin in the early thirteenth century and their importance for vernacular prose historiography, see Spiegel (1993: 55–98).

78 'Voil commencer l'estoire si cum li bons enpereires Karlemaine en ala en Espaignie par le terre conquere sore les Sarrazins. Maintes genz si en ont oi conter et chanter mes n'est si mensonge non ço qu'il en dient e chantent cil chanteor ne cil iogleor. Nus contes rimes n'est verais. Tot est mencongie ço qu'il en dient car il n'en sievent rienz fors quant par oir dire' (text and translation quoted from Spiegel (1993: 55); see also Mölk (1968: 100–2) for the text of the whole preface from a different manuscript).

of poetry that is vehemently proposed and historical truth that is defended through the translation of a Latin 'historiographic' work; here *estoire* indeed means primarily 'history' and only secondarily 'story'. Moreover, Nicolas ingeniously used the same people as his target of criticism as Chrétien had done some thirty years earlier, namely professional singers and storytellers. In the case of Chrétien it is the poet's artful verse that lends authority to the story, while in the case of Nicolas it is the historian's artless prose that validates the truth of the narrative, a situation radically different from the importance with which oral poetry as historical testimony was invested in Old Norse literature.[79]

In contrast to what has been described above for the various Frankish lands, Byzantine historiography presents us with a fairly – one might be tempted to say deceptively – homogeneous image. Historiography, based on the practices of Roman Imperial times, was cultivated assiduously and continuously from the fourth century onwards. On the one hand, historiographical discourse in the 'classical' mode opened up to various experimental developments,[80] while new subgenres, such as world chronicle and church history, emerged in order to cater to the needs of a Christian society.[81] In contrast to the French vernacular 'historiographic paradigm', Byzantine historians authorized in their prologues the truth of their narratives through different strategies, among which the 'critical assessment' of older sources figures prominently.[82] This assessment of older written sources was a specific trait of the chronicle, in which a panorama of world history was presented, starting with the Creation, leading to the Roman Empire and culminating mostly in the author's own time.[83] In order to see how historiography explores the twilight zone between history and fiction, we will examine three extensive verse narratives that were perceived by their authors and their respective audiences as history. Each of

79 See the contributions by Else Mundal and Slavica Ranković in the present volume.

80 See now the broader treatments by Taragna (2000) and Kaldellis (2004).

81 On Byzantine historiography, besides the more conventional overview in Hunger (1978: I, 241–504), one might consult the broad synthesis (including selected passages with commentary and substantial bibliography) by Karpozilos (1997, 2002 and 2009). On the literary qualities of Byzantine historiography one may read with profit the *Symbolae-Osloenses*-Debate led by Ljubarskij (1998) and the collection of essays in Odorico, Agapitos and Hinterberger (2006).

82 On historiographical *prooimia* in general, see Maisano (1985); on the twelfth century in particular, see Grigoriadis (1998).

83 That the Byzantines very well recognized the difference between 'history' and 'chronicle' as two distinct ways of narrating historical events is attested, for example, by the remarks of Photios in the *Bibliotheca* when he discusses ancient and Byzantine historians and chroniclers (Karpozilos 2002: 30–2).

these three works – a Byzantine, a French and a Persian one – stands at the beginning of a respective historiographic tradition in verse; all three works present a narrative that in differing ways constructs a form of 'national' history, not dissimilar to the grand project of Saxo's *Gesta Danorum*.[84]

The *Synopsis Chronike* ('Annalistic compendium') by Constantine Manasses (c. 1115–c. 1175), written for his patroness, the *sebastokratorissa* Eirene Komnene, in c. 1150–53, is a Byzantine world chronicle of the type described above.[85] In contrast, however, to all other chronicles up to his own time, Manasses composed his world history in 6620 fifteen-syllable verses. In his preface, the author explains his method of handling his sources (*SynChr* 21–6):

> Many composed histories and chronicles; they attempted to narrate correctly and truthfully yet, ultimately, wrote in contradiction to each other. I, however, having chosen those writers who seem to be the most exact and to keep more to the truth, shall fulfill your command to the best of my capacity.[86]

The chronicle begins with the creation of the world, goes through Hebrew, Egyptian, Greek and Roman history, and ends in 1081 with the rise of the young general Alexios Komnenos to the Byzantine throne. There is no single piece of original historical information in the *Synopsis* because the text is based in its entirety on a few easily identifiable sources, readily available around the middle of the twelfth century. Manasses does not defend himself in his preface or anywhere else in the chronicle for having chosen to write in verse rather than in prose. It seems as if a historiographically derivative verse-chronicle did not constitute an obstacle in historical truthfulness for

84 On this construction in the case of Saxo, see Lars Boje Mortensen's contribution in the present volume.

85 The editor of the chronicle (see Lampsidis 1988 and briefly Lampsidis 1996: xviii–xx) argued that the *Synopsis Chronike* was composed in c. 1140–42, that it had a bipartite structure and that it was revised in 1143–44 in order to be presented to the young Emperor Manuel after Eirene's disgrace. Reinsch (2007: 268–9) has now with serious arguments contested Lampsidis' dating; he has proposed that the chronicle was conceived as a whole textual unity and that it was composed in only one stage in c. 1150 and before Eirene's death in c. 1153. Be that as it may, neither of the two proposed dates influences the analysis that follows because in either case the chronicle was written in the first decade of Manuel's reign.

86 Πολλῶν ἱστορησάντων δὲ καὶ χρονογραφησάντων | καὶ σπουδασάντων μὲν εἰπεῖν ὀρθῶς καὶ φιλαλήθως, | ἀλλήλοις ἀνομοίως δὲ ταῦτα συγγραψαμένων, | ἡμεῖς, προχειρισάμενοι τοὺς μάλιστα δοκοῦντας | τῆς ἀκριβείας ἔχεσθαι καὶ μᾶλλον ἀληθεύειν, | τὸ κατὰ δύναμιν ἡμῖν ἀποπληρώσομέν σοι.

the patroness or for subsequent readers. In fact, the *Synopsis*, despite its having been composed for an aristocratic patroness, became the most popular chronicle in the centuries to come (with over 140 manuscripts and fragments), and was translated in 1336–38 into Old Bulgarian for Tsar Ivan Alexander (1331–73). The success of the *Synopsis* lies in its succinct and well-balanced presentation of historical information, as well as in its masterful handling of narrative through a distinctly novelistic and rhetorical discourse.[87] The techniques of this discourse Manasses had learned from Heliodorus and Tatius while writing his own novel *Aristandros and Kallithea*, now surviving only as a reconstructed 'excerpt collection' culled from three early fourteenth-century edificatory *gnomologia*.

Master Wace, an almost exact contemporary of Manasses, completed his *Roman de Brut* in 1155.[88] Both the French poet and his royal commissioner, Eleanor of Aquitaine, perceived the work as historical, since it was a translation of Geoffrey of Monmouth's *Historia Regum Britannie* (c. 1130–35). The author claims that 'Master Wace has translated it and tells it truthfully' (*Brut* 7–8),[89] thus adducing his own version of the historiographic paradigm. At a much later point in his narrative, Wace makes two further statements about the relation of history/truth to fiction/falsehood (Green 2002: 16–17). He first remarks that the tales told about Arthur's adventures are 'not all lies, not all truth, neither total folly nor total wisdom' (*Brut* 9793–4).[90] He then proceeds to distinguish his work from that of professional storytellers who recount mere wondertales and fables about Arthur (*Brut* 9795–8):

> The raconteurs have recounted so many yarns, the storytellers so many stories, to embellish their tales that they have made it all appear fiction.[91]

This discussion of Arthurian tales is part of a digression wherein Wace points to the splendours of Arthur's court that flourished because of the twelve-year period of peace at the beginning of the king's reign. It is during this 'great

87 See Lampsidis (1996: lv–lxv) (episodic structure, novelistic discourse, versification); Reinsch (2002) (rhetorical erotic discourse); Nilsson (2005 and 2006) (*ekphrasis* and compositional innovation).

88 See Frappier and Grimm (1978–84: II, 214–15) (no. 496); for a succinct presentation of the basic characteristics of Wace's narrative, see Green (2002: 176–7).

89 'Maistre Wace l'ad translaté | Ki en conte la verité.'

90 'Ne tut mençunge ne tut veir, | Ne tut folie ne tut saveir.'

91 'Tant unt li cunteür cunté | Et li fableür tant fablé | Pur lur cuntes enbeleter, | Que tut unt fait fable sembler.'

peace' (*grant pais*), Wace suggests, that Arthur accomplished his exploits that were gradually transformed into fables (*Brut* 9787–92).[92] In fact, this pause between the continuous warfare is the very historical niche in which Chrétien ingeniously placed his Arthurian fiction, starting with *Erec*. Just as Wace correlated the Arthurian court to the chivalric court of Henry and Eleanor, connecting in this way past and present, so did Chrétien use the 'historicity' of the Arthurian world as the necessary reference to his consistently fictional narrative. One probable reason for the utilization of Wace's Arthurian pause by Chrétien lies in the fact that both *Brut* and *Erec* were commissioned by the same patrons and were written at a distance of no more than fifteen years from each other. Thus, the Arthurian peace in Chrétien also correlates the Breton past to the Norman present through the courtly figure of King Henry Plantagenet.

Abulqasim Firdowsi (940–c. 1020) was born in a village near the city of Tus in Khorasan and lived most of his life there.[93] He was a *dihqan*, that is, a member of the indigenous landed gentry that partly survived the Arab conquest of Persia in the middle of the seventh century and that viewed itself as the repository of Iranian (pre-Islamic) traditions. It is the Samanid kings of Khorasan and Transoxania in the tenth century that, as the Abbasid Caliphate's power in Bagdad was diminishing, promoted a specifically Persian culture by commisioning translations, encouraging antiquarian interests and, most importantly, by using New Persian rather than Arabic as the official language at court; as a result, a court poetry of great brilliance began to flourish (Meisami 1987). It is in this socio-cultural context that Firdowsi started working on his great poem which he completed when he was seventy-one years old in 1011. The *Shahnameh* ('Book of Kings') is the oldest surviving and, most probably, the first of a series of *mathnawi* ('verse narrrative') in Persian.[94] The length of the *Shahnameh* is extraordinary by any standards, as it ranges, depending on the version, from c. 50,000 to c. 60,000 verses. But if one takes into account that the *mutaqârib* metre used by Firdowsi is a twenty-two-syllable verse with

92 *Brut* 9787–98 is also excerpted in Mölk (1969: 98).

93 For a detailed presentation of all available sources, see the entry on Firdowsi in the *Encyclopedia of Islam* 2 (1965), pp. 918–21 (Claude Huert and Henry Massé).

94 They are generically called 'epics' since the middle of the nineteenth century, but the term is somewhat misleading as it does not fit the three main types of such narratives: (i) a heroic war tale like Asadi's *Garshahspnameh*; (ii) a romantic tale like Gurgani's *Vis and Ramin*; (iii) a mystic tale like Sinai's *The Garden of Truth* (all three works belong to the first half of the eleventh century); on *mathnawi* as a metre and as a designation for longer narratives, see the respective entry in the *Encyclopedia of Islam* 6 (1991), pp. 832–5 (Johannes T. P. de Bruijn).

an internal rhyme after the caesura, thus resembling an eleven-syllable lyric couplet, the length is doubled in terms of Western versification. Beyond that, the poem's astonishing artistic qualities and the sheer force of its narrative breadth made it into a treasure house of Persian literature. Numerous poets up to the seventeenth century based themselves on larger sections of the *Shahnameh* for their own narrative tales, or picked up specific episodes to use as frames for their lyric poetry.

Organized around the rules of the Persian kings and punctuated by the poet's authorial interventions on the course of his tale or the fate of his heroes, the *Shahnameh* presents in a seamless narrative, the history of Iran from the mythical creation of the world up to the conquest of the land by Caliph Umar (634–44).[95] Similar to the narrative organization of the *Synopsis Chronike* and the *Roman de Brut*, the heroic tale does not present a 'universal' view of history. Firdowsi specifically concentrates on the very eastern parts of ancient Iran (i.e., today's Khorasan and western Afghanistan) and its major enemy, the kingdom of Turan to the north of the River Oxus. Thus, just like in the case of Manasses where the history of Ancient Greece is almost omitted and the chronicle practically moves from Ancient Egypt to the Trojan War and, then, directly to the foundation of Rome,[96] Firdowsi shifts the narrative without a break from the legendary kings of Ancient Iran to the story of Sekandar (Alexander the Great) and his conquest of Persia, omitting the history of the Achaemenid dynasty and its strong involvement with the Western lands of 'Rum', that is, Hellenic Asia Minor and Greece. In the introductory part of the *Shahnameh*,[97] composed as is usual for Persian literature by a variety of seemingly unrelated subjects, Firdowsi devotes a section on his sources. He says that the poet Daqiqi had found an ancient book and had decided to put it into verse, starting his narrative with King Gushtasp (the legendary Kavi Vishtaspa) who received Zoroaster at his court and espoused the sage's new religion. After Daqiqi's murder by a slave in c. 980, Firdowsi was given Daqiqi's unfinished work and the ancient book. He decided to incorporate the deceased poet's verses in his own work and to use the book (he always

95 For an excellent survey of ancient Iranian history up to 651, see Frye (1984).

96 On this attitude, see Jeffreys (1979).

97 Unfortunately, this introductory part has been completely omitted in the recent prose translation of the poem by Dick Davis (2006), who has also excised most of Firdowsi's poetological comments and authorial interventions (for similar passages in other Persian epics and romances excised by European translators, see Seyed-Gohrab 2003: 42 n. 54). Thus, the reader who wishes to get a complete picture of the poem and does not read Persian must go to the pioneering and still useful French translation accompanying the edition by Mohl (1838–78).

refers to it as *The Book of the Righteous*) as his principal source, purporting, like Wace, to follow it closely.[98] However, like in the case of Saxo Grammaticus, it is probable that the legendary material comes from oral tradition rather than from written sources, which also explains, again like in Saxo, the difference in narrative organization between the epic's 'first' (mythological) part up to the reign of Alexander and the 'second' (historical) part introducing the rise of the Sasanids.

Despite their different strategies in authorizing their narratives through the use of reliable historical sources (a single book as opposed to a selection from many writings), Manasses in the *Synopsis Chronike*, Wace in the *Roman de Brut* and Firdowsi in the *Shahnameh* view themselves as historians and not as writers of fiction. There are further similarities between the three poets: (i) the novel choice (dictated or not by a patron) of composing history in an accessible verse form (Greek fifteen-syllable verse, French octosyllabic rhymed couplet, Persian twenty-two-syllable verse) and in a fairly comprehensible linguistic medium (Old French vernacular, middle-level Medieval Greek, New Persian); (ii) the faithful adherence to the source material, even if the narrative has been shaped by various literary devices; (iii) the extravagant length of the three works.

Moreover, Manasses and Firdowsi also introduce a 'pause' in the narration of history, not dissimilar to the *grant pais* descriptively expanded by Wace from the mere reference of Geoffrey to it. Manasses, for example, rounds off the narrative of the chronicle's first part with the rise of Constantine the Great to the throne and the founding of Constantinople as the 'New Rome' of the now peaceful Christian Empire (*SynChr* 2291–318). The author then seamlessly creates a narrative pause by inserting a brief but rhetorically charged praise of the new capital in the form of a description (2319–26). The pause is brought to an end by an extended authorial intervention where Manasses defers further *laudes urbis* to a more appropriate time and leads his discourse back to its narrative purpose (2327–9).[99] However, in contrast to the Arthurian pause in Wace, the Constantinian pause in Manasses was never exploited for the placement of a fictional narrative in its confines. The four Komnenian novels, all written a few years before the *Synopsis* (i.e., between 1130 and 1145), had used the 'exotic' setting of a literary Hellenic antiquity to stage their fic-

98 The reign of Gushtasp, including the verses of Daqiqi on the introduction of Zoroastrianism, has been substituted in Davis (2006: 369–70) with the briefest of summaries.

99 The passage has been discussed by Nilsson (2005: 137–9) as to the function of the description.

tional narratives[100] because they had taken over the fictive contract set by their model texts. The Palaiologan romances, the earliest of which was written hundred years after Manasses's chronicle, never even employed any recurring 'historical' time and place to anchor their plots. Obviously, Emperor Constantine (306–37), well attested in all kinds of historical sources, could not function in the same way for the Byzantine rulers of the twelfth century as Arthur had for the Norman kings of England. On the one hand, Constantine had not been a *dux bellorum* magnified through some oral lore, nor had he been *a posteriori* invested with a chivalric image. On the other hand, he had very early on become a major saint of the Church and, thus, an unassailable model Christian ruler, while the Byzantines did not perceive in the historical continuum of the 'Roman' Empire any break that was in need of repair.[101] Emperor Manuel I Komnenos (1143–80), King Henry's contemporary and indirect dedicatee of Manasses's chronicle (*SynChr* 2506–12), did make a concerted effort to establish a highly extravagant imperial image that actually incorporated some Western chivalric elements, such as jousting tournaments, French dressing fashions, imperial falconry, and a superficial use of the notion of feudal vassalage.[102] However, this effort did not lead to any construction of a 'historio-fictive' Constantinian chivalric past and the concomitant production of a fictional narrative literature that would correlate the Roman past to the Byzantine present and that could have created Greek versions of *fin'amour* and *chevalerie*.[103] The notion of a feudal court culture with all its social accoutrements was still foreign to Byzantine concepts of kingship and its socio-cultural manifestations.

In the *Shahnameh*, Firdowsi does not focus on large-scale love stories until he reaches the reign of Bahram Gur ('the wild-ass hunter') who supposedly

100 Most recently discussed, but from quite different perspectives, by Jouanno (2005) and Kaldellis (2007b).

101 See the essays on various aspects of Constantine's Byzantine reception in Magdalino (1994).

102 One need only read Manuel's preparation of and active participation in a grand tournament at Antioch in April 1159, vividly described by Niketas Choniates (*Chronike Diegesis* IV.4.1–6; van Dieten 1975: 108.41–109.91 = Maisano and Pontani 1994: 244–9). On Manuel's imperial image during the first part of his reign, see Magdalino (1993: 434–54); on the Latin vogue at Manuel's court, see Agapitos and Smith (1992: 81–3); on the emperor's jousts Jones and Maguire (2002) with a translation and analysis of an anonymous *ekphrasis* of a tournament; on vassalage Agapitos (2006a: 128–9) with the older bibliography.

103 On these key concepts, see Kelly (1993: 121–7) with the older bibliography. They have also been discussed from a different perspective by Cupane (1986) in the case of the Palaiologan romances and their supposed failure to understand *amour* and *aventure*, a failure that resulted in unsatisfactory narratives (see my objections in Agapitos 2004b: 27–9).

reigned for sixty-three years.[104] Bahram is, in fact, the historical Varahran V (421–39). Most of the episodes narrated concern Bahram's astonishing hunting, drinking or love-making exploits, though there are some episodes concerning relations with other countries. After the young ruler has established himself, word reaches the various nations that Bahram is a pleasure-loving king. So, the emperor of China decides to invade Persia with the help of its vassal Turkic state of Turan; a complicated clash ensues in which, finally, Bahram himself brings about the victory over the huge Chinese and Turkish armies (Davis 2006: 647–51). At this point a 'pause' is introduced to mark the beginning of a long period of peace, in which Bahram secures the alliance of the Byzantine emperor (Davis 2006: 652–3). Firdowsi continues his tale by narrating further exploits of Bahram in India and his abduction of the Rajah's beautiful daughter. To a certain extent Firdowsi has filled his own 'pause' with an erotic-chivalric adventure of this Persian Don Juan. At the end of the Indian episode, the story returns to the shores of the 'pause', as Bahram sits peacefully and contemplates when he will meet his death (Davis 2006: 674–5).

In an act not dissimilar to Chrétien's use of the Arthurian pause in Wace, the great Persian poet Ilyas ibn Yusuf Nizami (1141–1209),[105] having been commissioned by the Seljuq ruler Alahuddin Körp Arslan,[106] rose to the challenge and decided to fill Firdowsi's Bahramian pause with an extended erotic-heroic story. On 1 August 1197 Nizami completed his fourth narrative tale, the *Haft Paykar* ('Seven Images'), in which he picked up the life of Bahram Gur basing himself on Firdowsi, as he explicitly states in the fourth chapter to his tale's introductory section (§4.24–25; Bürgel 1997: 26–7):

> What that sharp thinker had left half said, I said it all, pearls that he had only pierced halfway, I pierced them through and through, yet left what I deemed right and truthful in the form that I had found it.

In fact, only one fifth of the *Seven Images* is actually taken from Firdowsi. The

104 With minor omissions the whole section is translated in Davis (2006: 623–78).

105 On Nizami, see the bibliographies in Bürgel (1997: 411–14), Agapitos (2010: 169), as well as the overview of the poet's life, works and poetic achievement in Seyed-Gohrab (2003: 25–61).

106 Nizami refers to the commission in *Haft Paykar* §4.1–16 (Bürgel 1997: 25–6), he praises the sultan in §5 (Bürgel 1997: 30–4) and, finally, asks for his just reward in the tale's epilogue at §53 (Bürgel 1997: 318–22).

rest, according to Nizami, is taken from other sources (§4.27–29; Bürgel 1997: 27):

> Thus, then, I selected from secret books that lay scattered over the wide world, from writings in Arabic and Persian, the works of Bukhari and Tabari, next to some other scattered manuscripts, those pearls that were resting in their hideouts.

Nizami, like Chrétien in his defensive prologues to *Erec* and *Cligès*, takes pains to buttress the truth of his narrative by pretending to follow an old authority (Firdowsi), as well as using a selection of esteemed sources.[107] This obviously reflects the need to authorize a narrative that, though it has been placed in a historical niche, still remains a tale of fiction and will be perceived as such by its recepients. Despite the poet's explanations on his research, the overall result in *Haft Paykar* is Nizami's own invention as he emphatically declares in the opening of the seventeenth chapter, when he is about to introduce Bahram's first exploit in war (§17.1–2; Bürgel 1997: 78):

> Cease, oh sorcerer of words! For how long will you speak after the old words, for how long? Like a rose exude now your own perfume. Your mouth indeed pours forth perfume: your own mouth suffices!

Once Nizami has reached the 'pause' of the *grant pais* after the victory over the Chinese and the Turks, he changes course and omits the Indian episode. This is replaced by a very different and far more complex narrative that, moreover, seems to oppose Firdowsi's image of the eternally youthful hunter-lover king. Bahram, following a prophesy presented to him seven years before in a secret chamber of the magical palace Chawarnak (§15; Bürgel 1997: 72–5), proceeds to woo and to marry the seven princesses of the seven different lands of the world: India, Byzantium, the Maghreb (i.e., northwest coastal Africa), Russia, China, Khwarizm (a Turkic realm on the south coast of the Aral Lake), and Persia. He has a wise architect build a palace made of seven domed pavilions, each one alloted to one of the seven planets, their respective astrological colours and their respective days of the week. The seven princesses take

107 Nizami is referring to the grand collection of the Prophet's sayings (*hadith*) composed by the scholar Muhammad al-Bukhari (810–70), and the equally grand world chronicle of the famous scholar Abu Jafar Muhammad al-Tabari (838–923).

up residence and choose their domed pavillions. Bahram visits them, the one after the other, starting on Saturday – the day of the planet Saturn and of the colour black – by visiting the Indian princess. For seven days and seven nights the narrative repeats itself: Bahram and his chosen wife enjoy each other's company with food, music and love-making, before the king asks of each princess to tell a story from her land. It is only after seven years have elapsed that Bahram is forced to exit the 'pause', leave behind his royal brides and confront the harshness of the world, as the emperor of China invades the country for a second time (§39–40; Bürgel 1997: 281–8). It looks, then, as if the presence of a ruler (Henry and Körp Arslan respectively) who was interested to bolster his image by commissioning heroic-erotic narratives allowed in France and in Persia the development of a specific type of 'chivalric-amorous' romance that employed the filling of a historical 'pause' as one of its main authorizing devices. That this was not the case in Byzantium probably lies in the fact that the Komnenian novels were written for aristocratic cultivated women patrons who, along with the poets involved, were more interested in exploring antiquarian and learned fiction than in developing a new form of heroic-erotic tale that, at any rate, was irrelevant for bolstering any military image of their own.

Despite the absence of any attempt to fill the Constantinian pause in Manasses's chronicle with amorous-chivalric narrrative material, *amor et militia* do make a combined appearance in a famous but highly debated Byzantine narrative poem known as the *Digenis Akritis*.[108] It survives in a number of redactions, the two oldest of which are preserved in manuscripts **G** (Grottaferrata Z-α-XLIV, c. 1300) and **E** (Escorial Ψ-IV-22, c. 1480). These two poems represent diverging adaptations of equal textual 'value' because they were made from common but 'fluid' textual material for different audiences, in different places and at different times: **G** in the second half of the thirteenth century in Constantinople, **E** in the late fourteenth century possibly on the island of Crete. Both **G** and **E** (the former looking like a full-scale amplification, the latter like a substantial reduction) ultimately arose from a now lost, wholly hypothetical, poem ***δ** that was most probably composed in Constan-

108 For recent discussions of the complex problems surrounding the *Digenis*, see Alexiou (1985); Odorico (1995: xxi–liii); Jeffreys (1998: xiii–lviii); Odorico (2002: 15–67). However, Byzantinists and Neohellenists involved in these discussions have not studied the history of the respective debate in the case of the Old French *chanson de geste*, a debate going back to the middle of the nineteenth century (see Krauss 1978 and Lange 1983 with substantial bibliography). Even in a recent collection of papers on the *Digenis* (Beaton and Ricks 1993), the discussion continues to be conducted exclusively within the limited (and decidedly not interdisciplinary or comparative) perspective of 'Akritic' scholarship.

tinople during the first twenty years of Emperor Manuel's reign.[109] Theodore Prodromos addressed a satirical poem to the emperor, wherein he wears the mask of a novice monk and where he exposes various scandals at a Constantinopolitan monastery (*Ptochoprodromika* no. 4; Eideneier 1991: 139–75).[110] Early in the poem, he wishes for 'another Frontiersman' (Ἀκρίτης ἕτερος) to come and crush the corrupt abbot; at a later point, the poet refers to Emperor Manuel as 'the new Frontiersman' (τὸν νέον τὸν Ἀκρίτην).[111] The manner and the wording in which the two passages speak of the Frontiersman suggest that Prodromos was actually hinting at the hero of poem *δ. Moreover, Manuel systematically pursued between 1150 and 1160 an offensive strategy in northwestern Syria, that is, in exactly those regions that form the geographical core of the *Digenis Akritis*.[112] It seems probable, though far from certain, that the redactor of *δ used oral material from Anatolia (songs, legends, wonder-tales) in order to create by means of his rhetorical school training the 'biography' of a frontier hero, a type of narrative that I would term 'written primary epic'.

The case of *Digenis Akritis* gives me the opportunity to clarify my understanding of the differing – oral and textual – manifestations of epic as genre and discourse.[113] I see four types of epic: (i) as 'oral epic' *strictu senso* I understand a composition that has been taken down from oral performance, like the Serbian epics recorded in the early nineteenth century; (ii) a narrative like the *Iliad*, the Oxford redaction of the *Chanson de Roland* (c. 1130–70) or the *Nibelungenlied* (c. 1200) I would describe as a 'written primary epic', where a redactor has brought together oral material and presented it in a written form that to a very high degree retains the elements of oral-formulaic composition,[114] and *DigAkr* *δ could have been this type of text; (iii) such narratives as the Châteauroux/Venice redaction of the *Roland* in c. 8,000 rhymed verses (thir-

109 The proposal by Beaton (1996b) that *Digenis* might have been composed around 1100 within a Cappadocian 'lobby' at the court of Emperor Alexios I (1081–1118) cannot be supported from the sources.

110 Jacoby (1997: 527) has convincingly suggested that the poem could not have been written after March 1171 because a reference to cheese purchased in the capital's Venetian quarter must predate the Venetian's massive arrest ordered by Manuel and subsequent flight from the Empire. Thus, an approximate date between 1161 (the emperor's wedding to Mary of Antioch) and 1170 is highly probable.

111 *Ptochoprodromika* 4, 189–92 and 542–5.

112 On Manuel as 'New Frontiersman' in the fourth Ptochoprodromic poem, northwestern Syria and *δ, see Jeffreys (1993: 33–7).

113 This difference between genre and discourse is what Slavica Ranković in the present volume has described as the non-resolved tension between the 'attractors' of epic poetry.

114 On these elements, see now Foley (1988).

teenth century)[115] I would describe as 'written secondary epics', since they are written narratives that demonstrably based themselves on an existing text, even if they amplify, reduce or reshape it, and *DigAkr* **G** and **E** belong here; (iv), finally, narratives like Apollonius's *Argonautica,* Virgil's *Aeneid* or Ariosto's *Orlando Furioso* I would term 'literary epics', being texts conceived *ex nihilo* by their authors in a conscious intertextual and metapoetical dialogue with a codified epic tradition.

Be that as it may, *fin'amour* and *chevalerie* have nothing to do with what is to be found in the *Digenis.* Vaguely set during the times of the long-standing wars between the Empire and the Caliphate (ninth–tenth centuries), the poem tells of the story of an Arab emir, his exploits against the Byzantines, his falling in love with the captured daughter of a Christian general, their marriage, the subsequent birth of their son Basileios Digenes Akrites ('Imperial, the Frontiersman of Double Descent'),[116] the wondrous feats of the boy, his elopement with a general's beautiful daughter, their subsequent marriage, <his meeting with the emperor and his adulterous affair with a young girl; only in **G**>, Digenis's exploits against the *apelatai* ('bandits'), his bellicose/amorous encounter with the Amazon Maximou,[117] the building of his palace on the shores of the Euphrates, his sudden disease, his and his wife's deaths without any descendants. Even this catalogue-like summary shows that, despite the presence of war (especially in the beginning of the poem), the *Digenis* is not a *chanson de geste* in the style of the *Roland,* the most famous tale of how a Christian emperor and his barons fought against the infidels.[118] Neither is the *Digenis* a 'recreated' *chanson de geste* in the style of the *Poema de mio Cid* (c. 1200) about the brilliant warlord Ruy-Rodrigo Diaz de Vivar and his campaigns against Muslims and Christians in the east of the Iberian peninsula.[119]

In fact, the *Digenis Akritis* is closer in content, ideology and narrative style to the *Sîrat al-Muğâhidîn* ('Tale of the Holy Warriors'), also known as *Sîrat al-Amîra Dhât al-Himma* ('Tale of the Chieftainness Dhât al-Himma'), the oldest and longest among the Arabian prose epics dealing with the confronta-

115 See Steinsieck and Kaiser (1999: 399–401).
116 The name is etymologically explained at *DigAkr* **G** 4.48–53.
117 For an intelligent and convincing 'sexual' reading of the scene as presented in redaction **E**, see Kaplanis (2010).
118 See the balanced presentation of the *Roland* in Steinsieck and Kaiser (1999: 391–434) (with substantial bibliography) and more briefly in Short (1990: 5–25); on the *chansons de geste* and their construction of a 'masculine' genre, see the provoking analysis by Gaunt (1995: 22–70).
119 On the making of the *Cid,* see the excellent study by Smith (1983).

tion of Muslims and Christians at the Byzantine–Arab frontier.[120] The story of the *Dhât al-Himma* extends in very loosely handled historical time from the reigns of the Umayad Caliph Abd al-Malik (684–705) and the emperor Leo III (717–41) to the reign of the Abbasid Caliph al-Wâthiq (841–46). It presents in over 3,000 printed pages the stories of the heroine Fâtima (her warrior name is Dalhama or Dhât al-Himma, 'The Possessor of Ambition'), her black-skinned son Abd al-Wahhab, and the Sulaymian warrior al-Battâl, in conjunction with the fates of the Banû Kilâb Beduin tribe.[121] In particular, the numerous erotic stories (with or without violence and elopement) between Arab men and Byzantine women,[122] the astonishing warrior prowess of the heroine fighting with sword and spear on her steed,[123] the single-combat feats of the heroes against men and animals,[124] and the conversion of Christians to Islam[125] remind the readers of the equivalent scenes (even if on a smaller scale) in *DigAkr* **G** and **E**. It is an archaic and tribal world of war and love, very remote from feudal allegiance and military warfare as represented, for example, by the Oxford *Roland*[126] or the *Cid*.[127]

History is indeed omnipresent in *Roland, Cid, Digenis* and *Dhât al-Himma*, but it is employed in diverging ways. In the Oxford *Roland* no mention of truth or falsehood concerning its historical content is made. The poem was obviously seen by its primary recipients – the consolidated feudal aristocracy of France and England – as an inherently true historical account rather than as a fictive narrative with added historical elements. In the *Cid*, despite the presence of creative amplification and rewriting,[128] the historical outline of

120 On Arabian epic in general, see Lyons (1995, volume I, Introduction). For a broader study of the image of Byzantium (*bilâd al-Rûm*, 'land of the Rhomaioi') in learned Arabic literature, see El Cheikh (2004); on the image of Franks and Byzantines in the epic cycle, see Lyons (2001).

121 Extensive English summary in Lyons (1995: III, 301–504). For a broader study of the *Sîrat Dhât al-Himma*, see Ott (2003); for a comparison of the *Dhât al-Himma* with the *Digenis*, see the older study by Grégoire and Goossens (1934) and now Ott (2000).

122 §132–3: Miriam and Tayyibûn, Maimûna and Karfanâs (Lyons 1995: III, 453–6).

123 §24: Fâtima in single combat with her own son (Lyons 1995: III, 326–7); §92–94: Fâtima and the warrior Queen Karna (Lyons 1995: III, 402–5).

124 §14–5: the story of Sahsah, the Rûmî girl, the Christian monks and the three panthers (Lyons 1995: III, 316–18).

125 §137–8: a king and his city (Lyons 1995: III, 460–3).

126 See the battle of Rencesvals up to the death of the hero at *Rol* **O** 994–2396 (*laisses* 79–176).

127 See the extended episode of the campaign along the river Jiloca, ending with the defeat of the Count of Barcelona (*laisses* 46–63: vv. 851–1084).

128 For example, the scene with the nine-year-old girl in Burgos (*laisse* 4: vv. 21–64), the exchange of insults between the feudal lords during the judgement scene in Toledo concerning the shameful treatment of the Cid's two daughters by the Infantes of Carrion (*laisses* 140–149: vv. 3270–3389), or, more generally, the refocusing of Ruy Diaz's campaigning from Saragossa and Valencia towards Castile.

the hero's last ten years of his life remains intact. The sense of history is further buttressed by the presence of numerous details on exact geography or minor characters that are, in fact, fully attested. Even if the *Cid* gives the impression of a partially fictitious narrative, especially when compared to the earlier Latin sources, no such concern is ever expressed by its narrator within the text. The situation in the *Digenis* is different. When the story is about to focus on the boy Basil and his teenage exploits, the narrators in both redactions introduce extensive first-person comments on the truthfulness of their tale, while directly addressing their audiences (*DigAkr* **G** 4.4–47 and **E** 702–721). In a rhetorically structured antithesis, the 'truthful and attested' deeds of the emir and of his son[129] are juxtaposed to the 'false myths concerning Achilles and Hector' about which 'Homer and other Hellenes (i.e. pagans) lied'.[130] Within the Byzantine-Arab culture of the warrior tale, the appearance of Homeric pagan heroes causes an unexpected disjunction[131] and hints at the educated background of the two redactors and their respective audiences.[132] The presence of this narrative intervention in **G** and **E** suggests that the redactor of ***δ** had already introduced something similar in his narrative. This further suggests that, in contrast to the Komnenian novels and their wholesale fictional narratives set in 'Hellenic' times, the 'historical' tale of *Digenis Akritis* had to be buttressed as to its assumed truthfulness in order not to appear as fiction.[133] It is this explicit authentication device that, in my opinion, reveals the existence of a socio-cultural gap dividing the oral culture out of which the (lost) Anatolian Akritic tales emerged and the written culture framing the (equally lost) poem ***δ** as it was composed in the capital.

The type of literarization that we inferred as having taken place from the *Digenis* ***δ** to the *DigAkr* **G** and **E**, we can actually study in the case of the *Sîrat al-Amîra Dhât al-Himma*, which was at some point transformed into a historio-romantic tale, now called the *Sîrat Umar al-Numân*, and incorporated during

129 *DigAkr* **G** 4.36: τούτου δὲ πάντα ἀληθῆ καὶ μεμαρτυρημένα; **E** 721–722: ἀλλ' ἀληθεύουν ἐκ παντός· μηδεὶς οὖν ἀπιστήσῃ | ὡς λέγω τὴν ἀλήθειαν τοῦ θαυμαστοῦ Ἀκρίτη.

130 *DigAkr* **G** 4.27–28: παύσασθε γράφειν Ὅμηρον καὶ μύθους Ἀχιλλέως | ὡσαύτως καὶ τοῦ Ἕκτορος, ἅπερ εἰσὶ ψευδέα; **E** 719: ἃ Ὅμηρος ἐψεύσατο καὶ ἄλλοι τῶν Ἑλλήνων.

131 On the issue of the 'reception' of antiquity in Byzantine fiction, see the cautionary remarks by Odorico (2005a) based on this passage from redaction **G**.

132 They are clearly marked as readers in the case of **E** 712 (οἱ ἀναγινώσκοντες).

133 For a very different reading of these passages, supported by an uncritical use of ancient and medieval Greek texts, as well as Old French epic and romance, see Lasithiotakis (2005) who, along with other scholars, believes that the *Digenis* is a 'real story', i.e., an epic proper in the sense of Serbian historical tales.

the eighteenth century into the growing corpus of *Thousand and One Nights*.[134] Here we can clearly follow the process of adaptation from written primary epic to written secondary epic. The *Umar al-Numân* is closely based on the first section of the *Dhât al-Himma*, yet the story has been substantially condensed, the sequence of some episodes altered, historical details have been removed, names have been changed, the character traits of the heroes and the heroines have been drawn more fully, descriptive passages have been further developed, various fairytale elements have been added and, most importantly, amorous episodes have been substantially expanded.[135] However, the *Umar al-Numân* does not include the type of authentication device we observed in the *Digenis*, possibly because the tale's presence in *Thousand and One Nights* excluded any notion of it being 'true' history.

We will find another type of authentication device that signals a gap between an initially oral tradition and a subsequent written culture, and this type pertains to the translation of the *Roland* into Medieval German by the cleric Konrad (*phaffe Chuonrât*). The work, almost certainly commissioned by Duke Henry the Lion of Bavaria (ruled 1155–80) and his young wife Mathilda, daughter of Henry II and Eleanor, was written in c. 1170–72.[136] In his prologue, Konrad asks of God: 'Thou send into my mouth Your holy testimony, that I might avoid falsehood and write the truth' (*RoLied* 5–8).[137] In his epilogue the poet states: 'As it stands written in the book in the French language, so have I transferred it into Latin and thence translated it into German' (9080–3).[138] God's 'holy testimony'[139] and the French written source represent the unassailable authorities for Konrad's truthful poem in its doubly translated form. This is no more the written version of an oral tale embedded within in a specific socio-cultural context but a 'translated' textual narrative prepared for a different type of audience (Haug 1992: 75–80) and supporting the patron's penitential crusading ideology, in this case Duke Henry's journey to the Holy Land in 1172.

Wolfram von Eschenbach operated in a similar, even if far more complex

134 On the gradual expansion and complex textual formation of this collection well up to the early nineteenth century, see Grotzfeld and Grotzfeld (1984) and Irwin (2004).

135 Succinct presentation in Ott (2000: 141–4) and, in more detail, Ott (2003: 112–21) with the older bibliography.

136 For all relevant discussion I refer to Kartschoke (1996: 779–99).

137 'dû sende mir ze munde | dîn heilege urkunde, | daz ich die lüge vermîde, | die wahrheit scrîbe'.

138 'alsô ez an dem buoche gescriben stât | in franzischer zungen, | sô hân ich ez in die latîne betwungen, | danne in die tiutische gekêret'.

139 On *urkunde* (equivalent to Latin *testimonium*), see Kartschoke (1996: 628–9).

and sophisticated, manner in the prologue to his unfinished *Willehalm* (c. 1212–17), an adaptation of a now lost version of the *Chanson d'Aliscans* from the epic cycle related to Guillaume d'Orange (Bumke 2004: 375–90). In an extended address to the trinitarian God, the poet acknowledges through his own 'understanding' (*sin*) the power of the Creator who has strengthened 'the meaning and the word of the true script' (*der rehten schrift don und wort*) with his Spirit (*Will* 2,16–18).[140] Wolfram immediately rejects bookish learning and expressly relies on his own intellectual capacities (2,19–22):

> What stands written in books, I have no knowledge of it. In no other way am I learned: my understanding grants me what knowledge I have.[141]

He then proceeds to ask of God to grant him the 'not impious understanding' (*unlosen sin*) to tell of a splendid knight and his adventures of the soul and of the body (2,23–3,7). The poet finally reveals: 'Landgrave Hermann of Thuringia acquainted me with this here tale of him. In French he is called conte Guillaume d'Orange' (3,8–11).[142] Despite the ambiguous reference to having been acquainted with this story through his patron, it is obvious that Wolfram received a written version of *Aliscans* from the hands of Hermann. Wolfram, in his very own manner, makes an effort to mask the fact that the *maere* is a written source, because, not dissimilar to his authorial *persona* in *Parzival,* he promotes himself and his own *sin* as guarantors of truth.[143]

It comes therefore as no surprise that Jean Bodel (c. 1165–1210), famous as a poet of *fablieux, pastourelles,* a religious drama, and two long narrative poems (Rossi and Straub 1992: 15–27), employs the same devices in order to present to his audience a written epic tale based on a historiographical source. In the prologue to the *Chanson des Saisnes* ('Song of the Saxons') the poet boldly declares (*Saisnes* 1–5):

> He who has the leisure and the capacity to hear and to understand, let him

140 Konrad and Wolfram both frame the historiographic paradigm with the devices of prefacing a Christian *legenda,* a convention similar to the 'Apostolic' setting presented in the first chapter of Pseudo-Turpin introducing the narrative about Charlemagne and Roland.

141 'Swaz an den buochen stet geschriben, | des bin ich künstelos beliben. | niht anders ich geleret bin: | wan han ich kunst, die git mir sin.'

142 'landgrave von Duringen Herman | tet mir diz maere von im bekant. | er ist en franzoys genant | kuns Gwillams de Orangis'.

143 See Haug (1992: 179–96) and Bumke (2004: 358–75) for exhaustive discussions of this complex prologue.

> be quiet, if he wishes to listen to a good and valiant song of which the history books are witnesses and guarantors. No boorish storyteller should ever boast of such a song, for they do not know how to perform neither the verses nor the melody.[144]

Jean then continues with his famous distinction between the *trois materes* of Britany (Arthurian romance), Rome (antique romance) and France (epic tale), affirming emphatically the eternal truthfulness of the third (*Saisnes* 9–11):

> If the tales of Britany are delightful and pleasant, and those of Rome wise and instructive in understanding, those of France are true every recurring day.[145]

Once again, the programmatic declaration about reliable historical sources and the resulting veracity of the historical narrative is fully employed, in Jean's case connected with (i) a particular version of the criticism against 'boorish storytellers' as we have seen it in the case of Chrétien, Wace and Nicolas de Senlis (Green 2002: 12),[146] and (ii) the specific promotion of the interests of French royalty. The *topos* reflects the distance to the 'old' oral culture of the past and the need to authorize the 'new' written culture of the present; thus, fiction assumes the garment of history.[147]

One further characteristic trait of this move from oral epic to written secondary epic is the prominent appearance of a moralizing, outspokenly Christian, stance on part of the narrator as authorial *persona*.[148] Pfaffe Konrad, Wolfram von Eschenbach, Jean Bodel and the anonymous redactor of

144 'Qui d'oyr et d'entendre a loisir et talant, | Face pais, si escout bonne chançon vaillant | Dont li livre d'estoire sont tesmoing et garant. | Jamais vilains jougleres de cesti ne se vant, | Car il n'en saroit dire ne les vers ne le chant' (the text of the prologue is quoted from Mölk 1969: 6–7).

145 'Li conte de Bretaigne s'il sont vain et plaisant | Et cil de Romme sage et de sens aprendant, | Cil de France sont voir chascun jour aparant.' See the discussion of the passage by Green (2002: 138–40).

146 It should be kept in mind, of course, that Jean employs this device from the perspective of the narrator of a new type of *chanson de geste* (he calls it a *chançon rimee* with *riches vers nouviaus* at *Saisnes* 31–2) that oldfashioned storytellers (he refers to them as *bastart jougleour*, 'inept storytellers', at *Saisnes* 27) are not in a position to perform. Jean uses a very different *persona* when speaking in his *fablieux* as the professional *jongleur* he is; see, for example, *Le Sohaiz des Vez* (209–10): 'tant que lo sot Johanz Bodiaus, | uns rimoieres de flabliaus' (Rossi and Straub 1992: 152).

147 In a number of recent papers Franz Peter Knapp decisively rejects such a notion, allowing only for an either/or polarity between history and fiction (e.g. Knapp 2005: 243–9), though such an approach appears to me as too restrictive even for the supposedly limited perspectives of medieval artists and intellectuals.

148 See Paul Gerhard Schmidt's analysis of Pseudo-Turpin and *Dolopathos* in the present volume.

DigAkr **G** speak in their epic-like tales by means of a moralist discourse. God is systematically invoked, various actions and their results are commented upon in a distinctly moralizing tone, the Christian faith (shared by narrator and audience) is juxtaposed to the otherness of Muslims and pagans. In the case of *DigAkr* **G**, this moralist discourse is accentuated by the inclusion of an extremely high amount of gnomic pronouncements[149] that are not to be found in redaction **E**. The same device was employed to such an extent by Constantine Manasses in his novel and his chronicle that the two texts were profitably excerpted by compilers of *gnomologia*.[150] The presence of such *gnomai* in the Byzantine texts lends further authority to the 'moralist' narrative because commonplace didactic statements assume the function of proverbs that the audience is supposed to know or to recognize as such and therefore to accept as inherently true.[151] It is unfortunate that Manasses's *Aristandros and Kallithea* did not survive, for we would have been able to compare the overall effect of the presence of *gnomai* in the novel with their presence in the *Synopsis Chronike* and redaction **G** of the *Digenis Akritis*. Be that as it may, the massive presence of such commonplace *sententiae* in three contemporary Byzantine texts, written in three different narrative genres (erotic tale, world chronicle, warrior tale), clearly indicates the existence of a common ideological code of social communication that cuts across the boundaries of history, fiction and genre, and elevates the didactic aspect of medieval narrative into an aesthetic principle of literary authorization.[152] Furthermore, we have seen that the devices of authorization derived from medieval Latin historiography and employed by French and German authors of romances do not find their equivalent in the Byzantine texts of fiction. In fact, it is only the moralist *DigAkr* **G** that comes closest to the respective written secondary epics of the West, and it cannot be a coincidence that **G** is also closest to the rhetorical discourse of

149 See the studies by Odorico (1989) and Jeffreys (1998: xliii–xliv).

150 See Mazal (1967: 18–61); Lampsides (1985); Lampsidis (1996: lviii–lx).

151 For example, *DigAkr* **G** 3.284–5 (ἀγάπη γὰρ ὑπέρμετρος γεννᾷ πολλὰ τοιαῦτα | καὶ χαρὰ ὑπερβάλλουσα εἰς θάνατον ἀπάγει) derives from Heliodorus 2.6.4 (οὕτως ἄρα καὶ τὸ χαρᾶς ὑπερβάλλον εἰς ἀλγεινὸν περιέστη πολλάκις καὶ τῆς ἡδονῆς τὸ ἄμετρον ἐπίσπαστον λύπην ἐγέννησεν) and can be found in a number of Byzantine *gnomologia* (Odorico 1989: 149 no. 9), as well as in Manasses's *A&K* frg. 88 (οὕτω καὶ μέγεθος χαρᾶς νέκρωσιν οἶδε φέρειν); *DigAkr* **G** 6.650 (Θεὸς γὰρ ἀντιτάσσεται πᾶσιν ὑπερηφάνοις) quotes the Old Testament at *Prov* 3.34 (Κύριος ὑπερηφάνοις ἀντιτάσσεται) and is also found in numerous *gnomologia* (Odorico 1989: 149 no. 6). This point on the function of *gnomai* has been made by Morgan (1993: 202) in the case of the ancient novel, though the amount of proverbial *sententiae* there is far smaller.

152 On the function of such *gnomai* in the Komnenian novels and the Palaiologan romances, see briefly Agapitos (1993: 116–17).

the Komnenian novels. It is therefore significant to note that at the same stage of literary adaptation of the epic tradition, the Frankish and Byzantine lands converge in the ways of marking historicized fiction as authoritative truth.

VI. WAS FICTION AN ISSUE IN BYZANTIUM?

In the Western Middle Ages, especially from the late eleventh to the early thirteenth centuries, fiction was indeed a debated issue. On the basis of various ancient works such as 'Homer', Virgil, Lucan and the Aesopic fables, theoreticians either criticized fiction as false and deceiving its recipients or defended it on account of it being able to convey, in the words of Augustine, a 'form of truth' (*figura veritatis*), what developed on the basis of allegorical Bible interpretation as the theory of 'veiling' (*integumentum*).[153] To a certain extent, it is this scholastic discussion that forms an important background to the rise of vernacular fiction and the gradual development of a terminological vocabulary to designate fictive narrative.[154] It is in this context therefore that the statement of Abbot Baudri de Bourgueil (1046–1130)[155] has to be understood when, based on Ovid's slyly apologetic comment about poetic licence,[156] he excuses the love-letter poems he has composed by stating bluntly: 'Believe me: I do not speak the truth; I rather make everything up' (*Carm.* 85.39: *crede michi: non vera loquor, magis omnia fingo*).

If we are to judge from the available evidence, such a statement was irrelevant for Byzantine authors. I shall use two examples from the twelfth century that come close to the type of ethopoetic discourse composed by Baudri. In these two examples the same fictional performative representation as in Baudri (i.e., an ego-narrator as protagonist of his own 'story') does not lead to any excuse or defence of fiction. Theodore Prodromos composed a vernacu-

153 See the brief discussion in Green (2002: 153–5). For a translated selection of Latin commentaries discussing poetic fiction and *integumentum*, see Minnis and Scott (1991: 113–64); for a broader treatment, see Mehtonen (1996).

154 See the broad discussion in Green (2002: 1–17 and 134–53); more briefly in his contribution in the present volume.

155 On Baudri and the other two 'Ovidian' poets at the threshhold of the twelfth century (Marbod of Rennes and Hildebert of Lavardin), often referred to as the Loire poets, see, indicatively, Bond (1995) for a literary appreciation and Jaeger (1995) for a social reading of their literary production.

156 *Amores* iii 12.41–44: *exit in immensum fecunda licentia vatum | obligat historica nec sua verba fide: | et mea debuerat falso laudata videri | femina; credulitas nunc mihi vestra nocet*, 'Oh, creative poetic licence is boundless, and unconstrained by historical fact. You ought to have taken my praise of Corinna as fiction. Now your credulity's done me harm!' (trans. Peter Green, Penguin Classics, 1982).

lar poem with the title *To the Emperor Black-John*. The addressee is John II Komnenos (1118–43).[157] In the poem, Theodore described in an artfully buffoonesque manner the humiliating misfortunes he suffered from his wife, the formidable Matzoukina, and asked his patron for financial support. In the prologue he presents his poem with the following remark (*Ptoch* 1.6–7 + 9–11):

> Poor me, I had nothing appropriate to offer to your Majesty and virtuous Highness [...] except again a few non-metrical city verses: shy, playful but not shameless, for old men play as well, though in moderation.[158]

The poetic *topos* of old men playing moderately goes back to Gregory of Nazianzus (*Carmina* ii 1.39.45–6 and 54–6), with whose poems Theodore was intimately familiar. Contrary, however, to this weighty intertextual statement, the poet assumes the performative mask of a foolish and sexually deprived married old man (Alexiou 1999). Even so, no signal towards this ethopoetic device has been incorporated in the text. Obviously, the fictive quality of the poem's episodic narrative was not perceived as an issue needing apology or defence in front of an audience at the imperial court, even though the use of the *politikos stichos* in a burlesque context did.

The second example is the 'autobiographical' prologue of Nikephoros Basilakes (see also above, pp. 252–3), composed for an edition of his collected works. Though Nikephoros briefly refers there to his *progymnasmata* (Garzya 1984: 9.9–10), he makes no comment as to their fictionality because this also was not an issue within the rhetorical tradition in which the successful orator and teacher had been educated. Fiction, as presented in the three progymnasmatic types of *mythos* ('fable'), *diegema* ('narrative') and *ethopoiia* ('dramatic monologue'), had been already fully legitimized in the late Hellenistic rhetorical handbooks, of which those of Hermogenes (second century) and Aphthonius (late fourth to early fifth century) were widely used in the Byzantine school curricula.[159] Similarly, the extensive commentary on Aphthonius's

157 Εἰς τὸν βασιλέα Μαυροϊωάννην (*Ptoch* 1; Eideneier 1991: 99–107). *Mauroioannes* (Black-John or John Dark-Skin) is a pun on *Kaloioannes* (Good-John), a nickname given to the emperor by the inhabitants of the capital.

158 οὐκ εἶχον οὖν ὁ δύστηνος τὸ τί προσαγαγεῖν σοι | κατάλληλον τῷ κράτει σου καὶ τῇ χρηστότητί σου | [...] | εἰ μή τινας πολιτικοὺς ἀμέτρους πάλιν στίχους, | συνεσταλμένους, παίζοντας, ἀλλ' οὐκ ἀναισχυντῶντας, | παίζουσι γὰρ καὶ γέροντες, ἀλλὰ σωφρονεστέρως.

159 Hermog. *Prog.* 1, 2, 9 (Rabe 1913: 1–6, 20–2) and Aphth. *Prog.* 1, 2, 11 (Rabe 1926: 1–3, 34–6). On rhetorical theory and the commentaries on *progymnasmata* in Byzantium, see Hunger (1978: II, 75–91); on *mythos, diegema* and *ethopoiia*, see idem, II, 94–8 and 108–16. On Basilakes's *progym-*

progymnasmata written by John Doxapatres (c. 1040–50) defines this type of text as a 'preparatory exercise' for dealing with 'the exposition of fictional cases', αἱ τῶν πλασματικῶν ὑποθέσεων μελέται (Rabe 1931: 137.10). John Sikeliotes (early eleventh century) in his commentary on Hermogenes's *De ideis* remarks that 'since rhetoric is an art capable of imitating (i.e. representing) all beings and events, she therefore claims that she can deal appropriately also with the speeches [...] of persons and situations subject to her' (Walz 1968: IV, 248.3–7).[160] Thus, Michael Psellos, who had intelligently discussed *Charikleia* and *Leukippe*, had also quite a few things to say about the concepts of *metabole* ('change') and *mimesis*, and their importance in constructing a literary *persona* of the self.[161]

Going back to romance production in France and Germany, we can say that four literary devices, adopted by twelfth- and early thirteenth-century poets, were of great importance for the rise of vernacular fiction: (i) the detection of 'gaps' in previous historical narrratives, which provided a spatiotemporal niche for the setting of fiction, for example, exploiting the *grant pais* in the *Roman de Brut*; (ii) the move from an externally referential systemic frame anchoring fiction in history (the antique romance) to a self-referential semiotic code anchoring fiction in itself (the Arthurian romance);[162] (iii) the use of some sort of written source functioning as guarantor of truth within the historiographic paradigm; (iv) the use of a historically recognizable setting for a substantial part of the plot.

If we look for these four devices in Byzantine fiction, we will find that only the historically recognizable setting was actually employed. The four Komnenian novels and the *Digenis Akritis* did not squeeze themselves into any historical niche of an older narrative. On the one hand, the four novels entered into a complex intertextual dialogue with their ancient 'models' in order to produce highly artful and accutely subversive *dramata* of rhetorical and emotional display, an issue to which I shall presently return. Just like their ancient counterparts, the Komnenian novels referred to identifiable ancient historical markers, such as geographical settings (Abydos, Lesbos, Rhodes, Cyprus,

nasmata, see now Papaioannou (2007) (discourse of fictionality as 'drama') and Kaldellis (2007b) (performance of Hellenism).

160 ὥστ' ἐπειδὴ μιμητικὴ τέχνη ἡ ῥητορικὴ πάντων τῶν ὄντων καὶ γινομένων καταλλήλως καὶ τοὺς λόγους [...] τῶν ὑποκειμένων αὐτῇ προσώπων καὶ πραγμάτων μεταχειρίζεσθαι δικαιοῖ.

161 On these theoretical issues in Psellos, see Papaioannou (2003 and 2004); on the importance of rhetoric as literary theory for Byzantine intellectuals, see Katsaros (2002).

162 For points (i) and (ii), see Green (2002: 187–201) with the older bibliography.

Delphi, Pthia, Egypt, Tyre, Arabia) or nations (Greeks, Parthians, Libyans, Arabs), but these, of course, accentuated even more the exotic (*qua* fictive and wholly literary) world of the ancient Hellenes. Makrembolites in *H&H* went one step further and created his pagan setting out of blatantly fictional geographical markers. On the other hand, *DigAkr* **G** and **E** incorporated a number of recognizably contemporary historical markers,[163] thus evoking an Anatolian 'historical' frontier-land setting of its own, to be repeated only twice and on a very small scale in Byzantine literature, as we shall see further below (pp. 287 n. 191 and 290 n. 204). One hundred years later, when the Palaiologan romances emerge in the thirteenth century, their authors also did not seek a niche in some older historical narrative but developed a fictive world of their own, employing a broad variety of settings. Because each of the eight surviving romances has its own distinct setting with no intertextually signified 'historical' markers,[164] the notion of a self-referential semiotic code is not applicable. The Palaiologan vernacular romances may include contemporary historical details,[165] but these are of the same fictive verisimilitude as Chrétien's *Grece et Costantinoble* in the prologue of *Cligès* or Wolfram's massive Middle-Eastern geography in Book I of *Parzival* (13,16; 14,3; 14,5; 15,17–21: *Baldac... Babilôn... Ninivê... Marroch... Persîâ... Dâmasc... Hâlap... Arâbîe*).

How, then, was fiction perceived by its Byzantine recipients? I shall begin by examining the poetics of display in the Komnenian novels, in other words, their use of 'theatrical' (*qua* rhetorical) *apate* (ἀπάτη, 'deceit').[166] Let us take a look at two scenes from Prodromos's *Rhodanthe and Dosikles*. In Book 2, while recounting to his friend Kratandros how he succeeded in eloping with Rhodanthe, Dosikles talks about the visual and emotive power of dreams created by Night. Disappointed and exhausted, he falls asleep; in his dream he sees his beloved and talks to her. Prodromos introduces this brief scene as follows; Dosikles narrates (*R&D* 2.329–34):

> Of things done and of words spoken in daylight, Night recreates many phantoms and darkness-coloured visions; she fictively writes (*plasto-*

163 See the discussion in Jeffreys (1998: xxx–xli) with the older bibliography.

164 Such as naming King Arthur and placing the romance's opening time at Easter Sunday or Whitsun during the 'great peace' (*Erec* and *Yvain* respectively); see Schmolke-Hasselmann (1998: 41–7).

165 E.g. references to Persia, Armenia, Egypt and the Latins in *L&R*; Tarsus, Antioch and the Turks in *B&C*; the Francs in *Ach* **N**.

166 My understanding of 'theatrical discourse' in the novels is not what has been termed the 'dramatic element' in non-theatrical texts; on this concept and its potential use in Byzantine historiography, sometimes presented through theatrical discourse, see now Katsaros (2006).

> *graphousa*) only shades with her shade-writing finger and, then, introduces the apparition during sleep by means of a visual reflection; this is what happened to me at that time.[167]

Besides reflecting Prodromos's interest in Aristotelian dream theory (MacAlister 1990: 208–12), the passage presents Night as an artist who 'writes fictively' or, on account of the double meaning of the verb *grapho*, who 'paints fictively'.[168] The proposal to render here the verb *plastographeo* as 'to write/paint fictively', rather than by its conventional ancient meaning of 'to forge', finds support in Doxapatres's commentary on Aphthonius. Doxapatres explains the difference between a rhetor and a sophist (the latter being the designation accompanying Aphthonius's name in the manuscripts) in the following manner (Rabe 1931: 136.19–137.5):

> A rhetor is he who exerts himself in real judicial cases and at court, like Demosthenes; a sophist is also the writer of fiction (*plasmatographos*) who does not fight at court, like Libanius. Aphthonius then is called a sophist either because he makes students wise (*sophizon*) by expounding to them what concerns the art of rhetoric, or because he is a writer of fiction (*plasmatographos*) and not fighting at court, just like Libanius.[169]

Doxapatres's mention of Libanius is doubly appropriate since the Antiochene orator of the fourth century was not only famous for his model collection of fictional *progymnasmata*, but was also the teacher of Aphthonius (Liban. *ep.* 1065; *Opera* XI, 189 Foerster). Night, then, in *R&D* is the *plas(ma)tographos* who recreates for the novel's hero an intrafictive amorous encounter with his as yet unattained object of desire. Furthermore, it is the hero himself who

167 Τῶν πραγμάτων γὰρ καὶ λόγων τῶν ἐν φάει | εἴδωλα πολλὰ καὶ φάσεις νυκτιχρόους | ἡ νὺξ ἀναπλάττουσα καὶ σκιὰς μόνας | πλαστογραφοῦσα δακτύλῳ σκιαγράφῳ, | φέρει τὸ φάσμα τῇ καθ' ὕπνους ἐμφάσει· | οἷον κἀγὼ πέπονθα τῷ τότε χρόνῳ.

168 There are two further passages in the novel where dreams are represented in a similar manner and with a consistently similar vocabulary. In *R&D* 3.305–14 Dosikles explains to the frightened Rhodanthe the deceitful (*qua* fictive) nature of dreams created by Night; in *R&D* 9.241–50 Dosikles (again talking to Rhodanthe) wonders about the unexpected appearance of his and her parents in Cyprus, believing that he sees some dream or fictive painting (*plastographia*).

169 ῾Ρήτωρ μὲν γάρ ἐστιν ὁ τοῖς ἀληθινοῖς ἀγῶσιν ἐγγυμναζόμενος καὶ ἐπὶ δικαστηρίου ὡς ὁ Δημοσθένης, σοφιστὴς δὲ καὶ ὁ πλασματογράφος καὶ μὴ ἐπὶ δικαστηρίου ἀγωνιζόμενος, οἷος ἦν ὁ Λιβάνιος. Ὁ τοίνυν Ἀφθόνιος λέγεται σοφιστὴς ἢ ὡς σοφίζων τοὺς φοιτητὰς ἐκ τοῦ τὰ περὶ τῆς ῥητορικῆς τέχνης αὐτοῖς ἀναπτύσσειν ἢ ὡς πλασματογράφος ὢν καὶ μὴ ἐπὶ δικαστηρίου ἀγωνιζόμενος, οἷος ἦν ὁ Λιβάνιος.

knowledgeably discusses the fictive quality of Night's *skiagraphia*. This is an excellent example of poetological metalanguage embedded in the poetic text itself. Night introducing her fictive apparitions is a metaphor for the poet's own craft in creating fiction, a metaphor that Prodromos emblematically used when he referred to himself as a painter and to his creation as a painting in the epigram with which he dedicated his novel to his patron (on this poem, see below, pp. 325–6). At the same time, the willingly 'deceived' hero stands in for the novel's primary recipients who listen to the poet's recitation at the patron's literary *theatron* and who have willingly established with the author a contract of make-believe.[170] This is exactly what Dosikles expresses when, seeing Rhodamne alive in front of him, he exclaims: 'This thing is no deceit, no fancy of mine, no fancy or another plot of Fate!' (*R&D* 8.378–9).[171] Prodromos manifestly utilized the famous statement of Gorgias on tragedy – and which also constitutes one of the most succinct definitions of the author–audience contract (frg. B 23 Diels-Krantz):

> Tragedy <offered> a type of deceit wherein the deceiver is more righteous than the non-deceiver and the deceived more wise than the non-deceived.[172]

In Book 4, Prodromos introduces his audience to the most spectacular and comically grotesque symposium in all of Greek novelistic literature (4.111–417). The extended banquet scene is divided in three *epeisodia diegemata*, to use Psellos's terminology: (i) the miraculous 'birth' of living birds out of the belly of a grilled lamb and the subsequent dialogue between the pirate Gobryas (acting as host at the banquet) and the enemy envoy Artaxanes who falls for the culinary trick as being caused by the supernatural powers of the pirate leader Mistylos (4.111–208); (ii) the appearance of the wonder-maker (*thaumatourgos*) Satyrion who seemingly kills himself, only to be miraculously resurrected by Gobryas, and who then performs a hymn in praise of Mistylos (4.209–316); (iii) the description of a beautiful sapphire goblet that drops from the hand of the inebriated Artaxanes and breaks, while the sense-

170 For the signalled correlation of the protagonists as spectators of their own *drama* to the audience as listeners of Prodromos's novel, see Agapitos (1998b: 155–6).

171 οὐκ ἀπάτη τὸ πρᾶγμα καὶ φαντασία· | οὐ φαντασία καὶ Τύχης ἄλλο δρᾶμα.

172 ἡ τραγῳδία <παρέσχε> ἀπάτην, ἣν ὅ τ' ἀπατήσας δικαιότερος τοῦ μὴ ἀπατήσαντος καὶ ὁ ἀπατηθεὶς σοφώτερος τοῦ μὴ ἀπατηθέντος. The phrase comes from Plutarch's *De gloria Atheniensium* §5.348c (*Moralia* II.2, 129.11–19), a popular reading in Byzantium since the tenth century; on Plutarch's reception, see *Oxford Dictionary of Byzantium* 3 (1991), pp. 1687–8 (Alexander Kazhdan and Kenneth Snipes).

less envoy is carried away to sleep off his drunkenness (4.317–417).[173] Even from this brief summary it becomes clear that the banquet scene is based on theatrical *apate*. Gobryas as stage director and Artaxanes as spectator perform roles in which the former deceives and the latter is deceived. Gobryas first uses the miracle-working art of *haute cuisine* and then employs the miracle-working art of an actual performer to convey in a flamboyantly theatrical manner his master's power over inanimate and animate nature to the baffled envoy of the enemy king. Obviously, the banquet scene represents the exact opposite of the Gorgian *sententia* since Gobryas's plan was to truly deceive Artaxanes; in other words, the host did not establish a contract of make-believe with his guest. When bringing the second *epeisodion* to its conclusion, Prodromos himself openly signals that this inverted image of theatrical deceit is intentional (4.309–12 + 316):

> Thus Satyrion, good at playing the lyre, he who was fictively killed and had fallen as a false corpse, immediately arose on Mistylos's command (in accordance also with theatrical acting!) [...] <and> was quickly dismissed from the banquet.[174]

Through this device the poet reaffirms the fictionality contract with his audience. However, it is in the third *epeisodion* of the banquet scene that Prodromos openly asserts himself through the narrator's voice as the creator of fictional art. Artaxanes, already drunk and in a state of mental derangement (*R&D* 4.316: τὸν νοῦν σαλευθεὶς καὶ παρακεκρουσμένος), falls asleep before finishing the wine held in a precious sapphire goblet. The narrator intervenes with the following comment: 'For sleep likes to follow after stupor and is in some way related to extensive drinking' (4.322–3).[175] The goblet, belonging to Gobryas, slips from the hands of the sleeping envoy and breaks to pieces. The narrator interferes with yet another comment (4.327–30):

173 The first two *epeisodia* of the banquet have been exhaustively discussed as to their sources, rhetorical techniques, parodic and political intentions by Roilos (2005: 253–88); see also Kaldellis (2007a: 270–6). On cookery (*opsopoiia*) as another metaphor for the author's rhetorical art in the twelfth century, see now Kolovou (2007).

174 Οὕτως ὁ καλὸς εἰς λύραν Σατυρίων, | πλαστῶς φονευθεὶς καὶ πεσὼν ψευδὴς νέκυς, | αὖθις δ' ἀναστὰς τῇ κελεύσει Μιστύλου | (τῇ δραματικῇ ξυνδοκοῦν ὑποκρίσει) | [...] | τοῦ συμποσίου ταχέως ἀπηλλάγη.

175 Φιλεῖ γὰρ ὕπνος συνομαρτεῖν ταῖς μέθαις | καὶ συγγενής πώς ἐστι τοῖς μακροῖς πότοις. The immediate relation of drunkeness and sleep had been already expounded by Prodromos in the opening section of the novel's preceding book (3.1–43) where Dosikles narrates the 'funny' story of a drunken sailor dreaming of drinking even in his sleep (MacAlister 1990: 205–8).

> Gobryas felt deep sorrow on account of the broken goblet and judged the incident as an outstanding disaster; for the goblet was a beautiful sight for the beholder and made drinking far more pleasant.[176]

The remark on the object's beauty leads to an extended *ekphrasis* of the goblet (4.331–411).[177] The description is introduced in the following manner (4.332–6 + 341–3):

> The underlying material was sapphire stone that an ingenious and wise sculptor sculpted with his artist's finger and superimposed on it a shape of equal size; you can learn about it (should you have any desire to learn!) if you look carefully at trireme warrior ships. [...] The opposite part of the goblet's two sides had been well carved by the wise sculptor and had received numerous figures of images.[178]

On the one hand, the goblet as an imaginary object displaying a narrrative scene and, on the other, the object's wise creator stand in for the fictional narrative of display and its highly learned author respectively. The poetological correlation of the intrafictive sculptor to the extrafictive author is secured through the direct address of the narrator to the audience in his capacity as an expert interpreter of the visual arts ('should you have any desire to learn'). It need not be further emphasized that this is exactly the same intradiegetic role that the chief narrating voices assume in Longus (the author's *persona* in the opening scene at Lesbos, presenting the painting with the encoded plot of the novel) and in Tatius (the analysis by the author-narrator of the symbolically puzzling painting with the rape of Europa).[179] The narrator's initial comment on the beauty of the goblet for the beholder, the subsequent reference to the shape of the triremes, and the choice of a Dionysiac theme for the carving on

176 Ἀλγεῖ θρυβέντος τοῦ κρατῆρος Γωβρύας | καὶ συμφορὰν τὸ πρᾶγμα μυρίαν κρίνει· | καλὸν γὰρ ἦν θέαμα τοῖς θεωμένοις | καὶ τὴν πόσιν παρεῖχε γλυκερωτέραν.

177 The scene has been briefly discussed by Beaton (1996: 67) as implying that the power of art endures (see the critical remarks of Agapitos and Smith 1992: 42).

178 Ὕλη μὲν ὑπέστρωτο σάπφειρος λίθος, | ὃν εὐφυής τις καὶ σοφὸς λιθοξόος | λιθοξοήσας καλλιτέχνῳ δακτύλῳ | τὸν σχηματισμὸν ἀντέθηκεν ἡλίκον· | μάθοις ἂν αὐτόν, εἰ μαθεῖν ἔχεις πόθον, | εἰς τὰς τριήρεις ἐντρανέστερον βλέπων. [...] ἡ δ' ἀντίπλευρος τοῖν μεροῖν ἀμφοῖν θέσις | ἔξεστο καλῶς τῷ σοφῷ λιθοξόῳ | καὶ μυρίας δέδεκτο μορφὰς εἰκόνων.

179 On this specific function of the narrator in both the Hellenistic and the Komnenian novels, as well as the Palaiologan romances, see Agapitos (1999: 125 n. 76) and Agapitos (2004b: 41–2). On the broader poetological role of *ekphrasis* in ancient Greek and Byzantine literature, see now Mitsi and Agapitos (2006) (with extensive bibliography).

the goblet correlate the banquet's third *epeisodion* to an external and historically identifiable signifier (the trireme) and, simultaneously, to the specific intertexts underlying the scene: (i) the episodes in Tatius (*L&C* 2.1–3), where Leukippe practices by singing an erotic song before a brief banquet where Kleitophon tells the Tyrian version of the Dionysiac myth of the grapevine, and Leukippe's father offers for drinking a beautifully carved rock-crystal goblet with Dionysiac scenes; (ii) Theocritus's *Idyll* 1, where the goatherd offers to Thyrsis, as an exchange for the performance of a song, a beautifully crafted wooden cup that is described in detail (1.27–56). Prodromos retains the narrative frame of Tatius's banquet but expands the description of the goblet on the basis of Theocritus's cup. What Prodromos has done is (i) to remove any erotic element in the framing of the *ekphrasis*, and (ii) to create a burlesque and subversively erotic scene within the description: a young and sexually attractive Dionysus is presented fooling around with the Satyrs, and with flirtatious dancing Maenads caressing him. All of the above suggests that Prodromos inserted a seemingly irrelevant *ekphrasis* of an imaginary goblet – moreover, a goblet that has been smashed into pieces – in order to point once again to his audience that he is the creator of this narrative art of display and that he alone knows how to present and to explain the rhetoric of fictionality.[180]

Of course, the primary recipients of the Komnenian novels were highly educated members of the ruling family; moreover, Anna Komnene and her husband Nikephoros Bryennios were authors of ambitious and learned historiographical works, the *Alexiad* and the unfinished *Historical Material* respectively.[181] The patrons' knowledge of the ancient novels formed an essential part of the intertextual nexus on which the Byzantine authors based their semiotic code of fictive referentiality, a point to which I shall return below

180 On Prodromos's *persona* as a 'philologist' narrator of his novel, see Agapitos (2006a: 144–7). That Prodromos's goblet is imaginary within the novel does not mean that such an object was solely a literary device displaying the conceits of rhetorical *mimesis*. The literary and literate style of the text should not lead the modern reader to reject any relation of the described goblet to the poet's socio-cultural and economic realities (see my remarks on this aspect of *ekphrasis* in Agapitos, Hinterberger and Mitsi 2006: 46–8). Such luxury objects (carved out of rock crystal, in a way akin to 'sapphire stone') are attested in eleventh-century Fatimid Egypt and were disseminated from there to other Mediterranean markets (see Alcouffe 1984 and Hahnloser and Brugger-Koch 1985).

181 For example, the archaizing term 'trireme' used by Prodromos as an explicative simile for the goblet's oblong shape is systematically used by Anna in naval contexts. As with the goblet itself, however, this usage does not mean that the 'trireme' was not identified both by Prodromos and his audience as a *dromon*, the Byzantine long-hauled battleship *par excellence* and relative of the galley (see now the exhaustive study by Pryor and Jeffreys 2006).

(pp. 324–30). It is precisely on account of this intertextual nexus that fiction was accepted as such and signalled in the twelfth-century texts through the imagery of theatre and display.

The Palaiologan vernacular romances, which had for a long time been considered products of a popular culture, also show a high level of artistic consciousness, especially what concerns narrative, poetics and stylistics.[182] This is reflected in the consistent appropriation of some of the narrative devices[183] and the poetological metalanguage[184] employed by the four Komnenian authors who, as I have already indicated (p. 253), were systematically read in the thirteenth and early fourteenth centuries.

One literary feature unique to the Palaiologan romances and to the allegorical poems of the fourteenth century is the characterization of the text as narrative, so much so that the phrases employed both peritextually and intratextually add up to a terminological definition of a new genre.[185] Another literary feature of the romances not found in the novels is the explicit characterization of narrative as instruction, again to such an extent that, for example, *L&R* **α** and *Ach* **N** assume the form of handbooks in the *erototechne*, the 'art of love' (Agapitos 2004b: 46–50). Clothing narrative with the protective cover of beneficial instruction, even if this is in the amorous affairs of the body and of the soul, allows the Palaiologan poets to include and to explore such new subjects as the fantastic, the predominant narrative role of the heroine, sex, death, social and/or racial inclusion and exclusion. This device of constructing a didactic discourse of narrated action, rather than only a rhetorical discourse of represented display, is a feature common to the romances and the lives of saints, both genres dealing with 'fantastic' story matter that needs specific techniques of authorization.

One further trait of conscious fictionality is, as I have already hinted at, the use of setting as narrative space in structural, thematic and ideological terms. The Palaiologan romance does not employ one single overarching semiotic code like the Arthurian romance; however, the various texts build their narrative settings in a consistent and marked manner. I would distinguish four types of setting, where each type reflects in its own turn a correlative cultural

182 See Agapitos (1991, 1993, 2004b, 2006a).

183 E.g. *in medias res* opening, first-person perspective, encasement, parallel action, rhetorical stylistics.

184 E.g. poetry as visual art, astonishment and aesthetic pleasure.

185 Such phrases are ἐρωτικὴ ἀφήγησις and ἐρωτικὸν διήγημα ('narrative/tale of love'), διήγησις ἐξαίρετος ('exquisite tale'), ξενόχροος ἀφήγησις ('fantastic tale'), ἀρχή ('beginning'); for full references and a discussion of this issue, see Agapitos (2004b: 21–4 and 84–5).

ideology. For purposes of convenience, I shall refer to these four types as Occidentalism, Historicism, Antiquarianism and Utopianism. Let us look at some examples.

OCCIDENTALISM:[186] *Livistros and Rhodamne* is the most Byzantine among all of the romances as to its poetics, aesthetics and rhetorics, as well as its socio-political ideology. At the same time, it presents the reader with an overtly Western setting that, I would argue, in the eyes of the Byzantines conjures up the Franco-Levantine culture of the Outremer principalities. For example, the protagonists are 'Latins' (λατίνοι),[187] they are dressed in the latest Latin fashion, Latin customs are described, while the main part of the action takes place in Livandros and in Silvercastle, two fantastic Latin kingdoms, the latter of which appears to have extended diplomatic relations to the Armenian Kingdom of Litavia and to the Empire of Egypt. The presence of Armenians, Persians, Egyptians and Saracens intensifies the image of a society placed in a Middle-Eastern context. Upon closer examination this Franco-Levantine setting proves to be a construct. This can be seen, for example, in the explanation offered by Rhodamne successively to Livistros, to her father, and to Klitovon about the 'Latin customary law' of jousting for the hand of a noble lady (*L&R* **α** 2388–93, 2428–33, 3337–47). If the romance had been composed for a Greek audience under Frankish rule (as the early fourteenth-century Greek adaptation of the *Chronicle of the Morea* had been written in the Principality of Achaia), such an explanation would be unnecessary. Contrastively, the mere narrative reporting without any explanation of the peculiar ritual by means of which Livistros is crowned co-emperor of Rhodamne's father by being seated on a shield and then raised (*L&R* **α** 2488–94)[188] suggests that this exclusively Byzantine practice of the thirteenth and early fourteenth century did not pose a problem of comprehension for the romance's intended Byzantine audience. The inclusion of an explanation for a Latin custom and the exclusion of a similar explanation for a Byzantine custom indicates that the socio-cultural assumptions of the primary 'Byzantine' recipients and of the 'Latin' society presented in the romance do not coincide. This Occidentalism

186 I have coined the term as an opposite of Orientalism, both of them representing specific manifestations of constructing cultural alterity. Obviously, 'Orientalism' in this context is not to be understood in the way in which the term was used by Edward Said in his highly influential study (1978) in order to define the specifically imperialist and colonialist attitude of eighteenth- and nineteenth-century Europe towards the Near and the Far East; on Said and his *Orientalism*, see the broad appreciation by Prakash (1995).

187 On what the term signifies for the Byzantines up to 1200, see Kazhdan (2001).

188 On this ritual, see Agapitos (1993: 131) and Agapitos (2006b: 51–2).

is necessary to allow for the innovative tale to unfold itself by incorporating the 'exotic' image of the Latin West as an existing but not threatening Other. It is the same kind of culturally and ideologically prescribed technique that we detect in Chrétien's orientalist *Cligès*.[189] Thus, for example, the very end of the romance offers the same kind of explanation for an 'exotic' custom. On account of the 'adulterous' behaviour of Empress Fénice, all Byzantine empresses in times to come were kept in close custody, guarded by eunuchs (*Cligès* 6746–65). The peculiar practice at the women's quarters of the Byzantine imperial court had to be explained to a French audience or else it would remain incomprehensible. Such a practice, as we find it in *L&R*, where Rhodamne is always accompanied by her trusted eunuch Vetanos (*L&R* **α** 1260–4 *et passim*), needs no explanation for a Byzantine audience.

HISTORICISM:[190] In contrast to the 'Latin' *L&R*, *Velthandros and Chrysantza* systematically points to its Rhomaian identity. Singularly among the vernacular romances, the protagonist is defined as Velthandros the Rhomaian (Βέλθανδρος ὁ Ρωμαῖος) and he is a 'purple-born' prince (*V&C* 8 and 147), son of Rodophilos, the Rhomaian emperor (βασιλεύς). Thus, his place of birth is indirectly identified with Constantinople because empresses gave birth to their children in the 'Room of Purble Marble' situated in the capital's Holy Palace. It is to this place that Velthandros returns together with his wife Chrysantza, daughter of the (Latin) king (ρήξ, *rex*) of Antioch. The geography of the plot (the Western Anatolian plains, the Central Anatolian lands of the Turks, Tarsus, Latin Antioch), the Byzantine imperial apparatus, the intertextual evocation of the *Digenis Akritis*[191] and the references to the 'Rhomaian-born' characters (ρωμογενεῖς) anchor the romance in a distinctly historicizing setting. In my opinion, this setting reconstructs the empire's Anatolian parts during the reign of Manuel I Komnenos, when Byzantines, Seljuq Turks and Latin Crusaders co-existed in an uneasy political and cultural relation. This glorified setting, wherein the emperor's son succeeds in

189 On *Cligés*, see Kinoshita (1996: 331–54) and briefly Agapitos (2010: 160–4); more broadly on the 'appropriation' of Byzantium in medieval French literature of the twelfth century, see Wolfzettel (2001).

190 I use the term here as signalling the conscious effort to reconstruct a specific historical setting belonging to a socio-culturally and religiously related past of an author; this 'historicism' is not to be equated with modern conceptions of the historical novel (see Tomas Hägg's contribution in the present volume). For a different use of the term in relation to the Komnenian novels, see Kaldellis (2007b).

191 Compare the opening of the romance (the lonely hero singing with his lute under the nightly sky, the fight with the emperor's twenty-four kinsmen, the combat with the bandits) at *V&C* 120–232 with *DigAkr* **E** 622–645 (the hero and his lute, feats in combat with the bandits).

bringing back home a Frankish wife and in vanquishing the Turks, offers the necessary ideological support to the newly restored government in Constantinople in the late thirteenth century.[192] It is a setting not dissimilar to the historicist reconstruction attempted in the so-called aristocratic version of *Floire et Blancheflor* (c. 1150–60):[193] a Mediterranean Christian and pagan (*qua* Muslim) world with a Byzantine colouring is evoked and set at a time two generations before the age of Charlemagne and the supposed historical setting of the *chanson de geste*.[194]

A similar historicist strategy was developed by the Persian poet Ayyuqi in *Varqeh and his Cousin Gulshah* (c. 1030–50). The sad tale was culled from Arabian folklore and tells of two Beduin cousins who grew up together, fell in love but were only united in death. The romantic story is placed at the time of the Prophet Muhammad (i.e., in the early seventh century). It includes fierce battle scenes and individual combats between the Beduin warriors in northern Arabia and in Yemen, abduction of women between the tribes, a heroine who dresses like a man and performs warrior feats of astounding valour, as well as a developed urban setting far away from the desert.[195] Thus, the romance explicitly evokes the world of pre-Islamic Arabian epic for an eleventh-century Persian audience geographically and culturally far removed from the story's spatiotemporal frame.

ANTIQUARIANISM:[196] *The Tale of Achilles* is in many respects a unique narrative, because (i) it focuses – singularly among all Rhomaian and Frankish romances – on Achilles as its central character, (ii) it organizes its narrative by

192 There might even be an echo of the wedding of Manuel to his second wife, Mary of Antioch, and of the treaty signed with Kilidj Arslan II, Seljuq Sultan of Konya. Both events took place in 1161 and strengthened, at least temporarily, the emperor's position (on the political context at the time, see Magdalino 1993: 71–8). These possible echoes of the Komnenian age fit well in the reign of Michael VIII Palaiologos (Agapitos 1993: 131–2). Moreover, the main manuscripts transmitting the historiographical works of Niketas Choniates and John Kinnamos, both of whom refer to the two events of 1161, were copied in the late thirteenth century, thus providing the knowledge for such historicist echoes.

193 Edition of version I (a thirteenth-century redaction of the twelfth-century original) by Leclanche (1980). On the technical issues of the romance's two redactions, see Frappier and Grimm (1978–84: II, 120–2) (nos. 184 and 188); for a broader interpretation of *F&B*, see Clain-Legros (1992).

194 On the genre/gender issues involved in the deliberate combination of *chanson de geste* and romance in the case of *F&B*, see Gaunt (1995: 85–91); for an interpretation of the romance as employing Byzantine imagery in order to include Byzantium in the 'pagan' alterity of the plot, see Moore (forthcoming).

195 See Lavizzari (1992: 27–8, 82–90) (battle scenes); (29–31, 39–44) (individual combats); (16–17), (abduction of women); (44–51) (Gulshah as a warrior); (121–41) (urban setting: the king's palace in Syria).

196 The term is used here to describe a setting that purports to represent Graeco-Roman antiquity, thus situated outside the cultural and religious framework of Christian and Islamic societies.

means of a 'biographical' frame for the hero, (iii) it develops a love story with a tragic end for the protagonist couple,[197] (iv) it survives in three distinct redactions (Naples, London, Oxford) that were obviously prepared for quite different audiences at different times.[198] The romance is not translating any ancient text as do the three French *romans d'antiquité*, and therefore a comparison between an authenticating source and its medieval adaptation is not possible. The semblance of an antique setting makes its strongest appearance in the opening and closing sections of the Naples redaction. After the prologue (see below, pp. 315–16) and at the beginning of the story proper, Achilles's father is presented as a Hellenic king, lord of Thessalian Phthia and of the Myrmidons, as is Achilles himself later (*Ach* **N** 25–6, 27–8, 43, 55–6); at the end of the romance and after his wife's death, Achilles participates in the Trojan War and is treacherously killed by Paris (**N** 1861–901).[199] In the remaining romance, Hellenic antiquity is of minimal relevance to the setting or to the story: Achilles is presented as a Byzantine crown-prince wearing the appropriate court dress and riding a luxuriously caparisoned steed (**N** 366–85); Polyxena, Achilles's love and daughter of the enemy king, lives protected in a totally Byzantine garden (**N** 765–847), while she is dressed in the latest Frankish fashion (**N** 860–80);[200] once the couple has been married, a jousting tournament is organized at which a Frankish knight distinguishes himself until he is finally defeated by Achilles (**N** 1542–96).

Reading through the *Roman d'Enéas* (c. 1160), we see that the text constructs a French antique setting that is not dissimilar from a socio-cultural point of view to the Byzantine antique settting in the *Tale of Achilles*. The translation of Virgil's *Aeneid* sets, of course, a specific frame in which the adaptation has to operate. However, the extensive reworking of specific epi-

197 On these thematic, structural and generic innovations, see Moennig (1999: 14–7); Agapitos (2002: 216–22); Agapitos (2004b: 29–30); Theologitis (2004: 222–33).

198 See Smith (1988) on **O**, Smith (1991–92) on **N**, as well as Smith (1999) for a commentary of **N** (with substantial bibliography).

199 This so-called Trojan end is not to be found in the other two redactions and was viewed by older scholarship as an addition to the 'original' *Achilles*; see Smith (1999: 148–9) for a discussion of the problem.

200 The narrator specifically refers to the dressing style as Frankish at **N** 860 ('she loved to always wear a Frankish dress') and **N** 864 ('she had two low-reaching braids and a belt in Frankish style'). In no other of the Byzantine romances is female *haute couture* so explicitly characterized as Frankish, though some of the princesses (e.g., Rhodamne and Chrysantza) are actually dressed in Frankish style, because these clothes were seen as enhancing their sexuality (Smith 1999: 114–17).

sodes[201] or the addition of completely new ones[202] shows that the anonymous author (who never mentions his Latin source) was at pains to compose a story attuned to the tastes and the ideological context of his own times. This becomes manifest in the 'anachronisms' included in the poem,[203] such as the extended and wholly fantastic descriptions of the tombs erected for young Pallas, son of King Evander and companion of Aeneas, and for Queen Camille, ally and friend of Turnus. The two edifices (*Enéas* **D** 6472–591 and 7595–790 respectively), of astonishing artistry and luxury, reflect the ideal funerary housing of an aristocracy that placed the greatest importance on the coexistence of honour and beauty in death. Consequently, this aristocratic ideal expresses itself most clearly in the way in which 'war' is represented in the antique romances. In the *Enéas,* for example, the third battle (**D** 5672–6067), that includes the central episode of the confrontation between Turnus and young Pallas and the latter's unjust death (**D** 5700–847), is staged according to all technical practices of twelfth-century chivalric combat and their reflection in the *chansons de geste*. As a result, the ancient heroes appear as contemporary knights adhering to the customs of their military class. This epic-chivalric war setting in *Enéas* finds its equivalent in the *Achilles,* only there the war is staged according to Byzantine practice. Achilles and his army set out to stop the invading enemy king and his army; the battle starts out on a grand scale with complex tactic manoeuvering (*Ach* **N** 385–573). However, the battle ends with a series of single combats between Achilles, his companions and the sons of the enemy king (**N** 574–637) in the heroic style of akritic warfare as reflected in the *Digenis Akritis.*[204] The common interest in warfare as part of the antiquarian setting is filtered in the two romances through war imagery appropriate to and recognizable by the two societies for which the texts were composed. Thus, Roman antiquity in the *Enéas* takes on a French chivalric colour, while Hellenic antiquity in the *Achilles* presents itself with a Byzantine akritic flavour.

201 One might compare, for example, Book VIII of the *Aeneid* (Aeneas visiting the Arcadian Evander, while Venus arranges for Vulcan to prepare her son's armour and shield) with *Enéas* **D** 4382–900: the French author has transformed a steadily alternating narrative that consciously promotes variance into a continuous narrative that insists on structural unity.

202 The author has created with the help of Ovid's *Heroides* a splendid portrait of Lavinia in love and her amorous/courtly conversations with the hero in *Enéas* **D** 7921–9326. It is interesting to compare how Heinrich von Veldeke (*EneasRom* 260,7–306,34) expanded even further the amorous episode in his adaptation (see Kasten 2004: 90–4).

203 On these anachronisms in the *romans d'antiquité,* see the excellent study by Petit (1985).

204 On warfare in *Achilles* **N**, see Smith (1999: 101–7).

It seems that a similar process of differentiation in respect to different recipients took place, even if on a far smaller scale, in the case of Benoît's de Saint-Maure highly popular *Roman de Troie* (c. 1160–65) and its translation into vernacular Greek as *The War of Troy*, written in the first half of the fourteenth century in Frankish Morea. The importance of Benoît's poem for crusader ideology and its attested presence in the Levant have been sufficiently discussed.[205] It has been suggested that a series of changes in the Greek translation[206] could reflect the adjustment of a Hellenic subject, presented through a Frankish perspective, back to a more Greek context,[207] in this case the remnants of the old Byzantine gentry wishing to integrate themselves in the Frankish aristocracy of the Principality of Achaia (Jacoby 1986: 175–6). One such case is the description of the *chanbre d'alabaustrie* (conventionally called the Chamber of Beauties), placed at the very centre of the romance (*Troie* 14631–936), with its astonishing alabaster walls, its four columns and its four mechanical statues, yet another example of *automata* in French romance, ultimately deriving from Byzantine tradition.[208] The imagery, vocabulary and function of the four *automata* is a Western fantasy reflecting Oriental luxury. The equivalent scene in *WoT* (6288–415) retains the structure of the *ekphrasis*, but the translator has removed or abbreviated certain elements that do not fit into the Greek tradition of such descriptions.[209] However, there is something else that strikes the reader. The description of the chamber[210] is clothed with a vocabulary that closely resembles the equivalent vocabulary used in *Livistros and Rhodamne* for the description of Eros's courtyard with its wondrous buildings, its mechanical statues and the commanding figure of the God of Love himself (*L&R* **α** 285–358 + 429–565).[211] This vocabulary, that is fully functional in *L&R*, is used exces-

205 See Jacoby (1984: 633–6); Jacoby (1986: 170–4); Shawcross (2003: 136–45).

206 For an overview, see Papathomopoulos and Jeffreys (1996: liv–lxvii).

207 See Shawcross (2003: 143–5) and Lendari (2005: 96–103) for some examples.

208 On the Byzantine tradition, see Maliaras (1991: 137–71) (including discussion of vernacular texts); for the statues in the Chamber of Beauties, see Baumgartner (1988) and Croizy-Naquet (1994).

209 See, for example, the excised catalogue of the thirteen precious stones (*Troie* 14634–56 = *WoT* 6291–2), the highly abbreviated description of the first statue holding a mirror (14681–710 = 6300–04), or the shortened description of the wondrous incense-burner held in the hand of the fourth statue (14895–918 = 6390–400).

210 It is indicated by an appropriate rubric at 6287a: Ἔκφρασις τῆς τσάμπρας.

211 See, indicatively: λυχνιτάρια (*WoT* 6291 = *L&R* **α** 538), ἐρωτιδόπουλον (6300, 6305, 6322 = 435), ξενοχάραγος (6311, 6321, 6323, 6328, 6339, 6371, 6379, 6397 = 495), ἠχάδιν (6339, 6348, 6360 = 1066), τέχνη τοῦ τεχνίτου (6379 [*Troie* 14879–80] = 484–5), φοβερόν (6391 = 334), φρικτόν (6391 = 527). See also the following phrases taken from other 'ekphrastic' parts of *L&R*: αὐτόφια ξενοχάραγη (6402 = 2679), σμίξιν οὐκ ἔβλεπες ... τὸ ἔργον ὁ τεχνίτης (6408–9 = 1015–7).

sively but not inappropriately in *WoT*. In my opinion, this is an indication that the anonymous translator actually knew *L&R* in one of its redactions. Thus, the French Trojan War is rendered in its Greek form through the appropriate use of a poetic language that makes the text more easily communicable to its recipients. Whereas in the *Achilles* and the *Enéas* an ideological similarity is expressed in socially different ways resulting in an 'anachronistic' image of antiquity, in the *Troie* and the *Troy* an artistic similarity is expressed in stylistically different ways resulting in a Byzantinized version of a fantastic antique edifice of French invention.

The only example of fiction in Persian lands that presents its readers with an antique setting is *Vamiq u Adhra* ('The Lover and the Virgin') by Abulqasim Unsuri († c. 1040), court poet of Sultan Mahmud of Ghazna (998–1030) in eastern Persia. *V&A* is an adaptation (via Persian or Arabic) of *Metiochos and Parthenope*, an anonymous Hellenistic novel, possibly written as early as the first century BC. Unfortunately, both *M&P* and *V&A* have survived in a sadly fragmentary state.[212] Despite this problematic situation, the preserved portions of the Persian romance[213] include substantial elements that would make the readers recognize its Hellenic setting: the beginning of the story takes place in *Shamis* (Samos), where people from every island of the *Rum* (Greeks) have gathered to celebrate the wedding of King *Fuluqrât* (Polykrates); Love is depicted as an innocent-looking but pugnacious boy in the typical manner of the Hellenistic cupid; a musician plays an instrument called *barbât* (the Greek *barbitos*) and performs the songs of *Diyânus* (Dionysos); the instrument has been made in the likeness of the shell of a tortoise by the wise man *Hurmuz* (Hermes). Islam does not make an appearance as a religion in the fragments of *V&A*, though the literary conventions of Persian poetry are applied.[214] The setting remains an antiquarian reflection of a culture highly esteemed and intensely appropriated by Arabs and Persians,[215] yet far removed from their own surroundings.

212 See Hägg and Utas (2003) for an exhaustive study of the two texts with edition and English translation of all surviving fragments.

213 The sources consist (a) of a manuscript fragment amounting to c. 380 verses in *mutaqârib*, the same metre that had been used by Firdowsi; (b) extracts from various old Persian lexical works amounting to c. 150 verses. The verses in the manuscript fragment, though not forming a continuous narrative, most probably belong to the first part of the romance (Hägg and Utas 2003: 134–43).

214 For example, the description of Yânî, the young bride of Fuluqrât, follows the ekphrastic traditions of early Arabic poetry, incorporated in Ayyuqi's *Varqeh and Gulshah*.

215 See Rosenthal (1965) and, in a more historical perspective, Goutas (1998).

UTOPIANISM:[216] The early fourteenth-century romance of *Kallimachos and Chrysorrhoe* presents itself to such an extent as a wonder-tale that some scholars actually took this narrative strategy for real and went searching for the wonder-tale archetypus of the romance.[217] Far from it, *K&C* is a highly rhetorical and learned text of extreme narrative density.[218] The wonder-tale setting and its concomitant accoutrements include: 'once-upon-a-time' openings (25, 846, 2505), a 'barbarian' King with three sons (25–42), an enchanted castle (173–200), a monstrous man-eating Ogre (489–92),[219] a noble Rival King (846–60), buildings of the Hellenes (857), a mischievous old Witch (1066–9), a poisoned apple (1206–14), Fate personified (1334–40), a token ring (1722). All these devices serve to create a fantastic land where emotional and carnal love finds its fulfilment far away from a society in disorder[220] and in a magical world of amorous seclusion.[221]

A similar utopian setting is found in the anonymous *Partonopeu de Blois* (c. 1182–85),[222] a highly popular romance throughout medieval Europe.[223] This setting is encased within a 'French' setting placed in the remote times of Clovis, first Christian King of the Franks, three hundred years before Charlemagne. *Partonopeu*, similarly learned to *K&C* as to its intertexts and its literary aspirations (Fourrier 1960: 315–446), introduces a complex wonder-tale utopia: starting from an enchanted forest in the savage territory of the vast Ardennes (*Partonopeu* **A** 499–524),[224] the hero sets off on a magical

216 The term describes a setting that either lacks any concrete markers or includes markers of such an abstract or diffuse character that the plot cannot be anchored in some kind of 'historical' time.

217 For a critique of this approach, see Agapitos (1990: 257–9); Cupane (1995c: 47–9) suggests that the wonder-tale elements in *K&C* are similar to the fairy world of Arthurian romance.

218 Agapitos (1990: 259–68); (1991: 141–204, 240–3, 282–97).

219 It should be noted that the Greek *drakon* is not the lizard-like dragon of Celtic/Germanic mythology.

220 Civil war is about to ensue among the sons of the King for the succession (*K&C* 45–56), while in the land of the Rival King the lower classes are presented as living in poverty and squalor (1485–525).

221 For a succinct presentation of all these themes in the romance, see Agapitos (1993: 122–8); for the erotic element in particular, see Agapitos (1990: 268–73).

222 Excellent new edition by Collet and Joris (2005) of the late twelfth-century Arsenal redaction (**A**) together with the 'Continuation' from the Bern and Tours redaction (**B**/**T**); edition of the latter, considered until recently as the 'vulgate', by Gildea (1967–70). For the technical data, see Frappier and Grimm (1978–84: II, 172–3) (no. 372).

223 On its various adaptations from Spain to Iceland, see the studies collected in volume 25 of *Medievalia* (2004).

224 The author-narrator makes it explicit that there is a great difference between that ancient territory and the audience's contemporary county of Ardennes (**A** 505–8: 'Ele est ore molt escillie | Et par lius tot herbergie, | Mais a cel jor dont je vos cant | I par avoit de forest tant'; 'It is now much fragmented and in places much populated, but in those days of which I sing, it was covered with many forests'). Thus, he moves from a 'historical' present to a 'historicist' past, preparing the way for the shift into the utopianist setting. It is one of the many instances of the anonymous author's substantial narratorial interventions (see Walters 1992).

boat that takes him to an enchanted city and an enchanted palace where he meets a beautiful young woman. Gradually, the readers become aware that the luminous city is Constantinople (**A** 4561), that the palace situated at the mouth of the beautiful river Oire has been built by Melior (**A** 1763), empress of Byzantium (**A** 1330–40), the learned daughter of the previous emperor and an accomplished sorceress (**A** 4557–660).[225] This magical Byzantine utopia of power, peace and luxury[226] is far removed from and strongly juxtaposed to the Frankish society in disorder.[227] At the same time, the flavour of this fairytale Byzantium in *Partonopeu* is quite different from the exotic but historically recognizable Grecian empire in *Cligès*.

We find another variant of the utopian setting in Fakhruddin Gurgani's *The Tale of Queen Vis and Prince Ramin* (c. 1040–50). *V&R* is not only the most famous among the early Persian romances but is also a milestone in the development of the tropes and figures of Persian love poetry.[228] As Gurgani tells us in his prologue (§7; Morrison 1972: 18), he composed the poem obeying a request of Amid Abulfath Muzaffar, governor of Isfahan, appointed by the Seljuq Sultan Abu Talib Tughrilbeg (†1063). The sultan, his vizier, and the poet's patron are extensively praised in three separate chapters of the prologue (§3–4, 6; Morrisson 1972: 6–12, 14–16). Gurgani presents us with a scene where his patron asks him about the story of Vis and Ramin, admired by all in Isfahan. The poet explains to the governor (and vicariously to his readers) that the old story survives as a book in Pahlavi and is used by people to learn this ancient language. Gurgani indirectly suggests that it was written in unadorned prose, filled with 'meaningless expressions'. So, by command of the governor, he takes it upon himself to 'beautify this story as April the garden' (§7; Morrison 1972: 17–18). This is another variant of the 'old-book-translated/renovated' device for authorizing fiction (see above, pp. 254–8).

225 Cupane (1978: 237–8 n. 36) and (1986: 61–2) first pointed to a series of thematic/structural similarities between the first parts of *Partonopeu* and *K&C*.

226 On the 'Byzantine' setting, see briefly Bercovici-Huard (1982). The unpublished study by Joris (1992) was not available to me.

227 Inner strife breaks out at the death of King Clovis (**A** 1905–12), followed by an invasion of the pagan King Sornegur, resulting in a terrible war (**A** 2073–3834).

228 *V&R* survives in four manuscripts (**P**, **O**, **B**, **I**) with a fair number of variants between them, especially in the structuring of the chapters and the phrasing of the chapter headings. Massé (1959) and Davis (2008) offer French (prose) and English (verse) translations respectively based on **P O B**; Morrison (1972) bases his English prose translation on all manuscripts and quotes the rejected or accepted variants in the footnotes to the text. For my analysis, I have used Morrison's faithful translation of the complete text; in his elegant, but free translation, Davis has omitted the prologue and epilogue of the romance.

V&R takes its readers back to a Sasanian and Zoroastrian past,[229] geographically situated in medieval Khorasan and Isfahan, the far eastern regions of the ancient Iranian empire. The 'once-upon-a-time' opening of the story, where a mighty king celebrates his rule by giving a splendid banquet in a garden during springtime (§8; Morrison 1972: 19–20), emphatically introduces the utopianist wonder-tale imagery. Nobles from all the medieval provinces of Persia have gathered (e.g. Azerbaijan, Shiraz, Khorasan, Gurgan), counting among their rows heroes of Iran's legendary past (e.g. Bahram, Ruhham, Gushtasp). Beautiful princesses are accompanied by female attendants from the most famous exotic lands, such as China, Turkestan, Byzantium and the Maghreb (§9; Morrison 1972: 21–2).

The story itself is a complex tale of pure love, sexual desire, deceit and constancy, acted out among Shah Mubad, his younger brother Prince Ramin and Princess Vis, the daughter of the queen of Media.[230] Vis is forced to wed Mubad but loves Ramin. The young couple commits adultery, until, at the end, Mubad suddenly dies; the lovers ascend the throne of Marv and restore peace to the country. *V&R* is full of passages of astonishing descriptive power and emotive lyrical delicacy.[231] Moreover, the romance includes some of the same motifs that we find in *K&C* and *Partonopeu*: the kingdom is in civil strife and war figures prominently (§19–21, §60, §98–9), the king proves a scheming and violent tyrant (§27–8, §47, §54, §68), amorous affairs are conducted through intermediaries (§34–6, §40–2, §57–8, §78), the lovers enjoy their emotional and carnal union alone in a secluded castle (§63), and magic plays an important role in the development of the plot (§38). In no other romance from the whole of the medieval world are so many wonder-tale elements to be found joined together within the same plot as in these three representatives of romance utopianism.

Having examined the relevant Komnenian and Palaiologan narratives of love, we can confidently say that fiction was not a theoretical issue in

229 *V&R* §14 (the Sasanian custom of sibling marriage), §14 (the father of Vis is a descendant of the Sasanid royal dynasty), §40 (elements of Zoroastrian magic), §42 (reference to Khosrow and Shirin from Firdowsi's version), §54–5 (the Zoroastrian virginity trial by fire in the Temple of Fire at Marv), §48 (etymological explanation of geographic terms by recourse to Pahlavi).

230 Since the Western discovery of the romance, Romanists and Germanists have argued that the Persian Mubad-Ramin-Vis triangle is the actual 'source' of the Celtic Mark-Tristan-Iseult story. For a critique of this folklorist-positivist approach, see Bürgel (1990: 306) with the relevant bibliography.

231 *V&R* §29 (the astrological *ekphrasis* of the ominous night during which Mubad abducts Vis), §79 (a letter of Vis to Ramin, in which she declares her love and includes a series of ten letters to her lover on various topics concerning amorous behaviour).

Byzantium but a literary practice. The 'anxiety of fiction' that pervaded the first generation of romances in Frankish and Persian lands, as the 'old-book' authorizing device suggests (*Cligès, F&B, Troie, V&G, V&R*), did not trouble Rhomaian authors, given the complete absence of this device in Byzantine fiction. The acceptance of ancient model texts and of ancient rhetorical theory on fictional narratives allowed Constantinopolitan intellectuals in the Middle Byzantine period to redefine fiction for their own purposes and, ultimately, to compose fictional narratives in the second quarter of the twelfth century. By the late thirteenth century, the composition of 'tales of love', which looked back to the novel and epic of the bygone Komnenian age, as well as forward to contemporary Western and Eastern romances, allowed for fiction to flourish in the Palaiologan fourteenth century. However, while fiction in the twelfth century was perceived as a theatrical discourse of static display intended to 'deceive' its learned audience through a rhetorical reconstruction of *drama*, in the later centuries fiction was seen as a dynamic narrative whose power of make-believe lay in its exploitation of consciously staged, fantastic yet recognizably contemporary, settings. The way in which 'deceit' and 'make-believe' were realized in Byzantine fictional narratives brings me to the last part of my paper.

VII. CONTRACTS WITH THE AUDIENCE

In contemporary discussions of fiction, the notion of make-believe is seen as an essential feature in the acceptance of the 'fictive' by its recipients.[232] In theoretical terms, to make-believe suggests that, on the one hand, an author consciously constructs his text with a dual point of view and, on the other, a reader consciously receives this text with a similar dual point of view. This means that the author intends the reader both to 'believe' his text and to recognize this intention, while the reader simultaneously 'believes' the fictive text and recognizes it for what it is.[233] This bilateral dual perspective establishes a knowing collusion between author and reader, what has been termed

232 The notion of make-believe and its importance for ancient Graeco-Roman and medieval Franco-German audiences has been discussed by Morgan (1993) and Green (2002: 11–3 and 26–7) respectively (see also the broader analysis in Green 1994: 249–64).

233 On the theoretical problematization, see Newsom (1988: 1–12); Currie (1990: 28–35) ('tacit agreement'); Walton (1990: 209–89) ('participation'); Lamarque and Olsen (1994: 29–52, esp. 37) ('collaboration'); Melberg (1995: 51–84) (on *imitacion* in Cervantes). On the broader problem of the conventional opposition 'reality=truth vs. fiction=falsehood', its history in philosophical discourse and a new proposal towards a definition of the 'fictive', see Iser (1993: 18–51 and 158–291).

'fictive stance'; it forms the basis of a 'communicative contract' by means of which fiction is allowed to function.[234] Part of this contract is the construction of the reader in the text and the equivalent construction of the text by the reader, a dynamic concept of reader response developed by Wolfgang Iser and termed the 'implied reader'.[235] The implied reader is not to be equated either with the fictive audience in a text (Mr Franklin Blake reading the report written by Miss Clack based on her 'little diary' in Wilkie Collins's *The Moonstone*) or with the intended audience of an author (Collins's 'good readers in England and in America' from the preface to the 1871 edition of *The Moonstone*). Rather, both fictive and intended audiences are part of the broader concept of the implied reader because they belong to the mechanisms of constructing fiction itself within a literary culture.[236] The intended audience of fiction has been substantially discussed in the case of ancient Greek novels and their readership,[237] of Western medieval romances and their 'primary' recipients,[238] as well as of Byzantine novels and romances.[239]

For Western medieval listeners and readers the contract of make-believe and the resulting fictive stance was neither easy nor self-evident, as can be seen both in the criticism voiced by chroniclers and in the attempts of romance writers to bridge the gap between history (*qua* attested truth in the form of their authoritative source) and fiction (*qua* imaginative invention of their own) by using various devices. It will be useful to show how this tension is expressed in Western romance by analyzing an example from Chrétien de Troyes and Gottfried von Straßburg respectively. These two often discussed

234 See Lamarque and Olsen (1994: 43–4) and Iser (1989: 31–41) respectively.

235 Iser (1972: 57–93) and Iser (1976). Iser's proposal provoked substantial critical reaction but has been quite influential in understanding the communicative aspects of a text in a hermeneutic mode of interpretation (see, indicatively, the papers in Suleiman and Crosman 1980), rather than through a functional linguistic analysis, such as proposed by proponents of the speech-act theory (on Iser's theory and the resulting debate, see Iser 1989: 42–69 and Holub 1995: 326–34).

236 See Ong (1977: 53–81) ('The writer's audience is always a fiction') and Ong (2002: 100–2), refering, of course, to writers in the age of printing.

237 Hägg (1983: 90–101) and Hägg (2004), proposing a broad, not necessarily intellectual, readership of primarily female recepients; Bowie (1994 and 1996) opting for a restricted, rhetorically cultivated, primarily male readership.

238 The concept of primary reception for medieval German literature was introduced by Scholz (1980), whose study should be read in conjunction with the extensive review by Kartschoke (1983). Indicatively, one might refer to the following important studies: Zumthor (2000: 45–60) (on acoustic reception); Zumthor (1987: 245–68) (on performance and the audience as 'accomplice'); Krueger (1993) and Krueger (2000: 132–49) (on women readers of and in medieval French romance); Green (1994: 3–54 and 270–315) (on Middle High German literature); Coleman (1996) and Amtower (2000) (on late medieval England).

239 Agapitos and Smith (1992: 102–11); Cupane (1995a and 2003); Agapitos (2006b: 161–3) and, more broadly, Agapitos (2006a) with full bibliography.

passages will also serve to illustrate similarities and differences in the handling of fictive/intended audiences and the construction of the implied reader in the case of Byzantine fiction.[240]

Chrétien does not open *Yvain* with a 'poetological' prologue (as in *Erec* or *Cligès*), though he has some bitter words to say about the rapidly declining art and practice of Love in his days (*Yvain* 18–28). Instead, the poet introduces Arthur at the Feast of Pentecost. After dining, the king has surprisingly retreated to his chamber because 'it happened that the queen detained him', and has then fallen asleep (49–52), a humorous jibe at a sexual encounter between the royal couple. Some of Arthur's knights stand outside the royal chambers; an exchange of harsh insults takes place, in which the queen herself becomes involved. Because of these insults, Calogrenant, a handsome knight and cousin to young Yvain, refuses to continue narrating 'the tale not of his honour but of his disgrace' (60), until he is finally convinced to do so by the queen. He yields to her insistent demand and starts his tale in the following manner (142–74):

> Indeed, my lady <*i.e.* the queen>, what you order me to do is very difficult. Except for my fear of your anger, [142] I'd rather let one of my eyes be put out than to tell them <the other knights> anything more this day; I'll do what pleases you <the queen>, [148] though it causes me pain. Since it suits you <the queen, but also the knights?>, listen to me now!
>
> Lend me hearts and ears <the queen's, the knights's or someone else's?>, for words listened at that are not understood [152] by the heart are lost completely. There are those who hear something without understanding it, yet praise it; they have only the faculty of hearing, [156] since the heart does not comprehend it. The word comes to the ears like whistling wind, but doesn't stop or linger there; [160] instead it quickly leaves if the heart is not alert enough to be ready to grasp it. However, if the heart can take and enclose and retain the word when it hears it, [164] then the ears are the path and channel through which the voice reaches the heart; and the voice, which enters through the ears, [168] is received within the breast by the heart. So he who would hear me now must surrender heart and ears to me for I do not wish to serve you <the queen, the knights, someone else?> a

240 Due to the length of the passages discussed in this part of the paper, the texts will be quoted only in translation with reference to the original where necessary. The only exception is the romance of *Imperios and Margarona*, for which we lack any kind of satisfactory edition.

> dream, [172] or a fable, or a lie, which many others have served you; instead I shall narrate what I have seen myself.[241]

At the very end of his tale, when Calogrenant has described how, defeated by the Keeper of the Fountain in the forest of Brocéliande, he returned on foot to the house of his host, he remarks: 'And so I went, and thus I returned; upon returning I considered myself a fool. Now, like a fool I've told you what previously I have never wanted to tell' (575–8).[242] The whole opening sequence of *Yvain* is quite extraordinary in many respects (Hult 1994: 12–13). However, what interests us here specifically is the way in which Chrétien has invested an intrafictive situation of narrative performance – a knight telling a tale to a queen and a group of attending knights – with a set of four functions.[243]

(i) The 'scientific' explanation for listening and comprehending (153–68) clearly distinguishes between those who think that they understand and praise unwittingly, and those who actually do understand because they open their hearts and, thus, praise knowingly. The verbal similarity between 149–50 and 169–70 (a typical case of rhetorical linking) expressly accentuates in an acoustic manner Calogrenant's demand for full emotional and intellectual attention to his tale. Therefore, the passage reflects Chrétien's own attitude to the correct reception of fiction.

(ii) Furthermore, the passage forms an address of the poet to his intended primary audience. It has been convincingly shown that *Yvain* was being written at the same time as *Lancelot*, both of them at the court of Countess Marie de Champagne (*Lancelot* 1: *ma dame de Chanpaigne*).[244] The presentation of a noble lady (Queen Guenièvre) and an intelligent narrator (Calogrenant) within *Yvain* as fictive patroness and fictive protégé allows for the projection of this relation to the actual patroness (Marie) and the actual poet (Chrétien). By staging and interpreting this intrafictive situation of narrative performance, the compliment to the knowledgeable patroness and her court is duly payed,

241 The last two, very important, verses ('Dont maint autre vous ont servi, | Ains conterai che que je vi') are omitted in the Guiot codex (Poirion 1994: 343 n. b and critical apparatus at p. 1194). The translation by Kibler and Carroll (1991: 296–7) has been modified according to the edition by Hult (1994: 60).

242 'Ainsi alay, ainsi reving, | Au revenir pour fol me ting. | Si vous ai conté comme fox | çou c'onques mais conter ne vox.'

243 For a good discussion of the Calogrenant episode, see Green (1994: 254–5 and 263–4) with the older bibliography.

244 See Méla (1992: 9–11); Hult (1994: 9–10); Poirion (1994: 1170–1 (Philippe Walter) and 1235–7 (Daniel Poirion)) with the older bibliography.

while the poet's powerful and instructive art is extolled since Calogrenant's tale succeeds in immediately spurning Yvain to take revenge for his cousin's disgrace (579–87).[245] Chrétien has achieved this conjunction between fictive and intended audience by gradually shifting Calogrenant's narratorial addresses from the queen and the attending knights (142, 143, 145, 146, 147: *dame…vous…hui…vous…vous*) to an undetermined audience (149, 153, 169, 173, 174: *vous…tix…qui…vous…conterai*). In particular, the remark about not wishing to serve up a lie as others have done does not fit the fictive situation in front of the royal chambers because no one has contested the knight's story. However, the remark makes perfect sense if understood as the poet's criticism of his real or imagined competitors (see above, p. 254). At 169–74 it is Chrétien who speaks in the voice of Calogrenant.

(iii) This fluctuating movement between fictive and intended audience forms the frame for setting up a contract of make-believe. The contract is further strengthened through a clearly signalled intertextual reference that supports the poet's criticism about the fables 'served' by others as opposed to his 'true', because 'witnessed', tale. The hypotext to Calogrenant's story is a passage from Wace's unfinished *Roman de Rou* (c. 1160–75), a history of the dukes of Normandy.[246] Wace comes to talk about the forest of Brecheliant, 'much fabled about by the Bretons' (*Rou* 6396), in which a spring called Berenton is admired to such an extent that 'if what the Bretons say is true, it is a place full of fairies and many other marvels' (6409–11).[247] Wace decided to visit the place (6415–20):

> I went there searching for marvels, I saw the forest and I saw the land; marvels, however, I did not find. A fool I returned, a fool I went, a fool I went, a fool I returned: a folly, for which I considered myself a fool.[248]

The verbal similarities between Wace and Chrétien are unmistakable, while the parallel between the two narrators who have both 'seen' the forest and, at the end, consider themselves 'fools' in exactly the same words is striking.

245 One has, of course, to be aware of the often ambivalent position held by women, both historical and fictional, inscribed in texts written by men; see Krueger (1993: 33–67) (with substantial bibliography) for an analysis of female 'displacement' in *Yvain* and *Lancelot*.
246 The passage referring to the wondrous forest can be found in Mölk (1969: 99–100).
247 'La seut l'en les fees veeir, | Se li Breton nos dient veir, | E altres merveilles plusors.'
248 'La alai io merveilles querre, | Vi la forest e vi la terre, | Merveilles quis, mais nes trovai, | Fol m'en revinc, fol i alai, | Fol i alai, fol m'en revinc, | Folie quis, por fol me tinc.'

What is more striking, however, is the inversion of the experience. In the case of Wace, the fabled forest of marvels proves to be just a simple forest, while in the case of Calogrenant it is indeed the fabled forest of Breton lore and, thus, inherently true.[249] Wace's historiographical folly in believing ancient fables is substituted with Calogrenant's fictive folly in not believing the *matiére de Bretagne* out of which Chrétien's *Le chevalier au lion* has been shaped.[250] In other words, Wace is made to resemble the kind of recipient that Chrétien objects to at *Yvain* 153–6.

(iv) Finally, the conjunction of fictive and intended audience within the poem through the use of semantic ambivalence in the series of addresses by the intradiegetic and homodiegetic narrator[251] establishes the necessary blank space for situating the implied reader. Each and every listener or reader of the romance, irrespective of discerning or not the intertextual and socio-cultural game, can project themselves into the text and read it as an 'open work' (to use a phrase of Umberto Eco), investing it each time with a new meaning.

The other passage I would like to discuss comes from *Tristan*. After the hero's investiture and Gottfried's *excursus* on the German poets (4589–820),[252] Tristan reaches Cornwall, where he finds the kingdom in uproar due to the arrival of Morold, the mighty Irish knight, who has come to extract the heavy and shameful tribute owed. Finally, Tristan and Morold meet. Following a first exchange of blows (6833–65), Gottfried as the extradiegetic narrator intervenes with the following comment (6866–900):

> Now I have heard everyone declare (and indeed it stands in the tale) that this was single combat, and all agreed [6870] that no more than two were involved. But now I shall show that it was a general engagement between two whole detachments, and though I never read this [6875] in the tale of Tristan, I shall nevertheless make it credible. As the true version has

249 The truth of Breton lore has been already affirmed by Chrétien before the Calogrenant episode in relation to Arthur's eternally remembered fame (*Yvain* 35–8: '... Du roy qui fu de tel tesmoing | C'on en parole pres et loing; | Si m'acort de tant ad Bretons | Que tous jours mais dura ses nons; '... about the king whose fame was such that men still speak of him both near and far; and I agree wholly with the Bretons that this fame will last for ever'); see Hult (1994: 53 n. 1).

250 On the passage in Wace, see also Green (1994: 252–3); on the thematization of Breton lore and its shaping of the plot in *Yvain*, see Poirion (1994: 1171–8) (Philippe Walter).

251 Calogrenant narrates within the story and, at the same time, is a character of his own narrative. These terms for the narrating voice were coined by Genette (1972: 238–41 and 251–9); see also his clarifications in Genette (1983: 52–5 and 64–77).

252 On this famous passage, see, indicatively, Haug (1992: 219–24) and Palmer (2004: 534–45) (with full bibliography).

> always said and says today, Morold had the strength of four, [6880] making a force of four men. Such was the one side. On the other it comprised: first God; second Right; the third was their vassal [6885] and servitor, loyal Tristan; the fourth was Willing Heart, who works wonders in extremities. From the first four and the second, [6890] as best as I can, I quickly form two detachments, otherwise eight men.
>
> At first you thought this tale preposterous for saying that two companies [6895] on as many mounts should ever come to blows. But now you have learnt how in fact on either side four knights under one helmet – or a fighting strength of four – [6900] were met together here.[253]

Gottfried then proceeds to narrate the combat between the two extraordinary men. In this authorial intervention, the German poet has used a different stratagem than his French colleague in establishing the contract of make-believe. Gottfried openly points to common opinion (6866: *al die werlde*) and to Thomas's *Roman de Tristan* (c. 1170–73)[254] as the authenticating source that two knights fought that day (6867: *maere*; 6875: *Tristandes maere*; 6877: *wârheit*). At the same time, Gottfried declares that he has not read in his source his own 'incredible' proposition that, in fact, two whole companies of warriors met together. Despite this gap in his source, however, he intends to make his proposition 'credible' (6876: *wârbaere*). At the end of the intervention, he actually addresses his audience (6893: *iuch*; 6397: *ir'z*). He ever so gently scolds them about thinking his proposal to be 'preposterous' (6894: *ungevüege*), but now, through his explanation, they have been taught about his proposition's truthfulness (6897: *wâr*). Here also the contract with the audience has been established by a set of overlapping devices.

(i) The intertextual game with the source is not presented as competitive criticism, but as explicative amplification. The received opinion, therefore, is redirected to a different, wholly fictive, depiction of the clash between Tristan and Morold.

(ii) Through the juxtaposition of a pragmatic, and thus metaphoric, image of warrior prowess ('Morold had the strength of four knights') and a non-pragmatic, and thus metonymic, statement ('Tristan's four knights were God,

253 Translation with slight modifications quoted from Hatto (2004: 133); the passage has been briefly discussed by Green (2002: 8–9) with the older bibliography.

254 On the technical data, see Frappier and Grimm (1978–84: II, 206–8) (no. 464).

Right, the valiant vassal, and Willing Heart') the single combat has been transformed into a moral battle between brutal Might and loyal Right.[255]

(iii) The indeterminacy of the reference to common opinion ('everyone') and then to a non-descript audience ('you') creates the blank space for the insertion of the implied reader who, each time the romance is read, will have to negotiate its 'meaning' with the commanding figure of the authorial narrator and exegete.

(iv) Fiction can function in *Tristan* because of the explicit introduction – quite extraordinary in medieval romance – of plausibility. It is on the notion of *wârbaere* that the contract of make-believe between the poet and his audience is based. It is this very notion that elevates Gottfried to a *poeta doctus* (should the recipients have missed this point after reading the romance's prologue and the *Dichterexkurs*), who both reveals the techniques of his art and offers a key to its interpretation in an attempt to forestall 'incorrect' readings of the poem.

It will have to be repeated that the two passages (but also many others from Chrétien and Gottfried, as well as Hartmann and Wolfram) reflect the reaction of poets to the cultural constraint in the Middle Ages of having to defend 'fiction' as opposed to 'history' during the formative decades 1150–1220. This defence takes on the form of an explicit exegetical, almost didactical, attitude on the part of romance writers, especially Wolfram and Gottfried who stand under the 'anxiety of influence' (to quote Harold Bloom) of their French peers and their German predecessors.

If we turn to Byzantine fiction in order to examine contracts of make-believe and the construction of an implied reader, we find a very different situation, reflecting a far more relaxed attitude on the part of Greek poets. On the one hand, three of the four Komnenian novels do not have any authorial prologues or epilogues (*R&D, D&C, A&K*), while only Makrembolites's *H&H* includes a fairly complex narrative frame. On the other hand, most of the Palaiologan vernacular romances include authorial prologues and epilogues, as well as extensive narratorial comments; they form part of the dynamic narrativity of these texts.[256] Carolina Cupane (1995a: 89–91) has suggested (i) that these prologues show obvious thematic similarities to the French romances, (ii) that these thematic similarities are the result of immediate Western influ-

255 On metaphor and metonymy in poetic discourse, see Jakobson (1987: 95–114 and 301–17), in combination with the concise discussion of 'metonymy' in *The New Princeton Encyclopedia of Poetry and Poetics* (1993), pp. 783–5 (Wallace Martin).

256 Extensive analyses in Agapitos (1991: 41–128) and Agapitos (2004b: 26–37). For a very good discussion of the function of 'prologue' in medieval literature, see Evans (1999).

ence, and (iii) that the prologues of the Byzantine romances function exclusively as a literary *topos* in the sense used by Ernst Robert Curtius[257] and not as a reflection of a socio-cultural reality presupposing a public recitation of the texts at the stage of primary reception.[258]

However, a more detailed and less generalizing comparison between the prologues of the Byzantine and the French romances reveals (i) substantial differences in the structural organization and content of these opening passages, and (ii) substantial differences between the Byzantine prologues themselves. We might, on the one hand, say that the prologues of *Thèbes, Meraugis, Athis et Profilias* and *Le Castelain de Couci* are somewhat similar to *L&R* **α** and **V**, *V&C*, *Ach* **N**, *I&M* **N** and **V**. The prologues of *Erec, Cligès, Durmart, Le Bel Inconnu, Claris et Laris, Ille et Galeron, Partonopeus* and *Violette* seem further removed. The opening sections of *Yvain, Lancelot, Perceval* and *Beaudous* are quite different, while the prologues to beast tales (e.g. *Renart* in the redaction by Pierre de Saint-Cloud) or allegorical narratives, like the *Roman de la Rose*, are of a wholly different character.[259] On the other hand, we might say that *L&R* **α**, *Ach* **N**, *ByzIl* and *I&M* **N** resemble each other in some respects, while *V&C, I&M* **N** and *K&C* are also similar but in other respects. The prologue of *A&S* does not resemble any of the other texts, while *Ach* **O**, *F&P* and *WoT* have no 'poetological' prologues at all.

Concerning the prologues of the French romances, Beate Schmolke-Hasselmann (1998: 278–81) has shown that they display specific patterns which fall into three types of opening devices: (i) plunging straight into the action without a prologue, as in *Yvain* or *Yder*; (ii) a prologue including an address to a single recipient, as in *Lancelot* or *Le Bel Inconnu*; (iii) a prologue addressed to a general audience, as in *Meraugis* or *Durmart*. Now, it is possible that Byzantine writers of romance picked up the broader French practice of introducing a fictional narrative through some form of poetological prologue that included an address to a fictive or intended audience, though this practice also has a long-standing tradition in Byzantine hagiography and historiography (Agapitos 2004b: 49). Be that as it may, the question of where, when and how this

257 For a concise critique of the Curtian concept of *topos* with substantial theoretical bibliography, see now Constantinou (2006).

258 However, a few years earlier she was still thinking of an audience rather than a readership for Byzantine romance (see Cupane 1992: 303–5).

259 All of these passages, and many others, are easily accessible in Mölk (1969).

osmosis of French practice and Byzantine adaptation took place still remains unanswered.[260]

Based on recent research concerning the manuscript tradition, the reception and the chronology of the romances,[261] I would like to suggest that only *The Tale of Livistros and Rhodamne* and *The Outstanding Tale of Velthandros the Rhomaian* show tangible thematic and structural similarities to their French counterparts. Moreover, I would suggest that these similarities reflect specific historical realities that pertain exclusively to these two romances, namely, the socio-cultural context of Laskarid Nicaea around the middle of the thirteenth century in the case of *L&R* and of early Palaiologan Constantinople towards the end of the thirteenth century in the case of *V&C*.[262]

Let us look first at *L&R*. The prologue and epilogue of the romance form a coherent narrative frame in which the main narrator opens and closes his tale. This narrating voice is, on the one hand, extradiegetic (the chief act of narration takes place outside the confines of the actual story) and, on the other, intradiegetic and homodiegetic (the narrator is one of the characters in the story and also tells his own story). Prince Klitovon, nephew to the ruler of the Armenian kingdom of Litavia, addresses his tale to Queen Myrtane, the deceased king's daughter and successor, who is also (as we are to discover at a much later point) Klitovon's cousin and former lover (*L&R* **α** 3–26):

> Every sensitive person educated in love, reared and educated by the noble Graces, [5] tormented and oppressed by the madness of love, every noble lover, every person of a lower station, every goodwilled soul educated in

260 For example, Cupane (1999) pleads for the active influence of French romances in the fourteenth century, while admitting that there is no documentary evidence to support the assumption that the Byzantines could read (or comprehend acoustically) such romances or that there actually circulated manuscripts of such texts in Constantinople at that time. The situation with texts like the *Roman de Troie* and its attested presence in the Frankish East is, of course, quite a different matter.

261 Agapitos (1993, 2004a, 2004b, 2006a, 2006b); Agapitos and Smith (1994); Smith (1999).

262 On account of my own research over the past years, I have changed some of my opinions about fictive and intended audiences as expressed in Agapitos and Smith (1992: 102–11) (see also Agapitos 2004b: 85 for another change of opinion from what was proposed in Agapitos and Smith 1992: 50–1). Beaton (1996: 224–6) briefly discusses what he terms 'reception of the romances' (after having omitted the relevant section included in the first edition of his book; see Agapitos 2006b: 162 n. 9) and suggests, trying to defend his hypothesis of 1989, that oral presentation of the romances in the fourteenth century could be quite a legitimate way of primary reception. He further believes that most of the prologues where a young audience appears or the instruction motif is introduced date from the fifteenth century or later, thus pronouncing that the prologue of *V&C* is a later interpolation (Beaton 1996: 269 n. 118). Most of this cannot be substantiated by a detailed study of the available evidence.

love, and nobly graceful heart amorously disposed, let them join me to listen to a desire for love, an amorous tale that I wish to narrate.

[10] And you, lady Myrtane, queen of the Graces, amorously flowing fountain of good esteem, living embodiment of the Graces, mistress of Aphrodite, together with all the splendid land, the land of the Litavians, from your splendid relatives down to the people of a lower station, [15] men, noble women, old men, all the youths: let them come, let them arrive, let them gather together. For I intend, my lady Myrtane, to narrate today a strangely drawn tale of love and the toils endured by an outstanding man, [20] deeply suffering, deeply aching, tormented in love. From the tale and from the madness of desire everyone shall come to know the bitterness of love and to wonder at a man boorish in the ways of the world, how many misfortunes he bore, once he fell in love.

[25] Well then! Let me begin with the tale of love between Livistros the deeply suffering and the maiden Rhodamne.

On the level of poetics, the prologue offers an explicit statement about the character of this 'strangely drawn tale of love' (17: ξενοχάραγον ἀφήγημαν ἀγάπης). On the level of performance, the prologue stages an intrafictive situation of recitation wherein the narrator invites first 'every sensitive person educated in love' (3: πᾶς ἄνθρωπος εὐαιστητής, ἐρωτοπαιδευμένος) and then the queen, her relatives and the whole land of Litavia to listen to the tale he has to tell (8–9: νὰ ἀκούσῃ...τὴν θέλω ἀφηγεῖσται; 20: μέλλω...σήμερον ἀφηγεῖσται). The main narrator and the royal lady are not external to the romance's story (as, for example, Countess Marie and Chrétien in the prologue to *Lancelot*), but belong, even if not in the same proportion, to the characters forwarding the plot (similar to and yet different than Calogrenant and Guenièvre in *Yvain*). Following the brief statement about the story he has to tell (21–4) and its highly didactic value for the audience (how an outstanding nobleman but uneducated in proper social, *qua* amorous, conduct suffered when he fell in love),[263] the narrator introduces an internal title (25–6) and starts his tale.[264] The first-person perspective of the chief narrating voice, the fictive audience invoked and the use of verbs of telling and listening firmly establish the setting

263 On the didactic aspect of the narrative, see Agapitos (1991: 57–64). In my opinion (Agapitos 1991: 54–64; Agapitos 2004b: 49–50), this is not just a variation of the a-historical Curtian *topos* of *delectas-utilitas* (so Cupane 1995a: 89) which supposedly bears little significance to the culturally and ideologically prescribed narrative structure and meaning of hagiography and romance.

264 On the complex rhetorical devices of this opening, see Agapitos (1999: 112–14).

of an intrafictive public recitation. I have argued elsewhere that *Livistros and Rhodamne* is divided into four chapters,[265] that these chapters follow the same structural device (interruption of the narrative in the evening and resuming of it the next morning) and that this device can only function if the romance was originally intended for public recitation.[266] In the romance itself, the fictive situation of oral performance for forwarding the narrative is consistently maintained (Agapitos 1991: 51–4). At the moment, however, when Klitovon concludes the tale of the protagonist couple and his own story, he shifts his position from intradiegetic to extradiegetic narrator, as he addresses again his cousin Myrtane back at the court of Litavia (4579–81). The romance ends in the following manner (4587–601):

> And I, my wondrous lady Myrtane, I have narrated to you the toils of my friend, those that he badly suffered alone as well as together with me. [4590] But who will tell of the toils that I endured in this world, what other person will narrate my painful bitterness, who will tell of my injuries, write of my sufferings, who will narrate in detail my very own bitter experiences?
>
> Yet, some person who is sensitive to such things as [4595] feeling compassion for fellow sufferers, learning in pain, and narrating in his own words to other sufferers, let him tell, write in detail, search, examine carefully. Should he not be able to recount all of these events, I say that he should write most of it; [4600] and, simply, any lover who should wish to describe these events, let him adapt them as he pleases and desires.

The epilogue presents an extraordinary narrative situation since, imperceptibly, the extradiegetic narrator has again shifted his position, into becoming this time the *persona* of an authorial narrator who invites his extrafictive and thus intended audience ('some person', 'any lover') first to 'tell, write in detail, search, examine carefully' his story (4597: εἰπῇ, συγγράψῃ μερικῶς, γυρέψῃ, ψηλαφήσῃ) and, then, should these events prove too numerous, to 'adapt them as he pleases and desires' (4601: ὡς θέλει καὶ ὀρέγεται νὰ τὰ μετασκευάσῃ). This statement is the only one in the whole corpus of Byzantine fiction where the actual process of adaptation is explicitly described, while the fictive orality

265 The breaks are at *L&R* **α** 955, 2723 and 3816. The chapters are referred to in the respective rubrics as *logos* ('discourse/story') or *akousma* ('listening'), for example: Δεύτερος λόγος ἔρωτος Λιβίστρου καὶ Ροδάμνης (952), Τρίτον ἀγάπης ἄκουσμα καὶ ἀφήγησις καὶ λόγος (2720).

266 See Agapitos (1991: 269–71; 2002: 222–4; 2004c: 31–6; 2006b: 110–31).

of the narrated story is transformed into the fluid textuality of an 'open work'. Quite remarkably, the authorial narrator drops the intrafictive setting of a recited performance and thrice points to the tale as a written text by suggesting that a qualified prospective redactor (4594: ὁκάτις ἄνθρωπος ἔχων ψυχὴν εἰς τοῦτο) should 'write in detail' about his (the narrator's) sufferings,[267] these being the only references to writing in *L&R* that pertain to the actual process of the romance's composition.[268]

We do not find a single prologue in French (let alone German) romance that is strictly comparable to the prologue of *L&R*, and, as far as the epilogue is concerned, nothing even remotely similar can be adduced. One might briefly refer to three French examples in order to demonstrate differences and similarities. In the prologue to his *Meraugis de Portlesguez* (first quarter of thirteenth century),[269] Raoul de Houdenc first presents his ideal of 'good tales' (8: *bons contes*) and criticizes other romancers as 'versifiers of moralizing songs' (10–11: *rimeor de servantois*).[270] He then wishes to tell of a 'novel tale' (19: *novel conte*) about the deeds Meraugis – his hero – has performed. The poet clarifies to his audience that his is not a tale of peasantry but of nobility and that only noble and valiant listeners are worthy of hearing the words he shall narrate (27–28 + 30–31).[271] The extensive prologue of Jakemes to *Le Castelain de Couci et la Dame de Fayel* (second half of thirteenth century)[272] elevates Love to the driving force of the poet's wish to compose a tale in order to please lovers who would either read or listen to it (5–6).[273] The poet first criticizes disloyal lovers (17–22) and then attacks the uncouth and boorish minstrels and storytellers who have not learned how to tell of the beautiful tales that lovers praise and

267 *L&R* **α** 4592: τὰ πάθη μου συγγράψῃ, 4597: συγγράψῃ μερικῶς, 4599: νὰ τὰ συγγράψῃ. Echoing the opening lines of the romance, the narrator here characterizes himself as such a 'sensitive person', a sensitivity he has proven throughout the story by helping the hero and, finally, returning to his former love.

268 The acts of writing and reading figure very prominently in *L&R*, but they relate exclusively to intrafictive situations such as the writing and reading of letters, or the reading of inscriptions (see Agapitos 2006a: 126–34).

269 See Frappier and Grimm (1978–84: I, 388–9) for a summary and brief analysis, and II, 191–2 (no. 404) for all technical data; the whole prologue quoted in Mölk (1969: 37–8).

270 *Servantois* or *serventois* designates a strophic song of satirical, political or moral content; it was originally a genre of twelfth-century Provencal poetry.

271 'Il n'i a mot de vilainie, | Ainz est contes de cortoisie ... Nus, s'il n'est cortois et vaillanz, | N'est dignes dou conte escouter.'

272 See Frappier and Grimm (1978–84: I, 419–21) for an extensive summary, and II, 145–7 (no. 288) for all technical data; the whole prologue quoted in Mölk (1969: 61–2). On this quite astonishing romance, see Krueger (1993: 183–216).

273 'Pour les amoureus esjoïr | Qui le vorront lire ou oyr.'

delight in (31–38).[274] In the epilogue (8190–8266), Jakemes again expounds on Love, finally revealing that he has composed a tale for true lovers (8191: *conte des vrais amans*) in honour of a noble lady (8252: *dame gente*) who, however, is not directly addressed. The third example is Chrétien's prologue to *Lancelot* (c. 1170–75). Here the poet directly addresses his patroness Marie de Champagne who wishes him to compose a romance (1–2).[275] He indicates the title of his 'book' and explains that 'the subject matter and meaning are furnished and given him by the countess, and he strives carefully to add nothing but his effort and careful attention' (24–29).[276] No criticism of rivals appears here, no other audience is even hinted at, and only a discreet authorization of the story is established on account of the subject matter furnished by the countess.

Going back to *L&R*, we notice that in his prologue the anonymous poet has 'combined' the prologue addressed to a single recipient and the prologue addressed to a general audience (both of them directed in the French romances to intended audiences). However, he has hidden himself behind the *persona* of Klitovon and has transformed the intended recipients into an intrafictive audience. Moreover, no patron is mentioned, while Queen Myrtane (in contrast to Queen Guenièvre) does not command the narrator to tell his story. The poet does not enter into any form of rivalry with other writers of romances, nor does he defend his fictional narrative in any kind of way. On the contrary, the romance's epilogue accentuates the fictionality of the tale to a maximum degree, while the prospective lover as redactor is, in fact, the closest one gets to an explicitly formulated Byzantine version of Iser's implied reader. What remains of direct relation to the French tradition is the broader setting of an aristocratic court[277] as audience to a *romans* (≈ *aphegesis*), the notion that the poet will tell a *novel conte* (≈ *xenocharagon aphegeman*) and that the (male) audience should be sympathetic to this tale, in other words, that each one of the men should be a *vrai amant* (≈ *eugenes erotikos*). These poetological similarities are in tune with a series of thematic similarities to French allegorical and lyric poetry of the thirteenth century, especially what concerns the 'allegory of love' in the first half of the romance: Livistros's two dreams and the interior of the Palace and the Garden of Eros (*L&R* **α** 204–627 + 686–759),

274 'Et menestrel et jougleour ... Ce sont gent rude et paysant' (31 + 33).

275 'Puis que ma dame de Chanpaigne | Vialt que romans a feire anpraigne.'

276 'Del Chevalier de la charrete | Comance Crestïens son livre, | Matiere et san li dont et livre | La contesse et il s'antremet | De panser, que guere n'i met | Fors sa painne et s'antancïon.' On these highly debated lines see the discussion in Kelly (1992: 106–10) with the older bibliography.

277 E.g., *Erec* 20: devant rois et devant contes; *Perceval* 63: an cort real.

the exterior of the Silvercastle (1003–1252) and the interior of Rhodamne's apartments (2577–2644).[278]

The presence of such a high number of concrete similarities to French romantic and allegorical poetry in *L&R* is unique among all of the surviving Byzantine romances, but so is also the strong presence of purely Byzantine elements in the text (Agapitos 1993: 101–17). This innovative amalgam (Cupane 1999: 49) was created in the middle of the thirteenth century at the imperial court of Nicaea where Latin and Byzantine nobles co-existed under the high-spirited policy of John III Batatzes.[279] All of the intratextual indications suggest that *L&R* was publicly recited in imitation of the equivalent recitations of the twelfth-century novels at the aristocratic *theatra* of the capital, a further attempt of the Laskarids at resuscitating the lost Komnenian heritage. The romance's literary innovations and structural peculiarities cannot possibly be explained if we accept the traditional dating to the late fourteenth century, for by that time the whole system of education and literary production in the impoverished capital had broken down (Kyritses 2005), while there was no patron to be found in Constantinople that could have sustained the writing of such a long and complex text, or that could have held a literary salon that has otherwise left no trace in the sources.[280] However, it is highly unlikely that the intrafictive audience found in the romance is a hidden reference to a real audience at Nicaea, something similar to the discreet and ambivalent correlation of Marie and Chrétien to Guenièvre and Calogrenant in *Yvain*. The Armenian kingdom of Litavia functions as the necessary distancing stage for the presentation of the occidentalist fictional narrative (see above, pp. 286–7). What we do not find in the prologue and epilogue of *Livistros and Rhodamne* is a contract with the audience that is based on the notion of make-believe; fiction is accepted as such.

The situation in *Velthandros and Chrysantza* is somewhat different. As I have pointed out already (see above, pp. 287–8), this is the only romance

278 See Cupane (1973–74: 286–93) on the figure of Eros in *L&R*; Cupane (1978: 242–6) on the Castle of Eros in *V&C* and *L&R*; Cupane (1992: 292–303) on the allegory of Love in *L&R*.

279 On the situation in Nicaea after the death of Empress Eirene Laskarina and the marriage in 1241 of the fifty-year-old John to the thirteen-year-old Constanza/Anna of Hohenstaufen (illegitimate daugther of Emperor Frederick II), see Katsaros (2002: 255–60). A poem by Nicolas Eirenikos, performed as a musical piece at the wedding ceremony of John and Constanza in Nicaea, has survived in the Nicaean manuscript *Laur. Conv. Soppr.* 627 (Agapitos 2002: 208–9); on the poem's relation to the Hellenistic and the Komnenian novels, see Katsaros (2002: 260–8).

280 Cupane (2004: 440), who previously adhered to the later date, now accepts the possibility that *L&R* could have been written in the thirteenth century.

where explicit emphasis is laid on the hero and on his country being Byzantine. The authorial narrator opens his tale in the following manner (*V&C* 1–24):[281]

> Come! Attend a moment all you young people. I wish to tell you the fairest tale, an astonishing and highly varied story. Whoever wants to taste of its sadness and joy will also wonder at its account of daring and bravery.
>
> There was an emperor, a certain Rodophilos who had two sons, Philarmos and Velthandros, remarkable, glorious and born to the purple. Velthandros was the second born of Rodophilos, this mighty emperor. Well, Velthandros suffered a terrible grief. He was saddened by his father and scorned beyond limit. He even went into exile from his home. <The tale shall tell> how he left his native land, how he suffered woes with Chrysantza too, and how he bore the circular course of so much time and attained his father's rank. Though previously hated he came to be loved, he bore and gained the crown and diadem of imperial power. He became emperor and had as his fair wife the lady Chrysantza, the daughter of the mighty king of great Antioch. Well then, pay proper attention in order to hear the tale and marvel much. I shall not be proved a liar.

The narrator first addresses a general audience, specifically characterized as 'young people' (ὢ νέοι πάντες); he then offers a synopsis of the plot and, finally, concludes the prologue by making a comment about the 'truthfulness' of his story (23–4).[282] In my view, the consciously historicist setting of the romance needs, like in the case of the *Digenis Akritis*, this particular kind of excuse to defend its 'veracity'. *V&C* is the only Palaiologan romance where the authorial contract employs the device of make-believe through a reference to the binary opposition of 'truth-lie', and even so this reference appears only once in the whole text. In contrast to the brief statement in *L&R* about the toils of the hero, here the recipients are presented with a plot summary of seventeen verses that situates the tale in its 'historical' geography between Constantinople and Antioch.

This kind of summary, even if on a far smaller scale, is to be found in French romances that also have a 'historical' setting, such as the *Roman de Thèbes*, Benoît's *Roman de Troie*, Alexander's *Athis et Profilias* (early thirteenth

281 Translation quoted with some modifications from Betts (1995: 5).

282 Λοιπὸν τὸν νοῦν ἱστήσατε ν' ἀκούσητε τὸν λόγον | καὶ νὰ θαυμάσετε πολλά· ψεύστης οὐ μὴ φανοῦμαι.

century) set in Graeco-Roman antiquity,[283] and *Cléomades* (c. 1280–85) by Adenet le Roi set in the time of Emperor Diocletian.[284] The same approach, even if expressed in a very different poetic language, was used by Nizami in the long and highly complex prologue to his last work, the *Iskandarnameh* or 'Book of Alexander' (c. 1196–1204). The poet refers to his predecessor and the gaps he left in his grand book, the statement alluding once again to Firdowsi and his treatment of Alexander in the *Shahnameh*. Nizami includes a passage on the critical assessment of multiple sources in the historiographic mode,[285] thus differentiating himself from Firdowsi's epic 'one-book model', but approaching the Byzantine tradition as reflected in the *Synopsis Chronike* of Manasses. Nizami goes on to speak about the novelty of his own book and about the greatness of his subject (Alexander in his three functions as conqueror/ruler, sage and prophet), and then presents a succinct summary of the story.[286] The prologue ends with a forceful statement about truth and falsehood in narrative poetry, suggesting that sometimes 'falsehood', i.e. fiction, is closer to (philosophical or moral) 'truth' than historical correctness.[287] Obviously, I am not suggesting that the poet of *V&C* knew the French romances or the Persian tales. However, the similar treatment by near contemporary Persian, Byzantine and French poets of 'historical' subject matter embedded in a fictional narrative points to common ideological assumptions and their literary expression in three different 'medieval' cultures (Agapitos 2010).

Beyond the presence of the exegetic synopsis, the prologue of *Velthandros and Chrysantza* further underlines the didactic aspect of erotic narrative by constructing a teacher–pupil relation between the 'omniscient' narrator and his 'young' audience. This relation is encoded in the verb 'to admire' (5: νὰ θαυμάσῃ, 24: νὰ θαυμάσετε). In the romances the verb signals the astonishment of the recipient of a work of art – be it the listener of a tale or the viewer of a painting – whose meaning he is about to learn.[288] This didactic aspect is fully

283 Frappier and Grimm (1978–84: I, 278–80 and II, 74–5) (no. 16); prologue in Mölk (1969: 47–8).

284 Frappier and Grimm (1978–84: I, 463–4 and II, 71–2) (no. 4); prologue and epilogue in Mölk (1969: 62–4).

285 *Iskandarnameh* I, 69 with the German translation by Bürgel (1991: 37–8).

286 *Iskandarnameh* I, 49–50; I, 54–55; I, 67–73 (Bürgel 1991: 25, 28, 36–40).

287 *Iskandarnameh* I, 74–5 (Bürgel 1991: 40–1). Similar is Nizami's approach in the prologue to *Khosrow and Shirin*, his earliest 'historical' tale (see Bürgel 1980: 344–6 for a discussion of the make-believe contract there).

288 See Agapitos (2004b: 38–46) on *aporia* and the 'awe-inspiring mysteries' of art. Cupane (1995a: 86 n. 12) (objecting to Agapitos 1991: 57) thinks that the use of a 'liar' narrator here cannot be correlated to any notion of 'truthful instruction'.

confirmed in the romance's short epilogue. The authorial narrator explicitly includes an expanded paraphrase of an Old Testament moral saying: 'Let me then cease at this point. Let us attend to the words of the writer of Proverbs <16.17>. "If the beginning is good but the end is bad", as the sage remarks, "it makes the whole thing bad. But if there is good at the end of life, everything is good and the object of countless blessings". And I say "Amen! Amen!" and end my tale' (*V&C* 1342–8; Betts 1995: 30). Despite the small presence of narratorial vocabulary in the romance, this vocabulary consistently refers to the act of narration as 'oral' (Agapitos 1991: 50–1 and 57).

The Erotic Tale of Kallimachos and Chrysorrhoe presents us with yet another type of opening. Written in a style more 'elevated' than *L&R* and *V&C* (Apostolopoulos 1984), it addresses a single reader, a case unique among the vernacular romances. The authorial narrator introduces his *erotikon diegema* as follows (*K&C* 4–23):

> Nothing that happens on this earth, no action, no exploit does not partake of grief. Joy and grief are mixed, even blended together. Beauty and charm have their share of grief just as grief often has its share of joy. Fame, glory, honor, wealth, beauty, intelligence, learning, bravery, love, charm, noble appearance give sweet joy and pleasure; joined with them *you see* danger and malice, infirmities and obstacles which cause grief, not to mention the loss itself of what we long for. Desire deprived of its object shuns patience, and shows, one might say, no concern for other things. Love instils its charm into everything except separation and there alone it is filled with great bitterness. If, however, *you read* this writing and *learn* the matter of its verses *you will come to learn* through the deeds described therein the bitter-sweet pangs of Love. Such is the nature of Love: to sweeten in a mixed manner! But let our story turn to its main subject.[289]

The prologue presents itself as a collage of moral *gnomai* (Cupane 1995c: 58 n. 1). This admonitory discourse puts the recipient into the proper frame of mind concerning the understanding of the tale's 'main subject', namely, the 'bitter-sweet pangs of Love' (21: ἔρωτος γλυκοπικρὰς ὀδύνας). The use of *glykopikros* (a *hapax legomenon* in Byzantine vernacular literature and of extremely rare

289 Translation quoted with some modifications from Betts (1995: 37); verbs printed in italics are in the singular in the original.

occurrence in learned texts)[290] in combination with Love is, in my opinion, a direct allusion to Sappho's verses on Eros as a 'bitter-sweet creature' (frg. 130 L–P).[291] The poet of *K&C* could easily remember this fragment of Sappho because it is preserved in Hephaistion's short treatise on Greek metre, the basic handbook in Byzantine schools for learning metrics up to the fifteenth century (Hunger 1978: II, 50–1), and a major source for Demetrios Triklinios's work on his editions of the three tragedians in the early fourteenth century (Smith 1975: 111–12). Such an allusion should not come as a surprise from a poet who made use of the erotic epigrams from the *Greek Anthology*, freshly edited in 1299 by Maximos Planoudes, and who probably knew the great philologist's prose translation of Ovid's *Ars amatoria* (Agapitos 1990). On the one hand, any notion of make-believe or excuse for the wholly fictional character of the story is absent from this learned prologue. On the other hand, no other prologue of Byzantine romance offers such a generalizing moralist perspective on human life. Only one late instance from French verse romance can, to a certain extent, be compared to *K&C*. In the long prologue to the anonymous *Claris et Laris* (late thirteenth century),[292] the poet laments the baseness of his own times and describes how Sadness (*tristece*) has become queen of the earth, while goodness, honour and generosity have been lost.[293]

Beyond its prologue, *K&C* explicitly and consistently addresses itself to a readership. The narratorial vocabulary is always related to acts of reading and writing.[294] Moreover, the bipartite structure of the text (*K&C* 1–840 and 841–2607) is marked at the passage between the two parts by a strong signalling device: the narrator self-referentially reminds the reader of the prologue's 'main subject' of 'bitter-sweet Eros' (843–4).[295] Such a narratorial intervention can function only if the text is read rather than listened to (Agapitos 2004b: 27–9). Indeed, there is external evidence in the first quarter of the fourteenth century that solitary reading was an accepted way of enjoying fiction. The prolific poet Manuel Philes wrote a lengthy poem in which he interpreted in

290 See Kriaras (1969 ff.: IV, 316) and Trapp (1994 ff.: I.2, 320).

291 Ἔρος δηὖτέ μ' ὁ λυσιμέλης δόνει | γλυκύπικρον ἀμάχανον ὄρπετον ('Once again Love loosens my limbs and turns me giddy, bitter-sweet creature, irresistible'; trans. Denys Page, Oxford 1955).

292 Frappier and Grimm (1978–84: I, 395–6 and II, 107–8) (no. 128). The romance has a length of 30,370 verses and survives in a single manuscript of the late thirteenth century; it has not faired well among critics (see Kelly 1993: 63).

293 Prologue quoted in Mölk (1969: 43–4).

294 See the detailed analysis in Agapitos (2006a: 154–7).

295 'But what brings sweetness also brings bitterness, as you already have come to learn from the prologue' (ἀλλ' ὅπερ φέρει τὸ γλυκὺν φέρει καὶ τὴν πικρίαν, | ὡς ἔγνωκας, ὡς ἔμαθες ἀπὸ τοῦ προοιμίου).

an allegorical manner a romance (he calls it an 'erotic book' and it resembles *K&C* fairly closely) that was composed by prince Andronikos Palaiologos, cousin to the reigning emperor. Philes humorously describes two types of readers, one who is solely interested in the erotic plot, and one who searches for the story's hidden meaning.[296]

The prologues of *L&R, V&C* and *K&C* constitute three types of introducing romance in Byzantium. These three types are not correlated to the three types of French prologues, but represent a typology specific to different Byzantine socio-cultural and literary contexts from the middle of the thirteenth to the middle of the fourteenth centuries. The three types are: (i) a prologue introducing an intrafictive audience about to listen to a tale of love; (ii) a prologue addressing a general audience and offering a plot summary for a pseudo-historical narrative; (iii) a prologue stringing together moralist statements about the nature of Eros as presented in the book to be read by its recipients. All three types of prologues include, even if expressed with a different degree of emphasis, the basic notion that listening to or reading erotic tales is a process of instruction into the 'art of love'.

What we find in the other Palaiologan romances are, in my opinion, prologues that adapt and reshape the three types developed in *L&R, V&C* and *K&C* without recourse to French romance tradition. Two examples should suffice to demonstrate this process of adaptation. *The Tale of Achilles* (see above, pp. 288–90) focuses most powerfully on the devastating effects of Eros's negative power on humans.[297] The prologue runs as follows (*Ach* **N** 2–20):

> How shall I address Eros, how shall I name him? How shall I write about the primeval power and the strength he has? For he rends hearts asunder and withers souls, he burns youths before their time and utterly consumes them. Great is his strength, great the dominion of his command, his power is tremendous and his audacity awe-inspiring. Woe on him whom he will hold in his hands and seize him: he burns and inflames him, he wholly enslaves his mind.
>
> Yet, those of you who feel amorous Desire, those of you who have never been struck by the blow of Love, all of you now listen to this here very tale, so amorous and also so painful because of desire. Listen, that all of you might learn and be instructed how mighty Desire is and how

296 See Agapitos (2004a: 60–2; 2004b: 18; 2006a: 157–8); Odorico (2005b).
297 See the discussion in Smith (1992: 84–7) and Smith (1999: 80–3).

many things he can burn down. Listen, that you might learn about the immense strength and the power he has, that you might learn about his arrows, learn to pay obeisance to him and not to behave haughtily towards his terrible audacity. Accept him as your overlord and pay obeisance to him, [20] for he is a terrible and wondrous and great king!

In the prologue of the Naples redaction we detect a number of elements found in the three types discussed above: (i) explicit/implied address to a young audience (*Ach* **N** 5 ≈ *V&C* 1); (ii) direct address to those who have or have not fallen in love (**N** 10–11 ≈ *L&R* **α** 3–7); (iii) narration as instruction (**N** 14–17 ≈ *L&R* **α** 22–3, *V&C* 5 + 24, *K&C* 20–1); (iv) moralist discourse on the nature of Eros (**N** 6–9 + 14–20 ≈ *L&R* **α** 23–4, *K&C* 16–22); (v) narrative composition as a written process (**N** 3 ≈ *K&C* 20); (vi) the reception of the story as an oral process (**N** 12 ≈ *L&R* **α** 8–9, *V&C* 23). Thus, the prologue of *Ach* **N** not only does not resemble one of the three types of French romance prologues, it also does not resemble any of the three types of Byzantine romance prologues. As with the macrostructure of the Naples *Achilles*,[298] its prologue also constitutes a conscious mixture in order to innovate by deviating from the 'canon' established by *L&R*, *V&C* and *K&C*.[299]

In the romance's epilogue the specific moralist discourse of the prologue is transformed to a full-scale moral precept about the power of Death and the vanity of human affairs (*Ach* **N** 1914–26):[300]

And those who read this story here [1915] learn how the affairs of this world pass by. Beauty is of no avail to anyone, nor riches or courage, – *You speak the truth!* – Death withers everything, he always weaves for us the end, the affairs of the world are naught, everything is indeed a shade. [1920] – *How truthfully you have spoken!*

Behold the pleasantries of the world and the deceiver's graces, behold how all people in the briefest span of time come to pass. Beauty is of no

298 Rhetorical tripartite division of the text employing the device developed in *L&R*, use of the 'akritic' material from the openings of *DigAkr* **G** and *V&C*, use of the 'exchange-of-letters-and-songs' scene from *L&R*, use of the erotic bath from *K&C*, use of the ritualized premarital carnal union of the protagonists from *V&C*.

299 On this innovation as deviation in *Achilles* **N**, see Agapitos (2004b: 37).

300 The text's rubrics (written with red ink) are printed in italics. On the importance of the rubrics as an integral part of 'love romance' as a genre, see Agapitos (2004b: 24–6 and 87–8); on their narrative typology and their palaeographical and codicological characteristics, see Agapitos (1991: 95–103) and Agapitos and Smith (1994: 66–71).

> avail to anyone, nor riches or courage, Death gains everything, he always weaves for us the end; [1925] whatever man enjoys in this world during his lifetime, Death is its end, Death conquers it all.

The book teaches its readers about the frailty of human life and conduct. It is the rubrics that introduce here, for the first time in the romance, the notion of 'truth', though this truth is not related to the fictional character of the story but to the veracity of the moral precept. It is worth noting that this moral framework found in the Naples redaction is completely absent from the Oxford redaction of the *Achilles*, probably composed in the late fifteenth century. There is no prologue or epilogue in the short poem of 763 verses, various episodes have been omitted (e.g. the *ekphrasis* of the garden), others have been condensed (e.g. the exchange of letters), while no 'written' narrative vocabulary can be found. Thus, the story presents itself as a wonder-tale set in ancient times with no attempt to offer a peritextual key to its reading. All of this suggests that the Oxford redaction could be a reworking intended for an audience of listeners already familiar with the story of the 'byzantinized' Achilles.[301]

We have seen in the case of Gottfried's authorial intervention in the Morold episode how the German poet excuses the creation of his own fictive narrative. In the Byzantine romances, for example, *Kallimachos and Chrysorrhoe* or the Naples *Achilles*, the authorial narrator imposes himself most forcefully on his story, but does not offer any excuse for his fictional tale. One example should suffice to show this attitude. When the hero in the Naples *Achilles* has fallen in love with Polyxena, the narrator embarks on an extended description of the garden within the walled palace where the beautiful maiden lives (**N** 754–895). The *ekphrasis* culminates in the description of the princess herself. This description, which could have been used by the poet to excuse his fictional narrative (as Gottfried had done in his description of the two combatants), is introduced with the following authorial comment (**N** 851–5):

> For my intellect and my hand have given up writing about these things (i.e., the marvellous buildings and objects in the garden); so let my intellect be turned towards the delightful maiden. But who would have the power to tell everything in full detail? My mind is not able to assist me in describ-

301 See Smith (1988) and Smith (1999: 177–82).

> ing the maiden, for, whatever I might write about her, she will again defeat me.[302]

The 'professed incapacity of describing', combined with yet another statement about composition being a process of writing, serves only to accentuate the artifice of *ekphrasis* and the poet's power to control his artifact.[303] The acceptance of 'defeat' on part of the narrator obviously represents an inverted form of the poet's self-praise. Any suggestion that the beautiful maiden is a fictive construct of the poet (just as the eight combatants instead of two had been in Gottfried's poem) is absent since the authorial statement does not include any notion of make-believe.

The other example on the basis of which I would like to examine this combinatory use of the 'canonical' three types of Byzantine romance prologues comes from the unrhymed redaction of *Imperios and Margarona* (second half of fifteenth century).[304] The Greek *I&M* is a much abbreviated adaptation of the highly popular French prose romance of *Pierre de Provence et la belle Maguelonne* (second quarter of fifteenth century).[305] I have chosen for my analysis the still unedited text from ms. *Neapol. gr.* III-B-27,[306] because it preserves the most complete form of the unrhymed redaction, as well as representing, in my opinion, its textually oldest version. The prologue reads as follows (*I&M* **N** 3–15):[307]

> Καὶ πῶς νὰ γράψω ἐκ τὰς ἀρχὰς καὶ πῶς νὰ τὸ ἀφηγήσω,
> ἀφήγησιν πανέμορφην, ἐρωτικήν, μεγάλην,
> πῶς ἔπαθεν ἐκ τὰς ἀρχὰς ἡ θαυμαστὴ ἐκείνη,

302 Ταῦτα γὰρ ἐγκατέλιπεν ὁ νοῦς καὶ ἡ χεὶρ τοῦ γράφειν· | ὡς πρὸς τὴν κόρην τὴν τερπνὴν ὁ νοῦς μετατραπέντον. | Εἰς τὸ ἐκ παντὸς γὰρ κἂν ποσῶς τίς ἐξειπεῖν ἰσχύσῃ; | Οὐκ ἠμπορεῖ μου ὁ λογισμὸς νὰ ἀφηγηθῶ τὴν κόρην, | ἀλλ' ὅσα γράψω πρὸς αὐτήν, πάλιν νὰ μὲ νικήσῃ.

303 See Agapitos (2004b: 44–5 and 2006a: 158–62).

304 The romance survives in five distinct versions (**V**, **N**, **O**, **G**, **H**). On the manuscripts, see Jeffreys and Jeffreys (1971); on the distinction between 'redaction' and 'version' of a text, see Agapitos (2006b: 94–108). Only **O** and **V** have been edited separately (Lambros 1880: 239–88 and Wagner 1874 respectively); however, a critical edition proper is still missing since Kriaras (1955: 215–49) offers a conflated text based on an erratic mixture of all five manuscripts, making any serious close reading of the romance impossible. There exists also a younger redaction in rhymed couplets (**R**) which is transmitted only in chapbooks, of which the oldest surviving was printed in Venice in 1553 (old edition by Legrand 1880: 283–320 from a 1638 chapbook).

305 For a brief history of the French text and its numerous European adaptations, see now Chrysomalli-Henrich (2002: 371–80) with full bibliography; for a recent interpretative approach of the rhymed *I&M*, see Yiavis (2006).

306 Description in Smith (1999: 1–5); it is the manuscript also transmitting *Ach* **N**.

307 I have edited here the text directly from **N**, normalizing spelling and punctuation.

ἐκείνη ἡ πανεξαίρετος ἡ ὡραία ἡ Μαργαρώνα,
καὶ πῶς τὸ κυκλοχρόνισμαν ἐγύρισεν αὐτίκα;
Λοιπόν, νὰ γράψω καὶ νὰ εἰπῶ καὶ νὰ τὸ ἀφηγοῦμαι.
Ἐξενιτεύτην ὁ λαμπρὸς Πέρος ἀνδρειωμένος
ἀπὸ τὰ κάστρη τὰ ὥριζεν ἐκεῖνος ὁ πατήρ του,
καὶ πῶς τὸν ἐκατήφερεν τὸ θράσος τῆς νεότης,
τῆς ξενιτείας τὴν δούλευσιν πῶς ἐξαναγυρίστην,
ὕστερον ἐκατήντησεν (ἐκαντίντισεν **N**) εἰς τὴν ἰδίαν χώραν
καὶ τοῦ πατρός του τὴν αὐθεντία ἐκληρονόμησέν την.
Καὶ τί καὶ πῶς παθάνουσιν οἱ ἄνθρωποι τοῦ κόσμου.

How, then, shall I write from the beginning and how shall I narrate a narrative most beautiful, amorous, magnificent, [5] of how from the beginning that wondrous maiden, that most outstanding and beautiful Margarona suffered, and how the circular motion of years turned again? Well, let me write and tell and narrate! The splendid, valiant Peros exiled himself [10] from the walled towns commanded by his father; how did the insolence of youth bring him low, how did he change the slavery of exile, and then reached his own land and inherited the rule of his father! [15] Oh what and how do humans suffer in this world.

The prologue starts with an echo of the opening peculiar to *Ach* **N**, while the remainder, following the prologue of *V&C*, offers a somewhat awkward synopsis of the plot. The reason for the awkwardness of this synopsis possibly lies in the fact that the French original has no comparable prologue,[308] and that the plot of the Greek version develops along the biographical pattern found in the *Achilles* and *Florios and Platziaflore*.[309] The author of *I&M* **N** decided to include a prologue in the Byzantine tradition, just as he turned the late medieval French prose into Byzantine verse. Thus, the Greek poet says something about Margarona first, then intervenes with an answer to his initial hesitation of beginning his tale (*I&M* **N** 8 refers back to v. 3), and, finally, offers the briefest summary of Imperios's adventures, all of this resulting in a somewhat clumsy though not incomprehensible sequence. That the author had the

308 The prologue of *Maguelonne* **B** (c. 1438) starts with an invocation of Jesus Christ, and then includes a reference to the eleventh-century monastery of Saint Pierre de Melgueil and to the noble parents of the young Pierre (Biedermann 1913: 1–2).

309 The French original does not include an opening section describing the events leading to the birth, growth and upbring of Pierre.

prologue of *V&C* in mind can be inferred from the reference to the 'circular motion of time' (7: κυκλοχρόνισμαν), found as the 'circular course of time' in the older romance (*V&C* 16: κυκλοδρόμημα τοῦ χρόνου), both words being *hapax legomena* in Byzantine literature.[310]

The substitution of the French prose preamble with a Byzantine verse prologue and the addition of a 'biographic' opening in the Greek *I&M* is a clear indication of the strong presence of Byzantine romance tradition when authors dealt with texts coming from other languages. The prologues of the other three romances that were adapted from French, Italian and Ottoman originals respectively have undergone similar reworking. The long 'philological' prologue of Benoît's *Roman de Troie* (see above, pp. 256–7) about his Latin sources and the inadequacy of Homer (issues quite irrelevant to a Greek-speaking audience) has been omitted from the Greek *War of Troy*. The romance begins unannounced with an opening that resembles the respective wonder-tale opening of the main narrative in the Naples *Achilles* (*WoT* 1–2 ≈ *Ach* **N** 27–8).[311] *Florios and Platziaflore*, having omitted the brief preamble (an eight-verse stanza) of the Italian *Il Cantare di Fiorio e Biancifiore*, also starts unannounced with the main story.[312] Exactly the opposite happens in *The Tale of Alexander and Semiramis*, an early fifteenth-century Greek adaptation of a fourteenth-century Ottoman version of the story of Kalaf and Turandot.[313] A brief prologue in the tradition of Byzantine romance with a direct address to a listener is introduced (*A&S* **B** 1–3),[314] where no such structural element is to be found in the Ottoman original (Moennig 2004: 113–15). The address

310 See Kriaras (1968 ff.: IX, 33 and 35). The noun κυκλογύρισμαν found in *L&R* **α** 2539 means 'round contour' of a face, Rhodamne's in this case, and is not related to the passage of time.

311 The text in Papathomopoulos and Jeffreys (1996) conflates without reason the versions transmitted in two different manuscripts (**A** and **X**); on the two openings and the theories of interdependence proposed by various scholars based on faulty editions, see the sobering discussion in Smith (1999: 84–7).

312 *F&P* is transmitted in **V** and **L**; the opening survives only in **V** because one folio, which included a decorative heading and c. 35 verses, has been lost from the beginning of the text in **L**, a case similar to the lost beginning of the London redaction of the *Achilles*. The suggestion of Cupane (1995c: 464 n. 1) that the Greek redactor used a manuscript of the *Cantare* that lacked the opening stanza cannot be substantiated from the codicological evidence, since all but one manuscript of the *Cantare* transmit the opening *ottava*. It is possible that the omission of the preamble from *F&P* reflects the generally restricted presence of the narrator in this romance (Agapitos 2006a: 167–9).

313 On this process of adaptation, see Moennig (2004: 21–34). *A&S* survives in two distinct versions, **B** and **S**, of which the latter seems to be a draft for a prose adaptation; on the two versions and their 'archetypus', see Moennig (2004: 156–74).

314 'Listen again that I might tell you a story about love, what once upon a time the desire of love did to Semiramis, the Queen of the Syrians' (Ἄκουσον πάλιν νὰ σὲ εἰπῶ λόγον περὶ ἀγάπης, | τὸ τί ἐποῖκεν κάποτες ὁ πόθος τῆς ἀγάπης | τῶν Συριανῶν βασίλισσας, Σεμίραμης ἐκείνης).

to a listener is consistent with the 'oral' narrative vocabulary in the rest of version **B**, which was probably prepared for a monastic audience in the seventeenth century (Agapitos 2006a: 165–7). In the process of adaptation, be it the removal or the addition of a prologue, the contract with the audience does not include the notion of make-believe; fiction as a theoretical issue is not addressed.

We have to step outside the boundaries of romance to find some form of statement concerning fictional narrative. In *The Entertaining Tale of the Quadrupeds* (late fourteenth century),[315] one of the two surviving beast tales from Byzantium, its poet offers an excuse for the blatantly fictive character of the story.[316] The prologue and beginning of the tale run as follows (*DiegTetr* 1–16):[317]

> An entertaining tale of quadrupeds, for youngsters, students, and young men to read and to employ on account of its delightfulness; for it has been written to unite learning and pleasure, [5] yet note that these words have meaning, too, and importance. So understand exactly what they mean: when all the nations draw with us false peace, hoping by force of might to lead us into perdition, yet are we saved by just, inviolate oaths. [10] For God shares power out, as Judge of all. So here, my friend, let me set forth this tale.
>
> It was in the year six thousand and eight hundred and seventy and another three more years on the fifteenth of the month September, that all the animals did make assembly: [15] in one place all the clean, domestic beasts, the bloody and loathsome in another plain.

The prologue heavily accentuates the teacher–pupil relation between narrator and recipients by presenting its audience as young people and students, and by insisting that, though entertaining, the tale has a deeper meaning. This

315 The text has been edited by Tsiouni (1972) conflating all five surviving manuscripts; an edition by Manolis Papathomopoulos without critical apparatus and various interventionist corrections has been included in Nicholas and Baloglou (2003).

316 There has been a debate in recent years (see Nicholas and Baloglou 2003: 449–60) as to whether the prologue and the conclusion of the *Quadrupeds* are part of the original composition or later additions. I must admit that I cannot follow the excruciatingly positivist arguments of this debate aiming to superimpose a 'modern' logic and consistency to a medieval text, and this against all manuscript evidence. Therefore, I consider the prologue as belonging to the text.

317 Translation quoted from Nicholas and Baloglou (2003: 161) with some modifications of my own following different manuscript readings on the basis of Tsiouni (1972: 59–60).

meaning is immediately revealed to be an allegory for false peace between other nations and us; 'nations' (7: ἔθνη) probably refers in the Biblical sense to heathens (i.e. Muslims, but maybe also Latins), while 'us' (7: μεθ' ἡμῶν) characterizes the Greek-speaking Orthodox people. Following an authorial intervention about starting his tale, the poet abandons the wonder-tale opening[318] and places his story at a surprisingly exact date (*anno mundi* 15 September 6873 is *anno Domini* 1364), not more than a generation before the time of the poem's actual composition. This 'historical' exactitude is a form of make-believe, though at the same time, it probably underlines the subversively humorous character of the poem. Even so, fiction is not openly doubted or excused.

This happens in the last vernacular text to be discussed here, taken from the short-lived genre of allegorical narrative poetry (Cupane 1993). *The Consolatory Fable about Good and Bad Fortune* (second quarter of fourteenth century)[319] is a short poem narrating how a nameless Stranger seeks out the Castle of Bad Fortune in order to have his fate changed. The poet of the *Consolatory Fable* used to an astonishing extent shorter and longer passages from redaction **α** of *L&R* in order to develop the various themes and images of the allegorical narrative.[320] This is also the case with the poem's prologue (*LogPar* **L** 1+14–21):

> All of you, deeply embittered by Bad Fate [....][321] come, get together today, join me, [15] and I shall tell you about the painful sorrows of Bad Fate narrated to me by another endlessly tormented man. After I shall have narrated to you what he suffered, some of you should thank Good Fate since you have seen her benefactions and are holding her sweetness; [20] however, the others curse Bad Fate on account of your sorrow since you hold her evils and have drunk her bitterness.

Even a cursory comparison with the prologue of *L&R* **α** (see above, pp. 305–6) reveals the strong similarities of the two texts in their staging of an intrafictive

318 *K&C* 25 ('There was once a barbarian king…'), *V&C* 25 ('There was once a mighty emperor…'), *Ach* **N** 27 and *WoT* 1 ('There was once a king of the Hellenes…').

319 The poem survives in two distinct redactions, **L** and **O**, of which the former (edited by Cupane 1995c: 635–91) is used here. On the technical data of **L** (c. 1350–70), see now the summary of research in Cupane (2005: 281–6).

320 See the detailed analysis in Agapitos (2006b: 174–91).

321 *LogPar* **L** 2–13 is a long list of all those saddened by Bad Fate and gladdened by Good Fate.

situation of performance: (i) extensive list of an intended audience (*LogPar* **L** 1–13 ≈ *L&R* **α** 3–7 + 10–5); (ii) invitation to the audience to join the narrator (*LogPar* **L** 14 ≈ *L&R* **α** 8–9 + 16); (iii) a narrator who will tell the story of another person (*LogPar* **L** 15–16 ≈ *L&R* **α** 17–20); (iv) conclusion of the prologue with a reference to the narrative's didactic aspect (*LogPar* **L** 17–21 ≈ *L&R* **α** 21–4). Beyond the verbal similarities, the structural arrangement of the four constituent parts runs absolutely parallel in both prologues. In my opinion, the prologue of the *Consolatory Fable* is not yet another generic romance-like prologue,[322] but the product of a conscious intertextual dialogue conducted exclusively with *L&R*. The issue of fiction is not raised in the alllegorical poem's prologue, nor is it touched upon in the long and highly moralizing epilogue (*LogPar* **L** 717–47). It is, however, raised in a metrical colophon, found only in the Leipzig redaction. The colophon is not an invention of **L**, but existed already in the now lost exemplar (**λ**) from which **L** copied his text. Despite some serious textual problems, the main point of the colophon is quite clear (*LogPar* **L** 748–56):[323]

> This is a fable-like writing and a story about an unknown amorous yearning, a plot about a hidden love, as if by some strange-mannered person. [750] The author is peculiar, the thing is utterly bizzare; he narrates by means of a figment, the whole fable is strange. I have copied, but I have not subscribed to the fable as outstanding; for it is indeed lacking in desire, it is without a beautiful girl, the whole fable is about love, though unconquered by love. [755] So then, it is completed, the story has been copied out, and everyone who finds this writing, let him read it!

Scribe **λ**, as an engaged reader of the *Consolatory Fable*, expresses his disappointment about the allegorical poem. He consistently points out that the 'story' (748, 755: λόγος) is a 'fable-like writing' (748: μυθογραφή) and a 'fable' (751, 752, 754: μῦθος). Moreover, he suggests that the 'author' (750: ὁ συγγραφεύς) 'narrates by means of a figment' (751: λογοκινεῖ τῷ πλάσματι). The reason for the disappointment lies in the scribe's thwarted expectations about the poem's generic category, since its creator consistently used the typology of the

322 So Cupane (1995a: 165–6 and 1995c: 647 n. 3).

323 This important piece of evidence for reader response to and primary reception of romantic and allegorical narrative has been discussed, with a partly different understanding of the text's wording, by Cupane (1995c: 691 nn. 85–6; 2005: 290–3) and Agapitos (2004b: 18–20; 2006b: 165–7).

'tale of love' but did not include an actual love story. The poem, as **λ** candidly comments, is 'without a beautiful girl' (753: δίχως φουδούλαν), the characteristic *par excellence* of romantic narrative. It is the emphasis on 'figment' and 'fable' that interests us here. By using the conventional terms of school rhetoric for fiction (see above, pp. 277–8 and 279–80), the educated scribe places the allegorical poem on the side of 'falsehood' and, thus, decides to break his contract of make-believe with the author, even if he does not break off the copying of the manuscript. This sense of 'falsehood' is described by **λ** with a variety of words expressing negative images of alterity and absence: 'unknown' (748: ἀνεγνώριστος), 'hidden' (749: κρυφή), 'strange-mannered' (749: ξενότροπος), 'peculiar' (750: ἀλλότριος), 'bizzare' (750: ξενακουστός), 'strange' (751: ξένος), 'lacking' (753: ἀνεπιτήδευτος), 'unconquered by love' (754: ἀνερωτόληπτος). In the eyes of **λ**, alterity and absence define the anonymous poet's failed attempt at harmoniously correlating the non-erotic subject of his allegorical poem with the erotic discourse of romance. By using vocabulary pertaining specifically to *L&R* (Agapitos 2004b: 19), the scribe clearly signalled which 'tale of love' formed in his opinion the intertext of the *Consolatory Fable*.

It is almost an irony that the only explicit non-metaphorical reference to fiction in Byzantine vernacular literature comes from a reader of an allegorical poem whose author had admiringly read the most artful among the Palaiologan romances and whose literary experiment was condemned by the reader on the basis of that very romance. The intertextual dialogue between the *Consolatory Fable* and *Livistros and Rhodamne* leads us to look at intertextuality as a 'hidden' authorial contract with the audience in the Komnenian novels of the twelfth century. I have already discussed (see above, pp. 279–84) how Theodore Prodromos presents fictionality in *Rhodanthe and Dosikles* as part of his rhetorical and philological virtuosity that is displayed to and appreciated by his recipients. The learned discourse employed by all Komnenian novelists and their overt use of specific hypotexts was based on a common code of intertextual communication with their respective audience.[324] It is this semiotic code that fully captures (re-)creative *mimesis* ('imitation') and rhetorical *epideixis* ('display') as conducted in the aristocratic literary salons of the capital.[325]

One such quite extravagant example is the 'use' of *Charikleia* by Theodore

324 For such reader-response oriented approaches, see Agapitos (1998b), Nilsson (2001), Burton (2003), Jouanno (2005), Roilos (2005), as well as the collection of essays in Agapitos and Reinsch (2000).

325 On *mimesis* and *epideixis* in reading, writing and reciting the novels, see Agapitos (2006a: 135–52).

Prodromos and Niketas Eugeneianos. Prodromos has cut up, rearranged, shortened, lengthened and, ultimately, inverted the famous beginning of Heliodorus (*Aethiopica* 1.1–4) in the opening of his novel (*R&D* 1.1–70), restructuring it as a series of brief rhetorical *epeisodia*. This technique had already been described by Hermogenes when, in the case of reworking the plot of a given fable, he advised: 'It is sometimes necessary to expand fables and sometimes to contract them' (*Prog.* 1.13).[326] Eugeneianos went one step further in the opening of his novel (*D&C* 1.1–119) and proceeded to execute a similar textual operation on the beginning of Prodromos's novel. Thus, a new inversion took place in which, moreover, a passage from Longus's *Daphnis and Chloe* and Makrembolites's *Hysmine and Hysminias* respectively were incorporated, lending a lyrical and introvert tone to Eugeneianos's text as opposed to Prodromos's dramatic and extrovert narrative.[327] Such a display of rhetorical artistry could not have reached its full effect during a public recitation if the listeners were not familiar with the literary intertexts involved.

In the case of Prodromos this was explicitly expressed in a dedicatory poem of his novel to his patron. This poem, along with two shorter epigrams (one declaring Prodromos as author of the novel and one offering a brief summary of the plot), framed a miniature depicting the protagonist couple of his narrative; the textual and visual composition was probably placed on the opening left-hand page of the manuscript that the author presented to his patron, expecting an appropriate reward. The original manuscript perished, but the three poems have survived.[328] The patron in question was an anonymous *kaisar* ('caesar'), the highest title of the imperial court hierarchy given exclusively to the dignitary second in rank to the emperor. Elizabeth Jeffreys (2000) has shown that this *kaisar* was Nikephoros Bryennios (†1138), author of the unfinished *Historical Material*, recipient of a number of Prodromos's occasional works and husband of the princess Anna Komnene, herself an attested patroness of Theodore. The poem, written in high-level 'Homeric' hexameters, reads as follows (Agapitos 2000b: 175):

> My very own Caesar – for I, indeed, appropriate common good –, Caesar invincible, excellent, brave, Caesar to all of us, Caesar you, great glory to

326 χρὴ δὲ αὐτοὺς (sc. μύθους) ποτὲ μὲν ἐκτείνειν, ποτὲ δὲ συστέλλειν (Rabe 1913: 2.11–12).
327 For a detailed analysis of these passages, see Agapitos (1998b: 148–53).
328 See Agapitos (2000b) for a reconstruction of the dedication page and an edition of the three epigrams, previously thought to be one continuous poem.

> mortals, happy Caesar, Caesar mild in thought, wise Caesar, Caesar most noble, [5] your servant Theodoros, son of that Prodromos, having taken hold in his hands these here variegated colours has painted the image of Dosikles and Rhodanthe and begs of you, once you have looked at it, to judge it yourself. Do not, however, juxtapose my most recent work [10] to the beautifully painted panels and pleasant to see first models of Praxiteles, great in art, and also of Apelles, or I will have suffered in vain the demands of toil. Compare, then, my art to recent painters and quickly it will appear as not much worse than theirs.

Prodromos, exploiting the *topos* of the interrelation between writing and painting (see above, pp. 279–81) and through an inversion of Longus's preface, presents himself as a painter who submits his panel of variegated colours to his 'wise' patron for aesthetic appreciation. Interestingly enough, Prodromos asks of the caesar not to compare him to two famous artists of antiquity, the sculptor Praxiteles and the painter Apelles, but to (unnamed) recent painters of his own time. Theodore has here presented Bryennios with the interpretative key to reading his fictional narrative: Prodromos's 'very recent work' (τἀμὰ νεώτατα) is not to be compared to Heliodorus and Tatius as the 'first-born' novels (πρωτογενέθλοις), but to Eumathios Makrembolites who as author/ painter re-introduced the image of writing as painting in the chronologically first of the four Komnenian novels. While Makrembolites had sided with Tatius and his piquant novel, Prodromos, attuned to the more austere tastes of Nikephoros and Anna, sided with the dignified grandeur of Heliodorus.[329] This having been insinuated through the peritexts on the left-hand page of the dedication copy, the text itself of *Rhodanthe and Dosikles* opens on the right-hand page with the intertextual inversion of Heliodorus just mentioned above. For a patron, who in his own work quoted the very opening of the *Aethiopica* (*Historical Material* 1.16; Gautier 1975: 113.19–20), Prodromos's self-debasing (*qua* self-extolling) dedication and the beginning of his novel must have been a sufficient signal for the establishment of the necessary authorial contract and the acceptance of a work of fiction to be enjoyed at the highest level of learned craftsmanship.

A different intertextual strategy is used by Eugeneianos in an amusing passage from his *Drosilla and Charikles*. Having arrived at a village along the

329 For what has been presented here summarily, see the detailed analysis in Agapitos (2000b: 180–4) and Agapitos (2004a: 58–60).

coast from Palestine to Lebanon, Drosilla is informed in a dream that her lover Charikles is staying at the inn of a certain Xenokrates. Upon arriving there together with an old woman called Barylis, she finds Kallidemos, the young son of the innkeeper, who immediately falls in love with her. After Drosilla ironically rebukes him on his village background and feigns that she has a headache (*R&D* 6.292–301), Kallidemos retaliates by embarking on the lengthiest monologue of all ancient Greek and Byzantine novels: in over three hundred lines, only briefly interrupted by a sly remark of Barylis (6.559–64), the young villager tries to woo the heroine and convince her to marry him (6.332–643).[330] The monologue is structured in three parts, of which the first and third present the speaker's passionate *declaration d'amour* couched as a diatribe on the wild god's power (6.332–81) and the painful despair suffered by unreciprocated love (6.565–643). In the long second part (6.382–558), the speaker presents four *exempla* of 'persons of long ago who were united by love into one soul' (6.386–7). These are: (i) Arsake and Achaimenes and their unrequited passion for Theagenes and Charikleia respectively, taken from Heliodorus (6.386–402); (ii) Daphnis and Chloe's 'technically' protracted love affair from Longus (6.440–51); (iii) Hero and Leander's tragic love story from Musaeus's poem (6.472–91); (iv) the unrequited love of the Cyclops for the nymph Galatea and its sad end from Theocritus's *Idyll* 11 (6.503–39). Each *exemplum* is followed by the speaker's explicative commentary or amorous protestations. The four paradigms are introduced as a whole by the following remark (6.382–5):

> Oh maiden with the pearly-bright chest and the naturally golden-coloured locks sitting now next to me! Listen, then, and learn and comprehend the size of the waves, the torrents, the storms of my love.[331]

The rustic Kallidemos becomes the teacher of urbane Drosilla, while the horizon of expectations of the primary recipients is humorously inverted. Once again, this inversion can function only if the audience knows the four fictional texts from which the *exempla amatoria* have been culled, two of which (Heliodorus and Longus) are active hypotexts of Eugeneianos's novel. The insertion

330 The whole episode has been intelligently analyzed as to its intertexts by Burton (2003: 255–62).

331 Ἄκουε λοιπὸν καὶ διδάσκου καὶ σύνες, | ἡ νῦν παρ' ἡμῶν μαργαρόστερνος κόρη, | φύσει λαχοῦσα χρυσοβόστρυχον κόμην, | τὸ κῦμα, τὸν κλύδωνα, τὴν ζάλην ὅσην. I have rendered the rhetorically complex passage in a free manner; for a more literal translation, see Burton (2004: 127).

of characters from the ancient novels and other fictive works into a Byzantine fictional narrative is not only unique in medieval Greek literature, it is also the most explicit reference to the novelistic tradition that the Komnenian authors wished to evoke. Eugeneianos has, in this way, explicitly established an authorial contract with his audience that is based on the mutual acceptance of the ancient novels as a valid intertextual signifier of fictionality.

In my last example from the Komnenian novels, I would like to look at the end of Makrembolites's *Hysmine and Hysminias*. Ingela Nilsson (2001) has amply shown how Makrembolites used Tatius as the chief hypotext for his novel. In *Leukippe*, however, the initial opening narrative situation in Phoenician Sidon, where the authorial *persona* of Tatius meets the hero Kleitophon who, in his turn, becomes the intradiegetic and homodiegetic ego-narrator of the novel, does not reappear at the end of the novel. The story ends and the readers are left with the probably intended impression that author and hero have merged into one person. Makrembolites has shifted the narrative frame of his novel in such a manner that the hero Hysminias is from the very beginning the only intradiegetic and homodiegetic ego-narrator. He tells his story to a listener – he is called Charidoux – who by the end of Book 1 has merged with the audience of the novel. At the end of *H&H*, the audience is presented with an extended example of authorial closure that constitutes a singular case among Greek and Byzantine novels.[332] Following the wedding of the protagonist couple, Hysminias acknowledges that neither epic, poetry or rhetoric can actually describe the happy event; he prays to the gods and asks that 'no depth of forgetfulnes should obliterate this our story, no time eternal, no withering old age, no cup of oblivion mixed in Hades' (*H&H* 11.20.2).[333] This is an amplified variant of a *topos* recurring throughout Byzantine historiography (one need only read through the prefaces of Procopius, Theophanes Continuatus, John Skylitzes, Michael Attaleiates, Nikephoros Bryennios, Anna Komnene, and Niketas Choniates), but it is not a *topos* employed in erotic novels, that is, fictional narratives. The hero, at the very end of the story, expresses the wish that his fictive tale should be granted the same fate as historical narratives, namely the survival from oblivion because of its inherent didactic value. Hysminias asks of the gods to bestow on him and his wife some form of immor-

332 The passage has been discussed by Nilsson (2001: 52–3 and 74–8); Agapitos (2006a: 139–42).

333 μὴ βυθὸς ἀμνηστίας κατεπικλύσῃ ταῦτα τὰ καθ' ἡμᾶς, μὴ χρόνος μακρός, μὴ ῥυτίς, μὴ λήθης κρατὴρ ἐν Ἅιδου κιρνώμενος.

tality in the realm of mythical metamorphoses. The novel finishes as follows (*H&H* 11.22.4–23.3):

> So, if Zeus will not place our story among the stars, if Poseidon will not depict it on the waves, if Earth will not implant it in plants and flowers, let our story be set forth in evergreen trees and diamond stones by means of Hermes's pen and ink, and a tongue breathing the fire of rhetoric; and let someone from a later generation (καί τις τῶν ὀψιγόνων) eloquently expound this story and, as if on an immortal votive slab, forge through his words a golden statue.
>
> On the one hand, those among humans who are in love will accept our story on account of its many amorous charms; those who are virginal and modest will delight in our chastity; those who are compassionate will pity our misfortunes, and so memory of us will be immortal. On the other hand, we shall grace this writing and decorate the whole book both with amorous charms, as well as with everything else that adorns books and beautifies discourse; and the name of the book shall be *The Spectacular Love Story of Hysmine and Hysminias* (Τὸ καθ' Ὑσμίνην καὶ Ὑσμινίαν δρᾶμα).

At this final point, Hysminias emphasizes the double meaning of *graphe* as painting and writing (exactly the issue hinted at by Prodromos in his dedicatory epigram), and suggests that the love story will be written/painted by the pen and ink of Hermes and in a fiery rhetorical style. Even more so, he suggests that some person of a later age (*opsigonos*) will use this story to prepare through the power of words a golden statue that will function as an immortal votive slab. This *opsigonos*, obviously, can be no other than the author himself, who has in this manner inscribed his own person in the story's transmission. Thus, at the moment of closure, it is the story that has undergone a metamorphosis from the narrator's oral tale to the author's literary work of art in the form of a book. The narrator, now as the actual *persona* of the author, lists (by referring to Longus's preface) the intended audience of the novel: lovers, chaste virgins, people with compassionate hearts. He, then, suggests that the hero and the heroine will adorn the book with their charms and, finally, discloses in an authorial *sphragis* ('seal') the title of the work. This seal also validates the authorial contract set before the audience as the story has reached its end and they hold the finished product in their hands. The 'fictional' narrative of an amorous couple in a Hellenic wonder-tale land has become the 'true' book of

Makrembolites's erotic *drama* to be performed again and again by readers for times to come. Fiction is presented as something valuable and beautiful to be cherished by intelligent recipients. Furthermore, the text, through this device of shifting from the narrator's to the author's voice, has constructed its implied readers by explicitly incorporating them in the epilogue. It is therefore quite interesting to note that in *The Tale of Livistros and Rhodamne*, the only other Byzantine first-perspective romance, the same device is used, although, as it has been shown above (pp. 307–8), it has led to an even more open narrative closure. In other words, fictionality in Rhomaian lands was fully accepted and was not in need of defence. The type of authorial contracts of make-believe set in front of the recipients of *Hysmine and Hysminias* in the twelfth century and of *Livistros and Rhodamne* in the thirteenth century clearly mark the difference to the approach of the same issue in the case of romance in Frankish and Persian lands.

CONCLUDING THOUGHTS

The material drawn upon for the present paper has indeed been rich and highly varied, and, so, any attempt at offering some concluding thoughts will by necessity be more of a sketchy drawing than a finished painting. In this sense, I very consciously share the concern expressed by Marie de France (fl. 1170–90) when she states that 'the poet whose subject matter is the best, feels sorrow if his craft should fail the test' (*Guigemar* 1–2).[334]

The economic, social and cultural realities of the Latin West and the Byzantine East differ substantially in the eleventh and twelfth centuries, although, at the same time, we can discern specific cultural similarities that result from certain common ideological characteristics: for example, a new notion of military 'kingship'. However, such cultural similarities are of a momentary duration and will display only external traits of osmosis (such as in the second half of the twelfth century under Emperor Manuel Komnenos) should the two cultures not merge in some politically and administratively stable form. In other words, acculturation between Latins and Greeks occurred only in areas where the Latins took over the administration of formerly Byzantine territory. This can be clearly seen in Frankish Morea and Frankish Cyprus with their production of Franco-Byzantine art and of 'French' chronicles in the Greek

334 'Ki de bone matire traite, | mult li peise, se bien n'est faite' (Harf-Lancner 1990: 26).

language (such as the anonymous verse *Chronicle of the Morea* and Leontios Machairas's prose *Recital concerning the Sweet Land of Cyprus*), or in Venetian dominated Crete with its production of 'Italian' burlesque poetry in Greek (such as Stephanos Sachlikes's bawdy *Parliament of Whores*).

If examined dispassionately and with due consideration of the available evidence, the only time where some form of cultural osmosis between Greeks and Latins could take place under Byzantine administration was the Laskarid empire of Nicaea after its stabilization and the first six decades of Palaiologan government in Constantinople, in other words the hundred years between 1220 and 1320. The dynamic policy of Emperor John Batatzes, tangibly resulting in economic growth, diplomatic success and military expansion, allowed for a more differentiated and more confident attitude of the Byzantines towards the Latins, while the recapture of Constantinople and the stabilization of a relatively powerful state further strengthened their confidence. This confident attitude gave rise to a series of novel literary products connected to court life at Nicaea, such as Nicolas Eirenikos's marriage poem, Prince Theodore Laskaris's political and satirical orations, Nikephoros Blemmydes's mirror of princes, and George Akropolites's funerary poems and orations. It is here that *Livistros and Rhodamne* belongs, whose author had a very good knowledge of the Komnenian novels and an obvious familiarity with French romance tradition. The diplomatic relations of the Nicaean court with the Hohenstaufen and Angevin courts in southern Italy, the marriage of John III to Constanza, as well as the presence of numerous Latin mercenaries in the service of the Laskarid emperors[335] created the historically most tangible frame for a possible acquaintance of Byzantine literati with French amorous-chivalric stories as told by professional jongleurs accompanying the aristocrats and the warriors visiting or even staying in Nicaea and Nymphaion. Towards the end of the thirteenth century, the political confidence, the new economic conditions and the fully developed philological interests of Byzantine scholars gave the impulse for the translation of a number of Latin authors into Greek (from Ovid and Cicero to Augustine, Boethius and Thomas Aquinas) for various theoretical and practical purposes, such as teaching Latin at school or conducting theological disputes with Latin churchmen.

Beyond this historical context, the absence of clearly signalled linguistic distinctions in Byzantium should be always kept in mind. A poet like Theo-

335 On these, see Angold (1975: 81–2, 152, 185–6).

dore Prodromos, who wrote in 'learned' and 'vernacular' Greek, did not perceive these two (modern, at any rate) categories as separate languages, nor were there ever in Byzantium terms devised to describe, as in the case of *la lettre* (Latin) and *romans* (French), a distinction of languages, irrespective of how fluid that distinction might have been in medieval France or Italy. Moreover, in France, Germany and England the vernaculars were, initially at least, defined in respect to the problems posed by translating from Latin and developing an appropriate style. Thus, Theodore Prodromos cannot be compared to a poet like the Londoner John Gower (1330–1408), who composed lengthy and highly acclaimed poems in Latin, French and English. One should also point to the difference in the system of education between the Latin West and the Byzantine East. In the case of Byzantium, in particular, the presence of progymnasmatic fiction in Roman Imperial handbooks of rhetoric, the presence of novelistic models (constructed and read as a 'genre' of fiction since the ninth century), and the use of manuscripts joining together ancient Greek and Komnenian novels since the thirteenth century, created a basis for the acceptance of fiction quite different from the ambivalent attitude towards fictional narrative in the West.

In this sense, the differences in the approach to and composition of historiography are quite indicative. However, the similarities between Manasses's *Annalistic Compendium*, Wace's *Tale of Brut* and Firdowsi's *Book of Kings* as to the literary realization of their historiographical projects are an indication of what I referred to as common ideological characteristics. Yet, exactly these ideological and poetic similarities between the *Synopsis*, the *Brut* and the *Shahnameh* also reveal the differences in the social context of Angevin England, Komnenian Byzantium and Samanid-Ghaznavid Persia. The Constantinian pause, wherein the 'Roman' empire's official Christianization had been situated by Manasses, was not developed as the spatio-temporal *locus* for the anchoring of fiction in Byzantium's beaurocratic-monarchic society, whereas the Arthurian pause, into which the 'British' kingdom's great peace had been explicitly inserted by Wace, and the Bahramian pause, into which Firdowsi had situated the 'Iranian' kingdom's eternal peace, were fully exploited for the creation of a non-antiquarian type of fiction in Anglo-Norman feudal-hegemonic and Persian-Turkic tribal-hegemonic societies respectively. It is only in the area of epic narrative that we find a common ground concerning the excuse of fiction between the medieval West, Byzantium and the Arab East. While 'primary written epics' like the Oxford *Roland*, the *Cid* and the

Dhât al-Himma do not deal with fictionality, 'secondary written epics', like the Grottaferrata *Digenis*, Konrad's *Rolandslied* and the *Umar al-Numân* negotiate fiction with their respective audiences because they have to excuse the obvious literarization of their historical subject matter.

In Byzantium, fiction was not an issue theoretically problematized. The Komnenian novels incorporate the notion of fictionality as 'theatrical deceit' in a Hellenic setting, an intertextual device that fully presupposed the learned audience's fictive stance. The occidentalist, historicist, antiquarian or utopian settings in Palaiologan romance accentuate the fictionality of these texts but do not question it nor do they seek to authorize it in the overt and complex manner found in French and German romance of the twelfth and thirteenth centuries.

This absence of authorization becomes apparent when examining the contracts with the audience. In contrast to Chrétien or Gottfried, the notion of make-believe does not surface in the comments of Byzantine poets as authorial/narratorial *personae* of their works. In only two cases do we find statements about 'lies' and 'figments'. The poet of *Velthandros and Chrysantza* discreetly excuses the fictionality of his 'historical' setting, while the learned scribe λ as reader of the *Consolatory Fable* rejects the allegorical poem as a figment because it does not conform to the genre of love romance. On the contrary, the epilogues of Makrembolites's *Spectacular Love Story of Hysmine and Hysminias* and of the anonymous *Tale of Livistros and Rhodamne* show that fictional narrative was placed in front of the audience to be pleasurably admired or even creatively adapted. We can detect the different character of romance reception in late Byzantium from the late Middle Ages in the textual history of *H&H* and *L&R*. The manuscript transmission of these two first-person-perspective narratives, the most consciously artful creations of all of Byzantine fiction, is the largest in quantity and longest in duration, reaching well into the sixteenth century and comparable only to the manuscript transmission of Nizami's erotic-heroic tales. No French or German verse romance ever sustained such a length of textual history, despite the quantity of manuscript production close to the age of actual composition,[336] exactly because by the middle of the thirteenth century prose had essentially substituted verse as the chief medium of romance narrative in a changing social context where

336 See Busby, Nixon, Stones and Walters (1994) on Chrétien; Lachmann, Knecht and Schirok (2003: xxxi–lvii) and Bumke (2004: 249–55) on Wolfram's *Parzival*; Ranke and Krohn (1993: III, 321–6) on Gottfried.

knightly values were differently evaluated and practised.[337] This difference in manuscript transmission between Byzantium and the West attests, despite of or even because of the far smaller quantity of romance production in Rhomaian and Persian lands, to another, more relaxed and less involved, attitude towards fictionality in the 'periphery' of European culture before the advent of the Renaissance.

References

TEXTS

[*Ach*] *The Tale of Achilles* (or *Achilleid*).
Naples redaction (**N**): *Smith (1999), pp. 13–74; Cupane (1995c), pp. 324–442, with Italian translation.
Oxford redaction (**O**): Smith (1990); *Smith (1999), pp. 155–76, without critical apparatus.
London redaction (**L**): Hesseling (1919), pp. 93–125.

[*A&K*] Constantine Manasses, *The Love Story of Aristandros and Kallithea.*
Mazal (1967); *Conca (1994), pp. 689–777, with Italian translation.

[*A&S*] *Alexander and Semiramis*, Barlaam Monastery version (**B**).
*Moennig (2004), with German translation.

[*Alexander*] Ilyas ibn-Yusuf Nizami, *The Book of Alexander.*
*Bürgel (1991), only German translation.

[*Belis*] *The Tale of Belisarios*, redaction 'chi' (χ).
*Bakker and van Gemert (1988).

[*Brut*] Master Wace, *The Tale of Brut.*
*Weiss (2002), with English translation.

[*Cid*] *The Poem of the Cid.*
*Hamilton, Perry and Michael (1984), with English translation.

[*Cligès*] Chrétien de Troyes, *Cligès.*
*Méla, Collet and Gérard-Zai (1994), ed. Charles Méla, with French translation; Poirion (1994), pp. 170–336, ed. Philippe Walter, with French translation; *Kibler and Carroll (1991), pp. 123–205, only English translation.

[*D&C*] Niketas Eugeneianos, *The Love Story of Drosilla and Charikles.*

337 See the succinct discussion by Poirion (1978) and the broader overview by Lacy (2000) with recent bibliography.

Conca (1990); *Conca (1994), pp. 305–497, with Italian translation; Burton (2004), English translation with text of Conca (1994).

[*DiegTetr*] *The Entertaining Tale of the Quadrupeds.*
Tsiouni (1972); *Nicholas and Baloglou (2003), pp. 159–219, with English translation.

[*DigAkr*] *Basileios Digenis Akritis.*
Grottaferrata redaction (**G**): Trapp (1971); *Jeffreys (1998), pp. 1–235, with English translation; Odorico (1995), with Italian translation.
Escorial redaction (**E**): Trapp (1971); Alexiou (1985); *Jeffreys (1998), pp. 237–375, with English translation; Odorico (2002), pp. 71–168, only French translation.

[*Enéas*] *Romance of Enéas*, Paris I version (**D**).
*Petit (1997), with French translation.

[*EneasRom*] Heinrich von Veldeke, *The Romance of Eneas.*
*Ettmüller and Kartschoke (1997), with German translation.

[*Erec*] Chrétien de Troyes, *The Tale of Erec* (or *Erec and Enide*).
*Fritz (1992), with French translation; Poirion (1994), pp. 1–169, ed. Peter F. Dembowski, with French translation; *Kibler and Carroll (1991), pp. 37–122.

[*F&B*] *The Tale of Floire and Blancheflor.*
Leclanche (1980).

[*F&P*] *The Outstanding Tale of Florios and Platziaflore*, London redaction (**L**).
Hesseling (1917); *Cupane (1995c), pp. 464–565, with Italian translation.

[*HaftPayk*] Ilyas ibn-Yusuf Nizami, *The Seven Images.*
*Bürgel (1997), only German translation; Meisami (1995), only English translation.

[*H&H*] Eumathios Makrembolites, *The Spectacular Love Story of Hysmine and Hysminias.*
Marcovich (2001); *Conca (1994), pp. 499–687, with Italian translation.

[*Heinrich*] Hartmann von Aue, *Poor Heinrich.*
de Boor (1967), with German translation.

[*al-Himma*] *The Tale of the Holy Warriors* (or *The Tale of the Chieftainness Dhât al-Himma*).
Lyons (1995), vol. III, pp. 301–504 (extensive English summary).

[*I&M*] *The Outstanding Tale of the Admirable Imperios and the Maiden Margarona.*
Naples version (**N**): unedited.
Vienna version (**V**): Wagner (1874).
'Mixed' edition of all manuscripts: Kriaras (1955), pp. 215–49.

[*Iwein*] Hartmann von Aue, *Iwein.*
*Benecke, Lachmann, Wolff and Cramer (2001), with German translation.

[*Lais*] Marie de France, *Lais.*
*Harf-Lancner (1990), with French translation.

[*K&C*] *The Erotic Tale of Kallimachos and Chrysorrhoe.*
Kriaras (1955), pp. 29–83; Pichard (1956), with French translation; *Cupane (1995c), pp. 58–213, with Italian translation; *Betts (1995), pp. 37–90, only English translation.

[*K&Sh*] Ilyas ibn-Yusuf Nizami, *The Tale of Prince Khosrow and the Lady Shirin.*
*Bürgel (1980), only German translation.

[*Lancelot*] Chrétien de Troyes, *The Knight of the Cart* (or *Lancelot*).
*Méla (1992); Poirion (1994), pp. 505–682, ed. Daniel Poirion, with French translation; *Kibler and Carroll (1991), pp. 207–94, only English translation.

[*L&R*] *The Tale of Livistros and Rhodamne.*
Redaction 'alpha' (**α**): *Agapitos (2006b); Betts (1995), pp. 95–192, only English translation.
Escorial redaction (**E**): Lambert (1935).
Vatican redaction (**V**): Lendari (2007).

[*LogPar*] *A Consolatory Fable about Good and Bad Fortune.*
Leipzig redaction (**L**): *Cupane (1995c), pp. 635–91, with Italian translation.

[*al-Numân*] *The Tale of Umar al-Numân* from *Thousand and One Nights.*

[*Partonopeu*] *The Romance of Partonopeu de Blois.*
Arsenal redaction (**A**): *Collet and Joris (2005), with French translation; includes also parallel edition of the romance's *Continuation* in the Bern and Tours redaction.
Bern and Tours redaction (**BT**); Gildea (1967–70).

[*Parzival*] Wolfram von Eschenbach, *Parzival.*

*Lachmann, Knecht and Schirok (2003), with German translation; *Hatto (1980), only English translation.

[*Perceval*] Chrétien de Troyes, *The Tale of the Graal* (or *Perceval*).
*Méla (1990), with French translation; Poirion (1994), pp. 683–911, ed. Daniel Poirion, with French translation; *Kibler and Carroll (1991), pp. 381–494, only English translation.

[*Ptoch*] *The Poems of Poor Prodromos* (or *Ptochoprodromika*).
Eideneier (1991), with German translation.

[*R&D*] Theodore Prodromos, *The Love Story of Rhodanthe and Dosikles.*
Marcovich (1992); *Conca (1994), pp. 63–303, with Italian translation.

[*Roland*] *The Song of Roland*, Oxford redaction (**O**).
Short (1990), with French translation; *Steinsieck and Kaiser (1999), with German translation.

[*RolLied*] Pfaffe Konrad, *The Song of Roland.*
*Kartschoke (1996), with German translation.

[*RomTrist*] Thomas d'Angleterre, *Romance of Tristan.*
*Lacroix and Walter (1995), with French translation.

[*Shahnameh*] Abulqasim Firdowsi, *The Book of Kings.*
*Davis (2006), English prose translation; Mohl (1838–78), with French translation; Davis (1992), English verse translation of the Seyavash episode.

[*SynChron*] Constantine Manasses, *An Annalistic Compendium.*
*Lampsidis (1996).

[*Thèbes*] *Romance of Thebes*, London version (**S**).
*Mora-Lebrun (1995), with French translation.

[*Tristan*] Gottfried von Straßburg, *Tristan.*
*Ranke and Krohn (1993), with German translation; *Hatto (2004), only English translation.

[*ToT*] *The Tale of Troy* (or *Byzantine Iliad*).
*Nørgaard and Smith (1977); Lavagnini (1988), only Italian translation.

[*Troie*] Benoît de Saint-Maure, *Roman de Troie*, Milan version (**M^2**).
*Baumgartner and Vielliard (1998), abridged edition with French translation.

[*V&A*] Abulqasim Unsuri, *Vamiq and Adhra* ('The Lover and the Virgin').

Hägg and Utas (2003), edition of Greek and Persian texts with English translations.

[*V&C*] *The Outstanding Story of Velthandros the Rhomaian* (or *Velthandros and Chrysantza*).
Kriaras (1955), pp. 101–30; *Cupane (1995c), pp. 227–305, with Italian translation; Egea (1998), with Spanish translation; *Betts (1995), pp. 5–32, only English translation.

[*V&G*] Ayyuqi, *Varqeh and his Cousin Gulshah.*
Lavizzari (1992), only German translation.

[*V&R*] Fakhruddin Gurgani, *The Tale of Queen Vis and Prince Ramin.*
Morrison (1972), English translation; Massé (1959), French translation; Davis (2008), English verse translation.

[*Will*] Wolfram von Eschenbach, *Willehalm.*
*Schröder and Kartschoke (2003), with German translation.

[*WoT*] *The War of Troy.*
*Papathomopoulos and Jeffreys (1996).

[*Yvain*] Chrétien de Troyes, *The Knight with the Lion* (or *Yvain*).
*Hult (1994), with French translation; Poirion (1994), pp. 337–503, ed. Karl D. Uitti, with French translation by Philippe Walter; *Kibler and Carroll (1991), pp. 295–380, only English translation.

STUDIES

Agapitos, Panagiotis A. (1990) 'The Erotic Bath in the Byzantine Vernacular Romance *Kallimachos and Chrysorrhoe*', *Classica et Mediaevalia* 41: 257–73.

Agapitos, Panagiotis A. (1991) *Narrative Structure in the Byzantine Vernacular Romances: A Textual and Literary Study of Kallimachos, Belthandros and Libistros* (Miscellanea Byzantina Monacensia, 34), Munich: Institut für Byzantinistik und Neogriechische Philologie.

Agapitos, Panagiotis A. (1992) 'Byzantine Literature and Greek Philologists in the Nineteenth Century', *Classica et Mediaevalia* 43: 231–60.

Agapitos, Panagiotis A. (1993) ''Η χρονολογικὴ ἀκολουθία τῶν μυθιστορημάτων *Καλλίμαχος, Βέλθανδρος* καὶ *Λίβιστρος*', in Nikolaos M. Panagiotakes (ed.), *Origini della letteratura neograeca. Atti del secondo congresso internazionale 'Neograeca Medii Aevi'* (Biblioteca dell'Istituto Ellenico di Studi Bizantini e Postbizantini di Venezia, 15), Venice: Istituto Ellenico di Studi Bizantini e Postbizantini di Venezia, vol. II, pp. 97–134.

Agapitos, Panagiotis A. (1998a) 'Teachers, Pupils and Imperial Power in Eleventh-Century Byzantium', in Niall Livingstone and Yun Lee Too (eds.), *Pedagogy and Power: Rhetorics of Ancient Learning* (Ideas in Context, 47), Cambridge: Cambridge University Press, pp. 170–91.

Agapitos, Panagiotis A. (1998b) 'Narrative, Rhetoric, and "Drama" Rediscovered: Scholars and Poets in Byzantium Interpret Heliodorus', in Richard Hunter (ed.), *Studies in Heliodorus* (Cambridge Philological Society. Supplementary Volume, 21), Cambridge: Cambridge Philological Society, pp. 125–56.

Agapitos, Panagiotis A. (1999) 'Dreams and the Spatial Aesthetics of Narrative Presentation in *Livistros and Rhodamne*', *Dumbarton Oaks Papers* 53: 111–47.

Agapitos, Panagiotis A. (2000a) 'Der Roman der Komnenenzeit: Stand der Forschung und weitere Perspektiven', in Panagiotis A. Agapitos and Diether Roderich Reinsch (eds.), *Der Roman im Byzanz der Komnenenzeit. Ein internazionales Symposium* (Meletemata, 8), Frankfurt a.M: Beerenverlag, pp. 1–18.

Agapitos, Panagiotis A. (2000b) 'Poets and Painters: Theodoros Prodromos' Dedicatory Verses of His Novel to an Anonymous Caesar', *Jahrbuch der Österreichischen Byzantinistik* 50: 173–85.

Agapitos, Panagiotis A. (2002) 'Ἡ θέση τῆς αἰσθητικῆς ἀποτίμησης σὲ μιὰ "νέα" ἱστορία τῆς βυζαντινῆς λογοτεχνίας', in Paolo Odorico and Panagiotis A. Agapitos (eds.), *Pour une 'nouvelle' histoire de la littérature byzantine: problèmes, méthodes, approches, propositions. HERMENEIA. Actes du premier colloque international sur la littérature byzantine* (Dossiers Byzantins, 1), Paris: École des Hautes Études en Sciences Sociales, pp. 185–232.

Agapitos, Panagiotis A. (2004a) 'Ἀπὸ τὸ "δρᾶμα" τοῦ Ἔρωτα στὸ "ἀφήγημαν" τῆς Ἀγάπης: τὸ ἐρωτικὸ μυθιστόρημα στὸ Βυζάντιο (11ος-14ος αἰώνας)', in Christina Angelidi (ed.), *Τὸ Βυζάντιο ὥριμο γιὰ ἀλλαγές: Ἐπιλογές, εὐαισθησίες καὶ τρόποι ἔκφρασης ἀπὸ τὸν ἑνδέκατο στὸν δέκατο πέμπτο αἰώνα* (Ἐθνικὸ Ἵδρυμα Ἐρευνῶν. Ἰνστιτοῦτο Βυζαντινῶν Ἐρευνῶν: Διεθνῆ Συμπόσια, 13), Athens: National Research Foundation, pp. 53–72.

Agapitos, Panagiotis A. (2004b) 'Genre, Structure and Poetics in the Byzantine Vernacular Romances of Love', *Symbolae Osloenses* 79: 7–101.

Agapitos, Panagiotis A. (2006a) 'Writing, Reading and Reciting (in) Byzantine Erotic Fiction', in Brigitte Mondrain (ed.), *Lire et écrire à Byzance* (Collège de France – CNRS: Centre de Recherche d'Histoire et Civilisation de Byzance, 19), Paris: Centre de Recherche d'Histoire et Civilisation de Byzance, pp. 125–76.

Agapitos, Panagiotis A. (2006b) *Ἀφήγησις Λιβίστρου καὶ Ροδάμνης. Κριτικὴ ἔκδοση τῆς διασκευῆς «ἄλφα»* (Βυζαντινὴ καὶ Νεοελληνικὴ Βιβλιοθήκη, 9), Athens: Cultural Foundation of the National Bank of Greece.

Agapitos, Panagiotis A. (2010) 'From Persia to the Provence: Tales of Love in Byzantium and Beyond', in Panagiotis A. Agapitos, *Acme: Annali della Facoltà di Lettere e Filosofia dell'Università degli Studi di Milano* 63: 153–69.

Agapitos, Panagiotis, Martin Hinterberger and Efterpi Mitsi (2006) *Εἰκὼν καὶ λόγος. Ἕξι βυζαντινὲς περιγραφὲς ἔργων τέχνης*, Athens: Agra Publications.

Agapitos, Panagiotis A., and Diether Roderich Reinsch (eds.) (2000) *Der Roman im Byzanz der Komnenenzeit. Ein internazionales Symposium* (Meletemata, 8), Frankfurt a.M: Beerenverlag.

Agapitos, Panagiotis A., and Ole L. Smith (1992) *The Study of Medieval Greek Romance: A Reassessment of Recent Work* (Opuscula Graecolatina, 33), Copenhagen: Museum Tusculanum Press.

Agapitos, Panagiotis A., and Ole L. Smith (1994) 'Scribes and Manuscripts of Byzantine Vernacular Romances: Palaeographical Facts and Editorial Implications', *Hellenika* 44: 61–80.

Alcouffe, Daniel (1984) 'Islamic Hardstone-Carving', in David Buckton (ed.), *The Treasury of San Marco Venice*, Milan: Olivetti, pp. 207–27.

Alexiou, Margaret (1999) 'Ploys of Performance: Games and Play in the Ptochoprodromic Poems', *Dumbarton Oaks Papers* 53: 91–109.

Alexiou, Stylianos (1985) *Βασίλειος Διγενὴς Ἀκρίτης (κατὰ τὸ χειρόγραφο τοῦ Ἐσκοριάλ) καὶ Τὸ Ἄσμα τοῦ Ἀρμούρη. Κριτικὴ ἔκδοση, εἰσαγωγή, σημειώσεις, γλωσσάριο* (Φιλολογικὴ Βιβλιοθήκη, 5), Athens: Ekdoseis Hermes.

Amtower, Laurel (2000) *Engaging Words: The Culture of Reading in the Later Middle Ages* (The New Middle Ages, 32), New York and Basingstoke: Palgrave.

Angold, Michael J. (1975) *A Byzantine Government in Exile: Government and Society under the Laskarids of Nicaea 1204–1261*, Oxford: Clarendon Press.

Angold, Michael J. (1995) *Church and Society in Byzantium under the Comneni (1081–1261)*, Cambridge: Cambridge University Press.

Angold, Michael J. (1997) *The Byzantine Empire, 1025–1204: A Political History*, 2nd edition, London: Longman.

Angold, Michael J. (2002) 'The Decline of Byzantium Seen through the Eyes of Western Travellers', in Ruth Macrides (ed.), *Travel in the Byzantine World: Papers from the Thirty-fourth Spring Symposium of Byzantine Studies, Birmingham, April 2000* (Society for the Promotion of Byzantine Studies. Publications, 10), Aldershot: Ashgate, pp. 213–32.

Angold, Michael J. (2003) *The Fourth Crusade: Event and Context,* Harlow: Pearson-Longman.

Angold, Michael J. (2004) 'The Byzantine Empire, 1025–1118', in Dennis Luscombe and John Riley-Smith (eds.), *The New Cambridge Medieval History. Volume IV, Part II: c. 1024–c. 1198,* Cambridge: Cambridge University Press, pp. 217–53.

Apostolopoulos, Phaidon (1984) *La langue du roman byzantin 'Callimaque et Chrysorrhoé',* Athens: Academy of Athens.

Bakker, Wim F., and Arnold F. van Gemert (1988) *Ἱστορία τοῦ Βελισαρίου. Κριτικὴ ἔκδοση τῶν τεσσάρων διασκευῶν μὲ εἰσαγωγή, σχόλια καὶ γλωσσάριο* (Βυζαντινὴ καὶ Νεοελληνικὴ Βιβλιοθήκη, 6), Athens: Cultural Foundation of the National Bank of Greece.

Barker, John W. (1969) *Manuel II Palaelogus (1391–1425): A Study in Late Byzantine Statesmanship,* New Brunswick, NJ: Rutgers University Press.

Barzos, Konstantinos (1984) *Ἡ γενεαλογία τῶν Κομνηνῶν* (Κέντρον Βυζαντινῶν Ἐρευνῶν. Κείμενα καὶ Μελέται, 20a–b), 2 vols., Thessaloniki: Centre for Byzantine Research.

Baswell, Christopher (2000) 'Marvels of Translation and Crises of Transition in the Romances of Antiquity', in Roberta L. Krueger (ed.), *The Cambridge Companion to Medieval Romance,* Cambridge: Cambridge University Press, pp. 29–44.

Baumgartner, Emanuelle (1988) 'Le Temps des automates', in *Le Nombre du Temps. Mélanges en hommage à Paul Zumthor,* Paris: Champion, pp. 15–21.

Baumgartner, Emanuelle, and Françoise Vielliard (1998) *Benoît de Sainte-Maure: Le Roman de Troie. Extraits du manuscrit Milan, Bibliothèque ambrosienne D 55,* édités, présentés et traduits (Lettres gothiques, 4552), Paris: Le Livre de Poche.

Beaton, Roderick (1996a) *The Medieval Greek Romance,* 2nd edition, London and New York: Routledge.

Beaton, Roderick (1996b) 'Cappadocians at Court: Digenes and Timarion', in Margaret Mullett and Dion Smythe (eds.), *Alexios I Komnenos. Volume I: Papers* (Belfast Byzantine Texts and Translations, 4.1), Belfast: Queen's University Centre for Byzantine Studies, pp. 329–38.

Beaton, Roderick, and David Ricks (eds.) (1993) *Digenes Akrites: New Approaches to Byzantine Heroic Poetry* (Centre for Hellenic Studies, King's College London. Publications, 2), Aldershot: Ashgate.

Beck, Hans-Georg (1971) *Geschichte der byzantinischen Volksliteratur* (Handbuch der Altertumswissenschaft, XII.2.3), Munich: C.H. Beck.

Benecke, Gerhard F., Karl Lachmann, Ludwig Wolff and Thomas Cramer (2001) *Hartmann von Aue: Iwein.* Text der siebenten Auflage von Gerhard F. Benecke, Karl Lachmann und Ludwig Wolff, Übersetzung und Nachwort von Thomas Cramer, 4th edition, Berlin and New York: Walter de Gruyter.

Benton, John F. (1961) 'The Court of Champagne as a Literary Center', *Speculum* 36: 551–91.

Bercovici-Huard, Claude (1982) '*Partonopoeus de Blois* et la couleur byzantine', *Senefiance* 11: 178–96.

Betts, Gavin (1995) *Three Medieval Greek Romances: Velthandros and Chrysandza, Kallimachos and Chrysorroi, Livistros and Rodamni* (Garland Library of Medieval Literature, 98B), New York: Garland.

Bezzola, Retto Raymond (1963) *Les origines et la formation de la littérature courtoise en Occident (500–1200). Troisième partie: La société courtoise. Littérature de cour et littérature courtoise*, Paris: Champion.

Biedermann, Alfons (1913) *La belle Maguelonne*, Paris: Champion and Halle: Max Niemeyer.

Boissonade, Joseph François (1838) *Michael Psellus: De operatione daemonum. Accedunt inedita opuscula Pselli*, Nuremberg: Campe.

Bond, Gerald A. (1995) *The Loving Subject: Desire, Eloquence, and Power in Romanesque France*, Philadelphia: University of Pennsylvania Press.

de Boor, Helmut (1967) *Hartmann von Aue: Der arme Heinrich. Mittelhochdeutscher Text und Übertragung*, 2nd edition, Frankfurt a.M: Fischer Verlag.

Bowie, Ewen (1994) 'The Readership of Greek Novels in the Ancient World', in James Tatum (ed.), *The Search for the Ancient Novel*, Baltimore and London: The Johns Hopkins University Press, pp. 435–59.

Bowie, Ewen (1996) 'The Ancient Readers of the Greek Novels', in Gareth Schmeling (ed.), *The Novel in the Ancient World*, Leiden, New York and Cologne: E.J. Brill, pp. 87–106.

Brownlee, Kevin, Tony Hunt, Ian Johnson, Alastair Minnis and Nigel F. Palmer (2004) 'Vernacular Literary Consciousness c. 1100–c. 1500: French and German Evidence', in Alastair Minnis and Ian Johnson (eds.), *The Cambridge History of Literary Criticism. Volume II: The Middle Ages*, Cambridge: Cambridge University Press, pp. 422–71.

Brunner, Horst (ed.) (2004a) *Mittelhochdeutsche Romane und Heldenepen*, 2nd edition, Stuttgart: Philipp Reclam.

Brunner, Horst (2004b) 'Hartmann von Aue: *Erec* und *Iwein*', in Horst Brunner (ed.), *Mittelhochdeutsche Romane und Heldenepen*, 2nd edition, Stuttgart: Philipp Reclam, pp. 97–128.

Bryer, Anthony A. M. (1980) *The Empire of Trebizond and the Pontos*, London: Variorum.

Bürgel, Johann Christoph (1980) *Nizami: Chosrou und Schirin. Übertragung aus dem Persischen* (Bibliotheca Persica, 36), Zurich: Manesse.

Bürgel, Johann Christoph (1990) 'Die persische Epik', in Wolfhart Heinrichs (ed.), *Orientalisches Mittelalter* (Neues Handbuch der Literaturwissenschaft, 5), Wiesbaden: Aula, pp. 301–18.

Bürgel, Johann Christoph (1991) *Nizami: Das Alexanderbuch – Iskandarname. Übertragung aus dem Persischen* (Bibliotheca Persica, 37), Zurich: Manesse.

Bürgel, Johann Christoph (1997) *Nizami: Die Abenteuer des Königs Bahram und seiner sieben Prinzessinen. Aus dem Persischen übertragen und herausgegeben*, Munich: C.H. Beck.

Bumke, Joachim (1979) *Mäzene im Mittelalter. Die Gönner und Auftraggeber der höfischen Literatur in Deutschland 1150–1300*, Munich: C.H. Beck.

Bumke, Joachim (ed.) (1982) *Literarisches Mäzenatentum* (Wege der Forschung, 598), Darmstadt: Wissenschaftliche Buchgesellschaft.

Bumke, Joachim (1986) *Höfische Kultur: Literatur und Gesellschaft im hohen Mittelalter*, Munich: Deutscher Taschenbuch Verlag.

Bumke, Joachim (2000) *Geschichte der deutschen Literatur im hohen Mittelalter*, 4th edition, Munich: Deutscher Taschenbuch Verlag.

Bumke, Joachim (2004) *Wolfram von Eschenbach*, 8th edition (Sammlung Metzler, 36), Stuttgart-Weimar: Friedrich Metzler.

Burton, Joan B. (2003) 'A Reemergence of Theocritean Poetry in the Byzantine Novel', *Classical Philology* 98: 251–73.

Burton, Joan B. (2004) *A Byzantine Novel: Drosilla and Charikles by Niketas Eugenianos. A Bilingual Edition. Translated with introduction and explanatory notes*, Wauconda, IL: Bolchazy-Carducci.

Busby, Keith (1998) 'Foreword', in Beate Schmolke-Hasselmann, *The Evolution of Arthurian Romance: The Verse Tradition from Chrétien to Froissart*. Translated by Marie and Richard Middleton (Cambridge Studies in Medieval Literature, 35), Cambridge: Cambridge University Press, pp. xi–xlvi. [Revised translation of the German original, Tübingen: Max Niemeyer, 1980.]

Busby, Keith, Terry Nixon, M. Alison Stones and Lori Walters (eds.) (1994), *The Manuscripts of Chrétien de Troyes*, 2 vols., Amsterdam: Rodopi.

Cahen, Claude (1991) *The Formation of Turkey: The Seljukid Sultanate of Rum, Eleventh to Fourteenth Century*, London: Longman.

Chrysomalli-Henrich, Kyriaki (2002) ''Ιπποτικὰ μυθιστορήματα καὶ ἀφηγηματολογία: οἱ ἐκφάνσεις τοῦ ἀφηγητῆ καὶ ἡ δόμηση τοῦ χρόνου στὸ *Ἰμπέριος καὶ Μαργαρώνα*', in Panagiotis A. Agapitos and Michalis Pieris (eds.), *'Τ' ἀδόνιν κεῖνο ποὺ γλυκὰ θλιβᾶται': Ἐκδοτικὰ καὶ ἑρμηνευτικὰ ζητήματα τῆς δημώδους ἑλληνικῆς λογοτεχνίας στὸ πέρασμα ἀπὸ τὸν Μεσαίωνα στὴν Ἀναγέννηση (1400–1600). Πρακτικὰ τοῦ 4ου Διεθνοῦς Συνεδρίου Neograeca Medii Aevi*, Herakleion: University of Crete Press, pp. 371–96.

Clain-Legros, Henriette (1992) *La rose et le lys: Étude littéraire du Conte de Floire et Blancheflor* (Sénéfiance, 31), Aix-en-Provence: Presses Universitaires d'Aix-en-Provence.

Coleman, Joyce (1996) *Public Reading and the Reading Public in Late Medieval England and France* (Cambridge Studies in Medieval Literature, 26), Cambridge: Cambridge University Press.

Collet, Olivier, and Pierre-Marie Joris (2005) *Le Roman de Partonopeus de Blois. Édition, traduction et introduction de la redaction A (Paris, Bibliothèque de l'Arsenal, 2986) et de la Continuation du récit d'après les manuscrits de Berne (Burgerbibliothek, 113) et de Tours (Bibliothèque municipale, 939)* (Lettres gothiques, 4569), Paris: Le Livre du Poche.

Conca, Fabrizio (1990) *Nicetas Eugenianus: De Drosillae et Chariclis amoribus* (London Studies in Classical Philology, 24), Amsterdam: Gieben.

Conca, Fabrizio (1994) *Il romanzo bizantino del XII secolo. Teodoro Prodromo, Niceta Eugeniano, Eustazio Macrembolita, Constantino Manasse*, Torino: Unione Tipographica Editrice di Torino.

Constantinides, Costas N. (1982) *Higher Education in Byzantium in the Thirteenth and Early Fourteenth Centuries, 1204–ca. 1310* (Cyprus Research Center. Texts and Studies of the History of Cyprus, 11), Nicosia: Cyprus Research Center.

Constantinou, Stavroula (2006) 'Review of Thomas Pratsch, *Der hagiographische Topos* (Berlin 2005)', *Le Muséon* 119: 476–81.

Croizy-Naquet, Catherine (1994) *Thèbes, Troie et Carthage. Poétique de la ville dans le roman antique au XIIe siècle* (Nouvelle bibliothèque du moyen âge, 30), Paris: Champion.

Cupane, Carolina (1973–74) ''Ερως βασιλεύς: la figura di Eros nel romanzo bizantino d'amore', *Atti dell' Academia di Scienze, Lettere e Arti di Palermo*, ser. IV, vol. 33.2.2: 243–97.

Cupane, Carolina (1978) 'Il motivo del castello nella narrativa tardobizantina:

evoluzione di un'allegoria', *Jahrbuch der Österreichischen Byzantinistik* 27: 229–67.

Cupane, Carolina (1986) 'Topica romanzesca in oriente e in occidente: *avanture* e *amour*', in Cataldo Roccaro (ed.), *Il romanzo tra cultura latina e cultura bizantina. Testi della III settimana residenziale di studi medievali* (Biblioteca dell'Enchiridion, 5), Palermo: Enchiridion, pp. 47–72.

Cupane, Carolina (1992) 'Concezione e rappresentazione dell'amore nella narrativa tardobizantina: un tentativo di analisi comparata', in Arnaldo M. Babbi, Antonio Pioletti, Francesca Rizzo Nervo and Carlo Stevanoni (eds.), *Medioevo romanzo e orientale: Testi e prospettive storiografiche. Colloquio Internazionale*, Soveria Mannelli-Messina: Rubettino, pp. 283–305.

Cupane, Carolina (1993) 'Κατέλαβες τὰ ἀμφίβολα τῆς τυφλῆς δαίμονος πρόσωπα: il Λόγος παρηγορητικὸς περὶ Δυστυχίας καὶ Εὐτυχίας e la figura di Fortuna nella letteratura greca medievale', in Nikolaos M. Panagiotakes (ed.), *Origini della letteratura neograeca. Atti del secondo congresso internazionale 'Neograeca Medii Aevi'* (Biblioteca dell'Istituto Ellenico di Studi Bizantini e Postbizantini di Venezia, 15), Venice: Istituto Ellenico di Studi Bizantini e Postbizantini di Venezia, vol. I, pp. 413–37.

Cupane, Carolina (1995a) 'Leggere e/o ascoltare: note sulla ricezione primaria e sul pubblico della letteratura greca medievale', in Antonio Pioletti and Francesca Rizzo Nervo (eds.), *Medioevo romanzo e orientale: Oralità, scrittura, modelli narrativi. II Colloquio Internazionale* (Medioevo romanzo e orientale. Colloqui, 2), Soveria Manelli-Messina: Rubettino, pp. 83–105.

Cupane, Carolina (1995b) 'Λογοτεχνικὴ παραγωγὴ στὸ φραγκοκρατούμενο Μορέα', *Byzantinai Meletai* 6: 371–85.

Cupane, Carolina (1995c) *Romanzi cavallereschi bizantini. Callimaco e Crisorroe – Beltandro e Crisanza – Storia di Achille – Florio e Platziaflore – Storia di Apollonio di Tiro – Favola consolatoria sulla Cattiva e la Buona Sorte*, Torino: Unione Tipographica Editrice di Torino.

Cupane, Carolina (1999) 'Bisanzio e la letteratura della Romania: peregrinazioni del romanzo medievale', in Antonio Pioletti and Francesca Rizzo Nervo (eds.), *Medioevo romanzo e orientale: Il viaggio dei testi. III Colloquio Internazionale* (Medioevo romanzo e orientale. Colloqui, 4), Soveria Mannelli-Messina: Rubettino, pp. 31–49.

Cupane, Carolina (2003) 'Wie volkstümlich ist die byzantinische Volksliteratur?', *Byzantinische Zeitschrift* 96: 577–99.

Cupane, Carolina (2004) 'Il romanzo', in Guglielmo Cavallo (ed.), *La cultura bizan-*

tina (Lo Spazio Letterario del Medioevo. 3: Le Culture Circostanti, I), Rome: Salerno Editrice, pp. 407–53.

Cupane, Carolina (2005) 'Die Leipziger Fassung des Logos Paregoretikos peri Dystychias kai Eutychias', in Stephan Kolditz and Richard C. Müller (eds.), *Geschehenes und Geschriebenes. Studien zu Ehren von Günther S. Henrich und Klaus-Peter Matschke*, Leipzig: Eudora-Verlag, pp. 281–98.

Currie, Gregory (1990) *The Nature of Fiction*, Cambridge: Cambridge University Press.

Davis, Dick (1992) *Ferdowsi: The Legend of Seyavash.* Translated with an Introduction, Harmondsworth: Penguin Books.

Davis, Dick (2006) *Abolqasem Ferdowsi: Shahnameh, The Persian Book of Kings. A New Translation*, London: Penguin Books.

Davis, Dick (2008) *Fakhraddin Gorgani: Vis and Ramin. Translated from the Persian with an Introduction and Notes*, Washington, DC: Mage Publishers.

van Dieten, Jan Luis (1975) *Nicetae Choniatae Historia* (Corpus Fontium Historiae Byzantinae, 11), Berlin and New York: Walter de Gruyter.

Donnet, Dennis (1967) *Le traité Περὶ συντάξεως λόγου de Grégoire de Corinthe. Étude de la tradition manuscrite, édition, traduction et commentaire* (L'Institut Historique Belge de Rome. Études de philologie, d'archéologie et d'histoire anciennes, 10), Brussels and Rome: L'Institut Historique Belge de Rome.

Dyck, Anthony R. (1986) *Michael Psellus: The Essays on Euripides and George of Pisidia and on Heliodorus and Achilles Tatius* (Byzantina Vindobonensia, 16), Vienna: Verlag der Österreichischen Akademie der Wissenschaften.

Egea, Jose Maria (1998) *Historia extraordinaria de Beltandro y Crisanza. Estudio preliminar, texto griego, traduccion, notas y comentarios* (Biblioteca Neogriega. Serie Bilingüe de Textos Griegos Medievales, 1), Granada: Athos-Pergamos.

Eideneier, Hans (1991) *Ptochoprodromos. Einführung, kritische Ausgabe, deutsche Übersetzung, Glossar* (Neograeca Medii Aevi, 5), Cologne: Romiosyni.

El Cheikh, Nadia Maria (2004) *Byzantium Viewed by the Arabs* (Harvard Middle Eastern Monographs, 36), Cambridge, MA and London: Harvard University Press.

Evans, Ruth (1999) 'An Afterword on the Prologue', in Jocelyn Wogan-Browne, Nicholas Watson, Andrew Taylor and Ruth Evans, *The Idea of the Vernacular: An Anthology of Middle English Literary Theory 1280–1520*, Exeter: University of Exeter Press, pp. 371–78.

Ettmüller, Ludwig, and Diether Kartschoke (1997) *Heinrich von Veldeke: Eneasroman.* Nach dem Text von Ludwig Ettmüller ins Neuhochdeutsche übersetzt, mit einem Stellenkommentar und einem Nachwort von Diether Kartschoke, 2nd edition, Stuttgart: Philipp Reclam.

Fisher, Elizabeth A. (1994) *Michaelis Pselli Orationes hagiographicae*, Stuttgart and Leipzig: B.G. Teubner.

Foley, John M. (1988) *The Theory of Oral Composition: History and Methodology*, Bloomington, IN: University of Indiana Press.

Fourrier, Anthime (1960) *Le courant réaliste dans le roman courtois en France au moyen âge. Tome I: Les débuts (XIIe siècle)*, Paris: Nizet.

Frappier, Jean, and Reinhold R. Grimm (eds.) (1978–84) *Le roman jusqu'a la fin du XIIIe siècle. Tome 1: Partie historique. Tome 2: Partie documentaire* (Grundriß der Romanischen Literaturen des Mittlealters, IV.1–2), Heidelberg: Carl Winter.

Freeman, Michelle A. (1979) *The Poetics of translatio studii and conjointure: Chrétien de Troyes's 'Cligès'* (French Forum Monographs, 12), Lexington: French Forum.

Fritz, Jean-Marie (1992) *Chrétien de Troyes: Erec et Enide. Édition critique d'après le manuscrit B.N. fr. 1376, traduction, présentation et notes* (Lettres gothiques, 4526), Paris: Le Livre de Poche.

Frye, Richard N. (1984) *The History of Ancient Iran* (Handbuch der Altertumswissenschaft, III.7), Munich: C.H. Beck.

Gärtner, Hans (1969) 'Charikleia in Byzanz', *Antike und Abendland* 15: 47–69.

Garzya, Antonio (1984) *Nicephori Basilacae Orationes et epistulae*, Leipzig: B.G. Teubner.

Gaunt, Simon (1995) *Gender and Genre in Medieval French Literature* (Cambridge Studies in French, 53), Cambridge: Cambridge University Press.

Gautier, Paul (1975) *Nicéphore Bryennios: Histoire. Introduction, texte, traduction et notes* (Corpus Fontium Historiae Byzantinae, 9), Brussels: Byzantion.

Gebauer, Günther, and Christian Wulf (eds.) (1992) *Mimesis: Kultur–Kunst–Gesellschaft*, Reinbeck: RoRoRo.

Genette, Gérard (1972) 'Discours du récit: essai de méthode', in Gérard Genette, *Figures III* (Collection Poétique), Paris: Seuil, pp. 65–282.

Genette, Gérard (1983) *Nouveau discours du récit* (Collection Poétique), Paris: Seuil.

Gildea, Joseph (1967–70) *Partenopeu de Blois: A French Romance of the Twelfth Century. Volume 1: The Romance. Volume 2, Part 1: The Continuation in Mss T(BGLP). Volume 2, Part 2: Introduction and Commentary*, Villanova, PA: Villanova University Press.

Goutas, Dimitri (1998) *Greek Thought, Arabic Culture*, London: Routledge.

Green, Dennis H. (1994) *Medieval Listening and Reading: The Primary Reception of German Literature 800–1300*, Cambridge: Cambridge University Press.

Green, Dennis H. (2002) *The Beginnings of Medieval Romance: Fact and Fiction, 1150–1220* (Cambridge Studies in Medieval Literature, 47), Cambridge: Cambridge University Press.

Grégoire, Henry, and Robert Goossens (1934) 'Byzantinisches Epos und arabischer Heldenroman', *Zeitschrift der Deutschen Morgenländischen Gesellschaft* 88: 213–32.

Grigoriadis, Iordanis (1998) 'A Study of the *Prooimion* of Zonaras' Chronicle in Relation to Other 12th-Century Historical *Prooimia*', *Byzantinische Zeitschrift* 91: 327–44.

Grotzfeld, Heinz, and Sophia Grotzfeld (1984) *Die Erzählungen aus 'Tausendundeiner Nacht'*, Darmstadt: Wissenschaftliche Buchgesellschaft.

Hägg, Tomas (2004) 'Orality, Literacy, and the "Readership" of the Early Greek Novel', in Tomas Hägg, *Parthenope: Selected Studies in Ancient Greek Fiction (1969–2004)*, Copenhagen: Museum Tusculanum Press, pp. 109–140. [Paper originally published in 1994.]

Hägg, Tomas (2006) 'The Ancient Greek Novel: A Single Model or a Plurality of Forms?', in Franco Moretti (ed.), *The Novel. Volume 1: History, Geography and Culture*, Princeton and Oxford: Princeton University Press, pp. 125–55.

Hägg, Tomas, and Bo Utas (2003) *The Virgin and her Lover: Fragments of an Ancient Greek Novel and a Persian Epic Poem* (Brill Studies in Middle Eastern Literatures, 30), Leiden and Boston: Brill.

Hahnloser, Hans. R., and Susanne Brugger-Koch (1985) *Corpus der Hartsteinschliffe des 12.–15. Jahrhunderts*, Berlin: Deutscher Verlag für Kunstgeschichte.

Hamilton, Rita, Janet Perry and Ian Michael (1984) *The Poem of the Cid: A Bilingual Text*. Translated by Rita Hamilton and Janet Perry, introduction and notes by Ian Michael, London: Penguin Books.

Harf-Lancner, Laurence (1990) *Lais de Marie de France*. Traduits, présentés et annotés par Laurence Harf-Lancner, texte édité par Karl Warnke (Lettres gothiques, 4523), Paris: Le Livre de Poche.

Harris, Jonathan (2005) 'Political History 1204–1453', in Jonathan Harris, *Palgrave Advances in Byzantine History*, Basingstoke: Palgrave, pp. 58–67.

Hatto, Arthur Thomas (1980) *Wolfram von Eschenbach: Parzival*, Harmondsworth: Penguin Books.

Hatto, Arthur Thomas (2004) *Gottfried von Strassburg: Tristan, with the surviving fragments of the 'Tristan' of Thomas*, revised edition, London: Penguin Books.

Haug, Walter (1992) *Literaturtheorie im deutschen Mittelalter von den Anfängen bis zum Ende des 13. Jahrhunderts*, 2nd edition, Darmstadt: Wissenschaftliche Buchgesellschaft.

Haug, Walter, and Benedikt K. Vollmann (1974–85) *Ruodlieb: Faksimile-Ausgabe des Codex Latinus Monacensis 19486 der Bayerischen Staatsbibliothek München und der Fragmente von St. Florian.* Band I,1: Einleitung von Walter Haug. Band I,2: Tafeln (1974); Band II,1: Kritischer Text von Benedikt K. Vollmann (1985), Wiesbaden: Dr. Ludwig Reichert Verlag.

Haug, Walter, and Benedikt K. Vollmann (eds.) (1991) *Frühe deutsche Literatur und lateinische Literatur in Deutschland 800–1150*, Frankfurt a.M: Deutscher Klassiker Verlag.

Hesseling, Dirk Christian (1917) *Le roman de Phlorios et de Platzia Phlore* (Verhandelingen der Koninklijke Akademie van Wetenschappen te Amsterdam. Afdeeling Letterkunde, N.R. 17.4), Amsterdam: Koninklijke Akademie van Wetenschappen.

Hesseling, Dirk Christian (1919) *L'Achilleide byzantine publiée avec une introduction, des observations et un index* (Verhandelingen der Koninklijke Akademie van Wetenschappen te Amsterdam. Afdeeling Letterkunde, N.R. 19.3), Amsterdam: Koninklijke Akademie van Wetenschappen.

Hinterberger, Martin (1993) 'Sprachliche Variationsformen in volkssprachlichen metrischen Werken der spätbyzantinsichen und frühneugriechischen Zeit', in Nikolaos M. Panagiotakes (ed.), *Origini della letteratura neograeca. Atti del secondo congresso internazionale 'Neograeca Medii Aevi'* (Biblioteca dell'Istituto Ellenico di Studi Bizantini e Postbizantini di Venezia, 15), Venice: Istituto Ellenico di Studi Bizantini e Postbizantini di Venezia, vol. II, pp. 158–68.

Hinterberger, Martin (2001) 'Τὸ φαινόμενο τῆς πολυτυπίας σὲ δημώδη κείμενα', in Hans Eideneier, Ulrich Moennig and Notis Toufexis (eds.), *Θεωρία καὶ πράξη τῶν ἐκδόσεων τῆς ὑστεροβυζαντινῆς, ἀναγεννησιακῆς καὶ μεταβυζαντινῆς δημώδους γραμματείας. Πρακτικὰ τοῦ Διεθνοῦς Συνεδρίου Neograeca Medii Aevi IVa*, Herakleion: University of Crete Press, pp. 215–44.

Hinterberger, Martin (2002) 'Δημώδης καὶ λόγια λογοτεχνία: διαχωριστικὲς γραμμὲς καὶ συνδετικοὶ κρίκοι', in Paolo Odorico and Panagiotis A. Agapitos (eds.), *Pour une 'nouvelle' histoire de la littérature byzantine: problèmes, méthodes, approches, propositions. HERMENEIA. Actes du premier colloque international sur la littérature byzantine* (Dossiers Byzantins, 1), Paris: École des Hautes Études en Sciences Sociales, pp. 153–65.

Hinterberger, Martin (2005) ''Ο Ἀνδρέας Λιβαδηνός, συγγραφέας/γραφέας λογίων κειμένων, ἀναγνώστης-γραφέας δημωδῶν κειμένων: ὁ ἑλληνικὸς κώδικας 525 τοῦ Μονάχου', in David Holton, Tina Lendari, Ulrich Moennig and Peter Vejleskov (eds.), *Κωδικογράφοι, συλλέκτες, διασκευαστὲς καὶ ἐκδότες: Χειρόγραφα καὶ ἐκδόσεις τῆς ὄψιμης βυζαντινῆς καὶ πρώιμης νεοελληνικῆς λογοτεχνίας*, Herakleion: University of Crete Press, pp. 25–42.

Høgel, Christian (2002) *Symeon Metaphrastes: Rewriting and Canonization*, Copenhagen: Museum Tusculanum Press.

Holub, Robert (1995) 'Reception Theory: School of Constance', in Raman Selden (ed.), *The Cambridge History of Literary Criticism. Volume VIII: From Formalism to Poststructuralism*, Cambridge: Cambridge University Press, pp. 319–46.

Holzberg, Niklas (1995) *The Ancient Novel: An Introduction*. Translated by Christine Jackson-Holzberg, London and New York: Routledge.

Hörandner, Wolfram (1974) *Theodoros Prodromos: Historische Gedichte* (Wiener Byzantinistische Studien, 11), Vienna: Verlag der Österreichischen Akademie der Wissenschaften.

Hörandner, Wolfram (1993) 'Autor oder Genus? Diskussionsbeiträge zur "Prodromischen Frage" aus gegebenem Anlaß', *Byzantinoslavica* 54: 314–24.

Hult, David F. (1994) *Chrétien de Troyes: Le Chevalier au Lion ou Le Roman d'Yvain. Édition critique d' après le manuscrit B.N. fr. 1433, traduction, présentation et notes* (Lettres gothiques, 4539), Paris: Le Livre du Poche.

Hunger, Herbert (1978) *Die hochsprachliche profane Literatur der Byzantiner* (Handbuch der Altertumswissenschaft, XII.5.1–2), Munich: C.H. Beck.

Hunger, Herbert, and Ihor Ševčenko (1986) *Des Nikephoros Blemmydes Βασιλικὸς Ἀνδριάς und dessen Metaphrase von Georgios Galesiotes und Georgios Oinaiotes. Ein weiterer Beitrag zum Verständnis der byzantinischen Schrift-Koine* (Wiener Byzantinistische Studien, 18), Vienna: Verlag der Österreichischen Akademie der Wissenschaften.

Ilieva, Aneta (1991) *Frankish Morea (1205–1262): Socio-cultural Interaction between the Franks and the Local Population* (Historical Monographs, 9), Athens: St. D. Basilopoulos.

Ingledew, Francis (1994) 'The Book of Troy and the Genealogical Construction of History: The Case of Geoffrey of Monmouth's *Historia regum Britanniae*', *Speculum* 69: 665–704.

Irwin, Robert (2004) *The Arabian Nights: A Companion*, London and New York: Tauris Parke Paperbacks. [Originally published in 1994.]

Iser, Wolfgang (1972) *Der implizite Leser: Kommunikationsformen des Romans von Bunyan bis Beckett* (Uni-Taschenbücher, 163), Munich: Wilhelm Fink.

Iser, Wolfgang (1976) *Der Akt des Lesens: Theorie Ästhetischer Wirkung*, Munich: Wilhelm Fink.

Iser, Wolfgang (1989) *Prospecting: From Reader Response to Literary Anthropology*, Baltimore: The Johns Hopkins University Press.

Iser, Wolfgang (1993) *Das Fiktive und das Imaginäre: Perspektiven literarischer Anthropologie* (Suhrkamp Taschenbuch Wissenschaft, 1101), Frankfurt a.M: Suhrkamp.

Jacoby, David (1984) 'La littérature francaise dans les états latins de la Méditerranée orientale à l'époque des croisades: diffusion et création', in *Essor et fortune de la chanson de geste dans l'Europe et l'Orient latin. Actes du IXe Congrès international de la Société Rencevals pour l'étude des épopées romanes* (Padoue-Venise 1982), Modena: Mucchi Editore, pp. 617–46. [Repr. in David Jacoby, *Studies on the Crusader States and on Venetian Expansion*, Northampton: Variorum Reprints, 1989, no. II.]

Jacoby, David (1986) 'Knightly Values and Class Consciousness in the Crusader States of the East Mediterranean', *Mediterranean Historical Review* 1: 158–85. [Repr. in David Jacoby, *Studies on the Crusader States and on Venetian Expansion*, Northampton: Variorum Reprints, 1989, no. I.]

Jacoby, David (1997) 'Byzantine Crete in the Navigation and Trade Networks of Venice and Genoa', in Laura Baletto (ed.), *Oriente e Occidente tra medioevo ed età moderna. Studi in onore di Geo Pistarino* (Università degli Studi di Genova, Sede di Acqui Terme. Collana di Fonti e Studi, 1.1), Acqui Terme: Edizioni Universitarie, pp. 517–40. [Repr. in David Jacoby, *Byzantium, Latin Romania and the Mediterranean*, Aldershot: Ashgate Variorum 2001, no. II.]

Jacoby, David (2005) *Commercial Exchange across the Mediterranean: Byzantium, the Crusader Levant, Egypt and Italy*, Aldershot: Ashgate.

Jaeger, C. Stephen (1995) *The Envy of Angels: Cathedral Schools and Social Ideas in Medieval Europe, 950–1200*, Philadelphia: University of Pennsylvania Press.

Jakobson, Roman (1987) *Language in Literature*. Edited by Kristina Pomorska and Stephen Rudy, Cambridge, MA: Harvard University Press.

Jeffreys, Elizabeth M. (1979) 'The Attitudes of Byzantine Chroniclers towards Ancient History', *Byzantion* 49: 199–238.

Jeffreys, Elizabeth M. (1980) 'The Comnenian Background to the *romans d'antiquité*', *Byzantion* 50: 455–86.

Jeffreys, Elizabeth M. (1993) 'The Grottaferrata Version of *Digenes Akrites*: A Reassessment', in Roderick Beaton and David Ricks (eds.), *Digenes Akrites: New*

Approaches to Byzantine Heroic Poetry (Centre for Hellenic Studies, King's College London. Publications, 2), Aldershot: Ashgate, pp. 26–37.

Jeffreys, Elizabeth M. (1998) *Digenis Akritis: The Grottaferrata and Escorial Versions* (Cambridge Medieval Classics, 7), Cambridge: Cambridge University Press.

Jeffreys, Elizabeth M. (2000) 'A Date for *Rhodanthe and Dosikles*?', in Panagiotis A. Agapitos and Diether Roderich Reinsch (eds.), *Der Roman im Byzanz der Komnenenzeit. Ein internazionales Symposium* (Meletemata, 8), Frankfurt a.M: Beerenverlag, pp. 127–36.

Jeffreys, Elizabeth M., and Michael J. Jeffreys (1994) 'Who Was the Sevastokratorissa Eirene?', *Byzantion* 64: 40–68.

Jeffreys, Michael J., and Elizabeth M. Jeffreys (1971) 'Imberios and Margarona: The Manuscripts, Sources and Edition of a Byzantine Verse Romance', *Byzantion* 41: 122–60.

Jones, Lynn, and Henry Maguire (2002) 'A Description of the Jousts of Manuel I Komnenos', *Byzantine and Modern Greek Studies* 26: 104–48.

Joris, Pierre-Marie (1992) *Partonopeu de Blois: L'invention d'une autre scène pour le roman dans le dernier quart du XIIe siècle* (unpublished Ph.D. thesis), University of Geneva.

Jouanno, Corinne (2005) 'A Byzantine Novelist Staging the Ancient Greek World: Presence, Form, and Function of Antiquity in Makrembolites' *Hysmine and Hysminias*', in Stephanos Kaklamanis and Michalis Paschalis (eds.), *Ἡ πρόσληψη τῆς ἀρχαιότητας στὸ βυζαντινὸ καὶ νεοελληνικὸ μυθιστόρημα*, Athens: Stigme, pp. 17–29.

Jung, Marcel-René (1996) *La légende de Troie en France au moyen âge* (Romanica Helvetica, 114), Basel and Tübingen: Francke.

Jung, Marcel-René (1997) 'L'histoire grecque: Darès et ses suites', in Emanuelle Baumgartner and Laurence Harf-Lancner (eds.), *Entre fiction et histoire: Troie et Rome au moyen âge*, Paris: Champion, pp. 185–206.

Kahane, Henry, and Renée Kahane (1982) 'The Western Impact on Byzantium: The Linguistic Evidence', *Dumbarton Oaks Papers* 36: 127–53.

Kahane, Henry, Renée Kahane and Alfred Tietze (1958) *The Lingua Franca in the Levant*, Urbana, IL: University of Illinois Press.

Kaldellis, Anthony (2004) *Procopius of Caesarea: Tyranny, History, and Philosophy at the End of Antiquity*, Philadelphia: University of Pennsylvania Press.

Kaldellis, Anthony (2007a) *Hellenism in Byzantium: The Transformations of Greek Identity and the Reception of the Classical Tradition* (Greek Culture in the Roman World, 4), Cambridge: Cambridge University Press.

Kaldellis, Anthony (2007b) 'Historicism in Byzantine Thought and Literature', *Dumbarton Oaks Papers* 61: 1–24.

Kaplanis, Tasos A. (2010) 'Ὁ Διγενὴς καὶ ἡ Μαξιμοὺ στὴ διασκευὴ Ε: γλώσσα, παράδοση καὶ ποιητικὴ μιᾶς ἐρωτικῆς συνέντευξης', *Byzantina* 30: 83–100.

Karla, Grammatiki A. (2001) *Vita Aesopi: Überlieferung, Sprache und Edition einer frühbyzantinischen Fassung des Äsopromans* (Serta Graeca, 13), Wiesbaden: Dr. Ludwig Reichert.

Karpozilos, Apostolos (1997) *Βυζαντινοὶ ἱστορικοὶ καὶ χρονογράφοι. Τόμος Α΄ (4ος - 7ος αἰ.)*, Athens: Kanaki.

Karpozilos, Apostolos (2002) *Βυζαντινοὶ ἱστορικοὶ καὶ χρονογράφοι. Τόμος Β΄ (8ος - 10ος αἰ.)*, Athens: Kanaki.

Karpozilos, Apostolos (2009) *Βυζαντινοὶ ἱστορικοὶ καὶ χρονογράφοι. Τόμος Γ΄ (11ος - 12ος αἰ.)*, Athens: Kanaki.

Kartschoke, Diether (1983) 'Review of Scholz 1980', *Internationales Archiv für Sozialgeschichte der Deutschen Literatur* 8: 253–66.

Kartschoke, Diether (1996) *Das Rolandslied des Pfaffen Konrad. Herausgegeben, übersetzt und kommentiert*, 2nd edition, Stuttgart: Philipp Reclam.

Kasten, Ingrid (2004) 'Heinrich von Veldeke: *Eneasroman*', in Horst Brunner (ed.), *Mittelhochdeutsche Romane und Heldenepen*, 2nd edition, Stuttgart: Philipp Reclam, pp. 75–96.

Katsaros, Vasilis (1988) *Ἰωάννης Κασταμονίτης: Συμβολὴ στὴ μελέτη τοῦ βίου, τοῦ ἔργου καὶ τῆς ἐποχῆς του* (Κέντρο Βυζαντινῶν Ἐρευνῶν. Βυζαντινὰ Κείμενα καὶ Μελέται, 22), Thessaloniki: Centre for Byzantine Research.

Katsaros, Vasilis (2002) 'Ἡ ρητορικὴ ὡς "θεωρία λογοτεχνίας" τῶν Βυζαντινῶν', in Paolo Odorico and Panagiotis A. Agapitos (eds.), *Pour une 'nouvelle' histoire de la littérature byzantine: problèmes, méthodes, approches, propositions. HERMENEIA. Actes du premier colloque international sur la littérature byzantine* (Dossiers Byzantins, 1), Paris: École des Hautes Études en Sciences Sociales, pp. 95–106.

Katsaros, Vasilis (2003) 'Προδρομικοὶ "θεσμοὶ" γιὰ τὴν ὀργάνωση τῆς ἀνώτερης ἐκπαίδευσης τῆς ἐποχῆς τῶν Κομνηνῶν ἀπὸ τὴν προκομνήνεια ἐποχή', in Vasiliki Vlyssidou (ed.), *Ἡ αὐτοκρατορία σὲ κρίση(;). Τὸ Βυζάντιο τὸν 11ο αἰώνα (1025–1081)* (Ἐθνικὸ Ἵδρυμα Ἐρευνῶν. Ἰνστιτοῦτο Βυζαντινῶν Ἐρευνῶν: Διεθνῆ Συμπόσια, 11), Athens: National Research Foundation, pp. 443–71.

Katsaros, Vasilis (2006) 'Τὸ δραματικὸ στοιχεῖο στὰ ἱστοριογραφικὰ ἔργα τοῦ 11ου καὶ 12ου αἰώνα (Μιχαὴλ Ἀτταλειάτης, Μιχαὴλ Ψελλός, Εὐστάθιος Θεσσαλονίκης, Νικήτας Χωνιάτης)', in Paolo Odorico, Panagiotis A. Agapitos and Martin Hinterberger (eds.), *L'écriture de la memoire: la littérarité de l'historiographie. HER-*

MENEIA. Actes du troisiéme colloque international sur la littérature byzantine (Dossiers Byzantins, 6), Paris: École des Hautes Études en Sciences Sociales, pp. 281–316.

Kazhdan, Alexander, and Simon Franklin (1984) *Studies on Byzantine Literature of the Eleventh and Twelfth Centuries*, Cambridge: Cambridge University Press.

Kazhdan, Alexander (2001) 'Latins and Franks in Byzantium: Perception and Reality from the Eleventh to the Twelfth Century', in Angeliki E. Laiou and Roy P. Mottahedeh (eds.), *The Crusades from the Perspective of Byzantium and the Muslim World*, Washington, D.C.: Dumbarton Oaks Center, pp. 83–100.

Kelly, Douglas (1992) *The Art of Medieval French Romance*, Madison: University of Wisconsin Press.

Kelly, Douglas (1993) *Medieval French Romance*, New York: Twayne Publishers.

Kibler, William W., and Carleton W. Carroll (1991) *Chrétien de Troyes: Arthurian Romances. Translated with an introduction and notes*, London: Penguin Books.

Kinoshita, Sharon (1996) 'The Poetics of *translatio*: French-Byzantine Relations in Chrétien de Troyes's *Cligès*', *Exemplaria* 8: 315–54.

Knapp, Franz Peter (1977) *Ruodlieb: Mittellateinisch und Deutsch. Übertragung, Kommentar und Nachwort*, Stuttgart: Philipp Reclam.

Knapp, Franz Peter (1979) *Das lateinische Tierepos* (Erträge der Forschung, 121), Darmstadt: Wissenschaftliche Buchgesellschaft.

Knapp, Franz Peter (2005) *Historie und Fiktion in der mittelalterlichen Gattungspoetik (II). Zehn neue Studien und ein Vorwort* (Schriften der Philosophisch-historischen Klasse der Heidelberger Akademie der Wissenschaften, 35), Heidelberg: Carl Winter.

Kolovou, Foteini (2007) 'Die Rezeption der platonischen *Opsopoiia* in der byzantinischen Literatur', in Martin Hinterberger and Elisabeth Schiffer (eds.), *Byzantinische Sprachkunst. Studien zur byzantinischen Literatur gewidmet Wolfram Hörandner zum 65. Geburtstag* (Byzantinisches Archiv, 20), Berlin and New York: Walter de Gruyter, pp. 181–93.

Krauss, Helmut (ed.) (1978) *Altfranzösische Epik* (Wege der Forschung, 354), Darmstadt: Wissenschaftliche Buchgesellschaft.

Kriaras, Emmanuel (1955) *Βυζαντινὰ ἱπποτικὰ μυθιστορήματα* (Βασικὴ Βιβλιοθήκη, 1), Athens: Aetos.

Kriaras, Emmanuel (1969 ff.) *Λεξικὸ τῆς Μεσαιωνικῆς Ἑλληνικῆς Δημώδους Γραμματείας 1100–1669*, Thessaloniki: National Research Foundation and Centre for the Greek Language.

Krueger, Roberta L. (1993) *Woman Readers and the Ideology of Gender in Old French Verse Romance* (Cambridge Studies in French, 43), Cambridge: Cambridge University Press.

Krueger, Roberta L. (ed.) (2000) *The Cambridge Companion to Medieval Romance*, Cambridge: Cambridge University Press.

Kyritses, Dimitris (2005) 'Ἡ Ἅλωση τῆς Κωνσταντινούπολης καὶ τὸ τέλος τοῦ βυζαντινοῦ πολιτισμοῦ', in Tonia Kiousopoulou (ed.), *1453: Ἡ Ἅλωση τῆς Κωνσταντινούπολης καὶ ἡ μετάβαση ἀπὸ τοὺς μεσαιωνικοὺς στοὺς νεώτερους χρόνους*, Herakleion: University of Crete Press, pp. 161–72.

Lachmann, Karl, Peter Knecht and Bernd Schirok and (2003) *Wolfram von Eschenbach: Parzival. Studienausgabe.* Mittelhoch-deutscher Text nach der sechsten Ausgabe von Karl Lachmann, Übersetzung von Peter Knecht, mit Einführungen zum Text der Lachmannschen Ausgabe und in Probleme der 'Parzival'-Interpretation von Bernd Schirok, 2nd edition, Berlin and New York: Walter de Gruyter.

Lacroix, Daniel, and Philippe Walter (1995) *Tristan et Iseut: Les poèmes français – La saga norroise. Textes originaux et intégraux présentés, traduits et commentés*, 2nd edition (Lettres gothiques, 4521), Paris: Le Livre du Poche.

Lacy, Norris J. (2000) 'The Evolution and Legacy of French Prose Romance', in Roberta L. Krueger (ed.), *The Cambridge Companion to Medieval Romance*, Cambridge: Cambridge University Press, pp. 167–82.

Laiou, Angeliki (1972) *Constantinople and the Latins: The Foreign Policy of Andronicus II (1282–1328)*, Cambridge, MA: Harvard University Press.

Lamarque, Peter, and Stein Haugom Olsen (1994) *Truth, Fiction, and Literature: A Philosophical Perspective* (Clarendon Library of Logic and Philosophy, 26), Oxford: Clarendon Press.

Lambert, Jacoba A. (1935) *Le roman de Libistros et Rhodamné publié d'après les manuscrits de Leyde et de Madrid avec une introduction, des observations grammaticales et un glossaire* (Verhandelingen der Koninklijke Akademie van Wetenschappen te Amsterdam. Afdeeling Letterkunde, N.R. 35), Amsterdam: Koninklijke Akademie van Wetenschappen.

Lambros, Spyridon P. (1880) *Collection de romans grecs en langue vulgaire et en vers*, Paris: Maisonneuve et Companie.

Lampsidis, Odysseus (1985) 'Les "gnomologia" tirés de la Chronique de Konstantinos Manasses', *Byzantion* 55: 118–45.

Lampsidis, Odysseus (1988) 'Zur Biographie von Konstantinos Manasses und zu seiner Chronike Synopsis (CS)', *Byzantion* 58: 97–111.

Lampsidis, Odysseus (1996) *Constantini Manassis Breviarium Chronicum* (Corpus Fontium Historiae Byzantinae, 36), Athens: Academy of Athens.

Lange, Wolf-Dieter (1983) 'Chanson de geste', *Lexikon des Mittelalters*, vol. II, pp. 1703–7.

Lasithiotakis, Michalis (2005) '*Παύεσθε γράφειν Ὅμηρον... / ἆ Ὅμηρος ἐψεύσατο...*: Παρατηρήσεις στὸν πρόλογο τοῦ "μυθιστορήματος τοῦ Διγενῆ"' (G IV 27 κ.ἑ. /E 718 κ.ἑ.)', in Stephanos Kaklamanis and Michalis Paschalis (eds.), *Ἡ πρόσληψη τῆς ἀρχαιότητας στὸ βυζαντινὸ καὶ νεοελληνικὸ μυθιστόρημα*, Athens: Stigme, pp. 49–72.

Lauxtermann, Marc (1999) *The Spring of Rhythm: An Essay on the Political Verse and Other Byzantine Metres* (Byzantina Vindobonensia, 22), Vienna: Verlag der Österreichischen Akademie der Wissenschaften.

Lavagnini, Renata (1988) *I Fatti di Troia: L'Iliade bizantina del cod. Par. Suppl. gr. 926. Introduzione, traduzione e note* (Quaderni dell'Istituto di Filologia Greca della Università di Palermo, 20), Palermo: Istituto di Filologia Classica.

Lavizzari, Alexandra (1992) *Ayyuqi: Warqa und Gulschah. Aus dem Persischen übersetzt*, Zurich: Manesse Verlag.

Leclanche, Jean-Louis (1980) *Le Conte de Floire et Blancheflor* (Classiques français du moyen-âge, 105), Paris: Champion.

Legrand, Emile (1880) *Bibliothèque grecque vulgaire. Tome premier*, Paris: Maisonneuve et Companie.

Lemerle, Paul (1977) *Cinque études sur le XIe siècle*, Paris: Centre National de la Recherche Scientifique.

Lendari, Tina (2005) 'Ἐρωτικὰ μυθολογικὰ θέματα στὶς δημώδεις ἐρωτικὲς μυθιστορίες', in Stephanos Kaklamanis and Michalis Paschalis (eds.), *Ἡ πρόσληψη τῆς ἀρχαιότητας στὸ βυζαντινὸ καὶ νεοελληνικὸ μυθιστόρημα*, Athens: Stigme, pp. 87–111.

Lendari, Tina (2007) *Ἀφήγησις Λιβίστρου καὶ Ροδάμνης (Livistros and Rodamne): The Vatican Version. Critical Edition with Introduction, Commentary, and Index-Glossary* (Βυζαντινὴ καὶ Νεοελληνικὴ Βιβλιοθήκη, 10), Athens: Cultural Foundation of the National Bank of Greece.

Ljubarskij, Jakov (1998) '*Quellenforschung* and/or Literary Criticism: Narrative Structures in Byzantine Historical Writings', *Symbolae Osloenses* 73: 5–73.

Lock, Peter (1995) *The Franks in the Aegean 1204–1500*, London and New York: Routledge.

Loukaki, Marina (2002) 'Νικόλαος Καταφλῶρον καὶ Μιχαὴλ Χωνιάτης: Οἱ σχέσεις δύο λογίων τοῦ 12ου αἰώνα', in *Λόγια καὶ δημώδης γραμματεία τοῦ ἑλληνικοῦ μεσαί-*

ωνα. Ἀφιέρωμα στὸν Εὔδοξο Θ. Τσολάκη. Πρακτικα Θ΄ Ἐπιστημονικῆς Συνάντησης τοῦ Τομέα Μ.Ν.Ε.Σ. τοῦ Ἀριστοτελείου Πανεπιστημίου Θεσσαλονίκης (Μάιος 2000), Thessaloniki: Yiahoudis, pp. 161–71.

Loukaki, Marina (2005) *Discours annuels en l'honneur du Patriarche Georges Xiphilin.* Textes édités et commentés par Marina Loukaki, traduits par Corinne Jouanno (Collège de France – CNRS: Centre de Recherche d'Histoire et Civilisation de Byzance, 18), Paris: Centre de Recherche d'Histoire et Civilisation de Byzance.

Lyons, Frances (1980–81) 'Interprétations critiques au XXe siècle du Prologue de *Cligès*: la *translatio studii* selon les historiens, les philosophes et les philologues', *Oeuvres et critique: Revue internationale d'études de la réception critique des oeuvres littéraires de langue française* 5, no. 2: 39–52.

Lyons, Malcolm C. (1995) *The Arab Epic: Heroic and Oral Story-telling*, 3 vols. (University of Cambridge Oriental Publications, 49), Cambridge: Cambridge University Press.

Lyons, Malcolm C. (2001) 'The Land of War: Europe in the Arab Hero Cycles', in Angeliki E. Laiou and Roy P. Mottahedeh (eds.), *The Crusades from the Perspective of Byzantium and the Muslim World*, Washington, D.C.: Dumbarton Oaks Center, pp. 41–51.

MacAlister, Suzanne (1990) 'Aristotle on the Dream: A Twelfth-Century Romance Revival', *Byzantion* 60: 195–212.

MacAlister, Suzanne (1996) *Dreams and Suicides: The Greek Novel from Antiquity to the Byzantine Empire*, London and New York: Routledge.

Mackridge, Peter (1998) 'Byzantium and the Greek Language Question in the Nineteenth Century', in David Ricks and Paul Magdalino (eds.), *Byzantium and the Modern Greek Identity* (Centre for Hellenic Studies, King's College London. Publications, 4), Aldershot: Ashgate, pp. 49–61.

Magdalino, Paul (1993) *The Empire of Manuel I Komnenos, 1143–1180*, Cambridge: Cambridge University Press.

Magdalino, Paul (ed.) (1994) *New Constantines: The Rhythm of Imperial Renewal in Byzantium, 4th–13th Centuries. Papers from the Twenty-sixth Spring Symposium of Byzantine Studies, St Andrews, March 1992* (Society for the Promotion of Byzantine Studies. Publications, 2), Aldershot: Ashgate.

Magdalino, Paul (2004) 'The Byzantine Empire, 1118–1204', in Dennis Luscombe and John Riley-Smith (eds.), *The New Cambridge Medieval History. Volume IV, Part II: c. 1024–c. 1198*, Cambridge: Cambridge University Press, pp. 611–43.

Maguire, Henry (ed.) (1997) *Byzantine Court Culture from 829 to 1204*, Washington, D.C.: Dumbarton Oaks Research Center and Library.

Maisano, Riccardo (1985) 'Il problema della forma letteraria nei proemi storiografici bizantini', *Byzantinische Zeitschrift* 78: 329–43.

Maisano, Riccardo, and Anna Pontani (1994) *Niceta Coniata: Grandezza e catastrofe di Bisanzio (Narrrazione cronologica). Volume I: Libri I–VIII.* Introduzione di Alexander P. Kazhdan, testo critico e commento a cura di Riccardo Maisano, traduzione di Anna Pontani, Verona and Milan: Arnaldo Mondadori.

Maliaras, Nikos (1991) *Die Orgel im byzantinischen Hofzeremoniell des 9. und des 10. Jahrhunderts. Eine Quellenuntersuchung* (Miscellanea Byzantina Monacensia, 33), Munich: Institut für Byzantinistik und Neugriechische Philologie.

Maltezou, Chrysa A., and Peter Schreiner (eds.) (2002) *Bisanzio, Venezia e il mondo franco-greco XIII–XV secolo* (Istituto Ellenico di Studi Bizantini e Postbizantini di Venezia. Convegni, 5), Venice: Istituto Ellenico di Studi Bizantini e Postbizantini di Venezia.

Mann, Jill (1987) *Ysengrimus. Text with Translation, Commentary and Introduction* (Mittellateinische Studien und Texte, 12), Leiden and New York: E.J. Brill.

Marcovich, Miroslav (1992) *Theodori Prodromi De Rhodanthis et Dosiclis amoribus libri IX*, Stuttgart and Leipzig: B.G. Teubner.

Marcovich, Miroslav (2001) *Eustathius Macrembolites: De Hysmines et Hysminiae amoribus libri XI*, Munich and Leipzig: K.G. Saur.

Massé, Henri (1959) *Gorgâni: Le roman de Wîs et Râmîn* (Traductions de textes persans, 4), Paris: Les Belles Lettres.

Matschke, Klaus Peter (1971) *Fortschritt und Reaktion in Byzanz im 14. Jahrhundert. Konstantinopel in der Bürgerkriegsperiode von 1341 bis 1354* (Berliner Byzantinistische Arbeiten, 42), Berlin: Akademie der Wissenschaften.

Mazal, Otto (1967) *Der Roman des Konstantinos Manasses. Überlieferung, Rekonstruktion, Textausgabe der Fragmente* (Wiener Byzantinistische Studien, 4) Graz, Vienna and Cologne: Hermann Böhlaus Nachfolger.

Mavroudi, Maria (2002) *A Byzantine Book on Dream Interpretation: The 'Oneirocriticon of Achmet' and its Arabic Sources* (The Medieval Mediterranean, 36), Leiden and Boston: Brill.

McCash, June Hall Martin (1979) 'Marie de Champagne and Eleanor d'Aquitaine: A Relationship Reexamined', *Speculum* 54: 698–711.

Mehtonen, Päivi (1996) *Old Concepts and New Poetics:* Historia, Argumentum, *and* Fabula *in the Twelfth- and Early Thirteenth-Century Latin Poetics of Fiction* (Societas Scientiarum Fennica. Commentationes Humanarum Litterarum, 108), Helsinki: Societas Scientiarum Fennica.

Meisami, Julie Scott (1987) *Medieval Persian Court Poetry*, Princeton: Princeton University Press.

Meisami, Julie Scott (1995) *Nizami: Haft Paykar, A Medieval Persian Romance. Translated with an Introduction and Notes*, Oxford: Clarendon Press.

Méla, Charles (1990) *Chrétien de Troyes: Le Conte du Graal ou Le Roman de Perceval. Édition critique du manuscrit 354 de Berne, traduction, présentation et notes* (Lettres gothiques, 4525), Paris: Le Livre du Poche.

Méla, Charles (1992) *Chrétien de Troyes: Le Chevalier de la Charrette ou Le Roman de Lancelot. Édition critique d'après tous les manuscripts existants, traduction, présentation et notes* (Lettres gothiques, 4527), Paris: Le Livre du Poche.

Méla, Charles, Olivier Collet and Marie-Claire Gérard-Zai (1994) *Chrétien de Troyes: Cligès. Édition critique du manuscript B.N. fr. 12560*. Édition avec traduction, notes et introduction par Charles Méla et Olivier Collet. *Appendix: Chansons courtoises de Chrétien de Troyes*. Présentation, édition critique et traduction par Marie-Claire Gérard-Zai (Lettres gothiques, 4541), Paris: Le Livre du Poche.

Melberg, Arne (1995) *Theories of Mimesis*, Cambridge: Cambridge University Press.

Mergiali, Sophia (1996) *L'enseignement et les lettrés pendant l'époque des Paléologues, 1261–1453* (Ἑταιρεία τῶν Φίλων τοῦ Λαοῦ. Κέντρον Ἐρεύνης Βυζαντίου, 5), Athens: Association of the People's Friends.

Mertens, Volker (1998) *Der deutsche Artusroman*, Stuttgart: Philipp Reclam.

Minnis, Alastair J., and Andrew B. Scott (eds.) (1991) *Medieval Literary Theory and Criticism (c. 1100–1375): The Commentary Tradition*, revised edition, Oxford: Clarendon Press.

Minnis, Alastair, and Ian Johnson (eds.) (2004) *The Cambridge History of Literary Criticism. Volume II: The Middle Ages*, Cambridge: Cambridge University Press.

Mitsi, Efterpi, and Panagiotis Agapitos (2006) 'Εἰκὼν καὶ λόγος: Ἡ *ἔκφρασις* ἀπὸ τὴν ἀρχαία στὴ βυζαντινὴ λογοτεχνία', in Panagiotis Agapitos, Martin Hinterberger and Efterpi Mitsi, *Εἰκὼν καὶ λόγος. Ἕξι βυζαντινὲς περιγραφὲς ἔργων τέχνης*, Athens: Agra Publications, pp. 15–38 (text) and 165–74 (bibliography).

Mölk, Ulrich (1969) *Französische Literaturästhetik des 12. und 13. Jahrhunderts: Prologe, Exkurse, Epiloge* (Sammlung Romanischer Übungstexte, 54), Tübingen: Max Niemeyer.

Moennig, Ulrich (1992) *Die spätbyzantinische Rezension *ζ des Alexanderromans* (Neograeca Medii Aevi, 6), Cologne: Romiosini.

Moennig, Ulrich (1999) 'The Late-Byzantine Romance: Problems of Defining a Genre', *Κάμπος: Cambridge Papers in Modern Greek* 7: 1–20.

Moennig, Ulrich (2004) *Die Erzählung von Alexander und Semiramis. Kritische Ausgabe mit einer Einleitung, Übersetzung und einem Wörterverzeichnis* (Corpus Fontium Historiae Byzantinae. Supplementa Byzantina, 7), Berlin and New York: Walter de Gruyter.

Mohl, Jules (1838–78) *Le Livre des Rois par Abou'lkasim Firdousi* (Collection orientale, 2–8), 7 vols., Paris: Imprimerie Nationale (reprinted 1976, Paris: Jean Maisonneuve).

Moore, Megan (forthcoming) 'Boundaries and Byzantines in the Old French *Floire and Blancheflor*'.

Mora-Lebrun, Francine (1995) *Le Roman de Thèbes. Édition du manuscript S (London, Brit. Libr., Add. 34114), traduction, présentation et notes* (Lettres gothiques, 4536), Paris: Le Livre du Poche.

Morgan, John R. (1993) 'Make-Believe and Make Believe: The Fictionality of the Greek Novels', in Christopher Gill and Thomas P. Wiseman (eds.), *Lies and Fiction in the Ancient World*, Austin: University of Texas Press, pp. 175–229.

Morrison, George (1972) *Vis and Ramin. Translated from the Persian of Fakhr ud-Din Gurgani*, New York and London: Columbia University Press.

Mullett, Margaret (1984) 'Aristocracy and Patronage in the Literary Circles of Comnenian Constantinople', in Michael J. Angold (ed.), *The Byzantine Aristocracy IX to XII Centuries* (BAR International Series, 221), London and Oxford: BAR, pp. 173–201.

Necipoglou, Nevra (2000) 'Constantinopolitan Merchants and the Question of Their Attitudes towards Italians and Ottomans in the Late Palaiologan Period', in Cordula Scholz and Georg Makris (eds.), *ΠΟΛΥΠΛΕΥΡΟΣ ΝΟΥΣ. Miscellanea für Peter Schreiner zu seinem 60. Geburtstag* (Byzantinisches Archiv, 19), Munich and Leipzig: K.G. Saur, pp. 251–63.

Newsom, Robert (1988) *A Likely Story: Probability and Play in Fiction*, New Brunswick, NJ: Rutgers University Press.

Nicholas, Nick and George Baloglou (2003) *An Entertaining Tale of Quadrupeds. Translation and Commentary*, New York: Columbia University Press.

Nicol, Donald M. (1957) *The Despotate of Epiros 1206–1267*, Oxford: Clarendon Press.

Nicol, Donald M. (1984) *The Despotate of Epiros 1267–1479: A Contribution to the History of Greece in the Middle Ages*, Cambridge: Cambridge University Press.

Nicol, Donald M. (1993) *The Last Centuries of Byzantium 1261–1453*, 2nd edition, Cambridge: Cambridge University Press.

Nicolaou-Konnari, Angel, and Chris Schabel (2005) *Cyprus: Society and Culture 1191–1374* (The Medieval Mediterranean, 58), Leiden and Boston: E.J. Brill.

Nilsson, Ingela (2001) *Erotic Pathos, Rhetorical Pleasure: Narrative Technique and Mimesis in Eumathios Makrembolites' Hysmine & Hysminias* (Acta Universitatis Upsaliensis. Studia Byzantina Upsaliensia, 7), Uppsala: Institute of Classical Studies.

Nilsson, Ingela (2005) 'Narrating Images in Byzantine Literature: The *Ekphraseis* of Konstantinos Manasses', *Jahrbuch der Österreichischen Byzantinistik* 55: 121–46.

Nilsson, Ingela (2006) 'Discovering Literariness in the Past: Literature vs. History in the *Synopsis Chronike* of Konstantinos Manasses', in Paolo Odorico, Panagiotis A. Agapitos and Martin Hinterberger (eds.), *L'écriture de la memoire: la littérarité de l'historiographie. HERMENEIA. Actes du troisiéme colloque international sur la littérature byzantine* (Dossiers Byzantins, 6), Paris: École des Hautes Études en Sciences Sociales, pp. 15–31.

Nørgaard, Lars, and Ole L. Smith (1977) *A Byzantine Iliad: The Text of Par. Suppl. Gr. 926. Edited with Critical Apparatus, Introduction and Indexes* (Opuscula Graecolatina, 5), Copenhagen: Museum Tusculanum Press.

Ntourou-Eliopoulou, Maria (2000) *Οἱ Βυζαντινοὶ στὸ Φραγκικὸ Πριγκηπάτο τῆς Ἀχαΐας* (Τὸ Βυζάντιο καὶ οἱ ξένοι, 3), Athens: Goulandris Foundation.

Odorico, Paolo (1989) 'La sapienza del Digenis. Materiali per lo studio dei *loci similes* nella recenzione di Grottaferrata', *Byzantion* 59: 137–63.

Odorico, Paolo (1995) *Digenis Akritas. Poema anonimo bizantino*, Florence: Giunti.

Odorico, Paolo (2002) *L'Akrite: l'épopée byzantine de Digénis Akritas. Versions grecque et slave, suivie du Chant d'Armouris*, Toulouse: Anacharsis.

Odorico, Paolo (2005a) '... Ἅπερ εἰσὶν ψευδέα: Les images des héros de l'Antiquité dans le *Digénis Akritas*', in Stephanos Kaklamanis and Michalis Paschalis (eds.), *Ἡ πρόσληψη τῆς ἀρχαιότητας στὸ βυζαντινὸ καὶ νεοελληνικὸ μυθιστόρημα*, Athens: Stigme, pp. 31–47.

Odorico, Paolo (2005b) '*Καλλίμαχος* καὶ *Χρυσορρόη* κι ἕνας πολὺ μοναχικὸς ἀναγνώστης', in Elizabeth Jeffreys and Michael Jeffreys (eds.), *Neograeca Medii Aevi V: Ἀναδρομικὰ καὶ Προδρομικά. Approaches to Texts in Early Modern Greek*, Oxford: Exeter College, pp. 271–86.

Odorico, Paolo, Panagiotis A. Agapitos and Martin Hinterberger (eds.) (2006) *L'écriture de la memoire: la littérarité de l'historiographie. HERMENEIA. Actes du troisiéme colloque international sur la littérature byzantine* (Dossiers Byzantins, 6), Paris: École des Hautes Études en Sciences Sociales.

Ong, Walter J. (1977) *Interfaces of the Word: Studies in the Evolution of Culture and Consciousness*, Ithaca and London: Cornell University Press.

Ong, Walter J. (2002) *Orality and Literacy: The Technologizing of the Word*, London and New York: Routledge. [Originally published in 1982.]

Ott, Claudia (2000) 'Byzantine Wild East – Islamic Wild West: An Expedition into a Literary Borderland', in Panagiotis A. Agapitos and Diether Roderich Reinsch (eds.), *Der Roman im Byzanz der Komnenenzeit. Ein internazionales Symposium* (Meletemata, 8), Frankfurt a.M: Beerenverlag, pp. 137–46.

Ott, Claudia (2003) *Metamorphosen des Epos: Das Sirat al-Muǧâhidîn und seine Überlieferung* (University of Leiden: Research School of Asian, African and Amerindian Studies. Publications, 119), Leiden: Leiden University Press.

Palmer, Nigel F. (2004) 'Literary Criticism in Middle High German Literature', in Alastair Minnis and Ian Johnson (eds.), *The Cambridge History of Literary Criticism. Volume II: The Middle Ages*, Cambridge: Cambridge University Press, pp. 533–48.

Panagiotakes, Nikolaos M. (1995) 'The Italian Background of Early Cretan Literature', *Dumbarton Oaks Papers* 49: 281–323.

Papaioannou, Stratis N. (2003) 'Ἀπὸ τὴ ρητορικὴ στὴ λογοτεχνία: Ἡ ἔννοια τῆς μεταβολῆς στὸν Μιχαὴλ Ψελλὸ καὶ ἡ ἀναβίωση τῆς μυθοπλασίας', in Vasiliki Vlyssidou (ed.), *Ἡ αὐτοκρατορία σὲ κρίση(;). Τὸ Βυζάντιο τὸν 11ο αἰώνα (1025–1081)* (Ἐθνικὸ Ἵδρυμα Ἐρευνῶν. Ἰνστιτοῦτο Βυζαντινῶν Ἐρευνῶν: Διεθνῆ Συμπόσια, 11), Athens: National Research Foundation, pp. 473–82.

Papaioannou, Stratis (2004) 'Ἡ μίμηση στὴ ρητορικὴ θεωρία τοῦ Ψελλοῦ', in Christina Angelidi (ed.), *Τὸ Βυζάντιο ὥριμο γιὰ ἀλλαγές: Ἐπιλογές, εὐαισθησίες καὶ τρόποι ἔκφρασης ἀπὸ τὸν ἑνδέκατο στὸν δέκατο πέμπτο αἰώνα* (Ἐθνικὸ Ἵδρυμα Ἐρευνῶν. Ἰνστιτοῦτο Βυζαντινῶν Ἐρευνῶν: Διεθνῆ Συμπόσια, 13), Athens: National Research Foundation, pp. 87–98.

Papaioannou, Stratis (2007) 'On the Stage of *Eros*: Two Rhetorical Exercises by Nikephoros Basilakes', in Michael Grünbart (ed.), *Theatron. Rhetorische Kultur in Spätantike und Mittelalter* (Millenium Studien, 13), Berlin and New York: Walter de Gruyter, pp. 357–76.

Papaioannou, Stratis (forthcoming) *Michael Psellos: Rhetoric and Authorship*, Cambridge: Cambridge University Press.

Papathomopoulos, Manolis, and Elizabeth M. Jeffreys (1996) *Ὁ Πόλεμος τῆς Τρωάδος (The War of Troy). Κριτικὴ ἔκδοση μὲ εἰσαγωγὴ καὶ πίνακες* (Βυζαντινὴ καὶ Νεοελληνικὴ Βιβλιοθήκη, 7), Athens: Cultural Foundation of the National Bank of Greece.

Parani, Maria, Brigitte Pitarakis and Jean-Marie Spieser (2003) 'Un exemple d'inventaire d'objets liturgiques: Le Testament d'Eustathios Boïlas (avril 1059)', *Revue des Études Byzantines* 61: 143–65.

Peters, Ulrike (1981) *Fürstenhof und höfische Dichtung. Der Hof Hermanns von Thüringen als literarisches Zentrum*, Tübingen: Max Niemeyer.

Petit, Aimé (1985) *L'anachronisme dans les romans antiques du XII*e *siècle* (Centre d'Études Médiévales et Dialectales de l'Université de Lilles-III), Lille: Presses Universitaires de Lille.

Petit, Aimé (1997) *Le Roman d'Eneas. Édition critique d'après le manuscrit B.N. fr. 60, traduction, présentation et notes* (Lettres gothiques, 4550), Paris: Le Livre du Poche.

Pichard, Marcel (1956) *Le roman de Callimaque et de Chrysorrhoé*, Paris: Les Belles Lettres.

Pietsch, Effi (2005) *Die Chronographia des Michael Psellos: Kaisergeschichte, Autobiographie und Apologie* (Serta Graeca, 20), Wiesbaden: Dr. Ludwig Reichert.

Pignani, Adrianna (1983) *Niceforo Basilace: Progimnasmi e monodie. Testo critico, introduzione, traduzione* (Byzantina et Neo-Hellenica Neapolitana, 10), Naples: D'Auria Editrice.

Poirion, Daniel (1978) 'Romans en vers et romans en prose', in Jean Frappier and Reinhold R. Grimm (eds.), *Le roman jusqu'a la fin du XIII*e *siècle. Tome 1: Partie historique* (Grundriß der Romanischen Literaturen des Mittlealters, IV.1), Heidelberg: Carl Winter, pp. 74–81.

Poirion, Daniel (1994) *Chrétien de Troyes: Oeuvres complètes.* Édition publiée sous la direction de Daniel Poirion, avec la collaboration d'Anne Berthelot, Peter F. Dembowski, Sylvie Lefèvre, Karl D. Uitti et Philippe Walter (Bibliothèque de la Pléiade), Paris: Gallimard.

Polemis, Dimitrios I. (1968) *The Doukai: A Contribution to Byzantine Prosopography*, London: Athlone Press.

Prakash, Gyan (1995) 'Orientalism Now', *History and Theory* 34: 119–212.

Pryor, John H., and Elizabeth M. Jeffreys (2006) *The Age of the Dromon: The Byzantine Navy, ca. 500–1204* (The Medieval Mediterranean, 62), Leiden and Boston: Brill.

Rabe, Hugo (1913) *Hermogenis opera* (Rhetores Graeci, 6), Leipzig: B.G. Teubner.

Rabe, Hugo (1926) *Aphthonii progymnasmata* (Rhetores Graeci, 10), Leipzig: B.G. Teubner.

Rabe, Hugo (1931) *Prolegomenon sylloge* (Rhetores Graeci, 14), Leipzig: B.G. Teubner.

Ranke, Friedrich, and Richard Krohn (1993) *Gottfried von Straßburg: Tristan.* Nach dem Text von Friedrich Ranke neu herausgegeben, ins Neuhochdeutsche übersetzt, mit einem Stellenkommentar und einem Nachwort von Richard Krohn, 2nd edition, 3 vols., Stuttgart: Philipp Reclam.

Reardon, Brian P. (1991) *The Form of Greek Romance,* Princeton: Princeton University Press.

Reinsch, Diether Roderich (2001) 'Zu den Prooimia von (Ptocho-)Prodromos III und IV', *Jahrbuch der Österreichischen Byzantinistik* 51: 215–23.

Reinsch, Diether Roderich (2002) 'Historia ancilla litterarum? Zum literarischen Geschmack in der Komnenenzeit: Das Beispiel der *Synopsis Chronike* des Konstantinos Manasses', in Paolo Odorico and Panagiotis A. Agapitos (eds.), *Pour une 'nouvelle' histoire de la littérature byzantine: problèmes, méthodes, approches, propositions. HERMENEIA. Actes du premier colloque international sur la littérature byzantine* (Dossiers Byzantins, 1), Paris: École des Hautes Études en Sciences Sociales, pp. 81–94.

Reinsch, Diether Roderich (2007) 'Die Palamedes-Episode in der *Synopsis Chronike* des Konstantinos Manasses und ihre Inspirationsquelle', in Martin Hinterberger and Elisabeth Schiffer (eds.), *Byzantinische Sprachkunst. Studien zur byzantinischen Literatur gewidmet Wolfram Hörandner zum 65. Geburtstag* (Byzantinisches Archiv, 20), Berlin and New York: Walter de Gruyter, pp. 266–76.

Rohde, Erwin (1914) *Der griechische Roman und seine Vorläufer. Dritte, durch einen zweiten Anhang vermehrte Auflage,* Leipzig: Breitkopf und Härtel.

Roilos, Panagiotis (2005) *Amphoteroglossia: A Poetics of the Twelfth-Century Medieval Greek Novel,* Washington, D.C.: Center for Hellenic Studies.

Rosenthal, Franz (1965) *Das Fortleben der Antike im Islam,* Zurich and Stuttgart: Artemis.

Rossi, Luciano, and Richard Straub (1992) *Fabliaux érotiques: Textes de jongleurs des XIIe at XIIIe siècles. Edition critique, traduction, introduction et notes* (Lettres gothiques, 4532), Paris: Le Livre de Poche.

Said, Edward (1978) *Orientalism,* New York: Pantheon Books.

Schmolke-Hasselmann, Beate (1998) *The Evolution of Arthurian Romance: The Verse Tradition from Chrétien to Froissart.* Translated by Marie and Richard Middleton (Cambridge Studies in Medieval Literature, 35), Cambridge: Cambridge University Press. [Revised translation of the German original, Tübingen: Max Niemeyer, 1980.]

Scholz, Bernard F. (ed.) (1998) *Mimesis. Studien zur literarischen Repräsentation – Studies on Literary Representation*, Tübingen and Basel: Francke.

Scholz, Michael G. (1980) *Hören und Lesen: Studien zur primären Rezeption der Literatur im 12. und 13. Jahrhundert*, Wiesbaden: Dr. Ludwig Reichert.

Schröder, Werner, and Dieter Kartschoke (2003) *Wolfram von Eschenbach: Willehalm.* Text der Ausgabe von Werner Schröder, Übersetzung, Vorwort und Register von Dieter Kartschoke, 3rd edition, Berlin and New York: Walter de Gruyter.

Ševčenko, Ihor (1981–82) 'Levels of Style in Byzantine Prose', *Jahrbuch der Österreichischen Byzantinistik* 31: 289–312; 32: 211–38.

Seyed-Gohrab, Ali Ashgar (2003) *Laylî and Majnûn: Love, Madness and Mystic Longing in Nizâmî's Epic Romance* (Brill Studies in Middle Eastern Literatures, 27), Leiden and Boston: E.J. Brill.

Sideras, Alexander (1994) *Die byzantinische Grabreden: Prosopographie, Datierung, Überlieferung. 142 Epitaphien und Monodien aus dem byzantinischen Jahrtausend* (Wiener Byzantinistische Studien, 19), Vienna: Verlag der Österreichischen Akademie der Wissenschaften.

Shawcross, Teresa (2003) 'Re-inventing the Homeland in the Historiography of Frankish Greece: The Fourth Crusade and the Legend of the Trojan War', *Byzantine and Modern Greek Studies* 27: 120–52.

Short, Ian (1990) *La Chanson de Roland. Édition critique et traduction*, 2nd edition (Lettres gothiques, 4524), Paris: Le Livre du Poche.

Smith, Colin (1983) *The Making of the Poema de mio Cid*, Cambridge: Cambridge University Press.

Smith, Ole L. (1975) *Studies on the Scholia of Aeschylus. I: The Recensions of Demetrius Triclinius* (Mnemosyne. Supplementa, 37), Leiden: E.J. Brill.

Smith, Ole L. (1988) 'Notes on the Byzantine Achilleid: The Oxford Version', *Classica et Mediaevalia* 39: 259–72.

Smith, Ole L. (1990) *The Oxford Version of the Achilleid* (Opuscula Graecolatina, 32), Copenhagen: Museum Tusculanum Press.

Smith, Ole L. (1991–92) 'Some Features of Structure and Narrative in the Byzantine *Achilleid*', *Hellenika* 42: 75–94.

Smith, Ole L. (1999) *The Byzantine Achilleid: The Naples Version. Introduction, Critical Edition and Commentary.* Edited and prepared for publication by Panagiotis A.

Agapitos and Karin Hult (Wiener Byzantinistische Studien, 21), Vienna: Verlag der Österreichischen Akademie der Wissenschaften.

Spiegel, Gabrielle M. (1993) *Romancing the Past: The Rise of Vernacular Prose Historiography in Thirteenth-Century France*, Berkeley, Los Angeles and London: University of California Press.

Stavridou-Zafraka, Alkmene (1990) *Νίκαια καὶ Ἤπειρος τὸν 13ο αἰώνα. Ἰδεολογικὴ ἀντιπαράθεση στὴν προσπάθειά τους νὰ ἀνακτήσουν τὴν αὐτοκρατορία* (Ἑταιρεία Βυζαντινῶν Ἐρευνῶν, 7), Thessaloniki: Vanias.

Steinsieck, Wolf, and Egbert Kaiser (1999) *Das altfranzösische Rolandslied. Zweisprachig.* Übersetzt und kommentiert von Wolf Steinsieck, Nachwort von Egbert Kaiser, Stuttgart: Philipp Reclam.

Stephenson, Paul (2005) 'Political History 1025–1204', in Jonathan Harris (ed.), *Palgrave Advances in Byzantine History*, Basingstoke: Palgrave, pp. 39–57.

Suleiman, Susan R., and Inge Crosman (eds.) (1980) *The Reader in the Text: Essays on Audience and Interpretation*, Princeton: Princeton University Press.

Taragna, Anna Maria (2000) *Logoi historias: Discorsi e lettere nella prima storiografia retorica bizantina* (Hellenica. Testi e strumenti di letteratura greca antica, medievale e umanistica, 7), Alessandria: Edizioni dell'Orso.

Theologitis, Homere Alexandre (2004) 'Pour une typologie du roman à Byzance: Les héros romanesque et leur appartenance générique', *Jahrbuch der Österreichischen Byzantinistik* 54: 207–33.

Trapp, Erich (1971) *Digenes Akrites: Synoptische Ausgabe der ältesten Versionen* (Wiener Byzantinistische Studien, 8), Vienna: Hermann Böhlaus Nachfolger.

Trapp, Erich (ed.) (1994 ff.) *Lexikon zur Byzantinischen Gräzität besonders des 9.–12. Jahrhunderts*, Vienna: Verlag der Österreichischen Akademie der Wissenschaften.

Trillitzsch, Winfried (1964) *Ecbasis cuiusdam captivi per tropologiam. Die Flucht eines Gefangenen (tropologisch)*, Leipzig: Teubner.

Tsiouni, Viveta (1972) *Παιδιόφραστος διήγησις τῶν ζώων τῶν τετραπόδων. Critical Edition* (Miscellanea Byzantina Monacensia, 15), Munich: Institut für Byzantinistik und Neugriechische Philologie.

Türk, Emile (1977) *Nugae curialium: Le règne d'Henri II Plantagenêt et l'éthique politique*, Geneva: Droz.

Vollmann, Benedikt K. (1993) *Ruodlieb*, Darmstadt: Wissenschaftliche Buchgesellschaft.

Vryonis, Speros (1957) 'The Will of a Provincial Magnate: Eustathios Boilas (1059)', *Dumbarton Oaks Papers* 11: 263–77.

Wagner, Willhelm (1874) *Histoire de Imbérios et Margarona: Imitation grecque du roman français Pierre de Provence et la belle Maguelonne. Publiée pour la première fois d'après un manuscrit de la Bibliothèque Impériale de Vienne* (Collection de monuments pour servir a l'étude de la langue néo-hellénique, N.S. 3), Paris: Maisonneuve et Companie.

Walters, Laurie (1992) 'The Poet-narrator's Address to His Lady as Structural Device in *Partonopeu de Blois*', *Medium Aevum* 61: 229–41.

Walton, Kendall L. (1990) *Mimesis as Make-Believe: On the Foundations of the Representational Arts*, Cambridge, MA: Harvard University Press.

Walz, Christianus (1968) *Rhetores graeci. Volumina I–IX*, Osnabrück: Otto Zeller. [Reprint of the 1832–36 edition.]

Wehrli, Max (1997) *Geschichte der deutschen Literatur im Mittelalter von den Anfängen bis zum Ende des 16. Jahrhunderts*, 3rd edition, Stuttgart: Philipp Reclam.

Weiss, Judith (2002) *Wace's Roman de Brut: A History of the British. Text and Translation*, revised edition, Exeter: University of Exeter Press.

Wolfzettel, Friedrich (2001) 'Byzanz im lateinisch-französischen Mittelalter oder Literaturgeschichte der Bemächtigung', *Das Mittelalter* 6, no. 2: 83–108.

Yiavis, Kostas (2006) 'So near, yet so far: Medieval Courtly Romance, and *Imberios and Margarona*. A Case of De-medievalization', *Byzantinische Zeitschrift* 99: 195–217.

Zeydel, Edwin H. (1964) *Ecbasis cuiusdam captivi per tropologiam – Escape of a Certain Captive Told in a Figurative Manner: An Eleventh-Century Latin Beast Epic. Introduction, Text, Translation, Commentary and an Appendix* (University of North Carolina Studies in the Germanic Languages and Literatures, 46), Chapel Hill: The University of North Carolina Press.

Zumthor, Paul (1987) *La lettre et la voix: De la 'littérature' médiévale*, Paris: Seuil.

Zumthor, Paul (2000) *Essai de poétique médiévale [1972]*. Avec une préface de Michel Zink et un texte inédit de Paul Zumthor, Paris: Seuil.

Contributors

Panagiotis A. Agapitos is Professor of Byzantine Literature at the University of Cyprus.

Dennis H. Green was Professor emeritus of German at the University of Cambridge.

Tomas Hägg was Professor emeritus of Classical Philology at the University of Bergen.

P. M. Mehtonen is Associate Professor of Comparative Literature at the University of Tampere.

Lars Boje Mortensen is Professor of Ancient and Medieval Cultural History and Head of the Centre for Medieval Literature at the University of Southern Denmark and was Prof II of Medieval Latin at the Centre for Medieval Studies at the University of Bergen until 2011.

Else Mundal is Professor of Old Norse Literature at the Centre for Medieval Studies at the University of Bergen.

Slavica Ranković is Postdoctoral Researcher in Comparative Literature at the Centre for Medieval Studies at the University of Bergen.

Paul Gerhard Schmidt was Professor emeritus of Medieval Latin at the University of Freiburg.

Jonas Wellendorf is Assistant Professor of Old Norse at the University of California, Berkeley. He was Postdoctoral Researcher in Old Norse Literature at the Centre for Medieval Studies at the University of Bergen until 2011.

General Index